AMERICA'S CAPTIVES

AMERICA'S CAPTIVES

Treatment of POWs from the Revolutionary War to the War on Terror

PAUL J. SPRINGER

UNIVERSITY PRESS OF KANSAS

Published by the University Press of Kansas (Lawrence, Kansas 66045),
which was organized by the Kansas Board of Regents and is operated and funded by
Emporia State University, Fort Hays State University, Kansas State University,
Pittsburg State University, the University of Kansas, and Wichita State University

Library of Congress Cataloging-in-Publication Data

Springer, Paul J.
America's captives : treatment of POWs from the Revolutionary War to the War on Terror /
Paul J. Springer.
p. cm. — (Modern war studies)
Includes bibliographical references and index.
ISBN 978-0-7006-1717-3 (cloth : alk. paper)
1. Prisoners of war—United States—History. 2. Prisoners of war—Government policy—
United States—History. 3. United States—History, Military. I. Title.
UB803.S67 2010
355.1′2960973—dc22
2009044667

British Library Cataloguing-in-Publication Data is available.

Printed in the United States of America

10 9 8 7 6 5 4 3 2 1

The paper used in this publication is recycled and contains 30 percent
postconsumer waste. It is acid free and meets the minimum requirements of the
American National Standard for Permanence of Paper for Printed Library Materials
Z39.48–1992.

CONTENTS

PREFACE

My interest in American prisoner of war policy and practice began when I was an undergraduate student at Texas A&M University, an outgrowth of office discussions with Professor Arnold Krammer. I will be forever grateful to him not only for drawing my interest to the subject, but also for pushing me to attend graduate school and serving as a model of enthusiastic teaching that I aspire to emulate. In any academic endeavor of this magnitude, there are intellectual debts too numerous to mention. I am particularly thankful for the guidance provided by Professor Brian M. Linn. At times, he served as editor, motivator, challenger, and confessor. This book would not exist without his tireless hours of work. I also express special gratitude to professors Joseph G. Dawson III, Jonathan Coopersmith, David Vaught, and James Burk, each of whom read this work in dissertation form, and all of whom fulfilled a special role in the production of this work. At West Point, Dr. Roger Spiller and Dr. Robert Citino each set aside valuable time during their visiting professorships to mentor and develop my scholarly talents, including reading substantial portions of this manuscript and offering valuable suggestions to improve the finished product.

Financial support for the project was drawn from many sources, and I thank the history department of Texas A&M University, the Glasscock Center for Humanities Research, Andersonville National Historic Site, the Society for Military History, and the United States Military Academy at West Point for generous contributions. I received archival assistance of immense value from the respective staffs of the National Archives in Washington, D.C.; Archives II in College Park, Maryland; Sterling C. Evans Library in College Station, Texas; and Jefferson Library in West Point, New York. In particular, Alan Aimone and Edward Dacey provided extensive assistance in the final phase of this project.

Emotional support for years of graduate study came from uncountable individuals, but I am especially indebted to my fellow graduate students at Texas A&M, who proved to be lifelong friends as well as scholarly colleagues. In particular, Dr. Christopher Mortenson always knew the answers to my questions and maintained a steady balance at the most chaotic moments. More recently, Dr. S. Michael Pavelec has done yeoman's work in providing professional guidance, and Editor-in-Chief Michael Briggs has led me through the pitfalls of the publishing industry, doing his best to save me from myself.

Of course, the greatest support I have received has been the love of my family. No one has been more patient or long-suffering than my wife, Victoria, without whom I would have neither the curiosity to research nor the courage to write. I gratefully dedicate this book to her on the tenth anniversary of our marriage. The credit for this book belongs to each of these individuals; the errors are mine alone.

AMERICA'S CAPTIVES

Introduction

AMERICAN POW POLICY AND PRACTICE

In 1991, after the successful termination of Operation Desert Storm, the International Committee of the Red Cross pronounced the coalition prisoner of war (POW) camps, constructed and overseen by American military personnel, the best example of war captive treatment in history. Barely a decade later, another Red Cross report condemned the prison compounds at Abu Ghraib, Iraq, and Guantánamo Bay, Cuba, for inhumane conditions that might constitute international human rights violations. How could American treatment of enemy war captives devolve in such a short period? Was it simply an administrative failure, as alleged by some defenders of the detainee prisons of the war on terror? Did the nature of the latest war trigger an abandonment of the fundamental principles that have guided American wartime behavior for more than two centuries? The simple answer is that the allegations of torture and abuse that surrounded prison compounds in Iraq and elsewhere were the predictable, and to a certain extent natural, outgrowth of American wartime behavior.

Russell Weigley's groundbreaking work, *The American Way of War*, sought to identify the means by which American military and political leaders have pursued conflict. In particular, Weigley argued that the American approach to warfare has differed according to the enemy being faced. When facing a weaker opponent, the fundamental American strategy has been one of annihilation, a quick war to completely destroy the military capability of the enemy, by almost any means available. When facing a stronger foe, American military strategy has relied on attrition to grind down enemy military forces. Weigley's view has been repeatedly challenged, but never replaced, as the fundamental work of American military history.

Weigley's work, although foundational, largely ignored a key means by which American military forces have successfully annihilated and/or worn down enemy military capabilities: the capture of POWs. Forcing the surrender of field forces is the most economical and rapid means of removing enemy troops from the field without paying a corresponding toll in friendly casualties. In the American Revolutionary War, the battles of Saratoga, Charleston, and Yorktown served as major turning points in the conflict. Each resulted in the surrender of enemy field armies. Smaller captures at Trenton, Princeton, King's Mountain, and Cowpens maintained American morale and prolonged the conflict. In the Civil War, it was the surrenders at Fort Donelson, Vicksburg, and Appomattox that cemented Ulysses S. Grant in the pantheon of great American captains. In World War II, American forces took millions of German troops captive, greatly accelerating the collapse of Nazi Germany and reducing the number of Allied casualties by untold amounts. In the Pacific, American troops invested massive resources in psychological and propaganda operations to induce Japanese surrenders, rather than attempting to destroy Japanese forces in combat. Compelling the surrender of enemy forces has remained a consistent part of American wars for the entire history of the nation. Even in the cold war era, with preparations for nuclear war and the possibility of mutually assured destruction, the conventional military forces of the United States have planned for the capture of masses of enemy troops.

Unfortunately, almost no planning has gone into the question of what to do with enemy forces once they have surrendered in the field. The destruction of enemy combat power has been assumed to be the end, rather than the beginning, of American POW policy. Although American political and military leaders have paid lip service to the need to treat enemy captives with humanity and decency, they have rarely allocated the resources to do so in an adequate fashion. As such, the legacy of American POW treatment has been one of casual neglect, if not open abuse. Such negligence is not unique—prisoners of war have historically been among the most unfortunate of war victims. However, the United States, since its inception, has held the unique opportunity and capability to offer much more than simple humanity and decency to its captives.

American planners have typically struggled to react to the capture of enemy troops because the United States has never entered a major conflict prepared for the number of enemy prisoners taken. As a result, American treatment of enemy prisoners has often been improvised rather than carefully planned. The changing American concept of humanitarian behavior has guided the improvisation of American POW operations, but efforts to remain economically efficient have negatively influenced policy, as have reactions to enemy treatment of American POWs. Essentially, the United States has often conceded the initiative to the enemy in regard to POW policy.

The U.S. military has failed to incorporate POW lessons from each conflict, and has thus been unprepared for an influx of prisoners in each war. The problems have been compounded by the use of poorly trained units for guarding and maintaining POWs and by efforts to conserve resources used for the maintenance of prisoners. Typically the government has exercised little oversight over POW treatment and has turned over control of POWs to offices and organizations that only exist in wartime. In peacetime, the military has made little effort to prepare for POW operations.

Policy and practice are intertwined throughout the history of American treatment of POWs. Policy is theoretical; it creates guidelines for practices in the field that may not be applicable to every battlefield situation. It can exist without practice, as in the case of peacetime planning for the capture of prisoners of war or in the development of international law. Examples of policy guidelines include "Instructions for the Government of Armies of the United States in the Field" (1863) and the Geneva Convention Relative to the Treatment of Prisoners of War (1929). Practice is grounded in reality; it often does not follow prescribed policies. In the absence of clearly defined policies, practice can essentially replace policy. This was clearly demonstrated during the Mexican War, when generals Zachary Taylor and Winfield Scott both commanded armies that captured enemies without clear directives from the War Department about how to treat Mexican prisoners. At times in American history, policy and practice have come into conflict, when field commanders have deliberately ignored instructions regarding prisoner of war treatment.

Few attempts have been made to address the entire history of POW policy within the United States, although hundreds of works have addressed the events of a single war or the experiences of a single captive. This approach has been misleading when applied to POW policy over time because many of the authors began with the assumption that POW practices during a single conflict can be explained without the context of earlier and later wars. Although standards of treatment have evolved, many of the fundamental decisions regarding the treatment of captured enemies were made over two hundred years ago, and the underlying principles of POW treatment remain unaltered.

Three principles of American treatment of POWs are consistent from the Revolutionary War to the war on terror. The first principle is a dependence on reciprocal standards of POW treatment, including the threat of retaliation on enemy prisoners for perceived mistreatment of American prisoners. The United States has treated enemy prisoners in each war at least as well as the treatment received by American prisoners.

The second principle is a general attempt to adhere to accepted customs and international law regarding war. This concept includes a number of deliberate attempts to alter the accepted customs of warfare through the proposal of changes to international law designed to ameliorate the treatment of prisoners of war. Given that the United States has typically treated its captives better than American POWs have been treated, American attempts to improve the worldwide standards of POW care have certainly included an element of self-protection.

The third principle is one of general expediency. American treatment of enemy prisoners has often been dictated by doing what is quickest, simplest, or cheapest to maintain POWs at an acceptable level. To a certain extent, this is understandable. War, by definition, is not an easy or inexpensive undertaking, and a nation's priorities for war will not normally include a desire to coddle enemy captives who surrender on the battlefield. In almost every conflict, this desire for economy has not had dire implications for enemy captives, and although their existence might not have been comfortable, it also was not deliberately perilous. However, at times, the desire for economy has overridden the principle of maintaining the health and welfare of enemy captives, with the result that even when the United States had the capability and opportunity to keep its captives in excellent health, it failed to do so.

This study is organized chronologically, with one chapter devoted to each major war or significant period in POW affairs. This introduction, in addition to providing an introduction to the argument of the book, includes a general literature review and a brief discussion of American POW practices before the Revolutionary War. Chapter 1 discusses the American Revolution and efforts by the Continental Congress, Lieutenant General George Washington, and the individual states to create a consistent policy regarding POWs during the war. Despite the internecine nature of the conflict, American treatment of British prisoners was surprisingly lenient, particularly when the British behavior toward rebellious colonists is considered. The War of 1812, the subject of chapter 2, was another war against Great Britain; it was punctuated by threats of reprisals against prisoners for perceived mistreatment of POWs by the enemy, the virtual collapse of the War Department, and the establishment of a functional exchange cartel for officers and enlisted personnel.

Chapter 3 discusses the Mexican War and the difficulties faced by American commanders in the first war fought by the U.S. Army almost entirely on foreign soil. The most notable prisoner issue of the war, the execution of U.S. deserters caught fighting for Mexico, will receive special consideration. Chapter 4 argues that the American Civil War was a major turning point in the history of POW treatment by the United States. More than 400,000 prisoners were shipped to prison camps during the war, and 50,000 died in captivity as a result of the neglect of Union and Confederate officials. The Civil War is particularly interesting because Americans were both the captors and the captives, and yet prisoners were treated worse in that war than in any other American conflict. Chapter 5 details the changes in American policy and practice from the Civil War until World War I, including frontier warfare, the Spanish-American War, the Philippine War, and American participation in international efforts to ameliorate the conditions faced by prisoners of war. In World War I, the United States fought as part of an alliance and was forced to cooperate in forming POW policies. This resulted in a reconsideration of the requirements of coalition warfare and triggered further efforts to alter international law regarding prisoners.

Chapter 6 begins with a discussion of the changes wrought by the Geneva Convention of 1929. This multinational agreement heavily modified international law regarding prisoners, and the changes were reflected in some nations' treatment of prisoners during World War II. The chapter also compares the treatment of German and Italian prisoners taken in the European theater with the treatment of Japanese prisoners taken in the Pacific theater. Prisoner of war labor was the dominant issue of the war for American policies. Soon after the war, the Geneva Convention of 1949 made the most recent modifications to international POW laws. This convention governed American treatment of Korean and Vietnamese prisoners, discussed in chapters 7 and 8. In Korea, enemy prisoners were confined in a huge island prison at Koje-do, and no effort was made to exchange the prisoners or utilize their labor potential. In Vietnam, the U.S. military turned prisoners over to the government of South Vietnam for confinement, and it again used island prisons to hold thousands of prisoners in a single location. This system was repeated in the Persian Gulf War as a way of reducing the logistical difficulties of American units fighting overseas. Chapter 9 discusses the Gulf War of 1990–1991 and the treatment of prisoners captured in the war on terror and the Iraq War. These wars include a clear departure from the policy of adherence to international law regarding prisoners. The concluding chapter offers observations about United States approaches toward the issue of POWs in future conflicts.

This work is not designed to examine the treatment of prisoners of war in the United States at the individual level, except when such an examination can illustrate the general treatment of prisoners in the era. It is not an attempt to castigate the United States as a hypocritical nation, demanding adherence to international law from enemy nations while failing in our own efforts. Rather, it is designed to link the stated policy and goals of American POW policy to the actual practice of holding enemy captives. It is my contention that official American prisoner of war policy has remained relatively consistent for more than two centuries, but in practice, the application of that policy has been haphazard as a result of an institutional unwillingness in the U.S. military to incorporate the lessons of the past into planning for the future. Because American military institutions spend much of their time planning for the conduct of forces on the battlefield, they devote little time to planning operations beyond the battlefield, an area that naturally encompasses POW operations.

LITERATURE REVIEW

The issue of prisoners has greatly affected each of the wars in which the United States has fought, yet prisoners are often overlooked by works discussing the strategy and outcome of each war. When historians or analysts discuss captured troops, it is often in the context of atrocities or maltreatment allegedly committed by an enemy holding American prisoners. Rarely has any example of American malfeasance received more than cursory mention, with the exception of works discussing the experience of prisoners during the Civil War.[1] There are relatively few works devoted to a study of prisoner of war policies. Much more common are works describing the actual practice of keeping prisoners, typically a series of anecdotes from a single war or the memoirs of a former prisoner. Quite often, prisoners' journals and diaries are published long after the end of captivity, occasionally after the death of the author. In most cases, the journals are valuable to understand the conditions faced by prisoners, and they provide a way to evaluate wartime conditions.

In 1922, J. Fitzgerald Lee produced a brief article, "Prisoners of War," to argue the proper methods that should be followed by the United States for POW treatment during future wars. Lee's work was a response to the huge armies of World War I and the tremendous problems associated with the capture of tens of thousands of prisoners. He argued that without a well-planned system, nations would continue to be overwhelmed by massive captures in future wars, and needless suffering among captives would be the inevitable result.[2] Lee's work was followed by Herbert C. Fooks's *Prisoners of War*, a study of the international treatment of prisoners throughout history. Fooks organized his work topically, beginning with a definition of prisoners of war and ending with the liberation of prisoners. His work suggested that the Hague Convention of 1907 had provided insufficient protection for prisoners during World War I and should be replaced by a more comprehensive document.[3] William E. S. Flory's *Prisoners of War*, which provided a basic discussion of the evolution of international law regarding prisoners, focused almost entirely on the United States and Western Europe. Flory urged the

Allied nations of World War II to realize the importance of POW issues and to plan a system capable of holding millions of captured enemies. Like Lee, Flory believed that the problems faced in wartime were aggravated by the lack of planning for prisoners.[4]

In 1955, Lieutenant Colonel George G. Lewis and Captain John Mewha produced *History of Prisoner of War Utilization by the United States Army 1776–1945* for the Department of the Army. This work was one of the first general histories of American POW policy, with a special emphasis on the labor potential of captive enemies. Fully two-thirds of the work was dedicated to World War II because before 1943, the most common use of prisoners was for exchange, not for labor. Lewis and Mewha argued that such exchanges often proved detrimental to American war efforts, while the use of prisoners for labor was extremely helpful and even vital to the national economy. The authors concluded that American POW policy had never been adequately defined before an American conflict and that POWs have never been fully utilized as a labor force. Further, they believed that the U.S. government should plan an efficient labor system for prisoners of future conflicts.[5]

Immediately after the Vietnam War, A. J. Barker argued that modern war, involving the struggle for survival of competing ideologies, had complicated the problems of POWs and reduced the humanitarian component of POW care. Barker's *Prisoners of War* noted that with the rise of total warfare, the definition of a prisoner of war has become a major problem for powers at war. In Barker's view, the participation of guerrillas and freedom fighters had virtually nullified older definitions of POWs, and the perception of wars as matters of national survival ensures that attempts to regulate the conduct of warfare, through international agreements like the Geneva Conventions, became obsolete during conflicts. Barker pointed to World War II as the watershed event, when wanton violations of POW agreements occurred. He argued that the decline of POW treatment was simply one symptom of a general rise of barbarity during wartime. One major reason for the abuse of POWs was the failure of the principle of reciprocity after 1941. As Western powers have engaged Asian cultures, threats of reprisal have lost meaning, because "during World War II it became apparent that countries like Japan and the Soviet Union were not interested in Japanese or Russians who became prisoners of war."[6] In fact, these nations maintained an interest in their prisoners as agents of the war removed from the battlefield. Barker's work is extremely useful as a demonstration of the continuity of POW affairs. It is organized by events experienced by almost every POW, such as the moment of capture, interrogation, relationships with guards, and repatriation.

Howard S. Levie's *Prisoners of War in International Armed Conflict* contained a detailed legal evaluation of POW issues. The work included a brief discussion of the historical precedents of POW treatment, but focused primarily on an examination of the Geneva Convention of 1949 and its applications in modern warfare. Unlike Barker, who considered international agreements regarding prisoners to be virtually obsolete, Levie viewed the Geneva Convention as a vital document addressing almost every potential POW situation to arise in modern war. Levie's work explained how the provisions of the convention are to be put into practice. He did not attempt to draw conclusions about the history of American POW policy, preferring instead to create a set of guidelines to drive policy in the future, in the hopes of alleviating the suffering of the prisoners of modern war.[7]

Richard Garrett's *POW* examined the treatment of POWs from the Hundred Years' War to the Vietnam War, drawing conclusions about the experiences of POWs over the centuries. Organized chronologically, it focused primarily on the affairs of the United States and Europe, but it does not present an argument about the history of POWs in general, save that their lot in life was and is uniformly unpleasant. He described the experiences of prisoners in different wars primarily through anecdotal evidence, revealing that even as the size and scope of war broadened, the nature of prisoner operations from the perspective of the captive remained remarkably similar.[8]

The significance of this book within the literature of POW history is twofold. It is the first work since 1955 to present a comprehensive treatment of American policy and practice toward prisoners, with the goal of examining changes over time rather than focusing on a single war. It is also the first work to compare the stated goals of the United States regarding prisoners with the actual treatment received by captured enemies. All previous works have either focused entirely on one war or one aspect of POW treatment, or they have discussed only the experiences of a few prisoners, without any attempt to examine the bigger picture of American policy.

ANCIENT AND EARLY MODERN POW CUSTOMS

Before the seventeenth century, prisoners were typically killed or sold into slavery, depending on the whim of the battlefield victors. Prehistoric societies almost always executed captured foes, rather than spend their meager resources maintaining enemy warriors who contributed nothing to the captors' economy.[9] Some Native American tribes used capture as a means of increasing tribal numbers through the process of forced adoption. Others took captives for ransom or for ritual torture and execution.[10] In time, practices shifted throughout the world so that prisoners were typically enslaved rather than executed. The Greeks kept physically healthy prisoners for the slave markets or allowed captives to ransom themselves. The Romans used prisoners for labor, in rowing galleys, or in gladiatorial contests. The Romans rarely allowed ransoms because freed prisoners might again fight against the empire. In the Middle Ages, captured common soldiers still risked death or enslavement, but knights and nobility protected themselves with a code of chivalry that required participants to treat prisoners kindly and allowed them to ransom themselves. This behavior did not extend to wars fought with non-European populations; the Crusaders and their foes continued to kill and enslave prisoners.

In 1625, Dutch jurist Hugo Grotius codified the rules of warfare for the benefit of all nations in *De Jure Belli ac Pacis* (*The Laws of War and Peace*), and offered a more humane set of principles regarding POWs. He drew primarily on Greek and Roman philosophers, with occasional references to later events and practices. Grotius sought to establish the rights of nations to make war, as well as the responsibilities they bear as belligerents. His ideas publicized the plight of prisoners of war, but his suggestions for POW treatment were not universally accepted, and they proved to have a limited effect on European practices. Likewise, prisoners could expect few comforts from their captors and had no right to expect ransom or exchange. Grotius's work was the first real codification of the customs of warfare that specified when prisoners could be taken and how they should be treated.[11] He argued that prisoners were at the complete mercy of their captors and could be killed or enslaved at will, so the act of taking prisoners was a kindness, not a legal requirement. However, Grotius argued that by enslaving prisoners, the captor would benefit by sparing their lives. He thought that Christians should not enslave other Christians, and in the case of war between Christian nations, ransom should be the norm. Once a prisoner was taken, he was to be protected from harm, severe punishment, and excessive labor. In nations that did not allow the enslavement of prisoners, Grotius recommended exchanges or ransoms to free prisoners. The right of ransoms could be transferred between individuals or nations.[12]

The growth of national armies in the seventeenth century complicated the situation of POWs. At the end of the Thirty Years' War, the Treaty of Westphalia in 1648 provided that all POWs should be released and repatriated, without ransom or compensation. However, the use of ransom remained a popular practice well into the eighteenth century. Numerous attempts were made to specify a ransom for each military rank to simplify the process of regaining troops through payments. Simultaneously, exchanges became more common as belligerents began to forego the ransoms of prisoners of equal rank. Paroles became somewhat common during the seventeenth and eighteenth centuries, although they were reserved exclusively for officers. By giving his parole, an officer could be released to his own lines, to await formal exchange at a later date. The officer gave his oath not to participate in the conflict in any manner until properly exchanged. The parole system required mutual trust, but it offered the economic benefit of not forcing captors to maintain their prisoners until exchanges could be effected.

The ideas of Grotius were expanded and modified by Swiss philosopher and jurist Emmerich de Vattel, who published *The Law of Nations* in 1758. Like Grotius, Vattel sought to codify international law, with a particular emphasis on the laws of war. Regarding POWs, Vattel disagreed with Grotius on several major points. Vattel believed that a surrender must always be accepted, unless the enemy was guilty of an enormous breach of the laws of war.[13] He provided guidelines for the proper treatment of prisoners, arguing that prisoners should not be executed or enslaved unless guilty of a crime. They could be confined, but must be treated well; if a captor could not feed or guard them, they must be released on parole. Vattel argued that the state was bound to procure the release of its prisoners held by the enemy, either through exchange, ransom, or as an article in the treaty of peace. In his discussion of rebellions and civil wars, he argued all belligerents were bound by the laws of war as if separate nations.

As the concepts of exchange and parole became more common, institutions were created to oversee the POW system during wartime. During the Seven Years' War (1756–1763) England and France established a series of cartels, or agreements that allowed prisoners to be exchanged on a rank-for-rank basis. The cartels established commissions of representatives from each belligerent to keep records of prisoners captured, paroled, and exchanged by each side. Both sides presumed that at the end of the conflict, the nation with the balance of prisoners remaining after all exchanges were completed would be paid a ransom for the remaining prisoners. The cartel systems of the war were clumsy and required equal numbers of prisoners at specific ranks in order to function, but they demonstrated that enlisted personnel as well as officers could be exchanged during a conflict. Not surprisingly, the priority for exchange remained with officers; privates were often an afterthought within the cartel system.

European ideas about the treatment of POWs were transplanted to the New World by the colonial powers. The cartels created in Europe during the Seven Years' War were applied to fighting in North America, although with less regularity. Warfare in the colonial era did not closely resemble the European style of war, and the roles of colonial militias and native allies often complicated matters. The native allies recruited by European powers did not adhere to the rules of European warfare and refused to be bound by the European system. Likewise, Europeans and colonists did not view native enemies as equal opponents and rarely treated them as POWs.

The distinction between civilized and savage warfare is important to any discussion of American POW policy and practice. Grotius and Vattel each argued that the rules of warfare only applied to conflicts between civilized enemies. If an enemy did not follow the accepted rules and traditions of war, European armies did not feel restrained in their methods of warfare. Generally, the accepted rules of POW treatment were only applied between forces of European descent. Europeans who surrendered to native allies could not expect quarter, even when the allies were commanded by European officers.[14] Members of colonial militias, when captured by fellow Europeans, were often not considered worth holding for exchange, and they were often paroled to return to their homes and remain out of the fighting.

Even though the American colonies remained a part of the British Empire until the commencement of the American Revolutionary War, the British government did not provide many military forces to assist the colonists in their struggles with native populations. Rather, the individual colonies were left to devise their own approaches to govern warfare with the neighboring native tribes, with the result that no single policy existed for all of the colonies. Some common behaviors emerged, including a willingness to treat combatants and noncombatants alike, either through direct attacks such as raids on encampments or indirect attacks such as burning winter food stockpiles, placing the entire tribe at risk of starvation. Neither of these approaches to combat would be acceptable in Europe, but in North America, they were regularly used to compel a mass surrender, or simply to eradicate the enemy. Likewise, colonists often chose to execute the leaders of enemy tribes, to serve as a warning to other Native Americans in the region. Perhaps the most famous case in point was that of King Philip of the Wampanoag, who was captured in August 1676 after a yearlong search by colonial troops. Philip was beheaded and quartered. His head and hands were used to prove his demise, while the remainder of his body was hung from trees near the point of capture.[15]

Another common operational approach involved allying with other regional Native Americans to take advantage of ancient rivalries and blood feuds. Often, colonists rewarded their allies for behaving in nontraditional, brutal fashion. This was fully demonstrated in the Tidewater Wars, the Pequot War, the Tuscarora War, and the Yamasee War. In each case, English colonists purchased the services of native allies through promises of plunder and payment in manufactured goods. Soon after the successful conclusion of each war, the colonists then turned on their erstwhile allies, destroying them in a continual cycle of alliance, cooperation, and annihilation in the pursuit of more territory and resources. By the mid-eighteenth century, many native tribes relied on English colonists as a primary source of revenue and sustenance, earning payments for the delivery of enemy captives or scalps. Although prisoners brought in greater sums, the scalps proved far easier to transport, and they didn't offer the possibility of escape or resistance.[16]

Despite the bloody nature of colonial warfare, prisoners were taken by both sides on a regular basis. Many of the eastern tribes took prisoners as a means to increase the size and power of their society, integrating captives into their civilization through adoption customs. However, such adoptions typically pertained to women and children, rather than adult male combatants. Also, some tribes preferred to torture and then slay their warrior captives, which, when coupled with a lack of differentiation between tribal customs by many whites, led to a refusal to seek quarter by white fighters. Individuals not seeking quarter also did not offer it, and by the eighteenth century, raids to enslave Indians gave way to efforts to eradicate enemy tribes. As such, native conflicts exerted little influence over American prisoner of war policies in the colonial era and beyond, despite an almost constant state of conflict within the colonies.

The legacy of European POW practice is clearly visible in the American Revolutionary War. During that conflict, American commanders operated under the assumption that POWs should be protected from the ravages of war and maintained in anticipation of exchange with the enemy. Although Americans fighting for the cause of independence were not immediately viewed as legal combatants by the British, the existing system of POW captures, paroles, and exchanges was eventually applied to the war by both sides. This created a precedent that has affected American POW policy for over two centuries. The practice of implementing POW policies has changed, as should be expected with the changes in technology and society, but the underlying principles of American policy have remained consistent, striking a balance between humanitarian principles and political expediency.

1

STRUGGLING INTO EXISTENCE

The American Revolution

Like many of the officers of his generation, Ensign Thomas Hughes of the 53rd Regiment of Foot owed his commission to the social influence and financial contributions of his family. Hughes served during the 1777 Saratoga campaign under Lieutenant General John Burgoyne. While part of a detached unit of two companies stationed at Lake George, Hughes and his command awoke to a predawn fog on 18 September 1777. Suddenly, a party of approximately 600 militia, commanded by Colonel John Brown, burst forth onto the lakeshore, overwhelming the small garrison and capturing three officers and fifty privates. Hughes and his companions spent the next three weeks marching to Boston, where they began a confinement of nearly four years.[1]

As an officer, Hughes could give his parole not to escape a given area, in exchange for which he received a limited amount of freedom. Officers had to provide for their own housing and necessary supplies, often relying on credit from local merchants until they could receive their pay. Hughes managed to secure room and board for two silver dollars per week, living in the home of a Tory family. According to Hughes, "it consists of Father (who is almost deaf), Mother (a talkative old woman), and two daughters who are of the order of old maids, confounded ugly, with beards an inch long."[2] Hughes proved distraught to discover that his hosts had invited the servants to the dinner table, and that the Americans absolutely refused to launder his clothing. His days were spent wandering in the local woods with a fellow officer, returning to the home only for meals and to bed down in the garret, shared with the daughters, the servants, and another officer.

On 7 November, Hughes recorded his reactions to the surrender of Burgoyne's army. After confirming that the stories were true, he suggested that the United States would probably violate the terms of the agreement and prevent the British captives from returning to England. His prediction proved correct, and to his chagrin, it included his own fate along with the rest of the surrenders. Hughes's personality, readily apparent in his diary, proved incompatible with a series of hosts; in late April 1778, he wrote of his apprehensions that his hosts wished to murder him.[3] In May, he moved to Concord, where he received parole for the entire town, allowing him a certain degree of latitude in securing housing. He took a room in the home of a Mrs. Bliss, a woman with four sons serving in the war, two on each side. In June, Hughes became extremely ill, but he survived as a result of the care and diligence of his hostess and a local doctor, a mercy that took him by surprise. He soon moved to the home of the doctor, a professed Loyalist.[4]

The next two years of Hughes's parole reflected the life of a British officer without responsibilities to the regiment. He and his comrades continued to board with American citizens, accruing debts and making largely empty promises of repayment. Eventually, the U.S. Congress decided to gather British prisoners from the Saratoga campaign at Frederick Fort, Maryland, ordering Hughes and his comrades to report in the spring of 1780. There Hughes remained for almost a year, waiting for exchange. The exchange finally came in November 1780, when Hughes was informed he could return to New York once he had paid his personal debts, an undertaking that required yet another substantial loan. In June 1781, he finally embarked on the frigate *Confederate*, in command of a company of invalids en route to England, having spent nearly four years as a prisoner of war in Massachusetts, Rhode Island, New York, Pennsylvania, and Maryland.[5]

Hughes's story typifies the British officer POW during the Revolutionary War. Although his account provides some insights into the life of enlisted personnel, he simply did not care enough about the soldiers under his command to pay much attention to their often desperate situation. Like many of his comrades, Hughes often had to shift locations as a result of the vagaries of Congress, state governments, and the military situation in his region. He could offer his parole, which gave him an opportunity to improve his personal situation, but which also forced him to spend a great deal of money on his own upkeep—and which saved his captors a considerable amount of trouble. Hughes's tale is also important in that it offers a glimpse into the life of a captive from the Saratoga campaign. Unlike most prisoners of the revolution, these poor men did not get exchanged. Instead, they were moved around from site to site at the mercy of competing political and military interests. These interests formed the basis of American POW policies and practices during the war.

It should come as no surprise that American prisoner of war policy during the Revolutionary War changed constantly throughout the conflict. After all, no central government truly existed when the first shots were fired, and George Washington, the most important colonial military leader, did not assume command over the Continental Army until July 1775, a full three months after the engagements at Lexington and Concord. During the entire conflict, states ignored congressional requests and fought the war as they saw fit; likewise, militia units behaved however they chose, and they often refused to acknowledge any allegiance to the nation as a whole. Even within a single state or theater of the conflict, asserting control over the war proved virtually impossible for any specific entity.

Congress issued contradictory orders that were often ignored by field commanders and state governments. This created a poorly functioning system that made no attempt to utilize the labor or intelligence value of prisoners. Exchanges remained limited, unequal, and tedious throughout the war, and they often involved efforts by individual states to redeem their own captives for British POWs, regardless of congressional wishes. Enemy prisoners became victims of the system, although the situation faced by American prisoners remained at least equally unpleasant. The plight of prisoners influenced the outcome of the war, and was a factor in the British decision to seek a treaty and conclude the conflict.

American policy toward British prisoners of war consisted of a series of improvised measures created by Congress, influenced by the commander in chief of the Continental Army and individual state governments. Although Congress was not regarded as the supreme authority within the confines of each individual state, it served as a unifying body, attempting to create a coherent POW policy that coincided with the war aims of the individual states. Lieutenant General George Washington was under the command of Congress, but he was given great leeway in the daily operations of POW policies. His role was vital, particularly because he remained in command for the entire war while the membership of Congress changed.

The improvisational nature of American prisoner of war policy during the war is unsurprising, given that the Continental Army did not exist before the outbreak of fighting and that Congress was ill prepared to direct a war against Great Britain. Although specific policies and practices were improvised during the war, a few guiding principles consistently influenced American treatment of British prisoners. Prisoners represented different things to different colonial authorities. To Congress, prisoners did not maintain an intrinsic value, even as potential laborers. Their key value lay in their role as a diplomatic tool, a means to secure de facto recognition of the American government through diplomatic negotiations to create an exchange cartel. Washington saw the primary purpose of an exchange as a means to return veterans to the ranks of his army, which struggled to meet recruitment goals and certainly needed experienced officers. To individual states, the exchange of forces presented an opportunity to free state citizens from captivity, particularly those influential citizens who often served as militia leaders. Congress emphasized frugality in regard to POWs while adhering to the "recognized principles of humanity."[6]

Congress gave repeated instructions to Washington to seek an exchange cartel for prisoners on the basis of British recognition of U.S. sovereignty. For most of the war, the British refused to create a general cartel precisely to avoid this recognition. Thus the actual practice of prisoner exchange relied on negotiations for specific exchanges, not on a set of mutually recognized policies. States soon moved to enter separate negotiations with British commanders, often concluding lopsided agreements that sent thousands of British regulars and German mercenaries back into the enemy ranks, often for the release of a relatively small number of militia members, most of whom left service and simply returned home. The continual self-interest of the states frustrated Congress and Washington, who could do little to halt the separate exchanges.

The issue of prisoners received scant attention from Congress in the early years of the war because no true congressional military force existed to govern prisoners. Further, colonial militia forces had almost no history of taking prisoners and maintaining them for the duration of a conflict.[7] Colonial units facing the British Army were much more likely to feel bound by the laws and customs of war between civilized armies than when facing Native Americans in the field, as they had in previous colonial wars. Although Washington mandated humane treatment of prisoners by American forces, he had few means to enforce this dictate, and because he could supply neither guards nor provisions to assist in the safekeeping and maintenance of prisoners, his orders received scant attention, much less obedience, beyond the battlefield.

Even in the actual capture of prisoners, Washington exercised little control. A wide variety of American units took enemy prisoners during the war. The skirmishing of land forces and by the naval forces in service of the United States provided a slow but steady stream of prisoners, most taken in small engagements. Private American vessels (privateers) accounted for a great number of prisoners, particularly after Congress enacted bounties for enemy captives. Continental troops were present for the major American mass captures of enemy forces at Saratoga and Yorktown, but they had no means to maintain their captives and soon turned them over to state control. In these two campaigns, thousands of POWs were taken, rapidly taxing the ability of the Americans to supply and maintain them. Naturally, the British also took prisoners on a consistent basis, including captures at sea. Most Americans captured at sea were privateers, not members of the Continental Navy, and they were often effectively considered to be the equivalent of seaborne militia by state authorities. Like the American forces, the British took large numbers of prisoners on two occasions, once during the series of battles near New York in 1776 and secondly at the surrender of Charleston on 12 May 1780. Although exact numbers are unreliable, it is likely that the British maintained a favorable balance of prisoners during the first year of the conflict and for a brief period in 1780–1781. At all other times, the Americans probably held more enemy captives.[8]

Most of the works discussing the Revolutionary War contain at least some mention of POW issues, though few pay significant attention to prisoner affairs.[9] The most common topic is the treatment of American POWs, with particular emphasis given to the prison hulks that housed naval personnel and civilians. Herbert Aptheker argued that hundreds of Americans died because "the notorious corruption of 18th century British officialdom combined with typical aristocratic contempt and hatred for rebellious provincials to produce an inferno for the victims."[10] A common theme of the numerous prison narratives of Americans held by the British is the accusation of deliberate poor treatment.[11] Biographies of individuals associated with POW operations, such as Elias Boudinot, who served as the American commissary of prisoners for twelve months, have also provided an interesting view of the creation of POW policy.[12]

Most of the secondary works dealing exclusively with POWs during the revolution argue that American treatment of British prisoners was better than that given to American POWs, but they typically make use of only American sources.[13] Often, the authors analyze only a single aspect of the POW experience, without a discussion of the big picture, or they discuss Americans held by the British without mention of British prisoners.[14] The primary exceptions concern British prisoners taken at Saratoga and held in captivity for years despite a surrender agreement that promised them the opportunity to return to England immediately.[15]

DIPLOMATIC RECOGNITION, RECIPROCITY, AND THE EXCHANGE QUESTION

Although the United States naturally had an interest in regaining its citizens made prisoners by the enemy, there was a certain reluctance by both sides to actually agree to exchanges. Most prisoners held by the British had been captured aboard privateering vessels, and although they were American citizens, these prisoners were not in the direct service of the Continental forces. Also, enlisted personnel of the Continental Army captured by the British had often enrolled for a short period of service. In comparison, most army prisoners held by the United States were British regulars who served for an indefinite period, typically for life.[16] Because both sides agreed that all exchanges should be on a rank-for-rank basis for officers and a man-for-man basis for enlisted personnel, the British would gain much more from any exchange. Any British prisoners sent back to the British Army were likely to return to service within North America. Conversely, any American privates freed by exchange would most likely be near the end of their enlistment or would return to privateering. Unlike the enlisted ranks, American officers did not join the military for a fixed period, and Congress therefore placed great emphasis on the exchange of officers and avoided the discussion of exchanging privates whenever possible. The problems of exchange were exacerbated by Washington's insistence that American prisoners should be exchanged by date of capture, so that those held longest would be released first. Officially, he based this policy on humanitarian principles, but there was a practical component as well. If Washington agreed to seek the exchange of specific individuals regardless of the duration of captivity, he would be inundated with requests for special exchanges and privileged treatment. Instead, he quickly made it known that he would refuse all requests for prisoners to be exchanged out of order.[17]

The British treatment of prisoners was a determining factor in the treatment of prisoners by American captors. In addition to their usefulness for exchange purposes, British prisoners taken during the Revolutionary War were often viewed as a tool of retaliation, to prevent British commanders from treating captured Americans as treasonous subjects of the crown. Washington first threatened retaliation in an 11 August 1775 letter to General Thomas Gage, in which he noted, "I shall regulate my Conduct towards those Gentlemen, who are or may be in our Possession, exactly by the Rule you shall observe towards those of ours, now in your custody."[18] This letter, dated shortly after Washington assumed command, showed that he would base his initial

POW policy decisions on the behavior of the British toward American prisoners, but also leave all blame for mistreatment with the enemy. He soon wrote to Congress requesting instructions for the care and subsistence of captured enemy soldiers, because he believed their numbers would rise quickly. In the same communication, Washington recommended moving prisoners inland, away from the centers of British power in the colonies.[19] Much of Washington's knowledge of the British treatment of prisoners was provided by Elias Boudinot, who conducted an extensive investigation and tour of the confinement facilities in New York.[20] There, military and civil prisoners faced close confinement in prison hulks, where filth and disease claimed thousands of victims. At no time did American behavior toward British captives begin to compare with the conditions aboard the prison ships, even when British soldiers were locked into abandoned mine shafts or placed in city jails.

CONGRESSIONAL AND STATE AUTHORITY

The relationship between Congress and the states caused serious difficulties. On 9 April 1776, Congress requested that each state make lists of all prisoners they held and also that suppliers be paid on a regular basis for rations given to POWs.[21] Congress asked individual states to cease exchanging POWs within their power, as individual state exchanges undermined the power of congressional representatives to negotiate a general exchange cartel. For the most part, individual states ignored Congress and exchanged prisoners captured by their state militia forces for their citizens held by the British. Washington repeatedly requested that all prisoners be considered as a group to be exchanged against all American prisoners by date of capture, but he did not have the power to prevent the states' exchanges, even when the British captives had surrendered to Continental forces.[22] Many of the state exchanges included a desire to regain politically well-connected officers, and the question of fairness simply proved irrelevant as a result.

On 21 May 1776, at Washington's request, Congress created a set of general POW regulations. Most paralleled British norms for prisoner of war confinement. These rules were modified over the course of the war, but the spirit behind them remained fairly consistent, if often unenforceable. Officially, all prisoners held by the United States received rations equal to those issued to American troops on garrison duty. This policy departed from the British practice of issuing a two-thirds ration, believed to be sufficient for the maintenance of an enemy prisoner who performed no labor and thus expended little energy. Camp commanders segregated officers from privates, and all officers received parole unless specific orders were given for confinement. All American units under congressional control were to strictly observe surrender terms—an ironic demand, given the congressional habit of setting aside or unilaterally changing capitulation agreements, most notably after the Saratoga campaign. Where possible, a British agent supplied British POWS, although any prisoners out of the reach of a British agent were to be supplied by congressional funds. The families of any British prisoners could live with the POWs and received food and supplies in the same manner as the prisoners. Enemy prisoners could hire themselves out to private citizens within the locale of their confinement to support their families. Officially, no enemy POWs or deserters could enlist into American service.[23] Congress provided a standard form for paroles and reimbursement for the cost of lodging officers.

These general regulations provided a rudimentary guide for POW treatment, but they also proved completely impractical. States, not Congress, accepted nominal control over enemy captives, and the treatment meted out by each side varied. Some states chose to quarter enemy soldiers with the citizenry; others preferred separate compounds, normally military-style camps on the outskirts of large towns. Virtually every state allowed the recruitment and enlistment of enemy troops, occasionally even providing bounties to encourage the practice, as a reliable means to fulfill troop quotas. In addition to pursuing separate exchanges, states sometimes granted parole to enemy captives, regardless of congressional intentions.

In May 1776, Washington requested a congressional appointment for a commissary of prisoners, but Congress abandoned the day-to-day operations of POW care to the Continental Army and the states. Congress approved David Franks as the British agent for prisoners and tasked him with obtaining supplies for British prisoners at the expense of the British government. Given the congressional desire for economic frugality, it is surprising that Washington's request, on the grounds of both improving prisoner treatment and saving expenses, was not acceded to until 1777, when Washington offered the position to Elias Boudinot. Boudinot, a former member of Congress, was given the power to appoint deputies to provide necessary assistance and was granted control of all British prisoners regardless of location.[24] This control proved to be in name only. Without the funds needed to take over prisoner maintenance, Boudinot could request states' assistance, but he could not force their compliance.

In May and June 1776, Congress issued regulations designed to increase the number of British prisoners in American hands. There were simply not enough British prisoners to compel the British commanders to exchange captured Americans or to improve the treatment of American prisoners. Congress mandated that any individual taken in arms on a prize vessel, regardless of what vessel made the capture, was to be considered a POW. These prisoners were to be delivered to a U.S. marshal in any state, where they were held on an equal basis with other prisoners. On land, Washington was encouraged to employ native allies to capture British prisoners, using a bounty of one hundred dollars for officers and thirty dollars for privates to speed delivery to the Continental Army. Congress, which still held out hope of a general exchange cartel, forbade Washington from exchanging any prisoners without permission.[25] After the number of naval captures increased, on 5 August 1776, Congress voted to allow the navy and individual privateers to enlist any naval prisoners held by any state. Remaining naval prisoners were to be held by the states and exchanged for American prisoners from privateering vessels or the Continental Navy. British and German soldiers were still not allowed to join the Continental Army, and exchange of American seamen for British land prisoners was prohibited. On this last point, Congress would maintain its resolve for most of the war despite state protests.[26]

On 30 July 1776, Washington requested a definition from Congress of who should be considered a POW, including the status of sailors on merchant vessels flying the British flag. Initially, naval prisoners were only accorded POW status if captured on an enemy war vessel. In 1777, Congress declared any British subject serving as an officer, master, or mariner on any vessel, including merchant ships, to be a POW if taken by any American vessel. As with the decree of 21 May 1776, these prisoners could be delivered to any state as ordinary POWs. In 1781, Washington issued a final redefinition of prisoners of war to include only individuals taken in arms, and not civilians or members of militia captured unarmed. He wished to ensure that British commanders could not kidnap unarmed militiamen for the purpose of exchanging them for British POWs.[27]

THE CONVENTION ARMY

Near Saratoga, New York, on 17 October 1777, Lieutenant General John Burgoyne surrendered his forces to Major General Horatio Gates. At the stroke of a pen, the United States gained nearly 6,000 prisoners, almost half of them German mercenaries.[28] The Articles of Convention signed by Burgoyne and Gates specified that the prisoners were to be immediately marched to Boston, where British transports would be allowed to embark them for Great Britain. On the march, the enemy soldiers would be provisioned by the Continental Army at the same ration received by American soldiers. All expenses for the subsistence of prisoners would be paid by Britain before the embarkation of the convention troops. After reaching Europe, the convention troops would not be eligible to serve in North America for the remainder of the war, unless exchanged for American POWs.[29]

This short, simple agreement infuriated Congress, which was immediately critical of the terms granted to Burgoyne and soon accused the British of breaking the convention because they did not surrender all of the weapons and supplies mentioned in the agreement. No regimental colors had been surrendered, and the muskets turned over to American forces were both few in number and unfit for service.[30] To some politicians, these facts justified abrogating the entire covenant. Likewise, Washington informed Congress and Gates that the departure of the prisoners should be delayed, if possible, to prevent the troops from reaching England before spring. If the troops were allowed to depart before the end of the year, they might replace garrisons that could then be sent to America in time for the campaign season of 1778. On 8 January 1778, Congress voted to prevent the Convention Army from embarkation on the grounds that it had not received notification of the ratification of the convention by Great Britain. Much like earlier attempts to gain recognition by the British government, the requirement for ratification would implicitly recognize the United States as a sovereign power. Britain steadfastly refused to provide a ratification, and Congress was provided with a convenient excuse to keep the convention prisoners within America.[31] Rather than marching to Boston for the trip home, they marched off into years of captivity, privation, and continual recruitment offers from Continental Army representatives.

RENEWING THE QUESTION OF EXCHANGE

On 6 December 1777, Congress discussed the response of General William Howe to Washington's request for exchanges to commence. Howe insisted on a distinction between military prisoners and civilians held by the British authorities, allowing major differences in the treatment of each group. Congress wished all captives to be treated in the same humane fashion. In the preliminary negotiations at Amboy, New Jersey, Washington indicated his willingness to enter into an exchange of virtually any format Howe desired. Two months later, Washington reported to Congress that a man-for-man and rank-for-rank exchange system had been created, referred to as the Amboy Convention. Most importantly, negotiators created a composition system, allowing the exchange of officers and enlisted men of different ranks through a table of equivalencies. On 26 February 1778, Congress announced its eagerness for an exchange, yet blocked the ratification of the agreement until Britain agreed to pay all outstanding costs of upkeep for British prisoners. Congress ordered all states to forward accounts for prisoner upkeep, and it also demanded receipts from the quartermasters, provost marshals, and commissaries of prisons. The deadline for the receipt varied by location, with the latest deadline set at 1 June 1778. Even if the British agreed to the congressional demands, no exchange would occur before the summer of 1778. By delaying exchanges, Congress kept exchanged British troops from augmenting the forces already in North America in time for any summer offensives. For the next two years, Congress insisted on a general settlement of debts before the exchange of prisoners.[32] Not until after the fall of Charleston did British commanders begin to press the issue of general exchange, and with the balance of prisoners no longer in favor of the Americans, Washington informed Congress that he opposed a general exchange.[33]

When British commissioners refused to give in to the congressional demands for payment of prisoners' expenses, the exchange negotiations halted. Further complicating the issue, Congress demanded that any payments be made in specie, to prevent inflated continental currency from being used to discharge the debts, and removed David Franks as agent for British POWs because he had "abused the confidence reposed in him by Congress" by attempting to pass information across British lines.[34] Britain refused to appoint a different agent, and the lack of an agent caused great suffering among the British POW population. On 7 November 1778, Congress ordered that the commissary general of prisons reduce the rations issued to British prisoners to match the rations given to American prisoners held by the British at New York. Without an advocate in Congress, the prisoners and their needs were ignored in the ongoing diplomatic struggle.[35]

In the same resolution blocking the exchange, Congress again forbade the Continental Army from enlisting or drafting any British prisoners or deserters. As usual, most states simply ignored this prohibition and continued to enlist enemy prisoners in state regiments destined for Continental service.

In Washington's opinion, deserters were unlikely to remain more loyal in American service, and prisoners of war would return to the British at the earliest opportunity. In a letter to William Heath, Washington observed, "If we would wish to reinforce the Enemy with the whole of Mr. Burgoyne's Army, we can not pursue a mode that will be more effectual or more certain, than to enlist it into our service; but it may be done with less injury by sending them the Men, unarmed, without clothes and without paying them an exorbitant bounty." To prevent the practice, he recommended that recruiters be forced to pay for the losses caused by the desertion of any POWs they enlisted.[36]

Washington's aversion to exchange was primarily related to the possible return of enlisted men to the British Army. On 10 July 1780, he explained his opinion of prisoner exchanges to Congress. An exchange of officers, he believed, was worth pursuing because both sides would gain equally from the exchange, and the officers would no longer suffer in captivity. An exchange of privates, however, although sparing the prisoners further hardship, would damage the American military position because he anticipated taking the offensive. Because the United States could not afford to augment British manpower, Washington recommended sending supplies through the lines to American prisoners and halting exchange negotiations until after the campaign season. Congress, after considering the issue, instructed Washington to attempt a rank-for-rank general exchange of officers on 7 August 1780. After further consideration, Congress informed Washington that he could exchange officers by rank or by composition as he saw fit. Exchange was to be limited to officers only, chosen by length of captivity, and the first offer should be to exchange officers of the Convention Army, not militia officers. Washington immediately ordered Abraham Skinner, a deputy commissary of prisoners, to agree to a British request for a general exchange of officers. To delay any exchange of privates, Skinner requested a complete list of American enlisted personnel held by the British, including their corps and regiment. In response, the British insisted that any exchange include both officers and enlisted personnel, a proposition that Washington regarded as completely unprecedented and unwarranted.[37]

On 7 November 1780, Congress ordered Washington to exchange all Americans held by the British, including parolees, parole violators, captured militia, and Canadian hostages, as well as all American forces captured at Charleston, for members of the Convention Army and any other British prisoners available, rank for rank and man for man. When equal exchanges were not possible, the system of composition negotiated at Amboy in March 1778 could be used. Congress ordered that all expenses associated with British prisoners again be tallied, with the cost of upkeep for American prisoners in British hands deducted from the total and the remaining debt to be presented to British commissioners. If the British still refused to pay, Washington could offer exchange with the retention of British hostages to guarantee eventual repayment of the debt. If necessary, Washington could offer an exchange of hostages as surety that convention troops and their exchanges would not be used in the field before 1 May 1781. The British commissioners argued that the convention troops had never been prisoners of war and should have been returned four years before; they saw no reason to trade Americans for troops unlawfully held.[38]

Despite the differences in opinions, the negotiations resulted in substantial exchanges, and on 7 November 1780, Washington was able to report to Congress that almost every American prisoner held in New York City had been exchanged, primarily for officers of the Convention Army. The British government had concluded that the Convention Army would never be sent to England without an exchange of prisoners, and it decided to make the necessary agreements to regain their forces. Of the American POWs held at New York, every private and all but fifty officers were exchanged.

Regardless of congressional orders, Washington refused to exchange convention privates for Americans captured at Charleston before ascertaining the total number of prisoners held by the British in the South. Instead, he suggested trading all of the remaining American officers at New York for John Burgoyne, who remained on parole in England, and allowing Nathanael Greene to handle any negotiations involving the Charleston prisoners. Washington, alarmed by reports that Burgoyne was in ill health, noted that "his death would deprive us in exchanges of the value of 1040 private men or officers equivalent, according to the tariff which has been settled." Washington ordered Skinner to seek the exchange of Burgoyne because the British were unlikely to offer much in exchange for a corpse. The British refused to exchange Burgoyne by composition, and because they did not hold an American of equivalent rank, Burgoyne could not be exchanged.[39]

The congressional argument for exchanging the convention prisoners stated that Burgoyne broke the convention immediately after it was signed, and therefore the United States was not bound to release the prisoners. Congress wished Washington to quickly exchange the convention troops because convention prisoners were constantly escaping their confinement, traveling to New York, and being redrafted into new regiments to face American troops in the field. Officially, such behavior was forbidden by the second, third, and ninth articles of the convention, but in practice, neither side had faithfully adhered to the spirit or the letter of the document, and thus the British had few qualms about using escaped convention prisoners within their ranks. To prevent such duplicity, Congress ordered all convention prisoners to be placed in close confinement to prevent desertions and escapes. British officers of the Convention Army, whether on parole or not, were ordered to Simsbury, Connecticut, with the implied threat of imprisonment within abandoned mines, previously a form of confinement almost exclusively reserved for Loyalists. German members of the Convention Army were allowed to stay in Virginia, with officers allowed parole within Frederick County and privates confined to barracks near Winchester.[40]

Prisoner negotiations revealed the need for Congress to alter POW policies to suit the reality of the war situation. Through the end of 1779, British negotiators continued to refuse to even discuss the payment of outstanding prisoner upkeep debts and Congress continued to withhold permission for a general exchange. But in November 1779, the Board of War reported that individual states were exchanging prisoners without the sanction of Congress. The board requested that states stop these exchanges on the grounds that each local exchange undercut American repayment demands. The states ignored the congressional request and continued to negotiate exchanges for their own citizens.[41] In early 1780, Congress was finally forced to drop the demand for payment of debts before exchange, and on 13 January 1780, it renewed Washington's power to exchange prisoners as he saw fit. To assist him, it called for a new series of prisoner lists to be prepared by each state, to facilitate a general exchange of prisoners. To stop the individual state exchanges, Congress ordered all POWs delivered to the control of the commissary general of prisoners. In return, Congress agreed to allow any prisoners captured by militia forces to be exchanged for American prisoners from the same state, when possible. To augment its claim to enemy prisoners, Congress agreed to pay all upkeep, transport, and delivery costs for enemy POWs by reimbursing states for any expenditures made. All exchanges were still required to be soldier for soldier and sailor for sailor; no interservice exchanges were allowed. Because the British government refused to discuss debts incurred by British prisoners, Congress ordered that all prisoners allowed on parole had to pay their own personal upkeep costs before being exchanged. If the British government refused to pay for its prisoners en masse, perhaps individual soldiers would pay their own debts in the hope of exchange.[42]

PRISONERS IN THE SOUTHERN THEATER

While the war remained in New England and the middle states, Congress and Washington each maintained at least some influence over aspects of POW operations, if not actual control. However, the British decision to shift operations to the southern colonies in 1780 radically changed the nature of the prisoner issue in North America. Not only did Congress exert far less control in the Carolinas; the Continental Army, Washington's instrument of policy, surrendered en masse at Charleston on 12 May 1780. The relief force sent to South Carolina under Horatio Gates narrowly escaped annihilation at Camden less than three months later, eliminating any possibility that Congress or Washington could significantly exert control over events in the next phase of land operations. Instead, the decision to take and hold prisoners largely fell to individual militia commanders, some of whom showed little inclination to offer mercy to the enemy, particularly if the enemy consisted of Loyalist militia troops.

In some ways, the war in the Carolinas, particularly for the first half of 1780, followed the same patterns as the war further north. Unsurprisingly, battles in South Carolina involving linear formations of regular troops under tight control of officers did not devolve into wanton slaughter. Even when one side was routed, the probable result was the capture, rather than killing, of large numbers of troops, as demonstrated at the battles of Camden and Cowpens. This was also true during most of the sieges of the war in South Carolina. If the besieged chose to surrender, they could expect treatment in accordance with the customs and traditions of civilized warfare, such as the siege of Charleston. During the small engagements of militia forces in the South Carolina backcountry, the situation often proved far more grim. Officers often could not or did not exert firm control over their forces, with the result that allegations of refusing quarter became common as the campaign dragged on. Accusations of misconduct fueled calls for retaliation, with the result that a perception of intentional misconduct transformed into acts of deliberate slaughter.

A complicating factor was the nature of the militia war. The militia's knowledge of their neighbors meant that individuals could be targeted even off the battlefield. For example, on the night before Huck's Defeat of 12 July 1780, Whig militiamen captured Major John Owens, a subordinate of the much-hated British major Patrick Ferguson, asleep in his own bed.[43] Another key factor in the question of captivity or slaughter over the course of the South Carolina campaign was the leadership of the combatant forces.

Not only was the character of the leader and his adherence to the customs of warfare important, but also his ability to maintain control over his forces was a major factor. Thus, battles in difficult terrain or involving undisciplined militia were far more likely to include refusals of quarter than engagements involving regulars or open ground.

Although American POW policy in the northern and middle colonies could be controlled or at least influenced by Washington, his influence in South Carolina was minimal at best. This was amply demonstrated by American actions during the siege of Charleston. Washington favored abandoning the city in the hopes of saving the army commanded by Major General Benjamin Lincoln, though he did not go so far as to order Lincoln to evacuate. Lincoln's decision to stay was heavily influenced by the demands of the South Carolina state government, forcefully presented by Lieutenant Governor Christopher Gadsden. Lincoln refused to exercise his own judgment, with disastrous results. Eventually, Washington asked Congress to turn over all POW decisions in the South to Major General Nathanael Greene.[44]

Lieutenant Colonel Banastre Tarleton, commander of the British Legion and other forces, earned the sobriquet "Bloody Ban" early in the Southern campaign. During the siege of Charleston, he earned Clinton's approbation for his aggressive tactics and bold offensive actions. In particular, at Biggin's Bridge on 14 April 1780, he attacked a large detachment of Continentals and Whig militia, cutting off the last supply route for the besieged city garrison and capturing 100 soldiers in the process, along with horses, wagons, arms, and clothing. However, even Clinton admitted that only the difficult terrain in the area and the speed of the rebel withdrawal "prevented the slaughter which might else have probably ensued," lending weight to the American portrayal of Tarleton as an extremely sanguinary commander.[45]

On 12 May 1780, Lincoln agreed to surrender the city of Charleston to the British, and 245 officers and 2,326 enlisted personnel were made prisoners, radically altering the POW balance. When militia forces were included in the count, the surrender comprised 7 generals, 450 other officers, and 5,100 enlisted men. Before the fall of Charleston, British prisons in New York and Long Island held only 270 officers and 450 privates from the Continental Army. After the fall of Charleston, British commanders began to press the issue of general exchange, but with the balance of prisoners no longer in favor of the Americans, Washington informed Congress that he opposed a general exchange.[46]

The surrender terms that Clinton offered to Lincoln undoubtedly seemed generous to the victor. Although Lincoln's request to march freely out of the city in exchange for surrendering the capital was refused, Clinton did agree to release thousands of militia, taken under arms, on parole. After surrendering their weapons, these men left the city or returned to their homes, bound only by their oath not to serve against the crown. The Continentals taken in the city did not prove so fortunate. Lincoln's capitulation included the provision that all regular forces would remain in confinement until duly exchanged.[47]

It is quite likely that Clinton soon came to regret his generosity toward the militia, given the soon-to-change nature of the war. One shining example of this regret was Colonel Andrew Pickens, who was paroled after the fall of the city. He remained faithful to the agreement, living peacefully at home until his family was attacked by a gang of nominal Loyalists led by James Dunlap. Even though Dunlap was certainly not acting under the authority of Clinton, Pickens notified the British commander at White Hall Plantation of his intention to resume hostilities. For the remainder of the war, Pickens operated under the assumption that he would receive no quarter if taken prisoner once more.[48]

An infamous incident that set much of the tone for the backcountry war occurred at the Battle of Waxhaws on the afternoon of 29 May 1780. There, Tarleton's force of 270 men chased down almost 400 Virginia Continentals commanded by Colonel Abraham Buford. When Buford refused initial demands for surrender, Tarleton ordered a cavalry charge. The Continental volley did little to stop the charge, and Buford's men soon found themselves in the midst of a brutal melee. Unfortunately, one of the American shots struck Tarleton's horse, temporarily removing him from command. In the absence of their leader, and believing him dead, the legionaries furiously attacked Buford's troops, stabbing and slashing those trying vainly to surrender. By the time Tarleton regained control of his men, the toll was sickening. Tarleton had lost 5 killed and 14 wounded, while Buford's losses were 113 killed outright and 150 wounded, many mortally. Contemporary accounts accused British troopers of stabbing unconscious victims and pulling piled corpses apart to get at wounded men underneath.[49]

The perception of the Battle of Waxhaws and its aftermath fueled many subsequent events in South Carolina. According to the accepted laws of war, Buford's refusal to surrender meant that he and his troops could expect no quarter if Tarleton chose to attack. If his men threw down their weapons and begged mercy, Tarleton's dragoons were under no obligation to offer it, particularly if other members of Buford's party continued to resist. Although Tarleton's troops had no legal obligation to accept surrenders after

Buford's refusal, allegations of killing wounded enemy soldiers lying helpless on the ground quickly spread through the backcountry. Although there is no direct evidence that Tarleton planned or ordered the slaughter, the result was the same as if he had. Cries of "Tarleton's Quarter" began to arise from the throats of victorious Whig militia units in numerous small engagements throughout South Carolina, threatening to eliminate even the semblance of rules from the war in the South.

On 3 June, Clinton issued a proclamation that all prisoners on parole in South Carolina would be considered released from their parole on 20 June. However, there was one major stipulation that galvanized resistance to British control. All paroled prisoners were expected to take an oath of allegiance to the crown or be treated as rebellious subjects. Before the proclamation went into effect, Clinton boarded a ship to return to New York, leaving his subordinate, Charles Cornwallis, to deal with the ramifications. Cornwallis, in turn, attempted to repeal Clinton's proclamation and secure the POWs on parole outside of Charleston, but the damage was done.[50]

After the capture of thousands of Continentals at Charleston, British negotiators attempted to open discussions for a large exchange of POWs, but Washington resisted the temptation. While Washington and Clinton wrangled over the question of exchanges, British and Loyalist units throughout South Carolina engaged in a flurry of burning and looting, quickly transforming many would-be neutrals into partisans fighting for the rebellion. Not only did these depredations harden resistance, but they also triggered a series of reprisals, visited on both British regulars and marauding militia. Whig and Tory partisan bands began to ignore the traditional customs of war in the pursuit of vengeance and plunder. One notable example was Major William Davie, who quickly developed a reputation of offering no quarter. On 1 August 1780, near Hanging Rock, Davie's followers attacked a small unit of Tories, pretending to be fellow Loyalists until they were among the opposition. After trapping their quarry against a fence, Davie's troops slaughtered the entire outpost. At the same location just five days later, Brigadier General Thomas Sumter's militia band surprised a force of several hundred Tory militia and British regulars, killing and wounding 200 and capturing 73 more. Sumter, like Davie, had no way to maintain control over prisoners so close to enemy forces, but rather than slaughtering all of his enemies, he released them on parole.[51]

The Battle of Camden on 16 August 1780 followed the conventional pattern of linear warfare in the revolution. It was an extremely bloody affair for the rebel forces, with approximately 1,000 killed and wounded, and a further

1,000 captured. However, the massive losses of the Continentals and Whig militia were not due to any after-action slaughter by the British and their Tory allies; rather, they were due to the ineptitude of Major General Horatio Gates and the poor discipline of his troops. Camden demonstrated Cornwallis's willingness to take large numbers of prisoners when slaughter would be just as easy. Not only were hundreds taken immediately on the field, but hundreds more were rounded up from the scattered and fleeing Continentals and Whig militias. Cornwallis ordered them returned to Charleston, the heart of British power in the region, but he failed to order sizable detachments to guard the prisoners. As a result, many were able to escape captivity during the march to the capital, some by simply slipping away, others by the intercession of rebel partisans. A week after the Battle of Camden, Brigadier General Francis Marion's irregular force attacked a British unit of approximately 30 guards detailed to escort 150 Maryland Continentals. In the fight, Marion's men took 24 prisoners, including 2 officers. After freeing the rebel prisoners, Marion invited them to join his force in the hopes of increasing his forces, but many of the soldiers refused to obey his orders.[52]

In the aftermath of Camden, Tarleton's actions showed that he did not avoid taking prisoners, despite his bloodthirsty reputation. At Fishing Creek on 18 August 1780, Tarleton's troopers surprised Sumter's forces, killing 150 but capturing 300 more. In the engagement, the British dragoons also recaptured more than 100 prisoners held by the rebels. In contrast, that same day at Musgrove Mill, Loyalist militia forces lost 150 killed and wounded, with only 70 of their number taken prisoner by the partisan bands of Colonel Isaac Shelby, Colonel James Williams, and Colonel Elijah Clarke.

In the months after the Battle of Camden, much like the aftermath of the fall of Charleston, the war in South Carolina again devolved into a series of small engagements, primarily between bands of militia. Clinton believed that Tory militia forces would suffice to pacify the backcountry once the British regular forces established a series of fortified outposts throughout the region. One of the most notorious leaders of Tory militia forces, British major Patrick Ferguson, announced that if the rebellious citizens of the countryside "did not desist from their opposition to the British arms," he would "hang their leaders and lay their country to waste with fire and sword."[53] Ferguson's announcement did not pacify the countryside; rather, it galvanized rebel opposition by forcing everyone to choose a side. It also demonized Ferguson, who became a major target of partisan leaders throughout the state.

As the competing bands sought dominance of the backcountry, allegations of refusing quarter became increasingly common, as did other acts contrary to the traditional customs of civilized warfare. Most militia leaders had no formal training in the laws of war, and partisans who broke the rules of war on both sides seldom received any formal punishment beyond chastisement. Although they became subject to retaliatory acts, it is unlikely that this fact served as a deterrent, given the fact that they might be mistreated by the enemy regardless of their own actions. In addition to killing helpless enemies, torture and execution of prisoners became common. Whipping, tarring and feathering, hanging to the point of unconsciousness, and spicketing (driving a stake through the foot) all became disturbingly common occurrences as tools to extract information, but also as a form of brutal entertainment and revenge.[54] Although retaliatory executions were often threatened, they were not always carried out, in part because the threat of retaliation did not always serve as a deterrent. One example was the case of Colonel Isaac Hayne, a militia officer placed on parole after the fall of Charleston. After being accused of violating his parole, Hayne was executed despite threats of retaliatory measures from Nathanael Greene. Such threats did not stop the execution, nor did Greene order the execution of a British colonel held as a prisoner, despite his promises to do so.[55]

Ferguson's measures did little to demilitarize the region, and in the two months after Camden, neither Tory militia forces nor British regulars under Tarleton proved able to control significant sections of the countryside. Ferguson's movements served primarily as a magnet for smaller bands of Whig militia to coalesce, and after a prolonged pursuit, Ferguson's unit was surrounded atop a short hill, King's Mountain. The Whig militia bands were led by no fewer than eight commanders, with no single individual exercising authority over the entire group. After a series of advances and heavy firing, the rebels finally charged the hilltop, drawing Ferguson's men into a brutal melee and gunning down the hated Ferguson. The Tory militia, seeing their leader dead on the field, sought to surrender, but the rebel leaders proved unable or unwilling to stop their subordinates from commencing a general slaughter. Cries of "Tarleton's Quarter" and "Remember the Waxhaws" spurred the victorious troops forward. By the time the Whig leaders regained control over their men, 157 Loyalists lay dead, with another 163 grievously wounded. Only the difficulty of the terrain and the chaos of the battle prevented an even worse slaughter; by the end of the day, almost 700 were in captivity.[56]

On 9 November, Sumter's camp was attacked by a band of Loyalists under Major James Wemyss. The attack failed, and Wemyss was captured, along with a list of the houses his troops had burned. Rather than turning

Wemyss and the evidence over to his troops, Sumter chose to burn the list out of fear that his troops would kill Wemyss and his followers if they found out his responsibility for the attacks. Although this action demonstrated compassion on Sumter's part, it also showed that Sumter did not have complete control over his forces.[57]

In contrast to Sumter's uncertain control over his unit, Brigadier General Daniel Morgan maintained a disciplined mixed force of Continentals and militia. Morgan had seen service in virtually every theater of the Revolutionary War, and had spent time as a POW after being captured at the Battle of Quebec on 31 December 1775. After more than a year of captivity, Morgan was duly exchanged and returned to service, setting out to raise a rifle regiment. Morgan's Loyalist detractors argued that his methods were illegal, particularly because he encouraged his troops to target individuals, especially officers. At Bemis Heights, Morgan personally ordered a sniper to target Brigadier General Simon Fraser. When Morgan moved troops to South Carolina, Greene gave him an independent command. While harassing British and Loyalist outposts in the backcountry, Morgan's primary responsibility was providing intelligence to Greene regarding enemy unit positions and movements. Unsurprisingly, Morgan viewed enemy prisoners as a key source of information, and he consistently utilized interrogations of British and Tory prisoners to keep Greene informed of enemy movements.

At the Battle of Cowpens, Whig militiamen and Continental troops raised the cry of "Tarleton's Quarter" as the British formations disintegrated under heavy fire. However, Morgan and his officers, including Pickens, quickly moved to quell the cry that had come to signal the commencement of a massacre, and instead the victorious commander was able to report the complete defeat of Tarleton's forces with the capture of 29 British officers and more than 500 enlisted troops. A further 200 British wounded littered the field, safe from further injury thanks to Morgan's quick action. He ordered the officers sent on parole to Charleston, there to seek exchange for rebel officers held in close confinement. Pickens led the guard detachment that marched the enlisted troops to Salisbury, North Carolina, where their numbers almost offset the American losses at Camden.[58] The defeat at Cowpens greatly hindered Cornwallis's ability to pursue the various rebel groups operating in the Carolinas, and the lack of a subsequent slaughter removed the possibility of propagandistic cries for retaliation against Morgan and his men. Not every foe received such compassion from Pickens. His 1782 expedition against the Cherokee tribes of the Carolinas included an order to kill all adult males; only women and children were spared in the campaign.[59]

After Cowpens, Cornwallis decided to move his forces into North Carolina in pursuit of Greene's mixed force of Continentals and militia. He brought Greene to battle at Guilford Courthouse on 15 March 1781, where Greene sought without success to re-create Morgan's successful tactics from Cowpens. Like earlier open battles, the combat at Guilford Courthouse ended with the British regulars holding the field and hundreds of wounded soldiers littering the field. However, it was a Pyrrhic victory, and Cornwallis had few forces left after the battle to police his own wounded troops, much less any rebel prisoners. On the other side, one of Greene's aides accused Continental soldiers of executing British prisoners to avoid having them recaptured by the enemy.[60] After the battle, Greene moved back into South Carolina, fighting a series of small engagements that followed the pattern of the previous summer. On 8 September 1781, Greene's army fought the last major battle of the war in South Carolina, when they encountered Lieutenant Colonel Alexander Stewart's army at Eutaw Springs. In this fight, neither side made even a pretense of capturing enemy soldiers. The policy of recruiting enemy deserters had come full circle: at Eutaw Springs, the desperate combatants on each side expected to be executed if captured.[61] Although the British forces held the field at the end of Eutaw Springs, this battle signaled the failure of British attempts to pacify the South Carolina countryside, and the last British outposts in the backcountry were evacuated, leaving Charleston as the only significant British presence in South Carolina. The final British evacuation of Charleston occurred in December 1782, when thousands of Tory militia were abandoned to their fate.

In South Carolina, the conditions faced by prisoners once they reached captivity were not markedly different from POWs in other theaters of the war. However, the brutal nature of the backcountry fighting made the decision to take prisoners much less likely than in other regions. When allegations of refusing quarter erupted, retaliations followed almost immediately. However, it is important to note that not all of the backcountry engagements devolved into wanton slaughter. The intercession of strong leaders could prevent such atrocities, even when their subordinates seemed determined to eradicate the enemy forces. There was no ultimate factor in determining the question of surrender or slaughter, but the frequency of refusing quarter in South Carolina certainly distinguished the region from the rest of the Revolutionary War.

On 28 July 1781, a congressional committee reported that American prisoners in New York, primarily seamen captured aboard privateering vessels, continued to languish in terrible conditions. The British intent, according to the report, was to encourage enlistments in the Royal Navy. Congress considered such conditions tantamount to murder and threatened reprisals against British prisoners if the conditions were not alleviated.[62] To prevent American deserters from joining the enemy, Washington announced on 4 October 1781 that any captured in enemy lines at Yorktown would be immediately hanged.[63] This announcement repudiated the tradition of turning a blind eye to the enemy's possession of deserters by allowing their quiet removal during the surrender of a besieged location. Two weeks later, congressional threats of POW reprisals gained new weight with the surrender at Yorktown of over 7,000 British and German prisoners under Lord Cornwallis. Shortly after the surrender, Washington noted that the United States held a balance of prisoners sufficient to free all POWs held by the British, and he recommended to Congress that the new supply of prisoners not be squandered on exchange for American privateers.[64] He became incensed when Congress publicly ordered him to create a full, general exchange of all prisoners after secretly ordering that Cornwallis be held back from exchange. This order forced Washington to either reveal a secret decision of Congress to the enemy or be accused of treating falsely regarding prisoner exchanges.[65]

PRISONERS AFTER YORKTOWN

Despite frequent threats of retaliation, actually punishing enemy prisoners for mistreatment of American prisoners proved extremely rare. One exception was ordered on 3 December 1781, after the British authorities had ignored numerous complaints about the treatment accorded Henry Laurens, a former president of Congress. After his capture at sea, Laurens was imprisoned in the Tower of London and threatened with execution for treason. Congress was further infuriated by reports of American prisoners being imprisoned in English dungeons. Congress ordered the secretary of war to imprison British officers of high rank, including those on parole, and to send British prisoners to confinement in the notorious Simsbury mines, abandoned shafts used to house prisoners in horrid conditions. All officers allowed to return to England on parole, Burgoyne included, were recalled to North America immediately. Secretary of War Benjamin Lincoln also ordered all British enlisted POWs in America sent to Lancaster, Pennsylvania, to be placed in close confinement as a means to prevent desertion and escapes. German prisoners remained in frontier towns, as they were considered much less of a security risk, having proven much more tractable to their captors, and much less attractive to British exchange negotiators.[66]

Congress ordered the massive retaliatory efforts to compel the British to exchange Laurens for Burgoyne. Britain did not consider Burgoyne to be a prisoner of war under the terms of the Convention of Saratoga, and in any event, Burgoyne had been allowed to return to England on parole. Instead, the British government offered to exchange Cornwallis, still on parole in New York, for Laurens. When the offer of Burgoyne for Laurens was rejected, Congress exempted Cornwallis from exchange in any form.[67] It was unlikely that the British would ever agree to the Burgoyne-Laurens offer because such an agreement would essentially force Britain to release Laurens and receive nothing in return. Laurens assured his captors that Congress would agree to the offer of Cornwallis, and he was released from the Tower and allowed to assume ambassadorial duties in London. On 25 September 1782, Congress was notified that Laurens had negotiated for his own release in exchange for Cornwallis, regardless of congressional desires. Benjamin Franklin, serving as minister to France, had agreed to the exchange, forcing Congress to choose between disavowing the power of its most famous citizen and reversing its threat to hold Cornwallis indefinitely. Washington, annoyed by the behavior of Congress, demanded to know why Laurens had been released in Britain and allowed to resume his duties while Cornwallis was expected to remain on parole. In response, Congress asserted its authority to approve exchanges but allowed the matter to drop, and Cornwallis was duly exchanged.[68]

While the Laurens situation was being negotiated, Congress again gave Washington the power to negotiate a cartel regarding prisoners, on 18 February 1782. In this instance, Congress ordered Washington to seek a cartel of exchange that would include regulations protecting all prisoners, land or sea, and an exchange of captured private citizens. Naturally, Congress expected Washington to make another attempt to settle past POW accounts for the upkeep of enemy prisoners, but Congress no longer formally insisted on the payment of prisoner accounts before any general exchange. In fact, Washington had virtually universal control over prisoner negotiations, with the lone exception that Cornwallis could not be exchanged. Political pressure regarding exchange continued to mount, with states clamoring for Congress to make a general exchange agreement, even if not on optimal terms. To assist in the exchange negotiations, Congress announced a bounty of eight dollars for captured enemy deserters delivered to state control, to increase the available number of prisoners for exchange. States paid the bounty to individuals, along with reasonable charges for upkeep and transportation, and secured the prisoners until reimbursed by Congress. Washington remained uncertain of the relative importance of financial concerns compared with rescuing Americans from captivity, in part because Congress seemed to shift its focus often, and he suggested that exchanging American sailors for British soldiers might speed the negotiations.[69]

After Yorktown, the activities of the commissary of prisoners and all his deputies were placed under the control of the secretary of war, who was also given direct control over the security and safekeeping of enemy prisoners. This reassignment of the commissariat was necessary because other departments often failed to respond to requests made on behalf of prisoners. In an effort to save expenses, Congress repealed all resolutions and appointments regarding the commissary of prisoners in July 1782, effectively disbanding the department altogether, although Washington was empowered to appoint a temporary commissary as necessary.[70]

Throughout 1782, Congress returned to the matter of American prisoners enlisting in the enemy's forces. In particular, a large number of American naval prisoners had enlisted in the Royal Navy. In a similar situation, many German prisoners had expressed a desire to enlist in the Continental Army, or at least remain within the United States after the war, and in the meantime hire themselves out as laborers near their confinement locations. Washington thought that German prisoners could prove useful to the army, and he urged the secretary of war to allow German prisoners to enlist for three years. For their service, on 15 May 1782, Washington recommended a bounty of one hundred acres, received at the end of enlistment, and a guarantee of American citizenship.[71] On 5 June 1782, Congress authorized the secretary of war to recruit among German prisoners, with a bounty of eight dollars given to any new recruit. The former prisoners were treated as any new recruit in all respects, and could be counted against state recruiting quotas. Washington received direct control of any prisoners successfully recruited, to place them as he saw fit. While Germans obtained new opportunities, on 7 June 1782 the secretary of war was ordered to call in all British prisoners working with American citizens and to cancel all future work permits. Congress believed that the work program offered too many opportunities for escape. Most German prisoners had proven uninterested in returning to British service, but many British escapees had successfully reached their lines and joined new regiments.[72]

After canceling the work permits of all British prisoners, Congress returned to its demands for payment for POW upkeep costs. If Britain refused to pay past subsistence bills, the secretary of war was authorized to reduce rations given to enemy prisoners, although prisoners were to be kept healthy. Congress also planned to reduce any other costs associated with enemy prisoners, where possible. Washington was ordered to make a final demand for payment to Sir Guy Carleton, in New York, although Congress considered it unlikely that Britain would reverse its course and pay the demanded sums. Washington was reauthorized to make any partial exchanges, but no general officers were to be exchanged by composition, in the hope that the British government might pay for the return of its most prominent military captives.[73]

Just two weeks after revoking the parole of all prisoners and canceling work permits, Congress reversed itself and again opened the possibility of employing British prisoners. On 21 June 1782, Congress created a new POW labor system, designed to reduce escapes by relying on the financial interests of employers. Any British prisoner could be hired if the prospective employer deposited twenty French guineas into the Bank of North America. At the end of six months, the POW could sign an oath of allegiance and become a citizen of the state of his choice. Any prisoner who wished to labor but not obtain citizenship could hire himself out for a duration of one year, with a bond of forty French guineas paid by the employer. Congress hoped to reduce the costs of prisoners by allowing them to hire themselves out and provide for their own upkeep, while using the employers to maintain the security of the prisoners. By insisting on foreign currency, Congress could avoid the problems associated with wartime inflation and increase the supply of specie available for congressional expenditures.[74]

In many locations, employers ignored prohibitions against hiring enemy prisoners, and virtually no employers paid the high deposit for POW labor. Deputy commissaries of prisoners were court-martialed in York, Lancaster, and Reading, Pennsylvania, for allowing British prisoners to work without a bounty paid by the employers, but this did little to end the practice. On 3 July 1782, Congress concluded that any work programs would lead to additional enemy escapes, but no plan existed to reduce the problem. For this reason, the secretary of war was again ordered to recall all British prisoners and place them in close confinement. On 11 December 1782, another new labor policy was created, requiring a bond of one hundred pounds in Pennsylvania currency for the employment of a prisoner. Employers were also required to pay four dollars per month to the government, in addition to any wages paid to the prisoner, for the privilege of hiring any enemy POWs.[75]

Again, the regulations did little to fill congressional coffers, as few mechanisms existed to compel the obedience of citizens.

Through the end of 1782 and the first half of 1783, Congress considered the idea of a general exchange of prisoners, regardless of the number held by each side. In July 1782, Congress announced it was always prepared for a general exchange on just terms. At that time, the United States held more prisoners than the enemy, and thus a complete exchange could be an appealing proposition for the British. However, the legislature undertook negotiations to free all American prisoners on a man-for-man basis, rather than a complete exchange of all prisoners. Congressmen blamed the failure of negotiations for complete exchange on "the predetermination of Sir Henry Clinton to regain his captive soldiers, without regard to the enormous debt which had accrued and is daily increasing for their subsistence." Congressional negotiators also recognized that Britain "is now disabled by the loss of a veteran army which cannot easily be replaced." By retaining the extra British prisoners as little more than hostages, Congress might force a British payment for the subsistence of prisoners.[76]

After exchanging all American land forces in British hands for British soldiers, Washington proposed to Carleton an exchange of British soldiers for American sailors, with the caveat that British soldiers exchanged for sailors would not be eligible to serve in any capacity for twelve months. Washington argued that captured privateers in British hands were not directly engaged in the public service and would not necessarily return to their previous activities. On the other hand, British soldiers, if exchanged, could be employed immediately in North America or sent to aid operations in the West Indies, hurting the interests of American allies. Naturally, Washington attached a demand for subsistence repayments before the repatriation of British prisoners. Not surprisingly, Carleton refused the conditions offered by Washington, but he did agree to appoint commissioners to negotiate a general cartel.[77]

Washington named representatives to meet with the British emissaries, but the general cartel meeting was a dismal failure, in large part because the British commissioners were not given the power to bind Great Britain to any agreement beyond equal exchanges of prisoners, and they again refused to even discuss the matter of subsistence accounts. As a result, on 16 October 1782, Congress again ordered all partial exchanges to cease and directed the secretary of war to further reduce the costs of upkeep for enemy prisoners in any way possible.[78] Rather than a general cartel providing for the exchange of all prisoners, the commission only agreed to release captured medical and clerical personnel, and made them exempt from capture in the future.[79]

Shortly after the failure of the cartel commission, Congress ignored its own dictates and asked Washington to obtain the exchange of two American officers on 5 November.[80] Carleton was displeased by the failure of the cartel commission and blamed the failure on American demands for the repayment of subsistence debts. Washington described Carleton's response of 3 November as having "used an asperity of language so much the reverse of his preceding correspondence that many regard it as portending a revival of the war against the U.S." He forwarded Carleton's letter to Congress and included the suggestion that the United States should be more flexible in its demands.[81] On 18 February 1783, Congress relented and renewed Washington's power to approve exchanges. For the first time in the war, Congress also granted the secretary of war the power to make exchanges, in the belief that a different representative might have greater success in negotiations with Britain.[82]

In March 1783, the supreme executive council of Pennsylvania petitioned Congress to liberate all Pennsylvanians held by the British. The congressional response pointed out the logistical complications, particularly given the stated American desire to exchange prisoners by date of capture rather than by state of origin.[83] Despairing of the likelihood of a successful exchange negotiation, in April 1783, Congress extensively debated a proposal to free all enemy prisoners without exchanging them for Americans. Certain members of Congress believed the war was effectively over, and that housing and feeding enemy prisoners were a waste of funds. To justify their position, they argued that the ratification of the provisional peace treaty, which included the release of prisoners by each side, mandated that the United States release its captives. Other representatives pointed out the potential security hazards inherent in a proposal to release thousands of enemy troops without preconditions. After two days of heated debate, Congress decided that releasing all enemy POWs was premature and inadvisable. The primary argument against a general release of prisoners was economic: releasing the prisoners would probably reduce the effect of reimbursement demands presented to the British peace commissioners.[84]

The ratification of the Treaty of Paris officially freed all prisoners held by both sides. In an incident that summarized the entire POW experience of the war, on 1 July 1783, Washington wrote an extensive apology to Lieutenant Theodore Gebhard of Brunswick, explaining that Gebhard and the prisoners under his command had been liberated months earlier, but they had not been notified of the change in their status.[85] Gebhard's situation illustrates the fact that even after all of the negotiations for exchange and demands for

POW lists, the American system was still so disorganized that it could overlook an entire unit of enemy prisoners.

The American prisoner of war policy of the Revolutionary War was a constantly changing series of orders from Congress, often completely ignored by the individuals and states tasked with their implementation. The system often functioned poorly, and any efforts made to utilize prisoners for any purpose other than exchange proved mostly counterproductive. Throughout the war, humanitarian and economic concerns clashed, and together, they worked to ensure that exchanges were limited, unequal, and extremely time-consuming. Enemy prisoners endured difficult conditions while in captivity, but they were not subjected to worse circumstances than the members of the American military in the field. There were certainly inequalities in the system, but for the most part, enemies were relatively well treated. The United States lived up to Washington's decision to treat prisoners with decency and humanity, and at no time did the conditions used by the United States approach the horrors of captivity reported by prisoners of the British. Although the methods were improvised, virtually all of the goals of Congress and Washington with regard to POW policy were eventually achieved, at least in part because of the influence of prisoner negotiations, and although the prisoner issue did not determine the outcome of the war, the sheer number of prisoners taken by the United States influenced the British decision to end the war. Unfortunately, the American military soon forgot the lessons learned regarding POW policy, including how to house, feed, and maintain the health of prisoners. In the three decades between the Treaty of Paris and the new outbreak of war with Britain in 1812, the experiences of prisoners during the revolution were left behind. The army, reduced to an all-time low of only eighty troops in the immediate aftermath of the war, devoted little effort to preserving the records of the revolution, and no time to planning for future conflicts. Engagements in the Northwest Territory devolved into the traditional frontier warfare of the colonial era, where quarter could not be expected from either side. As a result, at the beginning of the War of 1812, POW policies had to again be created anew, and in many cases, the mistakes of the revolution were repeated in the later war.

2

THE FIRST DECLARED WAR

The War of 1812

In January 1812, W. B. Irish, Michael McClary, and James Prince all held the relatively unimportant government positions of U.S. marshals. All also pursued other careers; their marshal duties, although time-consuming, did not provide enough income to sustain their families, and they were undertaken more out of a sense of duty than any fiscal desire. However, when the United States and Great Britain went to war in that year, each man's position carried a responsibility for maintaining British prisoners, who soon began to arrive in large numbers at prison depots established throughout the American states. At each location, agents were appointed by the British to oversee the care of British POWs within the United States. Similar positions were created to ensure the safety and good health of captured American troops held by the British. These agents drew on the capturing government for funds to clothe and provision their charges. Each nation expected that the costs for prisoners would be included within any peace negotiations at the close of the war. In reality, British agents often drew loans from individual U.S. marshals of posts holding prisoners. These marshals were authorized to charge the U.S. government a commission of 2.5 percent on any sums advanced to British prisoners, an option used almost exclusively by officers. The government paid Prince, the marshal of prisoners in Massachusetts, a net profit of over $4,800 from 1812 to 1814 for what amounted to a part-time career. It requires very little imagination to understand why the secretary of war was inundated with requests for appointments to the position. The most important qualification for the post was the ability to loan large sums of money to the bankrupt American government, which was often slow in repaying its debts. According to the final accounting maintained in the records of the Treasury Department, as of 1 September 1815, Prince was due $92,674.52.[1]

Exacting payment from the United States government could become a frustrating process for many of the marshals. Irish, the marshal of

Pittsburgh, repeatedly complained that he had received no money for the upkeep of British prisoners in his care, and noted that he had "frequently had to borrow 4 & 5 hundred dollars of my friends," in addition to paying for the construction of barracks for the guards and prisoners. The system for payment remained unclear, with marshals requesting payment from many sources, including Commissary General of Prisoners James Mason, Secretary of State James Monroe, Secretary of War John Armstrong, and occasionally President James Madison. As McClary of New Hampshire noted in one letter, "as the prisoners are now delivered over the cost of their maintenance and all other charges it is expected will be paid." Not only had the marshal advanced funds to feed and house the prisoners, he had also paid the bounty authorized to privateer vessels to obtain the prisoners captured at sea and brought to Portsmouth. This letter, like many others of its kind, went unanswered by Monroe or his staff. McClary's financial woes continued for years. As late as 1817, he wrote to Stephen Pleasonton requesting payment for his services regarding British POWs. Pleasonton disallowed half of the accounts forwarded by McClary, largely on the grounds that they represented double charges. According to McClary, after the double charges were removed, the government remained in his debt for over $865, almost three years after the end of the war.[2]

Prince, Irish, McClary, and the other marshals illustrate a number of important points within the American prisoner of war policy. The system of maintaining prisoners through the use of civilian agents allowed the military establishment to utilize its manpower on the battlefield rather than at the prison compound. Prisoners in the War of 1812 were held in a number of different locations, preventing the possibility of a single swift British raid to free prisoners from American control. However, at each location for prisoners, the POWs were held in a fairly close concentration. This so-called concentrated dispersal allowed American leaders to minimize the number of United States personnel needed to guard prisoners and lessened the impact on local economies, while still spreading the British prisoners to a number of locations.[3]

RENEWED WAR WITH GREAT BRITAIN

When the United States declared war on Great Britain in 1812, it fought what many historians have dubbed the Second War of Independence. This conflict forced the creation of a cohesive policy for dealing with captured enemies. Before the outbreak of war, no formal international law existed that governed the capture and maintenance of prisoners of war.[4] Rather, most nations formed their prisoner policies primarily on the basis of expediency or arrangements created after the outbreak of hostilities. The conduct of American military forces was governed by articles of war approved on 10 April 1806, but the articles made no mention of POW treatment. In reality, the United States improvised practices throughout the war, with little thought to international law beyond the threat of retaliation for the mistreatment of American POWs.[5]

In much the same manner as the American Revolutionary War, the American government and military proved completely unprepared for the capture and maintenance of enemy prisoners. By the end of the conflict, the U.S. government had virtually collapsed, and the military had begun to improvise not only prisoner of war policies, but also almost every aspect of the war effort. Participants in the war were too far removed from the revolution to personally remember the practices of the earlier war, and the dissolution of the peacetime army in the intervening decades meant that the lessons of the Revolutionary War had to be relearned in the latter conflict. Despite the lack of planning and the frequent breakdowns of the POW system, the War of 1812 established many precedents for American behavior toward captives in subsequent conflicts. One of the most rapid and important changes during the war was the centralizing of POW operations. This reflected the role of a stronger federal government, and it avoided some of the difficulties caused by states pursuing independent POW policies. Other innovations included the use of prisoner of war labor, the concentration of prisoners in a small number of locations, and the refusal to repatriate POWs against their will at the end of the war. American commanders created a strict policy of retaliation for the mistreatment of American prisoners held by enemy forces, and they carried out retaliatory threats. Each of these tactics played an important role in shaping American POW policy for the next two centuries. Perhaps most importantly, all American POW operations remained under federal control, and a competent commissary general of prisoners, John Mason, assumed control of the rudimentary POW apparatus.

British practice in the War of 1812 was similar to that in the revolution, and Great Britain, which had been engaged in war on the European continent for much of the preceding decade, simply incorporated American prisoners into a prison system that already held 70,000 French prisoners by 1812. Devising a separate method for controlling American prisoners never occurred to British commanders, most of whom considered North America a secondary theater, a minor distraction in the war against Napoleon. British commanders chose to consolidate American prisoners at a few locations, most safe from any possible raid to free captives because of their distance from the North American theater. Halifax was the most common destination for American prisoners, particularly those captured on the Canadian frontier. Although the North American conflict presented a few complications, including the role of native allies and the status of captured slaves, it simply did not capture the attention of British leaders engaged in a war of national survival against France.

Although the War of 1812 remained an irritant to Britain, it consumed the attention, resources, and efforts of the entire American government and military. The question of legal recognition, so important to the Revolutionary War, did not complicate the War of 1812, and as such, exchange negotiations proceeded relatively quickly. The British government, desperate for troops to employ on the European continent and sailors to man the blockade of Europe, could not afford to leave military forces idle in American prison compounds. Instead, other issues came to define diplomatic negotiations of the war, beginning with the definitions of citizenship and naturalization.

CITIZENSHIP, IMPRESSMENT, AND IMPRISONMENT

One of the problems faced by the United States in the War of 1812 was the sizable percentage of American citizens in 1812 that had been born in Great Britain. Just as many Americans during the revolution had maintained loyalty to the British crown, American leaders feared the possibility of a large fifth column within the United States. A system was quickly instituted to keep track of the numerous "British subjects," loosely defined as any recent immigrant to the United States, or any individual who had not renounced British citizenship. U.S. marshals of every military district received orders to complete preprinted forms, sent for the same purpose, to identify and watch over potentially disloyal citizens. The forms, which served as a rudimentary form of visa, included a physical description of each subject, his or her location, and a provision that the document required renewal on a monthly basis for the duration of the war.[6]

According to English common law in 1812, all individuals born as British subjects remained so for their lifetime, regardless of residence or any naturalization processes in other territories. Thus allegiance was set at birth and could not be changed under any circumstances. By this reasoning, any Irish immigrants to the United States who took an active part in the war were guilty of treason against the crown. The American position was that a naturalized citizen was entitled to the same legal protections as a native-born citizen, and all naturalized Americans were free of any legal obligations to their native country. The issue was certainly important, given the large number of sailors on American vessels who were not born within the United States.[7]

The irreconcilable laws resulted in clashes between American merchant ships and the Royal Navy, which sought to reclaim British deserters serving on American ships by stopping and searching American vessels at will. As many as 25,000 British citizens served on American merchant ships in the early nineteenth century. Estimates of impressments suggest that up to 6,000 sailors were removed from U.S. merchant ships in the decade before the war. It is certain that some American sailors were mistaken for deserters and forcibly taken into the Royal Navy. The most notorious incident regarding impressments occurred on 22 June 1807, when the HMS *Leopard* demanded to search the USS *Chesapeake.* When the *Chesapeake* refused to submit to the search, the *Leopard* opened fire, forcing the American ship to surrender. After a thorough search of the ship, four sailors were taken from the *Chesapeake* as deserters. In 1811, two of the sailors were returned to the United States after almost four years of captivity. Of the other two sailors taken, one, a British sailor, was executed for desertion, and the other, an American, died in a hospital in Halifax. The *Chesapeake-Leopard* affair incited popular support for a war against Britain and was a major precipitating factor in the conflict.[8]

Before the outbreak of war, sailors from the United States and Britain often shifted allegiances. During the war, the practice continued because sailors were routinely offered the opportunity to switch sides rather than become a prisoner of war. On 17 May 1813, Colonel Thomas Barclay, British agent for prisoners of war, complained to Captain Stephen Decatur that some British prisoners had taken service on American ships. Barclay remarked, "It is unnecessary, I feel assured, for me to make any remarks on the impropriety of one nation taking the prisoners of war, subjects of another nation into its service." Decatur's somewhat bemused reply noted that this was not within his jurisdiction, but he also pointed out that "after the crew of the United States late Brig Nautilus were on board the Africa as prisoners of war many of them were tampered with & solicited to enter the British service & that five of them were actually entered & employed." Decatur then referred Barclay to the offices of John Mason, the American commissary general of prisons and prisoners.[9] With the British blockade of Europe in place for almost the entire War of 1812, the Royal Navy maintained a constant need for manpower. Extending the blockade to American ports only exacerbated the problem.

The two men with the greatest effect on American POW policy during the war were Mason and Barclay. Mason held his office for almost the entire war, and Barclay served as the agent for British prisoners for the first two years of the conflict. They maintained a steady correspondence throughout the war, discussing issues of mutual importance in regard to the British troops confined within the United States. The letters remained polite, but the men disagreed on virtually every aspect of POW treatment. In particular, Barclay was infuriated by the American decision to spread captives over many locations, a decision that inevitably made his duties more difficult. In a scathing letter to Mason, Barclay argued, regarding British prisoners, "they should be placed in regular established places, and not scattered over the whole United States, or permitted to go at large, or seduced into the American service."[10] Mason's chief complaint was that the British failed to pay the costs of prisoner upkeep, echoing the congressional complaints of the Revolutionary War.

During the War of 1812, American forces captured a total of 15,508 British prisoners, but only 5,765 of these prisoners were taken on land. Over 9,000 prisoners were captured aboard ships, including 1,485 on the Great Lakes, 2,905 at sea by public vessels, and 4,842 by privateers. A remarkable number of British prisoners were described in naval records as "retaken in Am. ship," suggesting that they were captured while manning prizes taken by British ships.

Of particular interest was the decision to turn all naval prisoners over to the control of the army. By transferring naval prisoners to army control, the U.S. military established a precedent, still in effect, that once captured, POWs would be guarded and maintained by the army. The lone exception to this policy occurred only briefly during the Spanish-American War. This policy not only freed naval personnel for service at sea, but also prevented the maritime service from negotiating separate exchanges. Much to the chagrin of the Royal Navy, it also slowed the transfer of exchanged sailors back to British control. Although the War Department maintained less detailed records of prisoners captured, a compilation of prisoners captured at sea and on land near the Canadian frontier is still in existence. This roster contains less individualized information than the final navy version, but it serves the useful purpose of confirming much of the data from the naval records.[11]

THE QUESTION OF TREASON AND CONFINEMENT OF HOSTAGES

After the disastrous Battle of Queenston Heights on 13 October 1812, a large number of American personnel were taken prisoner, including then lieutenant colonel Winfield Scott. The men were placed on boats to Halifax, the central British prisoner of war depot in Canada. During the trip, British officers mingled with the American captives and singled out those with a distinct Irish accent. Twenty-three men were pulled from the American prisoners to be sent to England to face trial for treason. Scott's arguments and appeals to the contrary proved useless. The plight of these "Irish traitors" occupied Scott's thoughts for the remainder of the war, and he used all of his influence in an attempt to win their freedom, or at the very least save them from the gallows. Scott was released on parole, and he immediately informed Secretary of War John Armstrong of the plight of the prisoners. On 2 July 1813, Sergeant Henry Kelly, one of the Irish Americans singled out, complained to Armstrong about the mistreatment the twenty-three men had suffered and included a list of grievances held by the prisoners and a roster of the men involved. This letter bolstered Scott's call for retaliatory measures to protect his troops.[12]

On 1 May 1813, Armstrong ordered Major General John Dearborn, commanding American forces on the Niagara frontier, to hold twenty-three British soldiers as hostages for the safety of the accused Irish traitors. These prisoners were confined at Greenbush Cantonment, New York. A list of the hostages was quickly forwarded to the British, in the interest of preserving the safety of the Irish American prisoners. The British response was to place forty-six American officers in close confinement, doubling the stakes of any retaliatory action. In an almost comical series of events, each side escalated, placing more officers and enlisted personnel into confinement as hostages.[13]

Neither the United States nor Great Britain showed any sign of compromise about the men being held as hostages, with each side threatening more dire actions, until the American agent for prisoners in London, Reuben G. Beasley, informed Secretary of State James Monroe that the Irish captives were treated in the same manner as all other American prisoners in England. Beasley's letter was received 27 June 1814, prompting Monroe to send Colonel Tobias Lear to meet with Colonel Edward Baynes to finalize a new exchange agreement. After the negotiations, the hostages held by each side were returned to their normal POW status, and they were eventually paroled for return to their homelands. Twenty-one Irish captives returned to the United States on 9 July 1815; the remaining two prisoners had died while in captivity.[14]

Despite the mutual decision to release the hostages from close confinement, some prisoners remained held in such a manner. On 9 August 1814, Barclay informed Mason that several British officers still held as hostages were expected to be made available for exchange. Barclay warned that "double the number of American Prisoners will once more be placed in a similar state of confinement in retaliation for these men" if they were not made immediately available. Despite efforts by both sides to ameliorate the conditions of captivity, the threat of retaliation remained constant for both sides.[15] Luckily, neither belligerent provoked the other into carrying out significant retaliatory acts.

On 28 September 1814, Mason wrote James Prince, the marshal of Massachusetts charged with maintaining British prisoners in that state, that 100 American seamen and 59 American soldiers had been deported to England from Canadian prisons on the charge of being English subjects. In the same letter, Mason ordered Prince to place six British naval officers and ten sailors in extremely close confinement in retaliation for British confinement of the officers and crew of a privateering vessel.[16]

Despite all threats, retaliatory measures by the United States primarily consisted of simply holding British prisoners as hostages against the safe treatment of American citizens. These hostages were typically confined in city or county jails, rather than in specially constructed federal prisons. This lessened the expense of maintaining the hostage prisoners, but it also presented a potential conflict of interest between individual states and the federal government. Because some state legislators, particularly in New England, had disagreed with the declaration of war, they resented any federal requirement to contribute to the war effort. This resentment erupted in Massachusetts in early 1814, when the state legislature passed a law ordering all British POWs held in city or county jails to be freed unless removed by the president within ten days. This law was not well received by the marshal of Massachusetts, James Prince, who protested that the British prisoners had never been placed into a county jail "without first ascertaining from the County Officer that the interest of the county will not be affected by their confinement therein." Prince advised Mason that the United States should consider removing prisoners altogether from state control, although he did not offer any practical alternatives.[17]

British troops placed in close confinement complained to Barclay that their health was in great danger as a result of their situation: they were not provided with soap, clean clothes, or the necessities of life. Particular emphasis was placed on the lack of tobacco in their confinement. The prisoners noted, "we at all times consider it not consistent with the character of a British Soldier to complain, we cannot help it at this time." Strangely, those prisoners of war did not blame the United States, but rather the British government, which had not maintained enough interest in the prisoners to see to their needs. According to one captive's letter, no British agent had been seen by the prisoners for four months, and during the previous visit, each prisoner had been given a single dollar to use for purchasing their necessary supplies beyond rations.[18]

In one of the strangest incidents of the war pertaining to prisoners, John Smith, the marshal of Pennsylvania, wrote a letter to Mason dated 29 April 1814, explaining the escape of nineteen officers held in close confinement in Philadelphia. These officers, who were designated for the retaliatory measures adopted by the United States, should have received extra attention from their captors. Despite the obvious importance of maintaining a careful watch over men held in close confinement, the guard personnel of the prison were reduced to four men, apparently without notifying the marshal. The officers somehow procured a saw and cut the iron bars covering the third-story mess window. The men then created a rope ladder from bedsheets and climbed to the ground on the night of 24 April 1814.[19]

EXCHANGE NEGOTIATIONS: THE CARTEL OF 12 MAY 1813

Near the end of the first year of war, British and American representatives met to discuss prisoners of war. Both sides argued that the conditions faced by prisoners of war would be best ameliorated by a policy of rapid exchange of prisoners. American commanders, desperate for veteran field forces, hoped to return POWs to service on the North American continent. The British, still fighting to depose Napoleon, needed to muster as many forces as possible as soon as they could be regained. American and British representatives held a conference at Halifax to discuss an exchange of captured naval personnel. The agreement was signed 28 November 1812 and allowed a complete exchange of all prisoners captured at sea. The Halifax negotiations served as the basis for a broader agreement. In early 1813, representatives of each government met again, at American insistence, to discuss prisoners taken in land engagements. Mason and Barclay represented their respective governments, expecting a quick resolution to negotiations in light of the successful naval exchange agreement.

After a few weeks of negotiation, Mason and Barclay finalized the cartel for the Exchange of Prisoners of War, commonly referred to as the Cartel of 12 May. The remarkably simple provisions of the cartel concerned only the welfare of prisoners of war. The first article stated that all prisoners, regardless of where captured, would be treated "with humanity conformable to the usage and practise of the most civilized nations during war." All prisoners were to be exchanged on a rank-for-rank or equivalency basis without delay. Rank equivalencies were provided for all conceivable prisoners held by either side. The system was adapted for naval use, and it was considered acceptable to exchange naval personnel for land forces—a major departure from Revolutionary War practices. The equivalency values of personnel greatly differed from those of the Revolutionary War, with the values of high-ranking officers significantly reduced, making the transfer of officers much more feasible.[20]

In theory, the new exchange equivalency system should have worked extremely well, particularly when compared with the older practice of rank-for-rank exchanges. The emphasis on exchange within the Cartel of 12 May should have created a system capable of quickly returning captured troops. In reality, however, the system proved unwieldy, largely as a result of the inefficiency of the men appointed as agents of exchange and the slow bureaucratic methods of keeping accurate records of each prisoner's status.[21]

Despite its functional problems, the table of equivalencies remained an unchanged part of American prisoner of war policy through the Civil War, when the last nonbattlefield, routine exchanges of prisoners involving the United States occurred. In records pertaining to the War of 1812, hundreds of exchange accounts still exist, typified by the exchange of Scott and 21 other American officers on 22 December 1812 for three British officers, 15 noncommissioned officers, and 141 privates. Scott's exchange demonstrated the utility of converting the value of each rank to a single commodity. Small-scale exchanges were common, but mass paroles of regulars were unusual during the war, as each side typically held prisoners for exchange via a formal cartel. The slow speed of communications, coupled with the large number of prisoners and considerable variety of locations in which they were kept, led to great difficulty in maintaining accurate records of British prisoners of war. Further complicating the issue was the number of individuals released at sea, and those who were never properly registered with a district marshal or a British subagent for prisoners of war.[22]

According to the cartel, any warship commander could approach a prisoner depot under flag of truce and demand an exchange of prisoners. If a certain prisoner was demanded, he could not be held back without good and sufficient cause for such detention. Lists of prisoners were to be prepared and exchanged by the agents for prisoners at each depot, to facilitate the exchange process. The only provision for stopping exchanges was in Article 14, which stated, "If either nation shall at any time have delivered more prisoners than it has received, it is optional with such nation to stop sending any more prisoners on credit until a return shall be made equal in number to the balance so in advance."[23]

Specific exchange locations were agreed on by each side, and cartel ships flying flags of truce were to be allowed into the designated harbors for the purpose of exchanges. The expenses of cartel ships were generally shared between the American and British governments. The standard rule of conflict was that the nation receiving its captured soldiers would bear the costs of their return, although the actual practice often relied on agreements for individual ships. One example was a proposal from Mason to Barclay to exchange via cartel all American prisoners at Halifax taken in Quebec for an equivalent number of British prisoners taken in Canada. The British were to outfit a vessel and transport the Americans to Salem, Massachusetts, where the British vessel would receive British prisoners and supplies at the expense of the American government. In the same letter, Mason suggested an exchange of prisoners from the vicinity of New Orleans for those held by the British in Nassau, with the two governments equally splitting all of the expenses incurred.[24]

Cartel ships required a great deal of preparation before embarkation; consequently, each side was well aware of when and where a cartel ship was due. Individuals used this knowledge to request the inclusion of specific prisoners on board particular cartel ships. The motivation and reasoning behind each request varied greatly, but almost all were granted "in the spirit of decency and common humanity."[25] At times, each side attempted to hold back certain individuals, usually officers considered exceptionally effective. For example, Sir George Prevost's subordinates advised him not to exchange Brigadier General William Winder, a skilled commander whose services to the United States would prove too valuable to allow his release. However, Prevost rejected the idea of holding Winder back, agreeing to his release.

Unsurprisingly, officers received preferential treatment for exchange. Dozens of letters were exchanged between Mason and Barclay proposing individual exchanges of certain officers. Typically, one or the other would send a list of officers he wished exchanged and ask for the demands of the other side in exchange. By the end of 1813, the system had engendered sufficient trust that Mason felt comfortable requesting the release of Samuel Cooper Hixon from his parole without providing an exchange. On 22 December 1813, Mason asked Barclay "simply to discharge from parole a released man on credit."[26]

The cartel carefully defined prisoners and the manner of their confinement. Only combatants in the direct service of the enemy nation could be held as prisoners of war. All noncombatants, including medical and religious personnel, as well as passengers on merchant ships, all women and girls, and boys under twelve years of age, were to be immediately released. Early in the war, captures of vessels at sea often included sailors from neutral nations, who were typically released under the condition that they no longer serve in the enemy's forces. To facilitate exchanges, lawful prisoners were to be held at designated prisoner of war depots, limited to six locations in British territory and seven locations in the United States.[27]

The cartel also specified that each nation was to provide each of its captives a daily ration of one pound of beef or twelve ounces of pork; one pound of bread; and four ounces of peas, six ounces of rice, or a pound of potatoes. Rations were supplemented by a small allowance of vinegar and salt. Each government clothed its own prisoners by appointing agents to oversee the needs of prisoners held by the enemy. The agreement also specified a system of parole, and each side swore that paroled prisoners would not serve in any capacity until a proper exchange had been completed.[28]

BOUNTY PAYMENTS AND CAPTIVITY CONDITIONS

As in the Revolutionary War, the U.S. government undertook measures to increase the number of British POWs. This included the offer of a cash bounty for all prisoners of war brought in by privateers. Before the creation of the bounty on 3 August 1813, most privateers released their captives on a neutral shore rather than bear the burden of their sustenance. The initial bounty of $25 per prisoner proved insufficient, and on 19 March 1814, the bounty was increased to $100 per prisoner. The prisoners were to be delivered to a district marshal, whose receipt allowed the privateer captain to apply for the federal bounty. Privateers applied to numerous offices in the hopes of obtaining bounties, but Mason received the most bounty applications. Bounties applied to any British sailors held as prisoners of war, but were expressly forbidden for any captured slaves, who were instead sold for the benefit of the privateer's crew. Once a bounty was applied for, privateers could not agree to private ransom offers from their captives. Thus, the bounty represented a guaranteed value for delivering prisoners and was at least somewhat more dependable than the negotiation of a ransom.[29]

Although the increased bounty turned captured British sailors into a valuable commodity, the bounty offer made no mention of standards of treatment. The original bounty of $25 was not sufficient to offset the cost of maintaining prisoners on privateering vessels. The $100 bounty made it fiscally possible for a privateering crew to profit by keeping prisoners, although negotiating a ransom could prove more profitable. The authority of the U.S. Navy and its regulations did not extend over private vessels, and the treatment of British sailors by privateers varied widely, prompting numerous allegations of mistreatment. One of the most notorious incidents, according to British prisoners confined aboard a prison ship at Charleston, occurred at the hands of the crew of the *Decatur.* Upon capturing the *Dominica,* American sailors abused the crew of the British ship, confining them in irons on deck during many days of "wet weather," refusing calls for quarter, and attacking individuals who had surrendered their arms. The marshal of South Carolina investigated the affair, and many prisoners alleged inhumane treatment. Strangely, one prisoner contradicted his comrades and testified that he could not have received better treatment at the hands of the Americans, "except to the plundering of the best part of my cloths [*sic*], money, my watch, gold chain, and 4 seals I have nothing to complain for." No record exists as to the results of the investigation, but it is unlikely that the alleged perpetrators received any punishment.[30]

Most British prisoners were held in camps scattered throughout the various states. However, in a practice dating back to well before the American Revolution, both the British and the Americans also used prison ships. The advantage of shipboard prisons rested on the ease of preventing escapes. The United States relied primarily on privately owned vessels for prison ships, leasing the ships on a daily or monthly basis. As late as February 1814, Michael McClary, the marshal of New Hampshire, asked Mason whether the prison ship at Portsmouth should be rented at $2 per day, or simply bought outright for the sum of $1,200. Conditions on the ships varied: McClary noted that prisoners under his care had received bedding but not blankets, as he was unsure of his responsibilities for prisoner comforts.[31]

By sending prisoners to many locations, the United States prevented a British attempt to free a large number of prisoners with a single attack.

However, dispersing captives to a number of holding sites vastly increased the problem of security. Prisoner escapes were often attempted, with varied results. In one interesting case at Camp Scioto, Ohio, two British prisoners attacked a sentinel while attempting to escape their prison compound. The sentinel shot and killed one of the attackers, and stabbed the other with his bayonet. A court of inquiry was convened to investigate the death, hoping to forestall any British retaliation. After two days of testimony, the court determined that the sentinel had committed no offense by shooting James Price during an escape attempt. A copy of the trial record was forwarded to Mason, "that you may with the greater facility, be able to justify the act, if necessary to the British Government."[32]

CAPTURING SLAVES

A particularly thorny problem arose as a result of the differing views held by Britain and the United States regarding slavery and the service of soldiers and sailors of African descent. Although slavery technically remained legal in both Britain and the United States, the nature of slavery in each location was quite different. Many sailors of African descent served in the Royal Navy, and as a result, no small number were captured by American forces. A total of 124 black sailors captured on British ships were reported on separate lists from white sailors; 47 were noted as slaves, and 3 were specified as "mullattoes." No record of any Africans captured on land can be found in the naval records, although this may simply reflect the less detailed army records used by the Navy Department to compile the final list of prisoners.[33]

Throughout the war, the British routinely raided the coastline of the United States, often capturing and retaining slaves. Frequently slaves were offered an opportunity to serve in the Royal Navy, especially when slaves were captured by the British aboard an American vessel. The manumission of slaves by British captains infuriated slave owners, who had no means to recover their former property. Mason noted that "the British officers in command at Halifax had separated from other prisoners, and refused to give up or exchange as prisoners of war, Slaves captured on the high seas in one of our vessels." Mason charged that the British captains on the coastline of the United States "were in the constant habit of receiving the slaves of our citizens on board British ships of war." These captains refused to return American "property" and tended to either employ the slaves aboard ship or transport them elsewhere in the British territories. As a result, Mason ordered all deputy marshals to retain any slaves captured at sea, regardless of ownership, to hold back from exchange against the return of American-owned slaves. Slaves captured by privateers, however, were ruled by Southern courts to be the property of the capturing vessel, and they were sold as prizes for the enrichment of the crew.[34]

Barclay repeatedly demanded the return of free black sailors captured by naval vessels and privateers, most of whom were sold into slavery regardless of whether they had previously been free. In one case, he requested the release of "16 Black men captured by the Holkar American Privateer and carried into New London." Barclay also mentioned "some Black Persons, Passengers in the British Sloop Hussar, captured by an American Privateer, and then, and still Prisoners in Savannah, these are also Non-Combatants." In Barclay's opinion, each of the above groups of captives should have been freed by the Cartel of 12 May and allowed to leave American captivity at their earliest convenience. After two weeks of inaction, Barclay again wrote to Mason requesting the release of noncombatants, including "the four black men who were manumitted by Mr. Dugan, and captured with Mr. Caruthers, particularly when you consider that a very large proportion of the American prisoners brought here in the *Magnet* were people of colour."[35] Just as Mason repeatedly failed to secure the return of captured slaves, Barclay failed to prevent the enslavement of captured free men.

Undoubtedly, the location where black prisoners were confined had a certain effect on their treatment. The marshal of South Carolina, Morton Waring, was accused by a British agent for prisoners of war, James Dick, of treating black prisoners inhumanely. In his own defense, Waring argued that the white British prisoners were the main source of difficulty in the prison, not the conduct of himself or the guards. In Waring's opinion, prisoners were to be kept "stirring as much as possible, this I knew would contribute to their health, Negroes in general are slothfully disposed." Thus the prisoners were ordered to undertake a number of mundane tasks, including cleaning the prison itself. Furthermore, Waring stated, "Since the release of the white Prisoners of war, I have never had any communication with Mr. Dick as British Sub Agent." Waring's defense proved effective in court, as the judge of the District of South Carolina, John Drayton, stated that Waring "is too much of a gentleman to use any such [harsh treatment] towards them [the prisoners]."[36]

To the eternal infuriation of Mason and other American officials, slaves taken by the British were almost never returned, even after the end of hostilities. According to English law, slaves who set foot in England were immediately made free. British authorities were unwilling to return freedmen to the status of slavery, regardless of American views on the matter. Despite the inclusion in the Treaty of Ghent of a provision forbidding the carrying off of private property, slaves were not returned to American custody, nor was compensation offered to their former masters. Eventually, the czar of Russia offered to mediate the issue, and the final decision about slaves taken in the War of 1812 was made on 11 September 1822. A claims board decided the average value of the slaves taken, and a definitive list of missing slaves was made by American and British representatives. Negotiations over reparations dragged on for several more years, with the British government agreeing to pay $1,204,960 by 1 August 1827, rather than return the freed slaves. This amount was considerably lower than that sought by American negotiators.[37]

NATIVE ALLIES

Another important aspect of the War of 1812 was the nature of the enemy forces. The United States and Great Britain each employed Native American allies in a form of quasi-coalition warfare. However, the Indian allies had a much harsher view of how prisoners of war should be treated. Those who survived to be taken prisoner by native allies could expect harsh treatment: nine soldiers taken prisoner at Fort Dearborn on 15 August 1812 complained they had "remained prisoners with the Indians upwards of nine months, suffering every hardship that human beings do endure from Cold, Hunger & Fatigue." In one of the most notorious POW incidents of the war, a group of American soldiers surrendered at the River Raisin near Frenchtown on 22 January 1813, with the understanding that all American POWs would be held by the British. The nonambulatory POWs were left under the "guard" of British native allies. Some of these prisoners were killed outright, while others were placed in the Frenchtown villagers' homes, which were subsequently set ablaze by the native allies. Approximately sixty American prisoners were killed in the River Raisin massacre. Other Americans captured at the River Raisin proved more fortunate and were ransomed from their Native American captors by the United States government. A few lucky individuals were purchased by local inhabitants, with the promise of reimbursement.[38]

Not surprisingly, the British and American forces chose to treat captured Native Americans differently from captured white troops. Native allies did not participate in the negotiation of the Cartel of 12 May, and did not feel bound by its provisions. Even after the formal acceptance of the cartel, the prisoner situation in the west depended on the independent decisions of commanding officers. In one interesting case, a white British army captain was captured while fighting with a unit of Native Americans. Captain Lorimier, who was held with the other members of his unit, announced to his captors that he was "un savage," causing Brigadier General John Boyd, commander of Fort George, to decide "his treatment should be the same as the others." Major General Francis Rottenburgh, the commanding general of the British Army of the Centre, complained that confining a British officer with his Native American troops was not an act of civilized warfare. After Rottenburgh's protest, Lorimier was moved to confinement with other British officers.[39] Rottenburgh's complaint never specified if the problem lay in confining an officer with enlisted personnel or in holding a British man with native troops. Most likely, the general found both concepts intolerable.

Lorimier's case was a small part of a series of letters between Boyd and Rottenburgh, in which Rottenburgh wished to exchange American and Indian prisoners for British soldiers and Indian ally prisoners held in the area. However, Boyd notified Rottenburgh on 4 September 1813, "The powers with which I am vested do not extend to the exchange of prisoners of war." Although technically true if the cartel was considered inflexible, Boyd's position certainly overturned traditional customs of European warfare and violated the spirit, if not the letter, of the cartel's provisions for rapid exchanges. The question of exchange rested with the president, the secretary of state, or the commander of American forces in the field. In the same letter, Boyd noted in regard to Indian prisoners, "They receive such treatment as the customs of war & the feelings of humanity dictate; and I cannot for one moment believe that any Americans in your possession will be placed in a situation likely to subject them to a usage that shall be in violation of both, & may lead to the most painful retaliation." The ever-present threat of retaliation remained in the letters between Rottenburgh and Boyd, and it also certainly resonated in the minds of all officers and enlisted personnel so unfortunate as to be captured by the enemy.[40]

REVISING THE SYSTEM

On 1 February 1814, Barclay submitted to Mason a list of proposed amendments to the Cartel of 12 May. A major portion of the amendments revolved around the question of rations issued to prisoners of war by the capturing nation. In his letter, Barclay reminded the United States of both the superior experience of Great Britain regarding prisoners of war and the fact that the majority of British attention remained in Europe. Barclay also accused the United States of moving too slowly to fulfill its commitments under the cartel. Barclay stated that the British government had shipped American prisoners to the United States in good faith immediately after signing the document, while the United States had used the same time to attempt the recruitment of British prisoners held in prison camps.[41]

Although Barclay and Mason's relationship had been for the most part amicable, despite their disagreements over interpreting the cartel, American officials viewed the British agent with some suspicion throughout the war, quite possibly with good reason. He was ordered to move from Harlem to Bladensburg in early 1814, to speed communications with the American government. His home in Bladensburg was visited by a number of British officers during the Chesapeake campaign, and numerous sources have suggested that he provided whatever intelligence he possessed, in violation of his duties as agent for prisoners of war. After being forced to move to Bladensburg, Barclay tendered his resignation as British agent for prisoners of war. He was promptly replaced by George Barton, who remained in his position for only a few months. The U.S. government, already strained beyond endurance by the demands of the war, had virtually disintegrated after the capture and burning of Washington, D.C. By the time Barton assumed his position, the War Department was bankrupt, Mason had lost any direct control over the POW situation, and diplomats were negotiating the end of the conflict. The final situation requiring his direct intervention was the disposal of prisoners held after the Battle of New Orleans. These prisoners, taken after the Treaty of Ghent had officially ended the war, remained in a form of diplomatic limbo for months, awaiting the decision of where and how they should be sent away from the United States. Barton showed a great deal of concern for the welfare of prisoners under his care and remained calm in his letters to Mason, in spite of the extremely slow workings of American bureaucracy.[42]

FREDERICK TOWN AND PITTSFIELD: THE SYSTEM IN PRACTICE

The requirements of confinement regarding British prisoners were fairly straightforward. A list of rules and regulations posted at Frederick Town, Maryland, on 14 September 1814 contained a list of guarantees by the

American government, particularly that "the prisoners will receive kind treatment." In exchange, each prisoner was prohibited to "pass the limits prescribed him, but by permission of an officer of the guards." Prisoners were banned from the use of "abusive language, obscenity, disobedience of orders, drunkenness, fighting . . . and other acts of insubordination." The prisoners were ordered to rise daily at sunrise to wash themselves and clean their barracks before breakfast. The dinner meal was served daily at one o'clock, and the prisoners were to be in bed by seven o'clock. The prisoners were allowed a certain degree of self-regulation: they were allowed to "divide themselves into messes, as may be convenient and agreeable to them and shall designate one person as head of each mess." Liquors were specifically forbidden to the prisoners without the explicit permission of the marshal. Other regulations included a daily sick call, a provision that the prisoners would launder their own clothes twice per week, and a promise that "the Ear of the Marshal will be open to all reasonable complaints and remedy promptly afforded. . . . The unreasonable will be disappointed."[43]

Guard regulations at Frederick Town were also clearly enumerated. The guard personnel consisted of two commissioned officers, two corporals, and forty privates, with half of the force on duty at all times. The guards' orders allowed only four prisoners out of confinement at any given time, to be guarded at all times by an armed soldier. Of particular interest is the final order: "No soldier must leave camp, but with leave of a Commissioned Officer, nor must any man abuse a Prisoner or strike him on any occasion, but such as the Laws will justify, as in the defense of his person, the prevention of escapes & preservation of the peace."[44]

An attached note to the commander at Frederick Town established the rations to be given to the prisoners on a daily basis. Each prisoner received half a pound of fresh or salted meat; one and a half pounds of wheaten bread; half a pint of peas or one pound of potatoes; and one tablespoon of salt per day. Disorderly prisoners could be confined or placed on two-thirds rations for up to ten days. The commander of the prison furnished clothing, blankets, beds, wines, spirits (despite their prohibition), sugar, molasses, tea, coffee, and camp kettles to the prisoners, with the eventual cost of the items to be paid by the British government. The regulations were in strict compliance with the Cartel of 12 May, although actual practice often differed slightly from the prescribed regulations.[45]

The conduct of American captors toward British prisoners of war varied somewhat by locale and depended partly on the disposition of individual American guard commanders. Overall, POW treatment appears to have been fairly lenient, and British officers in particular were pleased by the conditions of their captivity. The commander at Pittsfield, Major Thomas Melville, announced in a letter to Prevost that "the American Government will pride itself on giving the examples of liberality to its enemy." Melville complained that the British decision to ship all American forces captured in North America to Halifax had resulted in serious overcrowding and poor living conditions. He considered it an inhumane decision that might prompt American retaliation against British prisoners.[46]

Melville's compassion and leadership made the prison at Pittsfield one of the best locations where a British prisoner could be confined. Melville's record keeping was meticulous, as shown by a list of expenditures made by the prison for the upkeep of the hundreds of British POWs held in 1814. For the months of September through November, Melville spent almost $15,000 on rations for 924 British prisoners, and close to $20,000 to clothe the same prisoners in preparation for the winter. Melville served as both warden of the prison and agent for the prisoners kept within Pittsfield, appealing directly to Prevost for payment, in specie, of debts assumed while caring for POWs. The "Pittsfield Cantonment," located a few hundred yards from the village of Pittsfield, consisted of two barracks, each with twelve rooms and two stories. Each room was designed to house twenty prisoners in individual bunks. Officers lived in ten double rooms in the officers' quarters, with two mess rooms and a separate kitchen. A hospital and guardhouse completed the buildings of the compound.[47]

The Pittsfield Cantonment typified the prison compounds used by the United States during the war and could not hold more than several hundred prisoners at any time. Colonel Elisha Jenkins, who inspected a number of such compounds in 1813, notified Armstrong that the prisons were adequate to the provisions of the Cartel of 12 May, but he also recommended that POW regulations be formally furnished to the officers at each camp. Before then, the prison commanders had each maintained their own system. Jenkins was critical of the decision to house prisoners at Greenbush, New York, because "the inhabitants . . . are whigs, almost to a man," and they thus might prove sympathetic to the British prisoners confined in the area.[48]

According to most reports, both British and American prisoners received, for the most part, ample food, adequate clothing, and enough blankets for at least a minimum of comfort while detained as prisoners of war. One exception occurred in a disturbing report concerning prisoners held by the British at Melville Island. An American agent for prisoners of war, John Mitchell, notified Captain John Cochet at Halifax that prisoners had found tobacco, dirt, and ground glass in their bread rations. After a number of communications, Cochet informed Mitchell that although the foreign substances had been removed from the bread ration, the prisoners could not expect any better treatment until officially exchanged. Donald Hickey has argued that the British made captivity deliberately hard on maritime prisoners in the hope that captured Americans would enlist in the Royal Navy in exchange for their release from prison.[49]

Prisoner exchanges during the War of 1812, which began in 1812 and which were officially sanctioned by the Halifax agreement and the Cartel of 12 May, proved to be extremely complex and slow-moving affairs. British attempts to facilitate exchanges continued throughout the duration of the war but were often stymied by the United States. On 25 January 1814, Prevost proposed a general exchange of all nonhostage prisoners. Prevost's suggestion was almost a complete reversal of the Cartel of 12 May and a great departure from previous British policies. His willingness to meet at any place on the lines is of special interest because it signified a compromise from the previous British insistence on cartel ships for the delivery of prisoners of war to exchange depots.[50] Quite simply, the British government needed as many veteran troops as possible for the spring campaign of 1814, an invasion of France.

An exchange agreement was created according to Prevost's suggestions and was signed on 16 April 1814 by Brigadier General William H. Winder and Colonel Edward Baynes. This agreement included provisions to release all prisoners held by each side, regardless of rank, and to hold neither side responsible for any financial obligations to the other. All prisoners released by the agreement were to be considered exchanged and available for duty on 15 May 1814. The agreement, as negotiated by Winder, himself a former prisoner of the British, was rejected by President Madison on the grounds that the hostages should all go free as well, and modifications to the agreement were made and approved on 16 July 1814. Although each side had formally agreed to exchange all prisoners of war, the actual practice of exchange was an extremely time-consuming and difficult business. There was virtually no possibility that the prisoners would all return to their respective homes in less than one month. As late as 1 January 1815, Halifax held almost 2,000 American prisoners. Three months later, this number had dwindled to 420, demonstrating the slow speed of exchanges even after the war's termination.[51] According to the convention, all prisoners, with the exception of the twenty-three "Irish traitors," twenty-three British soldiers initially held as hostages, and forty-six American officers and noncommissioned officers held as hostages at Halifax, were to be released.[52]

ENDING THE CONFLICT

Although the Treaty of Ghent allowed for the final exchanges of prisoners, after the Battle of New Orleans, Major General Andrew Jackson arranged a battlefield exchange of prisoners with the British commander, General John Lambert. This agreement was sent to Washington for authorization before the release of the captives, allowing it to be incorporated into the final exchange process. Four hundred sixty-six men captured at New Orleans were returned to the British in exchange for Americans held throughout the Caribbean, primarily at Nassau.[53]

One of the most fundamental uses of prisoners of war, to the capturing power, is as a potential source of intelligence regarding the enemy's location, intent, and armament. The War of 1812 was certainly no exception to the age-old custom of questioning prisoners of war. During the war, the most useful sources of information often proved to be deserting members of the British military forces rather than members of units captured on battlefields. For obvious reasons, officers were a much more valuable source of information than enlisted personnel. However, the military leaders of the United States did not neglect the possibility of extracting useful information from individual soldiers, and regular reports of interrogations flowed into the hands of the commissary general of prisoners, the secretary of war, individual commanders, and the secretary of state. An excellent example of the interrogation of prisoners comes from the "Examination of British Deserters" received by American commanders shortly after the burning of Washington. In this brief document, Robert Gardner detailed the size of the British force, its origins, its intentions, and the general condition of the men within the force, all garnered from the brief interrogation of a number of British soldiers who deserted the British Army.[54]

Despite the focus on the rapid exchange of prisoners, cartel ships continued to sail for several months after the end of the war, with prisoners becoming increasingly anxious to return to their homes. In one incident, American prisoners aboard an American cartel ship, the *Mary Ann,* mutinied while returning from Plymouth, England, to Norfolk, Virginia. The prisoners revolted as a result of the poor rations provided for their voyage, and they refused to continue until their situation was improved. Further angering the passengers, the number of prisoners placed on the *Mary Ann* was lower than the number intended for exchange, without explanation from the British captors. Possibly the worst aspect of the journey for the returning prisoners was the destination: almost none of the prisoners were from Virginia. According to testimony from the master of the *Mary Ann*, on 2 June 1815, the prisoners seized control of the ship and set a new course for New York. Upon arrival, the crew discovered many small articles missing from the ship after the prisoners disembarked.[55]

Although exchange policies were designed to send prisoners back to their home countries as rapidly as possible, slow communications and limited transportation capacity drastically slowed the process. The result of this prolonged captivity was occasionally deadly, as shown in the case of the Dartmoor prison riot of 6 April 1815. More than three months after the Treaty of Ghent was signed, hundreds of American prisoners remained in terrible conditions at Dartmoor prison. They revolted against their captors, who opened fire, killing five Americans and wounding thirty-four. Dubbed the "Dartmoor massacre" in the United States, this unfortunate incident marked the last significant event in the prisoner of war history of the War of 1812.[56]

During the War of 1812, the United States made a deliberate effort to utilize POW labor. Individual British prisoners were allowed on an infrequent basis to practice some form of trade or craft, often for their own financial benefit. This practice allowed vital skills to be utilized by local areas while also motivating prisoners to contribute their labor to the enemy. At times, American captors compelled prisoner labor, rather than simply allowing it to occur. Barclay's letter of 26 May 1814 asked Mason to investigate the case of two British prisoners taken from the prison at Pittsfield, Massachusetts, by Melville, the deputy marshal of the post. Barclay complained that Melville removed the two prisoners and "either employed them himself, or suffered them to be employed by some of his friends as Servants or laborers." The crux of the matter was whether the prisoners had been returned to their regiment to be exchanged together. The notion that employing prisoners for labor was not allowed by international law did not seem to occur to Barclay, who was quick to complain of any real or perceived insult to the honor of captives under his nominal care. Although no international law specifically addressed the use of prisoner of war labor, it can be inferred that the use of captives for labor was acceptable, provided that the labor force was not withheld from exchange with other prisoners, and that officers were not forced to work.[57]

The prisoner of war bureaucracy established by the United States was hindered by the slow speed of communications and the unwillingness of individual commanders to overstep their responsibilities. As of 25 February 1815, a number of British officers remained confined in Raleigh, North Carolina, despite the end of the war and the nearby presence of their own ships near the American coastline. Barton asked Mason to direct the marshal of North Carolina "to permit all British officers in his custody to avail themselves of any opportunity to join their ships, which may present itself prior to the sailing of a cartel from Wilmington."

At the end of the war, the commissary general of prisoners was required by the Treasury Department to create a final account of all appropriations for the care and safekeeping of British prisoners. The United States Congress had appropriated $100,000 on 6 July 1812 for the commissary general. This was followed by an appropriation of $150,000 on 3 March 1813, an additional $400,000 on 24 March 1814, and a final $500,000 on 16 February 1815. When other expenses were added to the initial appropriations, the total bill for prisoner of war maintenance amounted to $1,194,425.32, submitted for payment to the government of Great Britain. This bill was counterbalanced by British costs for the upkeep of American prisoners of war, and it remained the subject of diplomatic negotiations for years to come.[58]

The legacy of the prisoner of war decisions made during the War of 1812 lasted through World War II. The most important decisions made during the war, and consequently the longest-lasting effects of the war with regard to POWs, were the decisions to practice strict retaliation for the actions of the enemy; the concentration of prison compounds; the use of prisoner labor; and the creation of a single POW command structure to house and care for all prisoners, whether captured on land or at sea. The United States adopted a system of maintaining prisoner agreements to a strict interpretation, even when simpler and more humane solutions were presented. The policy of returning all prisoners through proper channels remained in force for over one century, through the end of World War II, and was not ended until the armistice talks of the Korean War.[59] These aspects of prisoner policy, with modernization and some modifications, remained the foundation of American prisoner of war practice for over a century.

The prisoner of war decisions of the War of 1812 had a great effect on the Civil War and the world wars of the twentieth century. Strangely, these decisions had little effect on the prisoner of war policy implemented in the first international conflict involving the United States after the War of 1812. In the Mexican War, the United States radically altered its policy to suit the needs of a small army on foreign soil, surrounded by a hostile population. The lessons of the War of 1812 would not be truly implemented by the War Department for another fifty years, by which time few leaders remembered the problems of the earlier conflict. One lone exception, however, was Winfield Scott, who was appointed general in chief of the U.S. Army in 1841. Scott's personal command of the invasion of central Mexico provided a key thread of continuity between the wars.

3

PRISONERS ON FOREIGN SOIL

The War against Mexico

Antonio Lopez de Santa Anna, the self-styled Napoleon of the West, faced American troops in two separate conflicts in the mid-nineteenth century. First, during the Texas Revolution, Santa Anna led Mexican regulars on a campaign to pacify the upstart Texans, including his most famous triumph, the capture of the Alamo, in February 1836, where none of the defenders survived the final assault. Reportedly, Santa Anna ordered the accompanying band to play the *deguello*, a tune that signaled no quarter would be offered by his army. In the aftermath of the Battle of the Alamo, Santa Anna accused Texan forces of torturing Mexican prisoners of war to determine the size and strength of his army—an ironic position given his decision not to take prisoners. Barely two months after his victory, though, the situations were reversed, and it was Santa Anna seeking quarter from the Texan forces. His captivity remained remarkably lenient, including a brief period of house arrest at the Orozimba ranch, where he was repeatedly visited by General Sam Houston. After a brief stint in captivity, he received permission to travel to Washington, D.C., on parole, to visit President Andrew Jackson and discuss the possible annexation of Texas by the United States.[1]

One decade later, Santa Anna faced the U.S. Army in the field, primarily as a result of the 1845 annexation of Texas. He had not forgotten his treatment at the hands of Americans, and he personally saw to the maintenance of hundreds of American soldiers captured during the Mexican War. In one noteworthy instance, he extended a personal loan to American officers who had been exchanged, thus allowing them to return to American custody in relative comfort. Recognizing Santa Anna's worth as a political prisoner as well as the military leader of Mexico, Major General Winfield Scott ordered that he be captured at all costs, but Santa Anna, having already sampled American hospitality, escaped with his family, leaving Mexico for Jamaica in March 1848, one month after the treaty ending the conflict.[2]

LEARNING THE LESSONS OF 1812

Between the end of the War of 1812 and the beginning of the Mexican War, American military planners devoted little or no time to learning the POW lessons of the War of 1812. The wartime army was rapidly reduced in size, and most army regulars were sent westward for frontier duty. Officers educated at the United States Military Academy received scant training in the laws of war, and what they learned revolved around the definition of a just war, not ethical battlefield behavior.[3] Cadets read excerpts from Grotius and Vattel and discussed the customs of civilized warfare, but they received no practical training regarding the capture and maintenance of prisoners of war.

International law on prisoners did not change significantly during the first half of the nineteenth century, although practices in Europe became less humane during the Napoleonic wars, when the sheer number of prisoners led to deplorable conditions in England and on the continent. At the beginning of the wars, in September 1793 and May 1794, the French revolutionary government "prohibited ransoming of prisoners, and ordered that all émigré prisoners, and later British, Hanoverian, and Spanish captives as well, be shot as an 'example of the vengeance of an outraged nation.'"[4] Some commanders on each side maintained earlier customs, refusing to execute prisoners, but the number of prisoners taken on each side overwhelmed the systems designed to maintain them.[5] Revolutionary fervor and its calls for summary execution were common, and while prisoner exchanges occasionally occurred, no exchange cartels were used during the continual conflicts. Most enlisted captives were simply forced to wait for an end to the present conflict. Napoleon's practice of imposing a peace on a defeated enemy normally included the repatriation of prisoners, but the failure to decisively defeat Britain meant that the French and British maintained thousands of captives for years at a time. Likewise, Napoleon's rapid conquest and release policies utterly failed in Spain and Russia, with the result that thousands of prisoners from each conflict died in captivity. In the decades after the Congress of Vienna in 1815, when the Napoleonic wars officially ended, very little effort was made by any of the belligerents to evaluate prisoner practices.

INDIAN PRISONERS, 1815–1860

After the termination of the War of 1812, American military and political leaders once again confronted a domestic enemy, in the form of Native

American tribes. Indian policies from 1783 to 1815 had varied by administration, but all had been confronted by the possibility of conflict, coupled with a continual westward expansion of white control. In some locations, this movement remained relatively gradual, pushing native tribes steadily ahead of the frontier without resorting to open conflict. In other locations, it erupted into open warfare, with the relatively small U.S. Army augmented by local recruits and militia forces, as necessary. When Andrew Jackson won the presidency in the election of 1828, he brought frontier military experience into the office, having led the first expedition against the Seminoles of Florida in 1817. Although Jackson's foray proved largely unsuccessful, it certainly provided firsthand knowledge of the difficulties associated with Indian warfare.[6] Jackson's Seminole campaign failed to recapture escaped slaves living across the border in Spanish Florida, but it did spur the Spanish to negotiate the sale of the region to the fledgling United States. Of course, in addition to purchasing the territory, the American government obtained control over the inhabitants of Florida, including the demonstrably hostile Native American population.

Much of Jackson's presidency has been defined by his Indian policy, in particular his decision to order the removal of tribes from the southern states to the newly established Indian Territory in present-day Oklahoma. This policy met resistance from both the displaced tribes and the military officers ordered to carry it out, and nowhere was the resistance more deadly than the interior of Florida. The Second Seminole War, which began during Jackson's second administration but lasted through the presidencies of Martin Van Buren, William Henry Harrison, and John Tyler, proved extremely costly and was only partially successful in forcibly removing the Seminoles from their ancestral home. In addition, it proved damaging to the career of almost every military officer associated with the effort because the magnitude of the task was not matched by the government's commitment of resources. Although the army eventually claimed that more than 2,000 captives had been removed and sent west, the numbers are hard to prove.

The Second Seminole War established an important prisoner of war precedent for later Indian conflicts. In 1837, American forces captured King Philip and Hulata Mico, the key leaders of the Seminoles. Under duress, Philip sent runners to other tribal groups, whose respondents were then captured and used as hostages to compel further surrenders. Philip's son, Coacoochee, was forced to dupe Osceola and Coa Hadjo into surrendering to forces under Major General Thomas Jesup, who used a flag of truce to lure enemy leaders into negotiations, then seized the unarmed enemies. Once the primary leaders had been captured, they were sent to Fort Marion in St. Augustine, to be held against the behavior of their followers. Jesup's dishonorable approach had netted virtually every key leader of the opposition, yet all but Osceola escaped their captivity, returning to the swamps to continue the struggle.[7] Jesup's decision to hold Indian leaders in a single location, far from their followers, provided a blueprint for how to handle recalcitrant Native Americans who refused to remain confined on a reservation, subject to the vagaries of the federal government. Although the concept failed in practice, as a result of the Seminoles' willingness to starve themselves until they could shimmy through an eight-inch window in their prison cell, the idea of using Indian prisoners as hostages gained traction.

Other Native American conflicts with whites did not result in the decades of warfare experienced in Florida. In many cases, these wars lasted only a single campaign season. For example, the Black Hawk War of 1832 lasted only three months and largely pitted frontier militia forces against Sauk Indians. This conflict is now remembered primarily as the only military experience that President Abraham Lincoln held before entering the White House. In that conflict, the militia forces and Native Americans gave differing accounts of the use of white flags pertaining to parley or surrender. After several hit-and-run attacks, Chief Black Hawk decided that his enemies would not offer quarter, despite the fact that dozens of his followers had been captured and held by militia forces.[8] For their part, the militia, augmented by regulars near the end of the conflict, initially did not discriminate between combatants and noncombatants, treating all captives equally. After accepting the surrender of prisoners at every previous battle, the regulars proved unwilling to offer quarter at the Battle of Bad Axe, indiscriminately gunning down men, women, and children. This final victory concluded with the death of hundreds of Black Hawk's followers, at a cost of only five regulars killed and a handful wounded. In a short, sharp conflict, militia forces and federal regulars had clearly demonstrated that the laws of civilized warfare would not be applied to Indian conflicts on the frontier.[9]

PRISONERS IN THE MEXICAN WAR

American prisoner of war policy during the Mexican War differed significantly from previous experiences. No single POW policy governed the behavior of American commanders in the field; each commander established his own policy. The problems associated with holding prisoners while occupying foreign territory with a relatively small military force caused major generals Winfield Scott and Zachary Taylor to release thousands of captured enemies on parole. This policy saved the personnel and expense associated with maintaining prisoners, but on numerous occasions, paroled troops were found again fighting against American forces. Officially, the penalty for such duplicity remained execution, although the enforcement of such a punishment remained exceedingly rare. Occasionally, high-ranking officers were detained or even shipped to the United States to prevent their return to the battlefield, but for the most part, American troops quickly released any prisoners taken. Related to the question of prisoners of war in Mexico was the problem of desertion from the American army, and how to handle deserters caught fighting for the enemy. Although not strictly a POW issue, it certainly affected how American commanders defined a prisoner of war, and the ramifications of the decision influenced POW operations in the Civil War. Near the end of combat operations, American policy underwent a radical change when President James K. Polk ordered Scott to end mass paroles, and American troops began to hold significant numbers for a protracted period.

Pinpointing the exact number of prisoners taken in the war is virtually impossible because of the lack of accurate record keeping by the American forces and the decision to release almost all of the prisoners on parole. However, it is certain that the armies under Taylor and Scott each captured a sizable number of prisoners in several battles. By comparison, the Mexican Army captured a relatively small number of American troops. At no time in the war did Mexico have more than a few hundred American POWs, and American prisoners were quickly freed through the use of battlefield exchanges. Unlike the War of 1812, the United States maintained a positive balance of captures in Mexico for the entire conflict.

Many of the standard works discussing the war give no mention of prisoners despite the capture of thousands of Mexican soldiers in both the northern and southern theaters of the war. Often, prisoners are simply dismissed within lists of enemy casualties at specific battles, with no reference to the disposition of Mexican POWs.[10] The only captives to generate a significant body of literature were the San Patricio Battalion, composed largely of deserters from the U.S. Army. Most historians who mention Mexican prisoners argue they were insignificant to the outcome of the war and did not represent a substantial percentage of the forces engaged. Individual diaries and memoirs occasionally mention prisoners, but they do not consider them a central theme of the war.[11] One rare exception is George Wilkins Kendall's *Dispatches from the Mexican War*, which often refers to POWs, including lists of captured officers. Kendall was frequently critical of the POW decisions made by Scott in his advance on Mexico City, particularly when discussing the fate of the San Patricio Battalion.[12] Unit histories also rarely discuss POW issues, unless the unit being described had a specific connection to prisoners.[13]

THE INDEPENDENT REPUBLIC OF TEXAS

Some of the issues of prisoner of war treatment followed precedents created during the Texas War of Independence (1835–1836) and the skirmishes that followed between the Republic of Texas and Mexico. Texan leaders considered Mexican soldiers taken prisoner to be hostages rather than POWs, useful bargaining chips in the political fight for independence. By December 1835, the Texan forces held over one thousand POWs, most taken at the siege of San Antonio. In a somewhat surprising humanitarian gesture, these captives were freed, without giving their parole, when the Texan forces were unable to guard and feed them. They were allowed to return to their units, and they returned to service against Texan forces almost immediately.

The Mexican treatment of captured Texans was radically different: Santa Anna ordered that no prisoners be taken at the Alamo on 6 March 1836. On 27 March, he ordered the execution of all prisoners taken at Goliad: of the 445 prisoners, 342 were executed. The remainder escaped by running away at the commencement of the executions.[14] The Texans took their revenge at San Jacinto on 21 April 1836, where they clubbed, stabbed, and shot wounded and helpless enemies.[15] Despite these spontaneous executions, General Sam Houston retained 730 Mexican prisoners, including President Santa Anna, after the battle. The prisoners were sent to Galveston to work on fortifications or were assigned to individual citizens as laborers, while Houston used threats to force Santa Anna's legal recognition of the upstart republic. Negotiations to exchange prisoners dragged on for months, and the last Mexican prisoners did not leave Texas until May 1837.[16]

In the five years following its War of Independence, Texan forces launched two ill-advised major military excursions into Mexico, both of them dismal failures. The first was an attack on Santa Fe, begun 12 June 1841, launched in the assumption that local civilians would prefer to be part of the Republic of Texas rather than Mexico. The Texans were intercepted and disarmed by Mexican regulars, then sent to Mexico City for imprisonment. The Mexican government then responded to the unprovoked invasion by launching two punitive expeditions against San Antonio, capturing the city on 5 March 1842 and again on 11 September 1842. In each case, the Mexican invaders captured Texan prisoners before withdrawing across the Rio Grande. The second Texan attack involved three hundred volunteers who ignored Houston's order to remain north of the Rio Grande. Anticipating plunder, they attacked the city of Mier, where they were captured by two thousand Mexican troops on 25 December 1842. The captives marched to Perote, where they spent two years performing forced labor. These prisoners viewed themselves as prisoners of war, as they had been organized by the Texan government, but they were considered bandits by the Mexican government. Because Texas had not declared war on Mexico, the invaders had no legal right to claim POW status.[17] The prisoners attempted a mass escape on 11 February 1843. Mexican forces recaptured 176 escapees, then chose lots to determine which 17 would face execution as a warning against escape to the remaining prisoners.[18] Within the Texas legislature, several motions were made for an attack to free the prisoners at Perote, but cooler heads prevailed, and the prisoners were held without further incident until September 1844, when British and American diplomats requested their release.[19] Unfortunately, once freed, many of the Texan prisoners became Texas Rangers and volunteered their service during the Mexican War. In every theater of the war, Texas volunteers, especially Texas Rangers, earned a notorious reputation for brutality to prisoners and civilians, in many instances seeking some measure of revenge against their former captors.[20]

TAYLOR'S EXPEDITION IN NORTHERN MEXICO

Before the actual declaration of war, Taylor sent a party of dragoons to observe Mexican movements near the Rio Grande. Commanded by Captain T. B. Thornton, the unit was ambushed and approximately fifty soldiers surrendered on 24 April 1846. The American prisoners were immediately sent to Matamoras, where they reported exceptional treatment before being sent to the interior of Mexico. Generals Pedro de Ampudia and Mariano Arista housed and fed the officers of Thornton's command, who reported great satisfaction with the accommodations.[21] Despite all of the animosity between Texan and Mexican troops, the behavior of Mexican leaders toward American captives remained exemplary throughout the war.

After the battles of Palo Alto on 8 May and Resaca de la Palma on 9 May 1846, Taylor exchanged sufficient prisoners to obtain the release of Thornton's command. Before the exchange, the wounded Mexican prisoners were returned to their units in Matamoras; after the exchange was finalized, the remaining prisoners were released on parole. A few of the highest-ranking officers refused to give their parole, and Taylor sent them into confinement in New Orleans for the duration of the war. Along with the party of captive officers, Taylor sent a message requesting instructions for handling prisoners who refused to give paroles, and asking that they be well treated.[22] Secretary of War William L. Marcy commended Taylor for his decision to parole the POWs and conveyed the approval of President Polk as well.[23] He offered no guidelines for the treatment of future captives, deferring to Taylor's judgment on the matter.

As Taylor moved deeper into Mexico, Polk began to view prisoners of war as a way to "conciliate the inhabitants, and to let them see that peace is within their reach the moment their rulers will consent to do us justice."[24] Through Marcy, Polk ordered Taylor to counteract the attempts of Mexican newspapers to "prejudice and exasperate the minds of the people against us" by practicing kindness toward the populace and captured enemy troops.[25] Polk also ordered Taylor to interact with Mexican officer POWs as much as possible and to convey the wish of the U.S. government to begin peace negotiations, but not to actually open any negotiations. He was to inform the Mexican commanders of the willingness of the United States to create an "honorable peace, whenever such shall be their wish."[26]

Taylor acknowledged the president's wishes, but he complained that the use of volunteers made conciliatory efforts difficult because these uncontrollable troops continually committed excesses against the enemy citizens and property.[27] In the field, mounted Texans chasing Mexican guerrilla parties rarely took prisoners. They were far more likely to summarily execute any suspected guerrilla forces.[28] Rangers routinely abused and murdered Mexican civilians; even citizens serving as guides and interpreters were not safe from the Texas cavalry units.[29] Although Taylor believed his regulars could be trusted to accept surrenders and protect enemy captives, he did not have such faith in volunteers, particularly Texans who joined his force seeking revenge on the Mexican populace. Exasperated by the atrocities committed by Texans, he eventually requested that no more Texan troops be sent to augment his force in northern Mexico.[30]

Taylor's force moved quickly to besiege the city of Monterrey. This offered the possibility of a large number of enemy captives, particularly when Taylor demanded that the town's garrison surrender as POWs. He offered to parole them and send them to the interior of Mexico to await exchange, which would increase the balance of prisoners in favor of the United States without the unpleasant and expensive necessity of feeding and protecting the prisoners.[31] Mexico, which did not hold a significant number of American captives, would not be able to exchange the Monterrey defenders, assuming they followed their parole agreement; this would effectively eliminate a major field force at little cost to Taylor. To avoid an American army shelling or storming the lightly defended city, Ampudia agreed to Taylor's demands.[32] A few weeks after the surrender of Monterrey, Taylor discovered that a few American POWs had been held back from exchange and moved to San Luis de Potosí. He requested that the men be released and returned to American lines for exchange against an equal number of the men paroled at Monterrey. Santa Anna quickly acceded to the request and personally provided money and supplies for the men to travel from or to Monterrey.[33] After the Battle of Buena Vista, Taylor kept up his established pattern. He again negotiated a battlefield exchange, receiving Americans captured both before and during the battle in exchange for a mass parole of Mexican POWs.[34] Once more, a large field army was eliminated from the conflict without straining the American logistical system. For as long as the Mexican units maintained their promises to await exchange, Taylor's system functioned perfectly. Regrettably, Santa Anna ordered his troops to violate their parole as a necessary means to oppose Winfield Scott's invasion of central Mexico in 1847.

SCOTT'S INVASION OF CENTRAL MEXICO

Like Taylor, Scott used Mexican prisoners primarily for exchange, and he also sought to use them as a means to end the captivity of any Americans held by the enemy. Once all American captives returned to their lines, Scott offered parole to any remaining prisoners. This approach assumed that Mexican parolees would leave their units and return home to await a formal exchange that would likely never arrive. For example, after the battle at Cerro Gordo on 18 April 1847, approximately 3,000 prisoners were held for one day before being paroled.[35] After American victories at Contreras on 19 August 1847 and Churubusco on 20 August 1847, Scott again held approximately 3,000 prisoners.[36] Of these prisoners, most of the Mexican officers gave their parole not to fight against the United States for the duration of the war and were released. Most of the enlisted soldiers, including those wounded in the battles, were immediately released, although a small number were held as POWs and confined in several locations, to await exchange for the approximately 200 American POWs held in Mexico City. The American prisoners had been well fed and housed, but they had also been subjected to public ridicule by being paraded through the streets of the capital.[37] Despite the large American advantage in captured troops and the thousands of paroled Mexican soldiers awaiting exchange, some American soldiers had been held back from exchange. This was probably not a deliberate attempt to deceive Taylor and Scott. It is far more likely that the poor communications of the Mexican military led to confusion, and with the primary focus on halting Scott's invasion, these captives were simply lost in the shuffle.

Despite the practical difficulties associated with the upkeep and security of prisoners, on 31 May 1847, Scott was ordered to end his policy of complete paroles and to detain officers of the Mexican Army, either in Mexico or the United States.[38] Scott's orders to keep POWs in captivity may have been provoked by reports of the American POWs kept in Mexico City in violation of previous exchange agreements. During the assault on Mexico City, captured Mexican privates were not paroled; they were instead sent to Tampico, while officers were confined at Toluca.[39] The decision to retain POWs in captivity upset some Mexican leaders. Archbishop Manuel Posada y Gardu repeatedly asked Winfield Scott to parole all Mexican prisoners of war, but Scott pointed out that many prisoners taken at Veracruz and Cerro Gordo had rejoined the Mexican Army in violation of their parole.

The number of prisoners taken rose rapidly in the autumn of 1847, during the battles for Mexico City. As his forces closed in on the enemy capital, Scott realized that he could not simply release thousands of captives along his lines of supply and communication. During the final siege of the city, enemy POWs had to be temporarily confined. At Molino del Rey on 8 September 1847, the Second Pennsylvania Regiment was unavailable for battlefield duty because it had been detailed to guard 2,000 Mexican POWs during the battle.[40] In the battle, another 700 prisoners were taken. At Chapultepec Castle on 13 September 1847, more than 800 Mexican soldiers were captured. Once the capital fell, most of these prisoners were released after an oath not to bear arms for the duration of the war.[41] The last POWs taken by the United States during the war were captured with the fall of Mexico City, where Scott's forces captured almost 1,000 more prisoners.[42]

Scott's biographer, Arthur Smith, believed Mexicans violated their paroles under orders from their political leadership, and that many of the parole violators did not understand the legal meaning of their paroles.[43] Henry Halleck noted in 1861 that the Mexican government attempted to annul the paroles of captured Mexican troops and to force paroled soldiers to reenter the ranks. In response, Scott threatened to hang any soldier retaken after violating his parole.[44] Regardless of the reasoning behind parole violations, Scott did release

500 POWs on 22 December 1847, after asking Posada to use the Catholic Church to guarantee the paroles. Scott wished the church to refuse absolution to any parole breakers, and he also wished to use an oath of the church to enforce the paroles.[45] Posada entered the prisons to explain the purpose and rules of paroles to the POWs, and he personally administered the parole oaths to the prisoners.[46] The last Mexican POWs were released on 1 June 1848, when Major General Butler issued General Order No. 116, freeing all prisoners.[47]

The major exception to the general release of forces fighting for the Mexican Army involved a group of deserters from the U.S. Army. Desertion was a major problem during the war, and a larger percentage of U.S. regular forces deserted in the Mexican War than in any other conflict. Out of approximately 40,000 regulars, 5,331 deserted, with a particularly high number of immigrants among the ranks of the deserters.[48] With such high desertion rates, the army was forced to address the issue in such a way as to discourage further desertion. One way the U.S. discouraged desertion was to severely punish captured deserters. Another way was to prosecute Mexican citizens who encouraged American soldiers to defect or at least leave their present service. One example occurred on 19 June 1847, when Martin Tritschler, of Puebla, was executed after a military court found him guilty of "persuading or endeavouring to procure soldiers to desert the Army of the United States."[49]

Hundreds of immigrant deserters were enticed by promises of land or appeals to religion to join the Mexican Army, and they were organized into a unit called the San Patricio Battalion. The San Patricios participated in a number of engagements, but they were most notable during the advance on Mexico City. Mexico argued that the San Patricios had taken service with the Mexican government and that they were thus entitled to the legal status of prisoners of war. However, the San Patricios deserted the U.S. Army during wartime and enlisted in the service of an enemy government. Those who deserted after the declaration of war faced the ultimate punishment, and over seventy were executed after military trials in August 1847. Those who deserted before the declaration of war were branded on the cheek or hand and released. Their experience forced the U.S. government to devote at least a small effort to defining who should receive POW status.

CALIFORNIA AND NEW MEXICO

The campaigns to invade and conquer California and New Mexico were undertaken with little oversight from the War Department. In each location, a small American force moved in and established limited control over the territory. Each area was difficult to completely subdue because each contained guerrillas who fought against American occupation. As in Taylor's and Scott's invasions, American commanders were left to improvise their own POW policies for each location, with vastly different results. In California, captured guerrillas were well treated by American forces. After capturing Los Angeles, American units chose to withdraw from the area. In preparation, American and Californian commanders drafted an agreement to exchange all POWs and to excuse any past behavior by freed prisoners.[50] When fighting resumed in the area, Californian guerrillas surrendered to John C. Fremont after an agreement that all POWs on both sides would again be released, and all Californians would be protected by the American government and subjected to no punishment for resisting the occupation. This surrender, formalized 16 January 1847, marked the end of significant hostilities in the region.

In New Mexico, guerrilla resistance quickly followed the arrival of American troops. Prisoners captured in most locales were sent to Santa Fe for confinement and trial because American commanders in New Mexico considered guerrilla attacks to be criminal, not military, actions. A revolt in Taos in 1847 led to the capture of dozens of guerrillas by American forces, who accused fourteen of the prisoners of murder and ordered their immediate execution. The remainder were delivered to civilian authorities and placed on trial for a variety of crimes against the newly constituted government. Most of the prisoners were convicted and executed in March 1847.[51]

LEGACY OF THE WAR

Neither Scott nor Taylor had enough logistical support to maintain a large population of prisoners, nor could either spare the manpower to conduct prisoners to the United States to be held for the duration of the war. Thus the decision to release prisoners on parole was probably made for reasons of expediency and not for humanitarian purposes. However, Philip Berry argued in 1849 that Scott's decision to offer paroles was made "in consideration of the degree to which they [the Mexican prisoners] evinced those very qualities which rendered them formidable."[52] Berry's statement shows that at the time of the war and immediately after, Scott's decision was viewed as a sign of chivalry rather than necessity. In contrast, Robert Ripley criticized Scott's decision to parole Mexican prisoners, particularly after the Battle of

Cerro Gordo. Ripley argued in 1849 that Scott could have captured and held the entire Mexican Army after the battle.[53]

From a prisoner of war standpoint, the Mexican War is significant because of the large number of enemy troops captured in an offensive war fought almost entirely on foreign territory. The decision to allow mass paroles of thousands of enemy troops was a practical solution to the problem of caring for the POWs, provided the enemy soldiers could be trusted to uphold their paroles. For the most part, Mexican troops did follow the regulations of parole, although there were some instances of oath breaking. For all of the practical benefits of paroling captured enemies, it was also a decision brought about by necessity. The army simply could not provide for thousands of nonproductive, uncooperative prisoners. If a few of the released POWs rejoined Mexican forces in the field, they were a small minority, and facing them again on the battlefield was a small price to pay for depriving the enemy of the bulk of the paroled prisoners.

Prisoner of war operations in the Mexican War did not have a strong effect on the practices of the American Civil War (1861–1865), even though many of the commanders on both sides of the war served in Mexico. The lack of any sustained period of captivity for most Mexican prisoners meant that most American officers had no practical experience in dealing with prisoners. Even Major General Henry Halleck, who drew on many examples from the Mexican War in his 1861 work *International Law*, mentioned the war only once in his chapter on prisoners, noting that Mexican efforts to return paroled prisoners to the battlefield were a violation of the laws of war. Halleck reinforced the arguments of Grotius and Vattel by providing concrete examples of proper and improper behavior toward POWs.[54] In the Civil War, policies would again be improvised for the capture and maintenance of prisoners, with disastrous results.

4

BROTHER AGAINST BROTHER

The American Civil War

Lieutenant Colonel William Hoffman served in the military for his entire adult life. At West Point, he was a classmate of Confederate generals Robert E. Lee and Joseph E. Johnston, graduating in the middle of his class in 1829. Hoffman fought in the Black Hawk War, the Second Seminole War, and the Mexican War, receiving brevets twice in Mexico for gallantry in the field. He served on the frontier for much of his entire career, including detachments in Arkansas, California, Kansas, Louisiana, Missouri, Nebraska, New Mexico, and Utah. In December 1860, Hoffman finally attained his dream, receiving command of the 8th Infantry, U.S. Army, stationed in San Antonio, Texas. Unfortunately, shortly after his arrival, Texas seceded from the Union and joined the nascent Confederate States of America.

For a few months, a general state of unease existed between the rebellious Texan government and the federal forces within its borders. Although Hoffman took steps to prevent the outbreak of open hostilities, he had no authority to turn over federal property to Texas militia forces that demanded his surrender. On 16 February, hundreds of armed Texan volunteers seized the federal property in San Antonio. Hoffman voluntarily withdrew most of his forces to an encampment outside of San Antonio and awaited orders. Short of supplies and with no relief possible, Hoffman finally decided to surrender his command on the condition that they be allowed to return to the North on parole.[1]

Upon his return to the North, Hoffman solicited orders from the War Department for a position from which to contribute to the burgeoning war effort while still on parole. He scrupulously upheld the conditions of his parole, refusing an order to organize and train volunteers until duly exchanged.[2] Hoffman's exchange proved difficult to arrange because the Confederate authorities refused to individually exchange him for anyone of lesser rank, or to exchange him for a composition of lesser-ranking officers. Several proposals were exchanged and rejected by one side or the other before Confederate Secretary of War Judah P. Benjamin and General Robert E. Lee agreed to release Hoffman from parole upon the return of Captain Samuel Barron of the Confederate Navy.[3] After months of wrangling, Hoffman was formally released from his parole and exchanged on 27 August 1862.

Although his parole prevented field service, Hoffman longed to contribute to the war effort, and on 3 October 1861, Quartermaster General Montgomery C. Meigs recommended him to serve as the commissary general of prisoners and prisons while awaiting exchange. Three weeks later, Hoffman received orders for the position, which he occupied for the remainder of the war.[4] A victim of his own success, Hoffman petitioned repeatedly after his exchange for a position in the field, but his competence as the commissary of prisoners prevented his return to field command. Instead, he became the most influential person in determining the Union's prisoner of war policy for the Civil War, eventually overseeing the maintenance of hundreds of thousands of prisoners held in dozens of massive compounds throughout the North. Although he eventually received a brevet promotion to major general, he did not receive command of a regiment until after the war ended, finally returning to frontier service for three years after hostilities ended.

THE CIVIL WAR: AN OVERVIEW

In the American Civil War, both sides expected a short, almost bloodless fight, and thus neither the Union nor the Confederacy planned for the capture and imprisonment of tens of thousands of enemies. The result was an impromptu system of parole and exchange that was quickly overwhelmed by the influx of hundreds of thousands of prisoners. In 1863, both governments began stashing prisoners in massive prison compounds for safekeeping, with little attention given to the welfare of the prisoners. Exchanges were formally ended in May 1863 after each side made allegations of mistreatment and retaliatory threats. Each of these factors illustrated the danger of improvising POW policy to govern the maintenance of hundreds of thousands of prisoners during an ever-expanding, increasingly inhuman war.

Ironically, at the same time that exchanges ended, the federal government issued a new set of regulations, often called the Lieber Code, which included instructions to field commanders for the proper treatment of captured enemies. The code formed the basis for later international agreements but had little practical effect on the conditions faced by prisoners during the Civil War. As the exchange system faltered, prison populations swelled, increasing disease and straining supply systems to the breaking point. Mortality rates soared in the camps, which came to be little more than massive concentration camps for the incarceration of prisoners for the duration of the war. These camps had poor shelter, inadequate food supplies, and little medical assistance. By the end of the war, over 674,000 prisoners had been taken and over 400,000 incarcerated, of whom 56,000 died while in captivity. This mortality rate proved much higher than that faced by soldiers on the battlefield. From a survival standpoint, it was safer to fight than to be a captive in the Civil War.[5]

Unlike earlier American conflicts, the Civil War has produced a large body of work dealing with prisoners and POW policy.[6] *Prisoners of War and Military Prisons*, an early attempt to assess POW operations by both sides, was written by Asa B. Isham, Henry M. Davidson, and Henry B. Furness, all former members of the Union Army. Their work sharply criticized Confederate authorities for the suffering of Union prisoners and accused them of deliberately mistreating prisoners. They substantially inflated casualty figures for Union prisoners and argued that almost 39 percent of Union POWs died in captivity. In contrast, they minimized deaths in Union POW compounds, claiming that a mere 6 percent of Confederate prisoners died in captivity.[7] The work is useful because it combines a number of prisoners' diaries and journals to create a broad picture of prison life in the South.

A more balanced approach was William Best Hesseltine's 1930 *Civil War Prisons: A Study in War Psychology*, published in 1930. Hesseltine compared the experiences of Union and Confederate prisoners using the U.S. War Department's *Official Records* and a collection of personal narratives. He argued that neither the North nor the South deliberately mistreated prisoners. Rather, the high mortality rates were caused by the lack of exchanges during 1863 and 1864, which resulted in overcrowding and an inability to supply thousands of prisoners. Although Hesseltine did not blame either government for high mortality rates, he did argue that the Northern prisons were carefully constructed and well run, while the Southern prisons were "the result of a series of accidents."[8]

Hesseltine's work remained the only comprehensive study of Civil War prisons until the publication of Lonnie Speer's *Portals to Hell* in 1997. Speer found that the death rates in prisons on both sides were roughly equivalent, and that neither side planned adequately for prisoners. Speer considered Civil War prisoners primarily as victims of their captors, in particular as instruments of retaliation.[9] He argued that conditions were so awful in the prisons that "to have been killed on the battlefield might have been more humane."[10]

In 2005, Charles W. Sanders Jr. argued that the Union and Confederate leadership systematically mistreated captives during the war and then fabricated explanations for their behavior after the war. In his view, revisionist historians have refused to assign blame for the "darkest chapter of that conflict."[11] Sanders equated neglect with malign intent toward captives and assumed that presidents Lincoln and Davis were aware of prison conditions. Further, he believed not only that they had the power to solve POW problems unilaterally, but that they should have placed a higher priority on the maintenance of prisoners than on the supply of troops in the field.[12]

THE FIRST YEAR OF THE WAR

At the outbreak of hostilities, neither side had a formal process for holding prisoners, and the Union was undecided whether to consider Confederates to be POWs at all. The situation was analogous to that faced by Great Britain during the Revolutionary War, and like Britain, the federal government maintained that the enemy represented a rebellion against a legitimate government. Of course, this position could only be maintained if the war was quickly ended and the rebellion confined to a small number of ringleaders. After the federal losses in the summer of 1861, the Confederates held more prisoners than did the Union. Any harsh treatment meted out to Confederate prisoners could lead to retaliation against Union troops. The situation dictated that captured Confederates be treated as POWs, but because no formal policy existed governing the treatment of prisoners, Union field commanders improvised ways to maintain and guard prisoners and hoped that the War Department would clarify the situation.

Initially, the federal government placed captured Confederates in military fortifications along the East Coast. The most common destinations were Fort Delaware, Fort McHenry, and Point Lookout, Maryland. As the number of captives grew, the federal government slowly took steps to create a POW bureaucracy. After six months in the wartime post of commissary general of prisoners, Hoffman received a promotion to colonel, both as a reward for services rendered and to provide sufficient rank to work through the War Department bureaucracy. In this endeavor, Hoffman was both helped and impeded by his superior, Quartermaster General Meigs.[13] Meigs directed Hoffman that "the strictest economy consistent with security and proper welfare of the prisoners must be observed," a directive in keeping with earlier American POW practices.[14] On 17 June 1862, Hoffman was removed from Meigs's department and placed under the direct supervision of Secretary of War Edwin M. Stanton, while retaining the same title and function within the military establishment.[15]

Hoffman centralized POW operations, established regulations for prison camps, and decided where prisoners should be held within the Union. Virtually all POW correspondence went through Hoffman's office, including exchange negotiations, prisoner lists, camp reports, and subsistence orders. As the number of Confederate POWs grew, it became apparent that Hoffman's position required a higher rank to compel compliance from recalcitrant troop commanders. In 1864, Hoffman received a brevet promotion to brigadier general. In early 1865, he was brevetted to major general, although he reverted to the rank of colonel when he retired at the end of the war.

Captured federal troops were initially held in Richmond and Charleston in a series of improvised prisons, mainly empty tobacco warehouses and confiscated buildings. Hoffman's Confederate counterpart, Brigadier General John H. Winder, was named provost marshal of Richmond on 21 June 1861, a position that included control over the federal captives sent to the city's prisons. Winder's role expanded with the growth of the Confederate prison system. He was the de facto commissary general for prisoners, though the post was not formally created until 21 November 1864. Winder held this position until his death on 7 February 1865 during an inspection of the prison camp at Florence, South Carolina.[16]

The Union moved more rapidly than the Confederacy to create facilities to hold prisoners for protracted periods, realizing that the size and scope of the conflict would result in unprecedented numbers of POWs. In 1862, the Union converted a series of Volunteer muster camps into prison compounds, most located in the Midwest. The largest of these compounds were camps Alton and Douglas, Illinois; Camp Morton, Indiana; and Camp Chase, Ohio. Two additional locations were designated for federal prisoners paroled by the Confederacy and returned to Union lines: Camp Parole, Maryland, and Benton Barracks in St. Louis, Missouri. The Union prisoners remained at these camps under the supervision of the federal government until exchanged and returned to their regiments, a process that could take months or even years.

Despite negotiations to exchange prisoners and a rising number of captures by both sides, some commanders allegedly issued orders that prisoners not be taken. On 30 August 1862, Captain Joseph P. Reavis protested that two Confederate prisoners had been removed from a guardhouse for execution, by order of Colonel Albert Sigel. Reavis noted, "General, I know that we have orders from you to take no prisoners, but the spot where they are taken in my judgment is the place where you intended to have them executed; not after being placed under guard . . . taken forcibly from the guard-tent and mercilessly murdered."[17] An investigation found that Sigel had ordered no quarter given to Confederate irregulars who conducted raids into Union territory, commonly called bushwhackers, but had not ordered the execution of prisoners once taken.[18] Hoffman did not clarify the Union definition of legal prisoners of war until 4 December 1862, when he informed prison commandants that all enemy soldiers taken in arms were POWs, and that unarmed Confederate deserters, although not formally POWs, should be held for investigation as possible spies.[19] Before that time, field commanders made decisions independent of the War Department to define who a prisoner was and how he should be treated.

THE QUESTION OF EXCHANGE

On 11 February 1862, Stanton ordered Major General John E. Wool, the commander of Fort Monroe, to open negotiations with Confederate major general Benjamin C. Huger, commander at Norfolk, for an exchange of prisoners. Wool promptly notified Huger of his appointment, and Huger designated Brigadier General Howell Cobb to serve as the Confederate negotiator.[20] Wool and Cobb met on 23 February and quickly agreed that all prisoners on both sides should be exchanged, man for man, using the equivalency system adopted during the War of 1812. Any excess prisoners held by either side were to be released on parole.

Each side had a different reason to desire prompt exchanges. The Confederacy, heavily outnumbered by the Union, could not afford to have Union troops languishing in prison when they were needed on the battlefield. The Union, having lost the early engagements in the eastern theater, had lost more prisoners to the enemy and hoped to receive the excess on parole. Although paroled troops could not be sent back into Virginia for an advance on Richmond, they might serve in Union garrisons or on the western frontier, freeing nonparoled troops for frontline service. Also, in keeping with American traditions, neither side wished to bear the costs of feeding and maintaining enemy prisoners, whose presence tied down guard troops and who contributed no labor to the war effort.

After negotiations were ended, Cobb considered the matter finished, and the Confederacy immediately began to forward paroled prisoners to the front lines for the purpose of exchange. However, between Wool's appointment and the meeting with Cobb, the strategic situation regarding POWs had changed dramatically. On 16 February 1862, Fort Donelson surrendered, delivering 15,000 prisoners to Union control. Suddenly, the Union had a surplus of prisoners for the first time in the war, and Stanton did not wish to lose that advantage before the spring campaign. Officially, Wool claimed that because no exchange cartel had been signed, the agreement was in principle, not a practical plan to forward POWs for exchange. He stated that his orders had been changed just days after the agreement, and that the federal government would agree to exchanges but would not parole excess prisoners. Cobb was justifiably angry, but he had no means to compel the Union to live up to the agreement.

The two sides met again in June 1862 to negotiate a formal exchange cartel that would serve for the remainder of the war, rather than a single agreement to exchange the prisoners on hand. The negotiations were significant because they constituted a de facto recognition of the Confederate government as a sovereign power, something the Union had resisted for a year. The federal government sent Major General John A. Dix; the Confederacy sent Major General Daniel H. Hill. After several weeks of discussion, a formal cartel was signed on 22 July 1862 that governed the future exchange of prisoners.

The cartel consisted of six articles designed to create a simple, functional exchange system. The document did not formally recognize the Confederacy as a belligerent; instead, it dodged the issue, referring to Dix and Hill as "having been commissioned by the authorities they respectively represent."[21] The cartel stipulated that all prisoners, including those taken as privateers, would be exchanged either man for man or according to a system of rank equivalencies. The equivalencies were identical to the system included in the Cartel of 12 May 1813. In addition, prisoners from different branches of service could be exchanged for one another, and privateers could be exchanged for any other military personnel. All prisoners were to be paroled within ten days of capture and delivered to predetermined exchange points. Paroled prisoners could not serve in any military capacity until properly exchanged, including garrison, police, guard, and constabulary duties.

If each side had followed the provisions of the cartel throughout the war, the situation of POWs during the war might have been radically different. There would have been no need for the massive prison compounds and no allegations of deliberate mistreatment of thousands of prisoners. The cartel included a key provision: that "the stipulations and provisions above mentioned to be of binding obligation during the continuance of the war, it matters not which party may have the surplus of prisoners."[22] This provision proved inconvenient to each side at various times, and over the course of the next year, both the Union and the Confederacy moved to suspend all exchanges, but gradually the prisons in the North and the South became virtually empty. From July 1862 until May 1863, approximately 20,000 Confederate and 12,000 Union prisoners were exchanged.[23]

ENLISTING AFRICAN AMERICANS: THE END OF EXCHANGES

When the Union began to enlist African American regiments at the end of 1862, the Confederate response was shock and outrage. President Jefferson Davis, fearing such a move might incite a general slave insurrection, announced that white officers commanding black troops were subject to trial and execution for inciting a servile insurrection.[24] Any black troops taken prisoner were to be delivered to state control and punished according to the state laws for slaves caught bearing arms.[25] Field commanders issued orders that no quarter be offered to black troops or their white officers, including the message of Lieutenant General Edmund Kirby Smith, dated 13 June 1863: "I have been unofficially informed, that some of your troops have captured negroes in arms, I hope this may not be so, and your subordinates who may have been in command of capturing parties may have recognized the propriety of giving no quarter to armed negroes and their officers, in this way we may be relieved from a disagreeable dilemma."[26] The dilemma that Smith feared was effectively sanctioning the use of black troops by offering the legal protections given to white soldiers.

On 30 July 1863, President Abraham Lincoln announced that any soldier of the United States executed by the enemy in violation of the laws of war would result in the execution of a Confederate prisoner of equal rank. For any black troops placed into slavery, an equal number of Confederates would be placed at hard labor.[27] Lincoln sought to use the threat of retaliation to ensure that all Union troops were treated equally as prisoners of war. Union threats of retaliation did not have the intended effect, and captured black troops faced execution or slavery at the hands of Confederates, depending on the whim of the Confederate commander. On 25 September 1864, Major General Ethan Allen Hitchcock was informed that wounded black troops at the Battle of Olustee were executed on the field by Georgia regulars.[28] On 16 October 1864, Confederate slave owners were informed that 575 members of the United States Colored Troops (USCT), many former slaves, were employed on fortifications near Mobile, and that former owners could report to the city to claim their slaves.[29] On 12 October, Major General Benjamin Butler notified Colonel Robert Ould, Confederate commissioner of exchange, that 110 Confederate officers and men would be employed constructing a canal at Dutch Gap until an equal number of USCT troops were removed from construction parties building fortifications at Fort Gilmer.[30] On 19 October 1864, Lee defended the practice of reenslaving captured USCT soldiers, informing Lieutenant General Ulysses S. Grant that only soldiers who were slaves before joining the Union Army were required to work on fortifications. Grant responded by ordering Butler to remove the Confederate prisoners from the Dutch Gap Canal, but threatening to retaliate for any future mistreatment of Union prisoners, regardless of color or previous servitude.[31] In January 1865, O. O. Poppleton notified Butler that 569 black soldiers captured by Major General Nathan Bedford Forrest had been sent to Mobile and forced to work on the city's defenses.[32]

The Confederate decision to refuse quarter or exchange for black troops seems counterproductive to the modern scholar. Each Union soldier sent into slavery or killed not only invited retaliation on a helpless Confederate prisoner, but also prevented the return of desperately needed troops at a time when the Confederate system of conscription reached its height. To offer the legal protection of POW status, though, jeopardized the entire Confederate legal and social system. After all, if a black enemy soldier had to be given equal treatment as a white enemy, the concept of humans as property might be threatened or destroyed. Davis could not, or would not, abandon one of the key causes of the war to save the war effort as a whole, even if the lack of troops hastened the demise of the Confederacy.

On a number of occasions, specific mass exchanges were offered to alleviate the suffering of prisoners without raising the issue of the exchange cartel. On 7 December 1863, Major General Henry Halleck offered to exchange all federal POWs held in Richmond jails for their equivalents in federal hands. Lee refused the offer on the grounds that it did not precisely follow the system of the cartel.[33] In September 1864, Major General William T. Sherman refused the offer of Lieutenant General John Bell Hood to "release to him the prisoners at Andersonville in exchange for the soldiers taken from Hood in the Georgia campaign," even though Sherman would receive 30,000 federal prisoners in exchange for a fraction of that number of

Confederates.[34] Sherman feared that such a large influx of prisoners, incapacitated by disease and malnutrition, might slow the progress of his army and prolong the conflict.

Exchange was certainly an important consideration to the prisoners on each side. Rumors of possible exchanges circulated through every prison camp on a daily basis. Before 1863, POWs had a good chance of parole and eventual exchange, and this fact is reflected in prisoner narratives. When prisoner exchanges virtually ceased, the hope of exchange did not die. Rather, the rumors continued unabated, if unsubstantiated.[35] Prisoners attempted to remain abreast of new developments through newspapers and information brought in by new captives. Such information rarely proved accurate, and camp morale inevitably plummeted when rumors of a pending exchange proved false.

The Confederacy held the balance of prisoners for the first two years of the war, but with the prisons mostly empty in May 1863, the situation was about to change. Although the Chancellorsville campaign refilled the warehouses of Richmond, the Confederate advantage did not last long. Lee's Army of Northern Virginia gathered more captives on the march toward Gettysburg and even captured some Union forces during the battle. But these successes counted little when compared with the surrender of almost 30,000 Confederates at Vicksburg. When reduced to privates by the table of equivalencies, the capture of Vicksburg included 42,300 captives. Major General Ulysses S. Grant had no intention of trying to incarcerate and provide for so many captives while deep in enemy territory. Trusting in the previous year's cartel system, he ordered most of the prisoners paroled.[36]

On 20 October 1863, Confederate exchange commissioner Robert Ould requested that all prisoners be exchanged according to the provisions of the exchange cartel. He claimed that Sullivan A. Meredith, the federal commissioner of exchange, had verbally agreed to do so. Meredith denied such an agreement, countering that the Confederacy had declared thousands of prisoners exchanged without sending equivalent numbers back to federal lines.[37] Because Grant had released an entire army on parole, Ould sought only to return the Vicksburg troops to active duty, and to return the Union troops in rebel prisons to the North. Such an action would swell Confederate troop levels and reduce supply burdens. When Meredith refused the formal exchange, the Confederate government decided to keep its Union prisoners in confinement, hoping this would pressure Union leaders to uphold the cartel system.

When Stanton, Hoffman, Meredith, and Hitchcock refused Ould's request to exchange the Vicksburg prisoners, Ould opted to unilaterally declare the men exchanged and eligible to return to Confederate service. He announced that the men were considered exchanged because the Confederacy had delivered captured federal troops to City Point and had not received any prisoners in return. In response to Ould's announcement, Hitchcock urged Stanton to suspend all deliveries of Confederate prisoners until the Confederacy delivered enough Union prisoners to match the Vicksburg captures.[38] Major General Benjamin Butler responded to Ould's statement by declaring, "The Cartel is entirely annulled."[39] Each government had expected perfect adherence by the enemy and threatened retaliation for any breach of the cartel, but both sides violated the spirit and the wording of the cartel when it suited their purpose. In the end, the Union could afford a breakdown in the system much more easily, given the superior manpower reserves of the North.

The decision to halt exchanges, from Stanton's perspective, was a simple one, given that released Confederate prisoners were typically healthy enough to return to duty, while exchanged federal prisoners tended to be incapable of rendering service for months after returning from confinement. In the words of Charles Alfred Humphreys, a chaplain of the Second Maryland Cavalry, "Stanton was inflexible in adherence to his principle that in dealing with this question, *something* should not be given for *nothing*."[40] To support ending all exchanges, Hoffman sent Hitchcock a list of federal POWs on parole in the North. Thanks to the Vicksburg surrender, even if every federal prisoner in a Northern parole camp was declared exchanged, the Confederacy would still owe the Union 33,596 prisoners when reduced to privates by the system of equivalencies.[41] According to Hoffman's calculations, this number was roughly equivalent to the number of Union prisoners being held in Confederate prisons.[42]

RECRUITING THE ENEMY

Some individuals in both the Union and the Confederacy viewed POWs as a potential source of new recruits for their own military forces. Although international law did not allow captors to force POWs to enlist, there was no legal provision against a soldier voluntarily switching sides. American military history included many efforts to enlist prisoners, beginning in the Revolutionary War. Of course, any prisoner who switched allegiance was subject to trial and execution for desertion if recaptured, but thousands of prisoners still decided that switching sides was preferable to remaining in captivity. On 10 July 1862, Stanton ordered Robert Murray, U.S. marshal in New York City, to visit the city prisons and survey the captives, to determine whether any were willing to shift allegiances.[43] However, by 25 February 1863, Stanton had changed his stance, and he informed Hoffman that Confederate prisoners, even if willing to take an oath of allegiance, were not to be enlisted into federal ranks.[44]

Throughout the summer of 1863, federal policies regarding the recruitment of Confederate POWs wavered. In spite of Stanton's policy forbidding the recruitment of prisoners, approximately 600 Confederate POWs were enlisted into federal service from the prison population at Fort Delaware from May to August 1863. Many of these were detailed for service on the western frontier, to free troops for service against the Confederacy. Stanton made an important exception to his orders for prisoners who had been conscripted into Confederate service. On 20 June 1863, Stanton gave permission for major generals Ambrose Burnside, John M. Schofield, and Andrew Johnson to accept Confederate prisoners conscripted from the Tennessee region into federal service.[45] Hoffman announced on 2 August 1863 that enlisted men in the Confederate Army who claimed to have been impressed could be inducted into Union service if the examining officer believed the prisoner to be reliable.[46] Stanton again ordered on 26 August 1863 that no Confederate prisoners be enlisted, but within three days, he granted special permission for Major General William S. Rosecrans to enlist prisoners.[47]

Stanton faced pressure from state authorities as well as field commanders for the recruitment of prisoners. Governor Oliver P. Morton of Indiana asked permission to enlist 200 Irish POWs held at Camp Morton. Stanton acceded to the request, authorizing Morton to free the prisoners and enlist them in the 35th Indiana Regiment.[48] One year later, Lincoln authorized the recruitment of foreign-born prisoners held at Rock Island, Illinois, for service in Pennsylvania regiments.[49] Such recruitment contradicted the wishes of Grant, who advised that if such men were to be allowed into service, they should all be placed into a single regiment detailed for frontier service.[50]

In all, over 6,000 Confederate soldiers took the oath of allegiance and switched sides during the war. These men, officially known as United States Volunteers, were formed into six regiments and were commonly referred to as "Galvanized Yankees." These regiments saw service at more than fifty outposts along the western frontier, from St. Louis to San Francisco. They reopened the Overland Trail to the Pacific Coast, which had been closed by

Native American raids in 1864, and guarded stagecoach and wagon trains moving through hostile areas, and in the process, they fought dozens of engagements against Native American tribes.[51]

The Confederate government also sought to enlist federal POWs, although it did so with less success. The Confederacy did not have the alternative of frontier duty for enlisted prisoners, and thus federal troops who volunteered risked trial for desertion if recaptured. Confederate Secretary of War James A. Seddon was skeptical of the recruitment of federal prisoners, stating that "the Yankees are not to be trusted so far, or at all."[52] On 8 November 1864, 349 POWs enlisted from Camp Lawton, Georgia.[53] On 16 January 1865, Colonel J. G. O'Neil of the 10th Tennessee Regiment was authorized to enlist federal POWs for Confederate service. On 24 January, 192 prisoners enlisted, followed on 28 February by the enlistment of 138 prisoners.[54] The federal troops that did enlist in Confederate service deserted in high numbers, and most reported joining the enemy ranks out of desperation.[55] Most Union prisoners who entered Confederate service deserted at the first opportunity to enter Union lines, or they surrendered to federal units as quickly as possible. As these desperate ex-prisoners entered Union lines, the war was rapidly ending, and the conditions of captivity were becoming known to Union authorities, who declined to prosecute the individuals involved.[56]

THE LIEBER CODE

On 24 April 1863, the War Department issued the most important and detailed provisions for POW treatment in American history. General Orders No. 100, also known as the "Lieber Code" after its creator, Francis Lieber, consisted of 157 articles, "Instructions for the Government of Armies of the United States in the Field."[57] Lieber, a professor of history and political economy at Columbia College, had prepared a summary of international law regarding guerrilla warfare and forwarded it to Halleck, general in chief of the army, on 1 August 1862.[58] Impressed with the brevity and clarity of Lieber's work, Halleck ordered 5,000 copies of the sixteen-page pamphlet printed for distribution throughout the officer corps. On 13 November 1862, Lieber suggested the president create a committee to codify the laws of war, with Halleck as chairman. Lieber recommended that the committee define who should be considered a prisoner of war, and how prisoners should be treated by federal forces. On 17 December, Halleck invited Lieber to Washington to serve on a special board, chaired by Commissioner of Exchange Hitchcock, charged "to propose amendments or changes in the Rules and Articles of War and a code of regulations for the government of Armies in the field as authorized by the laws and usages of War."[59]

Of the 157 articles of the Lieber Code, 38 are devoted to the capture, maintenance, and release of prisoners of war. Lieber defined a prisoner of war as "a public enemy armed or attached to the hostile army for active aid, who has fallen into the arms of the captor, either fighting or wounded, on the field or in the hospital, by individual surrender, or by capitulation."[60] This included all soldiers, any individual rising en masse with the occupation of enemy territory, any citizen accompanying the army, and any partisan fighting detached from the main body of the army. Importantly, Lieber defined guerrilla activities as outside the laws of war. Any individuals who fought without being part of an organized army, without sharing continuously in the war, and occasionally returning to their homes or pretending to be civilians were not entitled to the privileges of prisoners of war.[61] The exclusion of guerrilla fighters from POW status remained a crucial, and controversial, element of international POW law through most of the twentieth century.

All prisoners of war were to be treated equally, according to rank, and could not be divided by class, race, or condition. Further, the code specifically forbade the enslavement of any prisoners of war. No unit of troops had the right to announce it would give no quarter, although any unit that gave no quarter in practice could expect none in return.[62] Once prisoners were taken, they were the property of the capturing government, not the capturing units or individuals. They could be placed in confinement, but they must be treated with dignity and respect, fed plain, wholesome food, and provided with adequate medical care. In exchange, the government could require prisoners to labor for the government benefit, according to their rank and condition. Regarding prisoners who enlisted with the enemy, the Lieber Code was clear: any member of the U.S. military who enlisted in enemy service and was recaptured was subject to trial for desertion.[63]

The Lieber Code did not supersede previous exchange agreements, nor did it unilaterally destroy the exchange cartel. Halleck noted in a letter to Hitchcock that the code "simply announces general principles which apply only in the absence of special agreements."[64] Paroles given by troops captured after the issuance of General Orders No. 100 that were not in accordance with the provisions of the exchange cartel were considered null and void, even if they followed the instructions provided by the Lieber Code. Halleck ordered Hitchcock to release any federal troops on parole in the North that had been paroled by the Confederates, on the grounds that their parole was illegal, and therefore they were not prisoners of war.[65] This action infuriated Ould, who asked that all prisoners on both sides be released from their paroles, and cited General Orders No. 100, Article 131, as justification.[66]

The code was not simply a series of orders; it was also a persuasive argument for how wars should be fought, noting that war was not an excuse for immoral behavior. It was realistic without being rigid; it prohibited certain activities, including cruelty, maiming, torture, and poisoning, but it allowed for military necessity and retaliation. Unlike earlier works on international law and the laws of war, which offered philosophical principles but little practical guidance, the Lieber Code was created specifically to govern armies in the field. It was the first time that a government clearly stated not only the expectations of its own forces, but also the rights and obligations of an enemy and an occupied civilian population.[67]

The effect of the Lieber Code reached far beyond the American Civil War. It was adopted almost unchanged by the British, French, and Prussian governments in the decade after the Civil War. The code also served as the basis for international attempts to codify the laws of war at the Brussels Conference of 1874; the Institute for International Law's manual of the laws of land warfare; and at the Hague conventions of 1899 and 1907.[68] Within the American military, the code governed army operations during the Spanish-American War and influenced doctrine in the 1914 Field Service Regulations.[69]

THE CAMP SYSTEMS

The Confederate prison camps for federal POWs were most characterized by two locations. The first was an assortment of prisons in and around Richmond, in particular on Belle Isle and at Libby prison. Despite their close proximity, the two prisons were vastly different. Libby was primarily reserved for Union officers, who received more food, larger living spaces, and better shelter. One enlisted prisoner noted, "Libby has a hard name, but it was the most comfortable of the six Confederate prisons of which I saw the interior."[70] Another observed, "Being an officer, I suffered but little in comparison with what was endured by the rank and file."[71] Many others commented that the treatment was markedly different between officers and enlisted men. Some claimed it was because of the stratification of Southern society, while others argued that the conditions within the camps were dependent on the whims of the commanding officers of the prison.[72] In any event, the prisons in Richmond, under the direct observation and control of Davis, Winder, and the Confederate War Department, never approached the reputation of isolated compounds created in 1863 and 1864, after the exchange system began to fail. These isolated compounds, initially designed to reduce the overcrowding in Richmond and the associated usage of limited food supplies to maintain enemy captives, soon became notorious for the neglect of prisoners held within their confines.

Without doubt, the prison most associated with the Civil War today was Camp Sumter, located near Andersonville, Georgia. Andersonville, as the prison was commonly known, was the largest of the Southern emergency camps, created to house prisoners a great distance from the battlefront, thus preventing any rescue attempts such as the cavalry raids on Richmond designed to free the prisoners at Libby. Andersonville was a great distance from any major rail hub, in the interior of the state, so supplying the camp was extremely difficult. Although Andersonville was not the only camp to experience massive supply shortages and high mortality rates, it was certainly the largest Confederate prison camp, and the conditions at Andersonville rivaled those at any other camp.

The prison compound at Camp Sumter was authorized in February 1864 and received its first prisoners on 24 February. Designated to relieve overcrowding in Richmond's facilities, it was slated to hold 10,000 prisoners. Initially, the camp consisted of a rough-hewn stockade wall enclosing seventeen acres, with guard platforms spaced around the wall. A "dead-line" was marked by a line of posts topped with a four-inch-wide plank, twelve feet inside the stockade. Any prisoner that crossed the dead-line was likely to be shot without warning. The only water supply for the prisoners was a slow-flowing creek that ran through the center of the stockade. No shelter was provided for any of the prisoners, beyond what they could improvise from materials they carried at the time of capture. As such, some prisoners slept within tents, some in holes covered by canvas, and some completely exposed to the elements.

The Andersonville prisoners resorted to desperate measures to survive their captivity. A gang of prisoners, commonly called the Raiders in prisoner journals, preyed on their fellow captives, robbing new arrivals of any cash or valuables that could be bartered with guards. They also stole clothing, blankets, and food from other prisoners for their personal use. Prisoners who resisted faced beatings or even murder at the hands of their supposed comrades in arms. On 11 July 1864, a different group of prisoners organized a posse and captured the leaders of the Raiders. The ringleaders were put on trial by their fellow POWs, found guilty of murder and robbery, and hanged for their crimes on a gallows provided by the prison commandant, Captain Henry Wirz. The bodies of the condemned were then interred in graves separated from fellow captives, a final symbol of their ostracism from the prison population.[73] The rest of the Raiders were forced to run a gauntlet between two lines of prisoners, who rained down blows with clubs and fists on them.[74] Although this vigilante justice broke the most organized victimization of prisoners, robbery and murder remained a constant threat in the captive population.

By August 1864, Andersonville had received more than 35,000 prisoners, reaching a total occupancy of 33,114 on 8 August 1864.[75] Although the compound had been expanded to encompass twenty-six acres, the crowded conditions allowed infectious diseases to spread rapidly. The camp water supply, fouled by its usage for bathing and latrines, greatly contributed to the suffering. Rations for the prisoners, always in short supply, were never issued for more than 11,000 prisoners on a single day.[76] The typical ration was unbolted cornmeal, which contributed to an extremely high rate of dysentery and chronic diarrhea within the POW population. Prisoners were susceptible to virtually any form of communicable disease, as well as dietary disorders such as scurvy and dysentery. In the month of August, over 100 prisoners died every day, with an all-time high of 127 deaths on 23 August 1864.[77] Medical facilities at Camp Sumter were virtually nonexistent; a trip to the hospital was a virtual death warrant, as 75 percent of prisoners admitted to the camp hospital died while patients.[78] Over the course of only nine months of operation, Andersonville housed 45,000 prisoners. A total of 12,912 did not survive to leave the prison, and thousands more died in transit to other camps or immediately after their release.[79]

The possibility of exchanging the prisoners at Andersonville arose repeatedly. The prisoners sent numerous requests to Stanton, Lincoln, and state governors, pleading for exchange. Civilians also petitioned for the release of the Andersonville prisoners, urging the federal government, "Fear not to make concessions, and to submit even to some degree of wrong, that you may achieve the God-like work of giving deliverance to the captives."[80] Sherman refused Hood's offer to exchange the entire population of Andersonville for the few thousand Confederate troops captured in the fighting around Atlanta, on the grounds that the exchange would overburden his logistics and delay the end of the war. The Union was certainly aware of the situation in Andersonville, as Sherman received regular reports from prisoners who escaped the camp and reached his lines.[81]

As Sherman moved through the South in his "march to the sea," Camp Sumter authorities became concerned that the Union troops would undertake a raid to free the prisoners at Andersonville. On 27 July 1864, Winder ordered artillery officers manning the batteries outside Camp Sumter, "upon receiving notice that the enemy has approached within seven miles of this post, open upon the stockade with grapeshot, without reference to the situation beyond these lines of defense."[82] Winder ordered the murder of thousands of prisoners rather than allowing their recapture by Union forces, a clear violation of the laws and customs of civilized warfare as understood by both sides. After Winder's death, his replacement as commissary general of prisoners, Colonel Henry Forno, issued a similar order for all prison camps in Mississippi, Alabama, and Georgia on 15 February 1865. Forno's order had only one key difference: written to prevent a general uprising among prisoners, it was legal because it was to be executed only in the event of a mutiny, and it did not order camp commanders to kill prisoners in response to an external threat.[83]

Compared with the depravity of Andersonville, it would be natural to assume that Union compounds would offer better treatment of prisoners. After all, the Union had a better logistical system, more industrial and agricultural production, and a higher population, all of which should have contributed to a humane, functional system. To assist in that goal, the Union first created a uniform set of regulations for POW compounds on 7 July 1862. The initial regulations called for prisoners to receive rations equivalent to those given Union Army troops in the field. The daily ration was to include bread, fresh beef or pork, beans or rice, potatoes, molasses, salt, sugar, coffee, and tea. A general prisoner fund was created for each camp for the improvement of camp life, and it was financed by withholding from rations all that could be spared without inconvenience to the prisoners and then selling the surplus. The fund could be used for table furniture, cooking implements, cleaning supplies, and construction materials. In an emphasis of the military hierarchy within the POW system, as well as the role of the federal government, prisoners could only be paroled or released by direction of the commissary general of prisoners under the supervision of the War Department.[84]

On 20 April 1863, the regulations were revised, requiring camp surgeons to submit semimonthly reports of POW deaths, including the name, rank, and unit of the dead prisoner. A statement of the prison fund from each camp was required on a monthly basis, including expenditures from the fund. According to the new regulations, the Union Army began to issue clothing to POWs as necessary. Any army clothing was acceptable, with all buttons and trim removed so prisoners would not be mistaken for Union troops. Clothing could be sent to POWs from family and friends, as long as it was gray or butternut in color. The regulations reiterated that no paroles or releases were allowed without the authorization of the secretary of war.

Through 1864, the federal government maintained prisoners at dozens of locations of varying sizes.[85] On 3 May 1864, field commanders were informed that all prisoners should be forwarded from temporary depots to a few permanent depots as quickly as possible. The principal depots were designated: Point Lookout, Maryland; Fort Delaware; Johnson's Island, Ohio; Camp Chase, Ohio; Camp Morton, Indiana; Camp Douglas, Illinois; and Rock Island, Illinois. All other locations were regarded as temporary depots. The War Department reiterated that it held all authority for paroles and exchanges.[86] The decision to forward the prisoners suggested that the War Department anticipated a renewal of exchanges, but such a resumption never took place.

On 1 June 1864, Hoffman directed camp commanders to reduce the rations in Northern camps to match those in Confederate prisons, and to stop allowing friends or relatives to send food to prisoners confined in the North. The daily caloric intake dropped in Northern prisons by over 30 percent.[87] He also ordered that only one suit of clothing was allowed for each prisoner, to be made of inferior quality.[88] Some Confederate prisoners saw the reduction as a malicious attack on their welfare, as one noted: "Every means was used to prevent our friends outside or at our homes from knowing our real condition."[89]

As in the Confederacy, the Union prisons segregated officers and enlisted personnel. The primary camp for officers was Johnson's Island, where prisoners reported fairly pleasant conditions, with ample diet, extensive privileges, and a generally comfortable environment. Indeed, William W. Ward reported that he gained a considerable amount of weight while imprisoned.[90] Most complaints revolved around the use of black troops as prison guards and the boredom of camp life. Rather than discussing survival, escape, or exchange, many officers' accounts focus on financial issues, particularly the fear of having insufficient funds to maintain a luxurious existence.[91]

While officers enjoyed a high standard of living in captivity, poor conditions for enlisted prisoners were certainly not limited to the South. The North had more resources and a greater capacity to house and feed Confederate prisoners, yet the overall mortality rate in Union prison camps was virtually identical to that in Confederate camps. The War Department received regular updates from the commanders and surgeons of prison camps.

On 19 August 1863, Stanton received a report from the commander of Fort Delaware that 180 Confederates had died from 1 July until 19 August, out of a population of approximately 10,000 prisoners. The report included a statement made by four Confederate surgeons held in the prison, who regarded the mortality rate as low for the size of the prison. The camp commander offered, "From my own observation, I consider the prisoners of war at this post in as good condition as it could be possible to keep them at any other place."[92]

In December 1863, Stanton requested Dr. Montrose A. Pallen to inspect the largest federal prison camps. Pallen reported that prisoners in all locations were living in tents without sufficient blankets to offset the cold of winter, but he also observed that prisoners received the same quantity and quality of rations as those provided to federal troops, including fresh bread each day and fresh beef five days a week. Pallen surmised that the high mortality rates in camp were not the result of federal negligence but rather the result of many Confederate prisoners being in poor condition before their arrival in camps. In addition, most had not been inoculated against smallpox, which had struck at each of the camps.[93] Although Union leaders might have felt compelled to maintain the health of enemy prisoners, they certainly never indicated a desire to improve prisoners' health before exchange.

The location most often compared to Camp Sumter was Camp Elmira, located in upstate New York. Both camps opened in 1864, included massive overcrowding, and had an abnormally high mortality rate. Elmira was initially constructed as a training depot for Union troops, but on 23 May 1864, Colonel Seth Eastman informed Adjutant General E. D. Townsend that the location was ideal for a prison camp: it had originally been built to house 3,000 recruits, but it was not in use at that time. Hoffman ordered Eastman to prepare for as many as 10,000 Confederate POWs, but Eastman incorrectly assumed the number would never exceed 5,000.[94] From July 1864 until July 1865, a total of 12,263 enlisted Confederate POWs were sent to Elmira, with the greatest number reported in August 1864, when prison returns contained 9,480 names. Much of the misery at Elmira was blamed on two major factors, both similar to Andersonville. The water supply was provided by a small pond that also served as a latrine sink. The lack of shelter also resembled Camp Sumter, as thousands of captives were exposed to the elements without adequate clothing, blankets, or shelter. Prison life at Elmira was tightly regimented; as one former captive stated, "Daily life at Elmira followed a routine as regular as clockwork."[95] This statement was a far cry from the mass chaos associated with Andersonville, where no effort was made to regulate the daily activities of prisoners, but the lack of shelter and a clean water supply paralleled the conditions there. Unfortunately, the mortality rate also proved similar. A total of 2,951 prisoners died at Elmira, for a total mortality rate of 24 percent, the highest rate of any Union prison camp, though lower than the mortality rate at Andersonville.[96]

FREEING THE CAPTIVES

As the war came to a close, the Union moved quickly to free all federal prisoners still held in Southern camps. Prisoners assumed that the surrender of the Army of Northern Virginia would mean a quick end to the war, but prisoners in the Trans-Mississippi region faced the possibility of months of further confinement. Prisoners at Camp Ford, Texas, were not informed of the end of the war. Their captors simply abandoned the walls of the camp after notifying the POWs that they had been exchanged.[97] No effort was made to arrange transportation for the POWs, or even to notify the Union of their location. One final disaster remained for the prisoners fortunate enough to survive Andersonville and other Southern prison camps. On 26 April 1865, the river steamer *Sultana*, built to carry fewer than 400 passengers, headed up the Mississippi River bearing over 2,000 former Union prisoners. At 2:00 A.M. on 27 April 1865, the steamer exploded, killing 1,900 passengers, almost all former prisoners.[98]

The Union moved less quickly to free Confederate prisoners, but on 21 July 1865, Hoffman ordered that all Confederate prisoners be released from federal parole camps and returned to their home states, with the exception of prisoners caught with Jefferson Davis and those held for special reasons, such as conviction of a crime committed while a prisoner.[99] All freed prisoners swore the oath of allegiance to the United States before they were released, and they gave their parole to be of good behavior and commit no act of hostility toward the United States. After release, all prisoners were transported to the point nearest their homes accessible by rail or steamboat.[100] By 20 October 1865, federal rosters listed only fifteen prisoners still in confinement. The number included four privates too sick to travel, a convicted spy, Davis, and two personal aides, Confederate Secretary of the Navy Stephen A. Mallory and Henry Wirz. All other prisoners had been released and returned home, without punishment for serving in the Confederate military forces.[101]

Of the remaining prisoners, only Wirz was placed on trial for his acts during the war. His trial was one of the first war crimes trials in history.

Despised by the federal prisoners in his charge, Wirz was indicted for murder and conspiracy to commit murder. After a trial of two months, he was found guilty on ten of the thirteen counts of the indictment. The court named Davis, Seddon, and Cobb as co-conspirators in the deliberate attempt to mistreat Union prisoners, but none of them was brought to trial on the charges. Wirz was executed on 10 November 1865, after pleas for leniency or a pardon were denied. Days after the execution, it was discovered that the most damning testimony of the trial was fabricated. The government's star witness, Felix de la Baume, received a written commendation from the trial commission for his testimony and obtained a clerkship in the Department of the Interior. On 26 November 1865, the *New York Tribune* identified de la Baume as Felix Oeser, a deserter from the Seventh New York. Oeser lost his clerkship and admitted that his testimony had been perjured.[102]

The Wirz family has argued for decades that Wirz was a scapegoat for the horrors of Andersonville and that he did his best to save as many prisoners as possible from conditions beyond his control. Wirz was the only member of the Andersonville command structure to be held accountable for the deaths of Union prisoners, despite his defense that he was not the highest-ranking authority at the prison and that he acted under orders from Winder.[103] Joseph Cangemi and Casimir Kowalski argued that postwar propaganda surrounding Andersonville, including the testimony given at Wirz's trial, provided a justification for harsh Reconstruction policies, and that the Northern public believed a deliberate effort to destroy Union POWs existed at Camp Sumter.[104] Whether he maintained malicious intent, Wirz certainly proved an incompetent administrator of prisoners. At the least, he proved guilty of gross negligence and a cold indifference to the conditions of captives under his control.

The Civil War illustrated the pitfalls of improvised POW policies during a war requiring almost total mobilization of the belligerent societies. As the pace of captures rose in 1862 and 1863, diplomatic breakdowns forced each belligerent to create holding facilities for thousands of prisoners almost overnight. These diplomatic failures occurred because political leaders sought to gain short-term advantages essentially by using POWs as hostages. Because of the lack of planning and the low priority given to prisoner welfare, these prison camps proved wholly inadequate to the task of maintaining the prisoners. Camp administrators on both sides tended to be incompetent, if not criminally negligent. General Orders No. 100 established a set of regulations for the capture and confinement of prisoners that governed military forces in the field for decades after the war and helped establish international agreements regarding POW treatment, greatly improving the lot of prisoners in conflicts around the world. Unfortunately, the Lieber Code was issued too late to solve the problems encountered during the Civil War and only applied to the forces of one side of the conflict. The horrors of the Civil War prison camps, particularly Andersonville and Elmira, left a lasting impression on the American military and the American public and served as an example of what could happen if POW policy continued to be improvised in future wars. In the conflicts after the Civil War, military commanders devoted at least some forethought to the problem of prisoners of war and sought to avoid the mistakes made by both sides during the war. Similarly, diplomatic efforts in the period after the Civil War sought to establish the precise rights of prisoners of war, and the responsibilities of capturing powers, before conflicts could erupt and cloud the issue.

Old Capital Prison, Washington, D.C. National Archives, Brady Collection, photo B-2292.

North side of Libby prison, Richmond, Virginia, May 1865. National Archives, Brady Collection, photo QM-552.

Camp Sumter, Georgia (Andersonville), on 17 August 1864. This photo shows the massive overcrowding of the prisoner population. National Archives, Brady Collection, unnumbered.

Camp Sumter, Georgia (Andersonville), on 17 August 1864. Over 33,000 prisoners were present in the camp at the time the photo was taken. National Archives, Brady Collection, photo 165-A-441.

Wounded Spanish prisoners at American hospital on San Juan Hill, 3 July 1898. National Archives, U.S. Army Signal Corps, RG 111, photo 165-SW-12A-9.

Spanish prisoners being exchanged for Lieutenant Hobson and his crew, 1898. National Archives, U.S. Army Signal Corps, RG 111, no number.

German enlisted prisoner of war camp at Is-sur-Tille, 13 August 1918. Bathhouse and workshop are visible on the left; barracks are on the right. National Archives, U.S. Army Signal Corps, RG 111, photo 18962.

German enlisted prisoners at noon mess, St. Sulpice, France, 14 August 1918. National Archives, U.S. Army Signal Corps, RG 111, photo 79145.

Interior 8. German POW camp kitchen at St. Sulpice, 14 August 1918. National Archives, U.S. Army Signal Corps, RG 111, photo 79143.

German enlisted men's barracks at the Officer Prisoner of War Enclosure, Richelieu, Indre-et-Loire, France, 21 April 1919. National Archives, U.S. Army Signal Corps, RG 111, photo 161628.

Interior of officers' bedroom at Officer Prisoner of War Enclosure, Richelieu, 21 April 1919. National Archives, U.S. Army Signal Corps, RG 111, photo 161625.

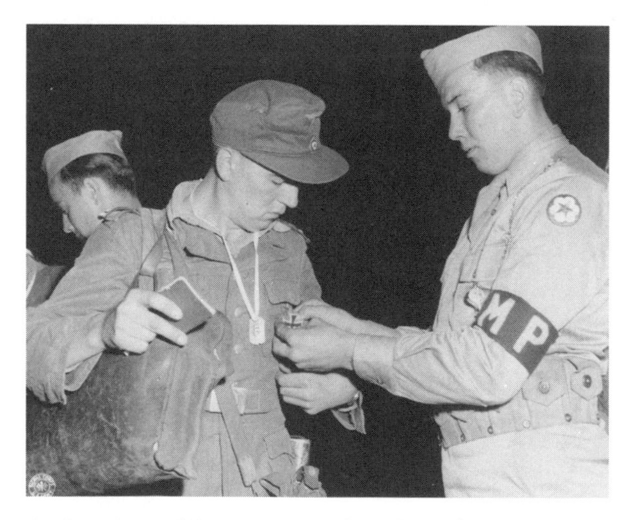

An American soldier removes an Iron Cross from a German prisoner of war, 1944. National Archives, U.S. Army Signal Corps, RG 111, photo 197669-S.

A military policeman stands guard in a watchtower outside a midwestern camp for German prisoners. National Archives, U.S. Army Signal Corps, RG III, photo 12254-PPA.

German prisoners working in the pulpwood industry. National Archives, U.S. Army Signal Corps, RG III, no photo number.

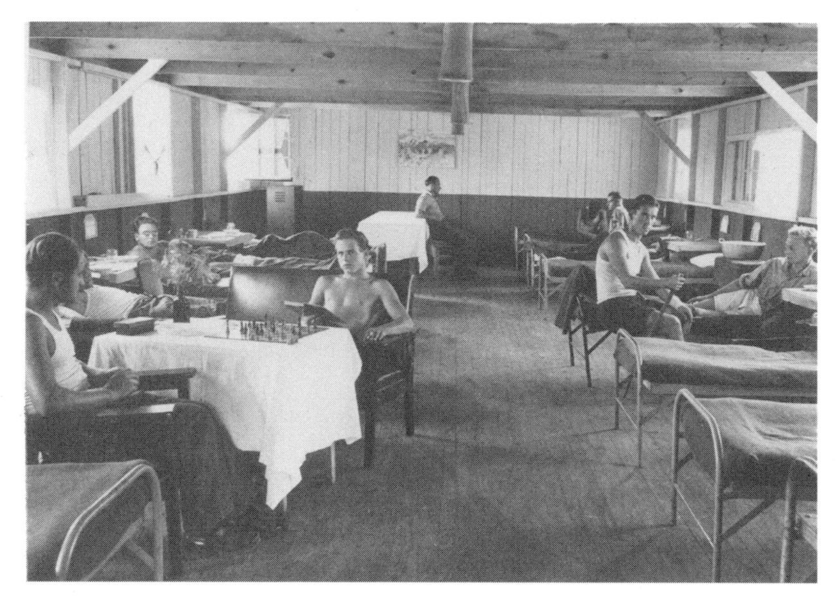

German POW camp hospital at Camp Polk, Louisiana. National Archives, U.S. Office of War Information, RG 208, photo AA-310K-15.

A German prisoner proudly displays his entry in a sand-sculpting competition. National Archives, U.S. Army Signal Corps, RG 111, no photo number.

German prisoners entertain themselves by performing a play for fellow prisoners and guard personnel. National Archives, U.S. Office of War Information, RG 208, photo 15616-FW.

Members of an Italian service unit rebuild a 40-millimeter antiaircraft gun at Erie Proving Ground, LaCarne, Ohio. National Archives, U.S. Office of War Information, RG 208, photo AA-311A-10.

Japanese prisoners emerge from a cave on Iwo Jima, 5 April 1945. National Archives, U.S. Army Signal Corps, RG 111, photo 205066-S.

More than 300 prisoners taken during the final day of organized resistance on Okinawa, 20 June 1945. National Archives, U.S. Office of War Information, RG 208, photo 43050-FMC.

Young Japanese prisoners captured on Okinawa who claimed to be eighteen and twenty, respectively. National Archives, U.S. Office of War Information, RG 208, photo N-42912-FMC.

Activities at a POW compound on Koje-do. The American officer with his back to the camera is Lieutenant W. M. Connor, chief of the psychological warfare section. National Archives, U.S. Army Signal Corps, RG 111, photo 375456.

A political demonstration within Compound No. 76 on Koje-do, 8 February 1952. National Archives, U.S. Army Signal Corps, RG 111, photo 393255.

The first communist prisoners are inspected before their transportation north as part of Operation Little Switch, the exchange of sick and wounded POWs, 15 April 1953. National Archives, U.S. Army Signal Corps, RG 111, photo 421803.

United Nations nonrepatriate camp at Tongjon-Ni, 27 August 1953, during Operation Big Switch, the voluntary repatriation of POWs. National Archives, U.S. Army Signal Corps, RG 111, photo 435784.

A Vietcong prisoner is escorted to an interrogation session, 2 October 1967. National Archives, U.S. Army Signal Corps, RG 111, photo CC-43814.

Vietcong prisoners inspect health and comfort items at Chu Lai, Vietnam, 1 November 1968. National Archives, U.S. Army Signal Corps, RG 111, photo CC-53535.

A Quan Canh guard holds a Vietnamese prisoner at gunpoint. National Archives, U.S. Army Signal Corps, RG 111, photo 594104.

Inside the barracks at the Phu Quoc prison compound, 20 October 1970. National Archives, U.S. Army Signal Corps, RG 111, photo 659256.

Captured Iraqi soldiers are guarded by U.S. Marines at Kibrit, Saudi Arabia, 25 February 1991. National Archives, Department of Defense Still Media Records Center, photo DM-SN-93-02250.

5

AMERICA BECOMES A WORLD POWER, 1865–1919

From 1865 until 1919, the United States engaged in a series of conflicts, both domestic and international, as it sought to pacify the interior of North America and gain respect as a world power at the same time. The treatment of two individuals, both deemed insurgents by the War Department, separated in time by a decade and in geography by half a world, demonstrate the variety of American POW treatment in this period. One, taken while leading a guerrilla campaign against white encroachment in the American Southwest, became the longest-held and most famous American military prisoner of the nineteenth century when he refused to collaborate with American authorities. The other, who was captured leading a guerrilla campaign against American conquest in the Philippine Islands, spent a short period in comfortable captivity and used his influence to end resistance and incorporate the islands into the American sphere of influence.

Geronimo was by far the best known of the Indian prisoners from the post–Civil War era. He and his followers fought a guerrilla war against white rule, ranging throughout the American Southwest and the wilderness of northern Mexico. However, Geronimo was not treated as a prisoner of war, even by the standards of the Lieber Code of 1863. Unlike other POWs, Geronimo received a trial under U.S. laws, after which he was exiled to Fort Pickens and forced to labor in violation of his surrender agreement.[1] After two years at Fort Pickens, Geronimo and his followers were moved to Mount Vernon Barracks, Alabama, where they remained for five years before being sent to Fort Sill, Oklahoma. Geronimo remained in limited captivity for the remainder of his life; he died in 1909 while still at Fort Sill. The War Department continued to file annual reports on the Apache prisoners at Fort Sill until 1913, when the survivors and their descendants were offered the choice of moving to Mescalero Reservation, ending the longest period of captivity for any group of POWs held by the American government.[2]

General Emilio Aguinaldo began his insurgent career fighting against the Spanish government in the Philippines. He proclaimed the independent Philippine Republic in 1899, and when informed that the United States had purchased the islands, simply returned to his guerrilla war with a new target. The capture of Aguinaldo became of prime importance to ending resistance on Luzon, the largest and most populous of the Philippine archipelago. After nearly three years of searching, a detachment commanded by Brigadier General Frederick Funston succeeded in tracking the self-styled president of the Philippine Republic and captured him on 23 March 1901. Aguinaldo was taken to Manila, where he received rooms and servants, guarded by American soldiers. He remained in captivity for less than a month before deciding to issue an open letter to the Filipino people, calling for them to lay down their arms and accept U.S. sovereignty.[3] Whereas Geronimo died in U.S. custody after more than two decades of captivity, Aguinaldo not only obtained his release from captivity, but lived to see the true independence of the Philippines, which was not granted until 1946.

MODIFYING INTERNATIONAL LAW

The period from 1865 to 1919 was punctuated by several international attempts to codify the laws of war, as well as conflicts involving the deployment of U.S. forces overseas. The founding of the Red Cross in 1864, the Declaration of Brussels in 1874, and the Hague conventions of 1899 and 1907 all served to alleviate the conditions faced by prisoners of war around the globe. The Spanish-American War in 1898 demonstrated the ability of the United States to capture and maintain thousands of prisoners in a humane fashion, if only for a short period of time, when leaders planned for the possibility of such captives. The Philippine War (1899–1902) showed the practical difficulties of applying a single code of conduct to guerrilla warfare in a wide variety of environments, and it illustrated that American POW practices did not always follow the prescribed policies for the treatment of enemy prisoners.

As for World War I, the United States joined the fighting more than two years into the conflict, when millions of prisoners already had been taken by all belligerents. U.S. officials were familiar with the conditions of captivity throughout Europe, as American representatives had accepted the role of protecting power for all of the major combatant nations, overseeing the needs of prisoners held by both sides of the conflict. The War Department made virtually no plans for the capture and maintenance of enemy troops, and thus was almost completely unprepared for the influx of prisoners with the entry of American troops into combat. As it had since the Revolutionary War, the army improvised a POW program, with the result that prisoners were inadequately sheltered and fed, and little effort was made to utilize the labor of prisoners held by American forces until after the end of the war.

SHAPING INTERNATIONAL LAW

Delegates from sixteen nations met in August 1864 to form a charitable society dedicated to alleviating the hardships of war for sick and wounded soldiers, regardless of nationality. The meeting resulted in the creation of the International Committee of the Red Cross. The mission of the Red Cross gradually expanded throughout the nineteenth century. By 1870, it included aiding prisoners of war held in the Franco-Prussian War by providing supplies and medical personnel to prison camps on each side of the conflict.[4] The influence of the Red Cross spread quickly in Europe, but in the United States, it did not become a factor in prisoner of war affairs until World War I.[5]

An international conference in Brussels in 1874 drafted a formal declaration of the laws of war to apply to all signatory states. This declaration was the first multilateral attempt to codify acceptable wartime behavior, particularly toward POWs. Although most of the signatories did not ratify the Declaration of Brussels, it provided the basis for the 1899 Hague II Regulations and the 1907 Hague IV Regulations regarding prisoners of war.[6] The Declaration of Brussels depended heavily on the Lieber Code, leaving unchanged many of the provisions regarding prisoners. Most importantly, it stated that prisoners were in the power of the enemy government, not the individual captors; prisoners could be forced to labor, but not on military works; and prisoners should be given food and clothing equivalent to those issued by the military of their captors.[7]

In 1899, international delegates again met at The Hague to consider the laws of warfare. Representatives of twenty-four nations adopted the Convention with Respect to the Laws and Customs of War on Land. Eight years later, forty-three nations sent representatives to another conference at The Hague to create a uniform code of conduct for military forces during war.

Each convention devoted seventeen articles to the treatment of prisoners of war, specifying how prisoners were to be captured and kept by belligerents. The provisions applying to prisoners did not differ significantly between the two conventions, with the unfortunate exception that the 1907 convention, which superseded the 1899 convention for all signatories, specifically stated that it would apply "only if all the belligerents are parties to the Convention."[8] Italy, Bulgaria, Serbia, Montenegro, and the Ottoman empire, all participants in World War I, did not sign the 1907 convention, thus the convention was not legally binding on the belligerents of the war.

The Hague conventions restated the principles of the Declaration of Brussels regarding captives. The hostile government, not the individuals or units that captured them, possessed the prisoners of war, who were to be humanely treated. Their captors could utilize their labor, but not in support of military operations.[9] Prisoners could not be legally transferred to the control of another government, a point that caused a great deal of contention between the American Expeditionary Forces and the Allied governments during World War I. Article 14 of each document obligated all belligerents to create a bureau of information for prisoners of war on the commencement of hostilities, to collect information from various governmental agencies, and to maintain an individual return for each prisoner. In a notable attempt to provide comfort to prisoners, these bureaus were to be given free postage and allowed to send and receive letters and parcels across battlefield lines for the improvement of the condition of prisoners. Relief societies such as the Red Cross could assist these bureaus in their efforts to ameliorate the conditions of captivity faced by all prisoners of war. Each convention explicitly stated that prisoners must be repatriated as quickly as possible after the conclusion of peace.

The United States incorporated the provisions of the Hague Convention of 1907 into the U.S. rules of land warfare and the army's field regulations, but did little to actually plan for the confinement of captured enemies. In 1913, as the threat of war loomed in Europe, the War College Division of the General Staff prepared a proposed general order for the treatment of prisoners, ready to be issued if the United States entered a conflict in Europe.[10] The order was never issued, primarily as a result of military operations along the Mexican border, where hundreds of Mexican nationals had been taken captive. These captives were referred to by the War Department as "interned prisoners," not prisoners of war. Any new regulations regarding POWs might create political problems for the American government by suggesting that a state of war existed with Mexico.[11]

THE FINAL PERIOD OF INDIAN WARFARE

After the termination of the Civil War, the United States Army rapidly demobilized and returned to its traditional duty of policing the frontier and enforcing the Indian policy of the federal government. Increasingly, this called for keeping native warriors on reservation lands and protecting overland migratory routes for settlers moving toward or through the frontier region. Conflicts with native tribes remained common, and as before the war, there was little room for prisoners in the behavior of postwar cavalry troops. Gone were the days of captivity narratives and forcible adoptions into Indian tribes. The enemy had changed, from the largely settled agricultural societies of the eastern woodlands to the subsistence hunter-gatherers of the plains. For the plains tribes, facing white encroachment on all sides, there simply was no possibility, even if there might have been a desire, to maintain captives. For their part, American troopers had no real interest in captives, except as negotiating points to compel native warriors to return to reservations. Many American soldiers, particularly officers, remained dismissive of the enemy, assuming that native prisoners had little intelligence value and would not uphold any agreements against future behavior.

Army life in the postwar era attracted a certain type of individual. The lifestyle consisted of low pay, harsh discipline, and hard work. "Duty" as a concept might have applied to officers, but it certainly did not motivate most of this time period's enlisted personnel. The frontier army had a great number of miscreants who couldn't function effectively in other institutions, as well as some individuals who truly enjoyed the lifestyle of the frontier army. It provokes little surprise, then, to discover that frontier soldiers saw little purpose in capturing enemy warriors, who might very well soon return to the battlefield. Instead, rampant killing was an option, and by destroying tribal settlements, warriors who escaped the fighting would be forced to concentrate solely on survival in the immediate future, rather than wreaking havoc on frontier settlements. Of course, the decision to kill carried its own penalties, including the obvious prevention of future surrenders. However, Indian victories were the rare exception, not the rule, and they did not tend to be accompanied by significant offers of quarter for their white enemies.

As an instrument of the federal government, the army could be expected to take the side of the citizens on the frontier, even when those citizens engaged in activities that openly violated agreements between the tribes and the government. As settlers moved in, they established farms, which radically altered the ecology of the Midwest, and which were in turn ravaged by the seasonal migration of buffalo herds. Given the dependence of many tribes on buffalo as a source of food, clothing, and shelter, the two world-views of plains Indians and white settlers simply could not be reconciled. Efforts to eradicate the massive buffalo herds, ostensibly for the protection of cropland and the establishment of transcontinental railways, had the unintentional side effect of destroying tribal livelihoods and provoking a backlash of conflict. In 1874, warriors of the Arapaho, Cheyenne, Comanche, and Kiowa joined together to fight against white hunters slaughtering buffalo on Indian lands near the Red River. They were treated as criminals and murderers rather than combatants, even though the "victims" had intruded onto protected reservation land and were directly threatening the existence of the tribe. When captured, the ringleaders were sent to Fort Marion in Florida after a brief period of captivity at Fort Sill, Oklahoma. While at Fort Sill, Lieutenant Richard H. Pratt of the Tenth Cavalry pushed unsuccessfully to have the leaders executed in front of their people as a warning against resistance.[12]

Other Native American tribes of the West that resisted assimilation or being forced onto reservations also came into conflict with American troops. Chief Joseph of the Nez Perce fought against U.S. Army cavalry forces while attempting to lead his people into Canada rather than remain under federal supervision. After a 1,700-mile march punctuated by skirmishes with American troops, Joseph agreed to surrender to the forces of Major General Nelson A. Miles in exchange for safe passage back to the reservation for his people. Instead, Joseph and over 400 followers were sent to Kansas, and later Oklahoma, after they had surrendered their weapons. Officially, this was done to protect them from neighboring tribes that had adhered to earlier treaties with the federal government. However, it also served as a warning to other tribal leaders who might resist confinement on a reservation.[13]

THE SPANISH-AMERICAN WAR

The United States declared war on Spain on 25 April 1898. Fighting followed in Cuba, Puerto Rico, and the Philippines, requiring the deployment of American forces around the globe in a variety of environments. Combat operations against Spain lasted for only three months, but in that period, American forces captured over 40,000 Spanish prisoners, most taken during the surrenders of Santiago, Manila, and Puerto Rico. The war was a departure from the improvised system of the Civil War for two reasons. First,

General Orders No. 100, issued in 1863, remained in force as the policy instrument guiding the capture and maintenance of enemy prisoners. Second, before combat operations, American commanders made specific plans to use the labor of prisoners captured in Cuba and Puerto Rico for the construction of roads in support of American combat operations.

Major General Nelson A. Miles, the commanding general of the army during the war, intended to besiege Santiago, on the southern coast of Cuba, and then march the army north, using Spanish prisoners taken at Santiago to build a road across the island. Miles assumed that a separate campaign in Puerto Rico would add 30,000 Spanish captives to the labor force, allowing construction to proceed at a rate of five miles per day.[14] Miles's plan was the first time U.S. forces had planned to use POWs before their capture in anything beyond a general sense.

Most of the works examining the Spanish-American War do not discuss prisoners, or they only mention the capture of prisoners taken at the capitulation of Santiago. Prisoners taken at other locations are often completely ignored.[15] Secondary works dedicated to the Philippine War primarily describe prisoners of war as victims of atrocities perpetrated by both sides.[16] Most treat the war as a single conflict, rather than a series of individual campaigns to pacify various regions of the Philippine archipelago. Stuart Miller argued that American soldiers murdered prisoners of war and civilians alike, attempting to frighten the population into submission, and were supported in their actions by commanding officers and the War Department.[17] David Bain blamed most of the reported atrocities on volunteer soldiers from the West, "who came to their adulthood on the American frontier."[18] Andrew Birtle noted that only a small percentage of Filipinos taken prisoner underwent any form of mental or physical abuse, but he also argued that summary executions were common if Filipinos were captured immediately after the murder of an American.[19] Brian Linn argued that the war varied greatly by location and cannot be treated as a single conflict; rather, it must be examined on a local basis.[20] He stated that most atrocities were committed by small groups engaged in counterinsurgency operations, and that senior officers, although aware of the actions of subordinates, did not actively pursue claims of American troops having violated the laws of war.[21]

The Spanish-American War was so short that even prisoners held in captivity until the war's end did not face significant hardships, and the number of prisoners held for more than one month was extremely low. Of the 40,000 Spanish prisoners taken during the war, more than half were taken in the capitulation of Santiago. The surrender of the city included a provision that the prisoners would be immediately transported to Spain, preventing their intended usage in road construction. The capture of Manila, with 14,000 prisoners, included equally lenient treatment and only a brief period of captivity. Fewer than 2,000 Spanish prisoners were transferred to the mainland of the United States, and all were naval personnel captured at sea. Because the United States had no official ambitions to annex Cuba, no effort was made to pacify the Cuban population or bring the countryside under American control.[22] To do so would have required a drastic alteration of American policy in Cuba; for the period of hostilities, Cuban rebels were considered allies against the common Spanish foe.

In Cuba, the first capture of prisoners occurred during the campaign to capture Santiago. The siege was complicated by the presence of a Spanish naval squadron, commanded by Admiral Pascual de Cervera. American naval forces blockaded Santiago on 27 May, and on 3 June, Lieutenant Richmond Hobson led an attempt to trap the Spanish fleet by sinking the USS *Merrimac*, an aged collier, in the entrance to the Santiago harbor. Hobson's efforts failed, and he and his volunteer crew were captured by Cervera's forces, the only American prisoners taken by Spanish forces during the entire war.[23]

U.S. Marines landed at Guantánamo Bay, Cuba, on 10 June, and an American army of more than 16,000 troops, commanded by Major General William R. Shafter, landed at Daiquiri, near Santiago, on 22 June. By 1 July, American forces surrounded Santiago and captured 120 Spanish prisoners at the Battle of El Caney. These prisoners reported surprise at the lenient treatment they received; for unknown reasons, they had expected no quarter from American forces.[24] Several of the Spanish prisoners were exchanged for Hobson and his crew on 6 July, and an additional twenty-seven wounded captives were sent to Santiago on parole.[25] Shafter later stated, "I have every reason to believe the return of the Spanish prisoners produced a good impression on their comrades."[26] In this, the treatment of wounded prisoners followed the example of the Mexican War, although there is no evidence that the similarity is anything more than a coincidence.

On 3 July, the Spanish squadron at Santiago emerged from the harbor and sought to escape the American blockade. Every ship under Cervera's command was sunk or set aflame, and Americans took 1,813 prisoners from the Spanish vessels. Captured Spanish officers, including Cervera, were delivered to the U.S. Naval Academy at Annapolis, Maryland. Enlisted prisoners of war were interned at the Navy Yard at Portsmouth, New Hampshire.[27] Included in the prisoners sent to Portsmouth were several volunteers of the irregular forces of the Spanish Army, captured by marines near Guantánamo. Prisoners taken by the navy and marines were held by the navy until the end of the war, and they were not transferred to the control of the army, as was the practice in previous and subsequent wars.[28]

While U.S. authorities shipped Spanish naval prisoners to America for confinement, an army under Shafter besieged Santiago. Shafter demanded that General José Toral, the Spanish commander of the Santiago military district, surrender the city to prevent further bloodshed in a futile defense. Toral requested instructions from the governor of Cuba, General Ramon Blanco, who referred the question of surrender to the Spanish government in Madrid. On 14 July, Miles notified Secretary of War Russell A. Alger of the terms of the proposed Santiago surrender. On 17 July, Toral surrendered the city, as well as all the troops within his military district, some at distances of up to 100 miles from the city. Almost 23,000 troops surrendered, in exchange for shipment to Spain at the expense of the United States. Because of the terms of the agreement, the plan to use POW labor to construct a road across Cuba quickly faltered.

On 20 July, the quartermaster's department opened bidding for a contract to transport the Spanish prisoners and their families to Spain. Of the ten bids received, only two were deemed to be responsible companies capable of fulfilling the contract. The Spanish Trans-Atlantic Company won the contract and was paid $55 per commissioned officer and $20 per enlisted person for transport. The first ship left Santiago on 9 August, and the last left Guantánamo on 17 September. All told, 22,864 individuals were delivered to Spain on sixteen transports, including 22,137 troops and 727 noncombatants, at a total cost of $513,860.[29] Prisoners awaiting transport were provided with ample rations and medical supplies, prompting one soldier to write a letter of thanks to his captors as he boarded the transport home.[30] This repatriation without requiring parole certainly differed from previous American POW practice. By quickly shipping prisoners home, though, American leaders not only created some goodwill in Spain, but also avoided the expenses associated with POW upkeep.

In keeping with the principle created at Santiago, on 27 July, the State Department, at the request of the secretary of the navy, John D. Long, used the British government as an intermediary to offer the release of all the Spanish prisoners taken during the destruction of Cervera's fleet. If the Spanish government agreed to send a neutral ship to Portsmouth to carry the sailors, they would be allowed to give their parole and return to Spain for the remainder of the war. Spain refused the offer on the grounds the Spanish military code "prescribed [a] penalty for prisoners of war obtaining release by giving parole not to bear arms against [the] enemy," and the sailors remained in captivity.[31]

On 12 August, diplomats met in Washington, D.C., and signed a peace protocol that ended all hostilities between Spain and the United States in all theaters of the war. Although formal peace treaty negotiations did not open until October, President William McKinley ordered that Spanish prisoners held in the United States be repatriated to Spain as quickly as possible. Once again, this decision offered both goodwill and economy. On 31 August, Cervera was informed that he should make arrangements for the transportation of all Spanish prisoners in the custody of the War Department and the Navy Department to Spain, which he did in a single shipment.[32] Not all of the prisoners desired to return to Spain; a few requested the opportunity to remain in Cuba.[33] Because the United States had no intention to annex Cuba, the American government left this decision to the revolutionary Cuban government, which offered no protest to the request.

Word of the 12 August cease-fire did not reach the Philippines in time to prevent an American assault on Manila on 13 August. After a brief engagement, the city capitulated, and 14,000 Spanish defenders became prisoners of war.[34] These prisoners remained in their barracks in Manila, and they could move about the city at will while awaiting repatriation to Spain. Few chose to leave their barracks area, preferring to remain in close quarters rather than mingle with the hostile Filipino population. The prisoners returned to Spain as quickly as transportation could be arranged, again at American expense.[35]

THE PHILIPPINE WAR

The Treaty of Paris that ended the conflict ceded possession of the Philippine Islands to the United States. This triggered a war in February 1899 between the occupying American forces and Filipino natives in the area surrounding Manila. The war expanded into an insurgency that occurred simultaneously in dozens of locations. General Orders No. 100 remained the governing policy for American commanders in their relations with Filipino natives. Unfortunately, as a result of lack of oversight, American practices regarding prisoners taken in the war varied by location, often depending entirely on local commanders, regardless of official policies. Portions of the instructions were reprinted regularly, to keep officers informed of the regulations regarding enemy prisoners and the civilian population, but few mechanisms existed to compel compliance.[36]

Of course, the Filipino insurgents were not bound by General Orders No. 100. To guide his followers, Aguinaldo issued "Instructions to the Brave Soldiers of Sandatahan of Manila" on 9 January 1899. This included an order to respect the lives and property of all civilians and to preserve the life of any soldiers who surrendered.[37] Antonio Luna issued a contrary order on 7 February, calling for insurgents to offer no quarter to American troops, but on 5 June, he was assassinated by followers of Aguinaldo.[38] Aguinaldo was informed in November 1899 that he would be held personally responsible for the behavior of units under his command.[39] Unfortunately, despite the regulations issued by American commanders and by Aguinaldo, reports of atrocities were common throughout the war, often involving the execution of prisoners by both sides.

American soldiers captured thousands of Filipinos in the fighting near Manila in 1899, and the city jails quickly began to fill to capacity. The provost marshal of Manila reported that 4,149 prisoners were held on 10 March 1900, and almost one third of the prisoners were sick, including 697 suffering from beriberi.[40] On 1 April 1900, President William McKinley offered to release thousands of prisoners if they agreed to swear an oath of allegiance to the U.S. government.[41] Prominent guerrilla leaders who refused to swear the oath were sent to Guam for the remainder of hostilities, easing the strain on the municipal jail system. The transfer of Filipino captives to Guam demonstrated that the U.S. government still regarded them as military prisoners, not criminals or traitorous subjects.[42]

On 20 December 1900, Major General Arthur MacArthur announced that any guerrillas or civilian supporters captured by U.S. forces would be held for the duration of hostilities but would not be granted POW status. Rather, they would be regarded as criminals punishable by the government for aiding the insurgency. In contrast, any guerrillas who voluntarily surrendered would be disarmed and paroled, without repercussions from the U.S. military.[43] It is important to emphasize that according to Articles 32, 52, and 82 of General Orders No. 100, MacArthur could regard insurgents as criminals rather than POWs, eliminating protection by the laws of war. MacArthur's pronouncement complicated the POW situation in the Philippines because the provost marshals received custody of all civil prisoners as well as POWs. U.S. military courts tried thousands of prisoners in 1901 and 1902 for a variety of offenses. However, by definition, POWs cannot be tried simply for being members of an opposing military force; they may only be placed on trial for offenses against the laws of war. By placing insurgents on trial, the army demonstrated that they were no longer considered POWs. Any guerrillas who did not continuously participate in the war could expect to be treated as common criminals.[44]

Between 5 May 1900 and 30 June 1901, MacArthur reported 1,026 contacts with insurgents. In the same period, 6,572 insurgents were captured in the field, and 23,095 voluntarily surrendered. Perhaps more importantly, 15,693 rifles were captured or surrendered in the same time period.[45] The number of prisoners held by the United States rose gradually until 1 March 1901, when MacArthur issued a notice to the people of the Philippines that the delivery of any serviceable rifle or revolver would be rewarded by the release of one prisoner, chosen by the person delivering the weapon.[46] To alleviate overcrowding, a prison was established at Olongapo on 7 March 1901, but the surrender of weapons proved so successful in reducing the prison population that the prison at Olongapo operated for only seven weeks.[47] On 28 March, U.S. forces captured Aguinaldo and brought him to Manila as a prisoner. MacArthur believed that the capture of Aguinaldo was the primary reason behind an increased rate of surrenders, particularly among insurgent leaders. He also hailed the surrender of Manuel Tinio as an important step in the pacification of the archipelago. To signal the importance of Tinio's surrender, on 19 April 1901, MacArthur ordered that 1,000 prisoners in Manila jails be offered the oath of allegiance in exchange for their release. As other insurrectionary leaders surrendered, MacArthur ordered similar mass paroles, effectively emptying the Manila prisons as resistance flagged.[48] By 31 May 1901, the provost marshal of Manila reported only 1,240 prisoners remained in the city.[49] The release of prisoners in exchange for weapons demonstrated to rebels that peaceful actions brought tangible rewards from the occupation forces. The decision to release large numbers of prisoners immediately after the surrender of guerrilla leaders proved that the American military did not seek to punish individual guerrillas; it only sought to pacify the insurrection, primarily by targeting leaders and holding them in captivity.

Sporadic guerrilla resistance continued through the spring of 1902, when the last insurgent commanders surrendered. On 16 April, Miguel Malvar and his remaining followers surrendered, ending resistance to American rule on the island of Luzon. Eleven days later, resistance on Samar ceased with the surrender of the remaining guerrillas on the island. On 16 June, military governance in the Philippines officially ended and was replaced by civilian government.[50] To conciliate the inhabitants of the archipelago, President Theodore Roosevelt issued a proclamation of peace and amnesty for all inhabitants of the islands except those convicted of murder, arson, and rape.[51]

The nature of the fighting in the Philippines—separate conflicts in remote locales by independent commands—prevented the existence of a single American POW practice, even with the policies established by General Orders No. 100. In particular, the treatment of prisoners at the time of capture varied greatly. In 1902, a Senate investigation revealed a disturbing pattern of prisoner abuse by American troops and native allies. Because American forces often could not distinguish between guerrillas and the civilian population, captured insurgents became an invaluable source of information regarding the populace. The most notorious form of abuse reported by American veterans was the so-called water cure, when a prisoner's mouth was pried open and gallons of water poured down his throat. The water cure produced a sensation of drowning or strangulation, and it was augmented by punching or kicking the victim's distended abdomen to expel the water.[52] Few prisoners subjected to the water cure could resist surrendering information after suffering its effects. Senate testimony provided by enlisted personnel contained numerous references to the use of the water cure in many locations—testimony provided by officers invariably denied having witnessed, ordered, or condoned such methods, which were explicitly forbidden by Article 80 of General Orders No. 100.[53]

In most locations, once U.S. interrogators determined that prisoners had no further intelligence value, they were held in guardhouses or outposts, usually in small numbers. American soldiers reported a high number of escape attempts, often accompanied by reports that a prisoner had been shot.[54] American commanders made no attempt to create a central POW enclosure or a series of large camps, preferring to place prisoners in existing installations. The treatment meted out to prisoners varied by location, but most American veterans who had observed prisoner treatment claimed that Filipino prisoners received rations, medical care, and lodging equivalent to that given U.S. troops, with the exception that the prisoners often received more rice and less meat, in accordance with their customary diet.[55]

Secretary of War Elihu Root contended that the United States fought with tremendous restraint in the Philippines, and that reports of the mistreatment of prisoners were isolated incidents, not a generally accepted behavior of American troops.[56] Brigadier General Robert P. Hughes echoed Root's sentiments, but he argued that American conduct became progressively more severe throughout the war, in response to the uncivilized behavior of Filipino insurgents. Major Cornelius Gardener noted that American troops looked down on Filipino natives as an inferior race, stating, "Almost without exception soldiers, and also many officers, refer to the natives in their presence as 'niggers' and the natives are beginning to understand what the word 'nigger' means."[57] Filipinos were also unfavorably compared to Mexicans, and they were deemed too cruel and untrustworthy to serve as officers in command of native troops.[58]

American military and civilian leaders quickly put aside or forgot the lessons of the Spanish-American War and the Philippine War with regard to prisoners of war. The conflict with Spain was too short to greatly affect American POW policy, and the only true legacy of the war was reflected in the decision by the Department of the Navy to intern German naval personnel taken during World War I in the United States, rather than shipping them to France, where German and Austrian soldiers were held captive. U.S. military officers deemed the guerrilla warfare lessons of the Philippine War to be irrelevant to the conventional warfare of World War I, but questions regarding the legal status of guerrilla prisoners again arose during the Vietnam War. In each conflict, American officers justified mistreatment of prisoners, particularly in the pursuit of intelligence gathering, by arguing that guerrillas were not protected by international law.

PRISONERS OF THE GREAT WAR

The international developments of the late nineteenth century had some effect on the belligerents in World War I, and although the Hague Convention of 1907 was not legally binding, most of the belligerents voluntarily promised to comply with the POW provisions. However, differing interpretations of the convention's articles ensured that the status of POWs in international law was far from settled by the experiences of World War I. To some observers, the Hague conventions were too lenient toward prisoners, as illustrated by J. M. Spaight in 1911: "Today the prisoner of war is a spoilt darling; he is treated with a solicitude for his wants and feelings which borders on sentimentalism. He is better treated than the modern criminal, who is infinitely better off, under the modern prison system, than a soldier on campaign."[59]

Although the historiography of World War I is voluminous, historians have given little attention to the role played by prisoners of war, particularly given the number of prisoners taken in the war. By the time the United States entered the war, the Central Powers held almost 3 million Allied prisoners, with more than half in Germany, and the Allies held more than 2 million, most of them in Russia.[60] Immediately after the armistice was signed, Carl P. Dennett, an American Red Cross commissioner, published *Prisoners of the Great War*, accusing Germany of failing to provide even the most basic necessities for prisoners to survive captivity. Dennett argued that American prisoners in Germany avoided the hardships suffered by prisoners of other nationalities because the United States maintained an interest in German camp conditions and took more prisoners than it lost; only the fear of retaliation led Germany to keep the American prisoners in good health.[61] Dennett's work remained largely unchallenged for decades, until the publication of Richard Speed's *Prisoners, Diplomats, and the Great War*. He argued that the United States had several years' advance warning and captured comparatively few prisoners, yet still struggled to adequately maintain its captives. According to Speed, if the war had continued for even a few more months, the American prison capacity would have been overwhelmed, with disastrous consequences.[62]

AMERICA AS A PROTECTING POWER

World War I commenced in Europe in August 1914. Within two months, almost 300,000 prisoners had surrendered. By 1 February 1915, almost 1 million men were in captivity, mostly Russian troops held by the Central Powers.[63] None of the belligerents were prepared for the huge influx of prisoners, and all were forced to improvise housing and security facilities for their captives. Diplomatic problems complicated the practical difficulties of feeding and housing prisoners. Although each government professed a desire to uphold obligations contained within the Hague conventions, they interpreted the obligations differently. Particularly troublesome were Articles 14 and 16, requiring the establishment of bureaus of information regarding prisoners. The British created a Prisoner of War Information Bureau in August 1914, and the French, Germans, and Austro-Hungarians opened agencies in September. Nominally, each fulfilled the requirements of international law, but they differed over what type of inquiries were legitimate (government or private), and whether prisoner lists should include the location of confinement. Disagreements soon arose over the interpretation of virtually every aspect of the convention. Each government felt obliged to protect its own prisoners held by the enemy, but no government had a means to assess the conditions of its own soldiers held as prisoners. Each side soon fell prey to rumors about the mistreatment of prisoners by the enemy, and threats of retaliation soon followed. As the front lines of the war stabilized, turning the conflict into a war of attrition, none of the major belligerents actively pursued the creation of a system of exchange, which might return vital manpower to enemy forces. Ironically, each side instead spent immense resources on confining prisoners in massive compounds.

The major powers of each side asked the United States, as a neutral nation, to serve as a protecting power. For the first three years of the war, the United States maintained relations with both sides, inspecting prison camps throughout Europe and distributing relief to prisoners regardless of nationality. The cost of American relief operations was charged to the benefiting power, and reports of inspections were provided to each belligerent, in the hope of preventing unnecessary retaliatory abuses. The first inspections were carried out on a reciprocal basis, with Britain and Germany expressing particular concern that the other might be unfairly abusing prisoners. Surprisingly, Russian authorities hindered the inspections the most, despite the fact that the Russian czar, Nicholas II, had sponsored the prewar Hague conferences. Russia held more prisoners than any other belligerent, with more than 2 million captures by the end of the war, most of them Austro-Hungarians. According to American inspectors, most of the abuses of prisoners in Russia were not deliberate acts, but rather the unfortunate side effects of an inefficient bureaucracy, a primitive transportation system, and an inability to provide sufficient supplies to war captives.[64]

In January 1915, the State Department offered to create a regular schedule of inspections throughout Europe, on the condition that each belligerent provide a statement of their POW policy to the enemy and that American representatives have access to prisoners at each location. The prisoners would be allowed to send written statements to their governments regarding the conditions of their captivity. The inspections began in April, with inspectors ordered to report the size and location of camps, the general conditions of captivity, and the specific needs of prisoners at each camp. The inspectors avoided critical commentary while writing inspection reports to prevent exacerbating diplomatic tensions between the belligerents.[65] American inspectors performed more than 600 inspections and were generally regarded as evenhanded in their evaluations of camp conditions, even by their future enemies. When the United States entered the war on 6 April 1917, Switzerland assumed the role of protecting power and continued the scheduled inspections of POW camps for the remainder of the war.

AMERICA AS A BELLIGERENT

Three factors complicated American policy during the war. First, the United States entered the war in 1917, after conflict had ravaged Europe for almost three years. Although American inspectors were familiar with the practices of European powers regarding prisoners, the American Expeditionary Forces (AEF) still had to create an entire prisoner of war system because the Hague conventions prohibited the transfer of prisoners between belligerents. American troops held any prisoners captured by American forces, under the direction of the provost marshal general, whose department existed only as a wartime institution.[66] This arrangement prevented any significant effort to plan ahead for the capture and confinement of enemy forces. Second, the United States joined Britain, France, and Russia in a coalition, but only as an associated power, not a formal ally. The British and French governments had announced their intention to follow the Hague conventions in 1914, and the United States was naturally expected to do so as well. However, because the conventions were not legally binding, American and German practices toward each other's prisoners were also governed by the treaty of amity and commerce signed by Prussia and the United States in 1785. This treaty included the provision that prisoners in any future conflict would be held in the United States or Prussia, not a third country. Third, because this was the largest overseas deployment to date for American forces, any prisoners maintained in Europe would only add to the logistical strain already imposed on American planners.

Previous American expeditionary experiences provided scant assistance —the deployment of forces to Mexico occurred on a much smaller scale, and the period of major combat operations against Spain ended before POWs could begin to have a major effect on resources or logistics. In Europe, however, the AEF failed to even supply most of its own heavy equipment. Any additional requirement, such as the care and guarding of tens of thousands of enemy prisoners, could only make the problem worse. Given that POW operations had not been a high priority for American commanders in any previous conflict, this offered the potential for a disastrous system like that created in the Civil War.

The AEF's leaders set their first priorities as training and deploying units to Europe, and therefore, the capture and maintenance of prisoners were not a high priority in the first months of American involvement in the war. On 5 July 1917, the War Department outlined the functions of the AEF General Staff, giving the provost marshal the duty of guarding POWs and maintaining records of their confinement, among many other duties.[67] A prisoner of war information bureau was not created until 30 November, and the duties of the provost marshal were not explicitly detailed until 10 December. However, American forces held very few prisoners at the end of 1917, and even though regulations for the treatment of captured enemies were not issued until 1918, Swiss observers found no cause for complaint.[68]

On 3 January 1918, the secretary of state asked the War Department whether prisoners would be shipped to the United States. The State Department feared that any attempt to remove German prisoners from Europe would be met with retaliation on American soldiers. An earlier shift of German prisoners from Britain to France had provoked Germany to threaten to ship British prisoners to Turkey or Bulgaria. The War Department requested that the State Department open negotiations with Germany regarding the disposition of prisoners of war; in the meantime, all prisoners captured by the AEF would be held in Europe by American guards.[69] On 23 January, the AEF General Staff asked the provost marshal general, Colonel William H. Allaire, what preparations had been made for the maintenance of prisoners. He responded that his department had yet to create a prisoner of war section. On 23 February, General John Joseph Pershing ordered the commanding general of the services of supply to select a camp location for German prisoners near the supply depot at Gièvres, where they would be put to work.[70]

THE LABOR CAMP SYSTEM

AEF regulations designated two primary functions for prisoners: as sources of intelligence and as sources of labor. After capturing prisoners, AEF officers forwarded them to division enclosures, where an intelligence officer selected prisoners for detailed interrogations.[71] All unselected POWs were transferred to a central enclosure, where they joined labor companies for employment on construction and repair work.[72] All prisoners received the same rations, bedding, fuel, and medical services as U.S. troops, including mandatory vaccinations.[73] Once assigned to a labor company, POWs worked six days per week at a rate of twenty centimes per day.[74] The initial regulations conformed to the requirements of the Hague Convention of 1907, although the treaty was not expressly mentioned in POW manuals until the July 1918 versions were issued.[75]

The manual established a table of organization for 50,000 prisoners—a remarkably accurate prediction, given that the AEF captured 48,280 prisoners during the war.[76] In addition to outlining the functions of staff officers within the Bureau of Prisoners of War, the manual specified that all prisoners would be disarmed, searched, and forwarded to division headquarters, to fill out identification cards and await interrogation. After initial questioning at the division level, prisoners were sent to a corps enclosure, searched again, and finally consolidated into an army enclosure. After a final search, the prisoners were sent to the Central Prisoner of War Enclosure No. 1 (CPWE-1). Eventually, eight central enclosures were created to deal with the influx of thousands of prisoners each week during the final offensive on the Western Front. As labor companies reached full strength, they departed the central enclosure and shifted to labor camps well behind the AEF lines. Initially, labor companies contained 400 men, but in 1919, each company was expanded by 50 prisoners. Eventually, 122 labor companies were created, each composed of 450 prisoners.[77]

While the General Staff was negotiating with the French for control of German prisoners, intending to utilize them for AEF labor needs, the secretary of war ordered that all German prisoners held by the AEF be transferred to the United States, on the grounds that the treaty of amity and commerce required internment in the continental United States.[78] Prisoners could fill labor shortages in agriculture created by the induction of millions of men into military service. The AEF General Staff requested that the secretary reconsider his plan, as the French and British governments would almost certainly protest the action, and the secretary relented, with the provision that no prisoners taken by the AEF be transferred to Allied control. The State Department had initially agreed with the secretary of war regarding internment locales, but then agreed that in the absence of any German diplomatic complaints, prisoners could be held in France by the AEF. Officers, who were exempt from labor requirements, were not mentioned in the War Department's instructions. The French government recommended that officer prisoners be shipped to the United States because they required guards and maintenance but did not contribute to the labor supply, but they were never transferred out of France.[79] In practice, the only German POWs interned in the United States were sailors captured at sea, who were sent to Britain for interrogation and then forwarded to the United States for internment.[80]

The first American camp for prisoners in Europe was not established until 28 April 1918, and it held accommodations for only 150 prisoners. On 14 May, the general staff requested that all captures made by American forces, many transferred to French control, be returned to American custody. The primary reason for the request was the fact that American prisoners were held in Germany, and the AEF wished to keep German prisoners to ensure the proper treatment of Americans.[81] The French government agreed and promised to forward any prisoners taken by American units to the American prison enclosure at Gièvres, but on 31 July, the provost marshal general pointed out that almost no prisoners captured by the AEF had actually been forwarded. On August 7, the French Army finally began the transfer of thousands of German prisoners to American custody.[82]

Most German prisoners held by the AEF were sent first to CPWE-1. The compound was initially a temporary installation near Tours, but in August 1918, a permanent facility opened at St. Pierre des Corps.[83] From June 1918 until April 1919, a total of 37,716 German POWs were processed at the facility. Some 32,000 received assignments to labor companies, and the remainder stayed in the camp or were forwarded to the Officer Prisoner of War Enclosure, as appropriate.[84] The camp consisted of eight separate enclosures, each a self-contained POW camp with barracks, mess halls, and infirmaries. Camp conditions were excellent for the prisoners. They received ample rations, fresh clothing, and thorough medical care. The diet varied by location; each labor company drew up weekly menus for the German POWs. A sampling of labor company menus for March 1919 showed that prisoners at every location received coffee, bread, meat, and vegetables on a daily basis.[85] Each enlisted prisoner worked nine hours per day, six days per week. When not working, the prisoners were given recreational opportunities, including sports, games, reading material, and musical instruments.[86]

Officers were forwarded from CPWE-1 to a separate prison facility near Richelieu. They did not perform labor, and they received a monthly allowance for the purchase of supplies beyond their daily rations.[87] They also received orderlies and cooks from the enlisted POW population. Every captured officer lived in a single compound, "a huge country estate . . . surrounded entirely by a stone wall ten feet high." Enlisted prisoners performed manual labor, but officers diverted themselves with dramatic productions, musical performances, and the opportunity to take college courses.[88] The officers enjoyed a comfortable lifestyle, including unsupervised nature walks, tailored clothing, and the opportunity to send telegrams to their families.[89] Unlike enlisted POWs, officers were allowed to consume alcoholic beverages, which were supplied by camp canteens.[90] The officer POWs took full advantage of their privileges, including running up tremendous debts at the camp canteen for credit purchases, eventually prompting the camp commandant to require cash for all sales.[91] Officers on nature walks reportedly broke tree limbs, uprooted saplings, and urinated and defecated in the chateau park, provoking the cancellation of all walks outside the enclosure.[92]

AEF headquarters received weekly reports from CPWE-1 detailing any POW deaths, transfers, or escapes. Many of the reports contained detailed information on individual prisoners, but the reports often proved a bureaucratic hassle rather than a useful tool. Field units reported the capture of thousands of prisoners that CPWE-1 did not receive, particularly after heavy activity in the American sector of the front. Almost 1,000 prisoners were reported missing in a single report on 3 October 1918; by November, 17,000 prisoners were in captivity but had not been individually processed. The American POW infrastructure proved incapable of keeping updated reports on prisoners as the rate of captures increased, greatly hindering the utilization of prisoner labor.[93]

The labor system for prisoners held by the AEF developed slowly, but by the end of the war, prisoners were employed in salvage work, construction of roads and camps, lumber production, sanitary maintenance, and freight handling.[94] Once the armistice was signed, the type and hours of work for POWs expanded. Prisoners could be required to work at night or on tasks previously considered too dangerous for compulsory labor, such as the disposal of high explosives.[95] Within the labor companies, prisoners received rations and supplies identical in quantity and quality to those issued to U.S. troops. Every captive was inoculated against various diseases, and they received the same medical and dental care as that furnished American soldiers. Laborers were paid a daily wage in canteen script that could be spent on luxury items. Prisoners could send two letters per week, subject to censorship by American officers, and could receive an unlimited number of letters and packages.[96]

INTELLIGENCE-GATHERING OPERATIONS

Perhaps the most important use of prisoners during World War I, for both sides, was as a source of intelligence.[97] Local raids to capture prisoners were common along the Western Front. As prisoners were brought into Allied lines, they were briefly questioned and forwarded to divisional headquarters. At each level, interrogators asked POWs for biographical information for identification purposes, followed by questions about unit strength, morale, and enemy intentions. Interrogators inquired about the specific location of machine gun emplacements, divisional headquarters, and artillery batteries. They inquired about divisional movements, as well as which units manned the trenches at the time of capture. As each interrogation was completed, individual reports were forwarded to corps headquarters. American commanders did not expect extensive intelligence from individual soldiers, but they hoped to gain useful information from the aggregate data collected from the combined interrogation reports. As reports corroborated one another, AEF headquarters obtained a fairly accurate estimate of enemy strength, morale, and intentions. Most prisoners refused to willingly provide useful information to American interrogators, but few realized the potential intelligence value of even small details gleaned by their captors.

In September 1918, Captain Charles A. Willoughby proposed that interrogators focus primarily on identifying characteristics of a prisoner's uniform and speech patterns, rather than on the information actually supplied by the prisoner. He noted that most German army corps recruited territorially, so a prisoner's dialect could serve as a way to test the veracity of many of his statements. By learning which German units were in the vicinity, American commanders could anticipate enemy actions, regardless of the statements made by prisoners, who were often found to be lying about troop movements or units in the area.[98] Willoughby's idea offered a new means of utilizing POW interrogations, even if it came too late to offer practical use in World War I. The idea that enlisted enemy captives might provide more than immediate tactical information dramatically altered future American approaches to prisoner interrogations.

At the end of the war, the United States repatriated its prisoners before any Allied nation, but it did not do so immediately after the end of hostilities. The Hague Convention declared that "after the conclusion of peace, the repatriation of prisoners shall be carried out as quickly as possible," but the Allies did not rush to return their captives.[99] In contrast, the armistice of 11 November 1918 required Germany to begin the repatriation of Allied POWs immediately, without reciprocity. Even after the signing of the Treaty of Versailles in June 1919, repatriation of German prisoners was delayed for months. On 7 September, the AEF began sending German POWs home, a process that required only seventeen days, thanks to the relatively small number under American control and the short distance to travel.[100] All officers traveled through Gièvres en route to Germany; enlisted personnel were collected at Is-sur-Tille for repatriation.[101]

The POW experience in World War I demonstrated that the Hague conventions of 1899 and 1907, although mitigating the conditions faced by prisoners, were not sufficient and required substantial revisions. In particular, the international regulations governing the treatment of prisoners needed specific guidelines for the signatories to guarantee equal treatment of prisoners. Also, the requirement that all belligerents be signatories before the provisions became binding set a diplomatic standard prohibitively high. World War I was especially important to the evolution of American POW policy because it was the first time that the War Department performed a thorough postwar assessment of its POW practices. The commanders of each central enclosure and labor company submitted reports to the adjutant general detailing the history of their POW organizations, and these reports became the basis for American practices in World War II. They also served as examples of a functional system of camp and labor organization for American officers to follow in the next world war.[102]

6

AMERICA BECOMES A SUPERPOWER

World War II

Georg Gaertner, a twenty-two-year-old member of the Afrika Korps, surrendered to American forces during the Battle of Tunis on 13 April 1943. He spent more than two years as a prisoner of war in Texas and New Mexico, laboring primarily to help bring in crop harvests, while also serving as a translator and liaison within his camps. Upon learning that he faced repatriation to his hometown in East Prussia, an area overrun and occupied by Soviet troops, Gaertner decided to escape his prison compound at Camp Deming, New Mexico. On 21 September 1945, Gaertner slipped under the barbed-wire enclosures and fled to a nearby train track, leaping inside a rail car that eventually carried him to San Pedro, California. He remained a fugitive from the Federal Bureau of Investigation for the next forty years, until he finally contacted Professor Arnold Krammer, author of *Nazi Prisoners of War in America*, to orchestrate his formal surrender. Although the FBI had not officially forgotten about Gaertner, by 1985, the search for him had long since ended. Nevertheless, he formally surrendered on 11 September, ending the longest escape in the history of American POW operations.[1]

Gaertner, like many German POWs, reported boredom as the worst aspect of life in a prison compound. The prisoners were allowed to entertain themselves with sports, books, and games, and even the labor requirements did not prove too onerous. To put POW labor in perspective, Gaertner's autobiography notes that prisoners received eighty cents per day in camp scrip, enough to purchase eight packs of cigarettes or eight bottles of beer in the canteen. Given the wartime rationing in the United States, it is unsurprising that many citizens accused the federal government of coddling their prisoners. According to Gaertner, the life of POWs became markedly more unpleasant after the German surrender, as news of the Holocaust and the Malmedy Massacre reached American audiences. However, even in the last few months of his captivity, he was well fed, provided with excellent shelter and medical care, and required to work only a few hours per day.[2] Gaertner's story typifies that of German prisoners held in the United States from 1943 to 1945; even the relative ease of his escape mirrors the experience of thousands of POWs in America.

The United States captured more POWs during World War II than in every other American conflict combined, a total of more than 7 million German, Italian, and Japanese prisoners.[3] Most American POW policies during the war concerned German prisoners. This was almost certainly a question of numbers, as the vast majority of all captures were German soldiers. The War Department utilized prisoner of war labor on a wider scale than ever before, primarily in POW camps established throughout the continental United States. The POW experience of the war changed markedly at the end of the war. Most captures were made in the final months of the war in Europe, as Allied forces rapidly advanced into Germany. The capture of millions of German soldiers overwhelmed American planners, with the result that European prison camps served primarily as short-term holding pens for prisoners awaiting repatriation or transfer to labor facilities, and did not follow the labor-first guidelines of American camps in the United States.

Much of the historiography of American POW operations during the war has focused on three key issues: utilizing enemy labor, efforts for politically reeducating prisoners, and allegations of deliberately mistreating captives. George Lewis and John Mewha provided the most extensive discussion of the POW labor program, devoting ten chapters to all aspects of POW labor during the war. They argued that the labor program was vital to the American economy, and that it was the first successful application of enemy prisoner labor in American history. In particular, they noted that Americans employed prisoners in the harvest of dozens of different crops and in hundreds of industrial applications.[4] Their discussion of the labor utilization of prisoners makes virtually no mention of the opposition of labor unions to the use of prisoner labor in nonagricultural work.

Judith Gansberg's *Stalag USA* focused primarily on the American reeducation program for German prisoners established in 1944. The program, discussed in greater detail below, was designed to train bureaucrats for the postwar administration of Germany. Gansberg relied primarily on interviews with the commanders of the Special Projects Division (SPD) of the provost marshal general's office, the unit created to supervise the education program, and she considered the effort a complete success. Ron Robin also examined the SPD, but in *The Barbed Wire College*, he argued that the program produced an "intellectual backlash" among the prisoners selected for administrative training and led the trainees to resist indoctrination efforts while maintaining a facade of accepting American ideals. Robin demonstrated that the internal records of the SPD showed very little progress in reeducating prisoners, but the records were later modified to suggest that it was an unmitigated success.[5] *The War for the German Mind*, by Arthur L. Smith Jr., argued that American reeducation programs must be viewed as part of a larger Allied reeducation effort, in which each nation sought to influence postwar Germany through repatriated POWs. He believed that American and British efforts aimed primarily to instill democratic principles in the German mind, but the Soviet program was designed to turn Germany into a communist nation.[6]

The most comprehensive discussion of German prisoners held by the United States is *Nazi Prisoners of War in America*, by Arnold Krammer. Krammer argued that German prisoners in America received better treatment as captives than as soldiers in Europe. He demonstrated that German POWs humanized the war for millions of Americans and served as a vital source of emergency labor. Krammer devoted particular attention to the political ideology that dominated many of the POW camps in the United States, with fanatic Nazi prisoners terrifying their comrades into resisting American camp commanders. He considered the decision to remove the most fervent Nazis from camps and intern them separately as the turning point in the German POW experience in America.[7]

Perhaps the most controversial work in the historiography of POWs during World War II is James Bacque's *Other Losses*, published in 1989. Bacque accused General Dwight D. Eisenhower of conspiring to murder over a million German POWs at the end of the war through starvation and neglect. Bacque based his accusation on a single question presented in his interview of Colonel Philip S. Lauben, who subsequently retracted his statement as a misunderstanding.[8] The accusations provoked a conference, hosted by the Eisenhower Center at the University of New Orleans, where several papers effectively dismantled Bacque's thesis. In particular, other scholars criticized Bacque for deliberately misreading documents discussing the transfer of prisoners from various army commands and the release of prisoners without formal processing. In each case, Bacque assumed that the prisoners, listed as "other losses" on official records, had died in captivity, despite ample evidence that they had simply been moved from one Allied army command to another or been transferred to a different nation's control, a practice forbidden by the Hague conventions but allowed by the Geneva Convention of 1929, and thus legal during World War II.[9]

A major trend in World War II POW historiography has been a series of regional studies primarily focusing on German camps in the United States. Some focus on the events at a single camp, such as John Hammond Moore's *The Faustball Tunnel*, or the experiences of a single prisoner, such as Reinhold Pabel's *Enemies Are Human.*[10] Others examine a number of camps in a single state, such as Allan Kent Powell's *Splinters of a Nation* or David Fiedler's *The Enemy among Us.*[11] Lewis H. Carlson's *We Were Each Other's Prisoners*, a collection of interviews of former American and German prisoners, compared captivity on opposite sides of the Atlantic Ocean and found a high degree of similarity in the experiences of prisoners held by each side.[12] These detailed studies are excellent sources of information on specific camps or individuals, but they rarely provide more than a cursory examination of the broad picture of American prisoner of war policy.[13]

REVISING INTERNATIONAL LAW

In the aftermath of World War I, dozens of nations sought to prevent or mitigate future wars through treaties and voluntary arms limitations. In 1922, for instance, the Washington Naval Conference limited naval construction and precluded a naval arms race similar to the one experienced before World War I. The Locarno Pact of 1925 secured Germany's western frontier, defined by the Versailles Treaty, to head off any future conflict. In 1928, sixty-five nations signed perhaps the most optimistic treaty in history, the Kellogg-Briand Pact, renouncing war as a means of settling disputes. In 1929, a conference at Geneva met to create a new set of international regulations governing the capture and maintenance of prisoners of war, replacing the Hague conventions of 1899 and 1907.

The Geneva Convention of 1929, in effect during World War II, included the key provision that it applied to all signatories whether or not their enemy had signed the convention. According to the convention, all captured enemies needed to be moved from the battlefield as quickly as possible, and thereafter given rations and accommodations equal to those supplied to the captor's own forces. Every belligerent agreed to create a prisoner of war information bureau, to allow camp inspections by a neutral nation, and to limit the types of labor that would be required of prisoners. The Geneva Convention forbade the use of POW labor on any project directly connected to war operations, including the transport of material to combat units. No dangerous or degrading labor assignments could be given to prisoners of war. Officers could not be compelled to work, and noncommissioned officers could be assigned only supervisory work.[14] Of the major belligerents of World War II, only the USSR and Japan did not sign the convention. The USSR announced in 1941 that it would adhere to the Hague Convention of 1907 regarding prisoners. Japan indicated in 1942 it would follow the major provisions of the convention but in practice ignored the convention whenever the agreement proved inconvenient.

AMERICA AS A CAPTOR

When World War II began in Europe in 1939, the United States maintained its neutrality. As in World War I, each of the belligerents created POW systems long before American entry into the war.[15] Although the United States formally declared war against Japan on 8 December 1941 and against Italy and Germany on 11 December 1941, enemy captives remained relatively few throughout 1942. In August, the United States agreed to the transfer of 50,000 prisoners from British prisons to alleviate overcrowding, but by the end of the year, the United States held fewer than 2,000.[16] Thirty thousand prisoners arrived in May 1943, most shipped from the North African theater, followed by 50,000 prisoners in August. The number of prisoners in the United States slowly rose but did not truly climb rapidly until after the Allies invaded Normandy. As Allied forces closed on Germany, the number of German captives rose more rapidly than American logistics could handle. American planners expected 60,000 prisoners in the first three months of combat after the Normandy landings, but by 1 September, almost 200,000 were captured and sent to the United States.[17] In all, almost 400,000 German prisoners were sent to the United States during the war.[18] Shipments of prisoners to the United States overwhelmed the transportation network. Immediately after the surrender of Germany, all transportation of German POWs to America halted.[19]

There are no exact figures available for the number of German prisoners taken by the United States, although most estimates place the number between 3 and 5 million. This lack of specific numbers is partly because many German prisoners were captured, disarmed, and immediately released at the end of the war rather than processed into POW camps.[20] The provost marshal general's office stated in 1947 that the peak number of prisoners in U.S. custody was reached in June 1945, when almost 3 million POWs were in captivity in Europe. This number did not include prisoners shipped to the United States for confinement, prisoners transferred to other nations, or captives disarmed and released from custody.[21] Compared with the millions of captured Germans, barely 50,000 Italian prisoners were taken by American forces, most during the North African campaign.[22]

ITALIAN PRISONERS IN AMERICA

Initially, there was little difference in the treatment of German and Italian prisoners. The first large groups of each came from combat in North Africa, and they arrived at the same time in the United States. American commanders segregated the two groups and shipped them to large holding compounds, where they awaited assignment to labor camps. Most of the Italian POWs captured by American forces during the entire war came from North Africa. An agreement with Great Britain ensured virtually every prisoner taken in the region, German and Italian alike, remained in American custody.[23]

The status of Italian prisoners radically changed with the forced resignation of Benito Mussolini on 25 July 1943. An armistice, signed 3 September, ended the state of war with the Allies, and on 10 October, Italy declared war on Germany. The Allies accepted Italy as a cobelligerent, creating a strange situation. Could the Allied powers consider the Italian prisoners they held as prisoners of war? The armistice required Italy to release all captured Allied troops, but it did not mention the disposition of Italian POWs. In December 1943, the American and British governments suggested that nonfascist Italian POWs should be allowed to volunteer for noncombatant service units, although they would still be legally considered POWs. Italian prime minister Pietro Badoglio rejected the idea, but the Allied governments proceeded to implement the system over his protests.[24]

On 13 March 1944, Lieutenant General Brehon Somervell, commander of the Army Service Forces, ordered the creation of Italian Service Units (ISUs), volunteer units of Italian POWs in the United States. By 31 May, 180 ISUs existed, with over 1,000 Italian officers and 33,614 enlisted volunteers.[25] The units worked primarily on military posts nationwide, usually at tasks not allowed by the Geneva Convention for prisoners of war. These tasks included service at ordnance and supply depots handling munitions, performing salvage and reconditioning work, and loading military supplies at ports for shipment overseas.[26]

In exchange for service, ISU members received limited parole benefits not extended to ordinary prisoners, including the opportunity to work without military supervision. They had more recreational opportunities than German POWs, and at many locations, ISUs fraternized regularly with American civilians. ISUs stationed near large Italian American communities enjoyed home-cooked meals, sightseeing tours, and dances attended by American hostesses.[27] Dozens of ISU members married American women while still prisoners of war, despite a War Department prohibition against the practice.[28] Hundreds more returned to the United States and married Americans after the war, or sent for American brides to join them in Italy. The privileges extended to the ISUs created a "coddling" controversy, and some Americans were angered that men captured while fighting against the United States enjoyed luxuries not available to American troops overseas.[29] ISU volunteers received one final privilege over ordinary Italian prisoners: they were designated for the earliest repatriation as a reward for their service. Virtually all ISU members returned home by the end of 1945, although some non-ISU prisoners remained in captivity in the United States until March 1946.[30]

PRISONERS FROM THE RISING SUN

Japanese prisoners were taken in much fewer numbers than Europeans, and few were shipped out of the Pacific theater of operations. The primary reason that few of the Japanese prisoners taken in the Pacific were shipped to the United States was an agreement that Australia would hold all Japanese prisoners who had no significant intelligence value.[31] The war was almost over before the capture of significant numbers of Japanese prisoners. By 20 August 1945, fewer than 20,000 prisoners had been captured by U.S. forces in the Pacific, and only 5,000 had been sent to the United States for confinement and interrogation.[32]

John Dower argued that Japanese unwillingness to surrender, combined with Allied disinterest in taking prisoners in the Pacific, ensured that few Japanese captives were taken in the Pacific.[33] Dower's thesis is supported by memoirs and contemporary accounts of American service personnel.[34] Simon P. MacKenzie bolstered Dower's thesis by stating that American marines executed Japanese prisoners in the Pacific rather than burden themselves with prisoner care.[35]

Japanese prisoners resisted surrender because of indoctrination by the Japanese military and expectations of mistreatment after capture. Most Japanese army recruits believed death was preferable to capture.[36] The provost marshal general and the Office of Strategic Services operated under the same assumption.[37] Ironically, because Japanese commanders assumed their troops would not surrender, enlisted soldiers and sailors received no instruction regarding the proper behavior of POWs. Consequently, during interrogations, Japanese prisoners often proved willing to answer questions about morale, strength, and troop placement of enemy forces because they had never been instructed to resist interrogation. The most effective propaganda aimed at inducing Japanese soldiers to surrender was designed by Japanese prisoners. Allied propaganda efforts finally began having a measurable effect on Japanese troops in the summer of 1945.[38]

Even as the war drew closer to the Japanese Home Islands, unit cohesion remained strong. Whereas in North Africa and at Stalingrad, hundreds of thousands of prisoners surrendered en masse, in the Pacific theater, surrenders of more than a handful of prisoners at a single time remained exceedingly rare. On the Eastern Front in Europe, German and Soviet forces had an approximately equal number of troops killed and captured, but the Japanese wartime ratio was over thirty killed for every prisoner who surrendered.[39] This was primarily a function of Japanese unwillingness to surrender, not an Allied resistance to taking captives; only one-third of all Japanese prisoners surrendered intentionally. Most of the rest were incapacitated by wounds or illness, or became separated from their units and blundered into Allied forces. It is worth emphasizing that more than half of all Japanese prisoners captured in the war were naval personnel plucked from the ocean after surviving the sinking of their ships.[40]

There simply were not enough prisoners taken in the Pacific theater to have a significant effect on American POW policy. The 12,194 prisoners captured in the Southwest Pacific area in 1945 before the surrender of Japan were a far cry from the millions of German prisoners captured in North Africa and Europe. Most Japanese prisoners were penned in holding camps scattered throughout the region, and the Allies made little effort to utilize their labor. On 2 September 1945, approximately 100,000 Japanese prisoners surrendered in the Philippines as part of the surrender of the Japanese empire, but their captivity was brief. Japanese prisoners were repatriated almost immediately after the end of the war. Half of all Japanese prisoners were home by the end of 1945, and all returned to Japan by the end of 1946.[41]

PRISONER INTERROGATIONS

As in World War I, prisoners provided a wealth of intelligence to American commanders. A systematic effort by all belligerents to interrogate prisoners taken in all theaters commenced with combat operations in 1942 and continued throughout the war. Initially, American interrogators followed British practices when questioning enemy prisoners.[42] Early interrogations focused on troop strength, unit movements and intentions, enemy morale, and enemy supply situations. American commanders realized that extensive questioning of every prisoner was unrealistic because the average enlisted prisoner had almost no knowledge of planned operations or troop strength. As such, American officers sought to identify prisoners having high rank or detailed knowledge who could be separated and subjected to lengthy interrogations. Although most prisoners were sent to camps in the United States by sea, prisoners with valuable information were airlifted to special interrogation camps, designated in official communications only by postal box numbers. Forts Hunt and Tracy, near Washington, D.C., were used for European prisoners. Japanese prisoners of special interest were flown to Byron Hot Springs in California.[43]

By 1944, senior staff at the departments of War and Navy gave American interrogators weekly lists of topics of interest, with a particular emphasis on military technology.[44] American military engineers desired detailed information about the development of jet propulsion, rocket motors, and guided missiles.[45] The Army Medical Corps requested information on Japanese plans for biological warfare, especially efforts to infect water supplies with harmful bacteria.[46] Psychological warfare officers studied POW interviews for signs that enemy morale was flagging and that surrender demands were having an effect.[47] In the spring of 1945, as Germany neared collapse, surveys of POWs were used to determine the political mind-set of Germans regarding the Nazi Party, the United States, the Soviet Union, and the likelihood of continued resistance after the surrender of Germany.[48]

German prisoners who identified themselves as anti-Nazi often emerged as subjects of special interest for American interrogators. These prisoners were considered more reliable sources for evaluating the effect of Allied operations on German morale, the effect of bombing campaigns on the civilian population, and the possibility of a communist takeover in postwar Germany. Many of these prisoners supplied intelligence voluntarily, in an effort to assist the Allies in the destruction of the Nazi regime. In particular, the prisoners revealed a gradual decline in German troop morale after the D-day invasion of 6 June 1944 and a growing lack of faith in Adolf Hitler's leadership. They also reported increasing supply shortages resulting from Allied bombing raids and estimated the extent of damage to major German cities from the aerial campaign.[49]

POW CAMPS IN AMERICA

The provost marshal general's office maintained responsibility for prisoners of war, as it had in World War I. On 5 October 1944, the office issued regulations to all POW guard personnel governing every aspect of prisoner operations. The instructions, "Enemy Prisoners of War," were contained in a War Department technical manual known as TM 19-500, which was updated during the remainder of the war. The manual replaced the earlier improvised regulations, which varied by service command. It ordered all POW guard personnel to follow the Geneva Convention, both in spirit and letter.[50] The manual only explicitly applied to POWs held in the United States; operational theater commanders could apply the regulations as they saw fit, although all theater of operation POW camps were defined by the manual as temporary.[51] In the United States, the manual's primary consideration for the placement of POW camps was the ability to use POW labor to the maximum extent possible.

American commanders segregated POW camps by nationality. Eventually, German POW camps were also separated by political ideology, as American officers sought to separate fanatical Nazis from politically neutral or anti-Nazi prisoners. In camps for Japanese prisoners, captives of Korean and Formosan ancestry were separated as "a necessary step in preventing violence and possible bloodshed."[52] Prisoners in each camp elected spokesmen to serve as liaisons with American authorities and neutral-nation camp inspectors.[53]

In the camps, prisoners expressed surprise at the amount of food, clothing, and space they received. Some perceived the lenient treatment as an American attempt to curry favor in the event the Axis powers won the war. In fact, the Geneva Convention caused enemy prisoners to receive more food, clothing, and living space than they were accustomed to: they were receiving these items in equal quantities to those received by American forces. As with the ISUs, some American civilians complained that German prisoners were coddled by the government, enjoying luxuries not available to the American public as a result of wartime shortages. In addition to food, clothing, and housing, enemy prisoners received exceptional medical care, including monthly medical inspections, immunizations, dental care, and psychological counseling.[54]

The Geneva Convention specified that all prisoners should receive intellectual and physical diversions as much as possible, and American camp commanders soon provided sporting equipment, reading materials, and musical instruments to their charges. Prisoners formed athletic leagues, bands, choruses, and acting troupes for their own entertainment, and they often invited American personnel to their performances. Prisoners could pursue higher education if they so desired: several American universities offered correspondence courses for prisoners, and in 1944, the German Reich Ministry of Education offered high school and university credit for courses taken while held as a prisoner of war.[55] Prisoners received extensive mail privileges. Each was allowed to send two letters and four postcards per week, subject to military censorship, and could receive an unlimited number of letters, postcards, and parcels.[56]

German POWs became so comfortable in the United States that they deliberately provoked American authorities on many occasions, risking administrative punishment by playing pranks. In one incident, German prisoners painted a swastika on a turtle in Florida and jokingly informed their guard that the turtle was a Nazi sympathizer. Other prisoners painted, carved, and drew swastikas and other German symbols on virtually any available surface, continually provoking American personnel while maintaining their identity as German soldiers. Most historians have viewed this behavior as an effort to uphold military discipline among the prisoner population, although Omar Bartov argued that this type of behavior represented the prisoners' devotion to ideology.[57]

Political sentiments in the camps often dominated camp life. Fanatical Nazis sought to exert control over fellow prisoners by threatening reprisals against any POW who expressed anti-Nazi sentiments. The provost marshal general's office attempted to separate anti-Nazi prisoners from camp populations and hold them in separate facilities, but this effort was often frustrated by the prisoners. As a rule, ardent Nazi Party members held all of the leadership positions within each camp. They were almost invariably chosen as camp spokesmen for communicating with American officials. Noncommissioned officer POWs showed the greatest devotion to Nazism and held the highest ranks in most German POW camps. They often censored or banned books in the prison libraries that they considered anti-Nazi, in particular targeting books by Jewish authors.

The German POW population organized kangaroo courts as a means of keeping control over anti-Nazi prisoners. These courts, also called honor courts, met to determine whether any prisoners were guilty of treason against the Reich. *Newsweek* reported one trial in February 1945, in which Corporal Johann Kunze was tried, convicted, and beaten to death by his fellow prisoners. Kunze's killing provoked a court-martial of five German prisoners, who were convicted of murder and executed in July 1945. Kunze's death was not an isolated incident; murders, assaults, and forced suicides continued even after the surrender of Germany.[58]

As a result of Nazi atrocities within the camps, the provost marshal general's office reversed its policy of attempting to segregate anti-Nazi prisoners and instead decided to isolate the most ardent Nazis from the prisoner population. These fanatical adherents to Nazism proved easy to distinguish because they seemed eager to prove their fervor to captors and comrades alike. The War Department constructed a special maximum-security prison at Alva, Oklahoma, for these intractable prisoners. Simultaneously, a campaign to reeducate and "denazify" the camps commenced. A gradual adjustment of camp environments ensued, with the introduction of pro-democracy reading materials and films, and the creation of the SPD to oversee the reeducation effort.

THE SPECIAL PROJECTS DIVISION AND DENAZIFICATION

Two U.S. Army officers, Lieutenant Colonel Edward Davison and Major Maxwell McKnight, commanded the SPD and assembled a team of intellectuals and educators at Fort Kearney, Rhode Island, to direct the denazification effort. The group called itself "the Factory" in official and nonofficial communications and made great efforts to remain secret. Prisoners deemed sympathetic to the reeducation cause were sent to Fort Kearney to assist in the effort to modify the ideology of their fellow prisoners. Once an educational program was created, the SPD expected to provide a crash course in democracy for up to 20,000 cooperative German prisoners in the hope that they would form the nucleus of a new political system in postwar Germany and aid in the occupation effort.[59]

One of the SPD's first projects was to create a national German POW newspaper, *Der Ruf* (*The Call*). It was written and published at Fort Kearney for national POW distribution. To avoid the appearance of propaganda, *Der*

Ruf was sold at prisoner canteens rather than simply given to the prisoners. The first issue appeared on 1 March 1945 and sold 11,000 copies. By 15 October, over 70,000 copies of each issue were sold in the camp canteens. Although sales of the paper steadily increased, some prisoners found it disturbing, recognizing its propaganda value and subtle attempts to undermine or destroy their loyalty to Germany.[60] Dozens of camp newspapers were created by POWs across the country, and the Factory monitored each for evidence that the general mind-set of German prisoners was being affected by the SPD's denazification efforts. The Factory identified a gradual transformation of the editorial practices of many camp newspapers, suggesting that prisoners were becoming more receptive to the principles of democracy and individual freedom.

The Factory included four other sections to influence POW thinking. The Film section reviewed radio programs and films before they were offered to prisoners. The Translation section conducted surveys of the German POW population and translated pamphlets into German for distribution among the camp populations. The Camp Administration section monitored general camp conditions and maintenance, and the Review section analyzed materials submitted by government agencies and the SPD for use with the German POWs, such as labor training manuals for certain industries.

The existing education system in the POW camps expanded under the SPD because classroom instruction offered a perfect environment for indoctrination. Many written works banned by the German government became available in the camps, and the Factory created a series of paperback books, the *Bucherreihe Neue Welt* (New World Bookshelf), incorporating traditional classics of American literature as well as works by Jewish authors. The books, sold through camp canteens, often sold out in a matter of hours. Bored prisoners purchased virtually any printed material, and even textbooks and manuals sold quickly at the canteens. English-speaking prisoners were allowed to subscribe to certain American newspapers and magazines, supplementing their exposure to American culture and ideals.

The deliberate attempt to reeducate and recondition enemy prisoners on an unprecedented scale certainly violated the spirit, if not the letter, of the Geneva Convention. Although it proved extremely successful in the short term, providing thousands of eager converts to serve as liaisons between occupying forces and the civilian population of postwar Germany, it also established a slippery slope regarding POW treatment. After all, if it was acceptable for American captors to remake enemy prisoners in their own image, what would stop future enemies from attempting the same type of reeducation among American captives? In both the Korean War and the Vietnam War, American POWs were bombarded by continual political indoctrination attempts by the enemy, justified by the American system of World War II.

THE POW LABOR PROGRAM

The enlistment of millions of young men through the massive expansion of the armed forces ensured that the possibility of filling wartime production quotas in many industries would be virtually impossible. As working hours in factories producing airplanes, munitions, and other war materials increased, the available number of workers rapidly declined. The federal government did not order draft exemptions for essential workers until March 1943, by which time the situation was already on the verge of disaster. A War Manpower Commission (WMC) report in the summer of 1943 noted that the United States was running out of laborers for vital industries, and that unemployed women represented the last major group eligible for recruitment into the workforce. Between July 1943 and July 1944, 700,000 women would be required for the workforce, and an additional 200,000 would be needed for the armed forces.[61] By 31 August 1943, over 100,000 POWs were interned in the United States. Most were eligible for work details. Although the labor of prisoners certainly could not solve all of the manpower problems of the WMC, it became an increasingly important source of unskilled labor within certain employment sectors as the war continued.[62]

Beyond the obvious difficulties associated with language barriers, the prisoner workforce proved frustrating to American employers as a result of differences in work attitudes between American and European laborers. Ironically, the extreme efficiency of German laborers was often an issue. Employers frequently complained that German output was lower than that of American workers because they spent more time perfecting a task. Thus, the workmanship of the Germans was often considered superior to domestic workers, but their raw production was lower.[63] A report of the WMC noted, "Efforts to have them hasten or short-cut or to be slip-shod in their methods are resented." In comparison, the Italian attitude was reported as "converse to those of the Germans. He is singing, happy-go-lucky."[64]

Early POW labor contracts were negotiated between camp commanders and employers without the official sanction of the WMC as the result of an oversight by the War Department authorizing camp commanders to hire out prisoners to local employers. These early contracts gave labor unions ample reason to fear the intrusion of prisoner labor into domestic markets. According to a 1943 WMC investigation, prisoners of war were being employed in direct competition with free labor, at wages far below the prevailing rates in many areas.[65] As a result of union protests, an agreement was reached with the War Department granting the WMC control over all POW labor contracts for labor outside of military installations. The American Federation of Labor (AFL) representative to the Labor-Management Committee of the WMC persisted in his complaint that all POW labor was a threat to domestic free labor, with the result that Paul McNutt, chairman of the WMC, agreed to bring "all questions involving the type of work on which prisoners of war are to be used and the conditions of their employment to the Committee for its advice and recommendations."[66] Despite orders to WMC regional directors that no POW labor could be used in place of free labor during labor disputes, labor unions remained wary of POW labor usage throughout the war.[67] Historians Byron Fairchild and Jonathan Grossman considered labor unions a major hindrance to the successful use of prisoner labor, but they also argued that the number of prisoners in the United States could not greatly affect wartime labor shortages.[68]

Americans initially employed prisoners solely on military installations, performing mundane tasks related to their own upkeep and basic base maintenance duties.[69] Before prisoners could begin laboring outside of the prison camps, the War Department and the WMC created a complicated system for assigning prisoners to various projects. Before receiving any prisoners, an employer applied to the local representative of the WMC for a certificate of need, which demonstrated that no local supply of free labor was available. The employer was required to prove that prisoner labor would not be detrimental to free wages and would not result in a decline in working conditions. The request was then forwarded to the local military authorities, who met with the representatives of the Department of Agriculture to determine the number of prisoners needed for a given task. If the request was approved, an employer entered a contract with the War Department for a period of not more than three months. The employer paid the War Department the prevailing wage rate for free labor and could not rely on prisoner labor as a long-term solution to labor shortages. Despite all of the drawbacks to the system, farmers across the country deluged the WMC with requests for laborers. The War Department responded by altering the system of housing the POWs for the convenience of the labor program, establishing a network of branch camps, satellites of the main prison camps in the nation. The camps moved labor closer to the neediest agricultural regions in the country and made the transportation of prisoners to work sites practicable.[70] Prisoner labor was first committed to aid in the harvesting of agricultural crops, tasks that had previously been performed in large part by migrant workers, most of whom were not represented by organized labor. Prisoner labor was quickly committed to agricultural projects throughout the nation.[71] Weekly reports to the WMC demonstrate that prisoner labor had an immediate effect on agricultural production, beginning in the summer of 1943, primarily in crop harvests and canning operations.[72]

The use of prisoners in agriculture, like the earlier use of prisoners on military installations, was not met with much organized hostility by American unions. In one rare exception, members of the Southern Tenant Farmers Union called for picketing cotton plants processing cotton picked by POWs.[73] Despite their complaints, the use of prisoner labor continued to rise in agriculture. By late 1944, more prisoners were employed in agriculture than were directly employed by the military. Although prisoners had some trouble adapting to tasks they had never performed before, particularly in the cultivation of cotton, their labor proved essential in the harvesting and production of vital staple crops. In an agricultural capacity, the POW labor program must be considered an unqualified success.

Farmers were not the only employers suffering from a lack of labor; factories were also understaffed, and soon industrial employers began requesting assistance from the War Department. Organized labor was a much more important part of the industrial workforce and could potentially create insurmountable difficulties for the WMC. The first major union opposition to POW labor came in the meatpacking industry. Initial arguments against the use of prisoners revolved around the possibility of captured enemies sabotaging the nation's food supply. However, the fundamental issue was not the potential adulteration of meat packaged by prisoners, but rather the threat that prisoner labor presented to unions. Prisoners employed in meatpacking were not required to pay union dues, even in plants staffed entirely by union members. In December 1943, members of the Amalgamated Meat Cutters and Butcher Workmen, a subsidiary of the American Federation of Labor (AFL), argued that the union was owed twenty-five cents in weekly dues from each prisoner working at the Seabrook Farms plant. The plant refused to garnish the wages paid to the War Department and suggested that the union request its dues be paid by the army. In the ensuing debate, the union representative admitted, "Our real concern is that more prisoners may be brought in from time to time until our contract won't be worth the paper it's written on, because there will be more prisoners than union members."[74]

The prisoner labor represented a very real threat to the power, and even the existence, of the AFL at Seabrook Farms. At other plants, legal arguments were presented to demand a cessation to prisoner labor. At the Jerpe Commission Company in Omaha, union leaders reported that the company had violated Executive Order No. 8802 by "not employing negroes in the freezers or elsewhere in [the] establishment."[75] Therefore, according to the union, the company had not exhausted all of the free labor sources in the area and should be excluded from the use of prisoners of war. The War Department worried that prisoners might attempt to sabotage the nation's food supply while working in the meatpacking industry, but no evidence of sabotage occurred at any meatpacking plant employing prisoners.[76]

The WMC considered the union position as an example of "being shortsighted and taking a position which in the long run may very well boomerang and bring discredit on the organized labor movement."[77] In the opinion of regional WMC director Frank Rarig, Americans held as prisoners of war would be furious on returning to the United States and learning of union opposition to the use of Axis prisoners' labor.[78] The War Department refused to bow before the demands of the union but was hesitant to provoke a larger engagement. To alleviate the situation, the WMC undertook a recruiting campaign to draw workers into the meatpacking industry, allowing prisoners to be reassigned to other industrial sectors. The meatpacking dispute, although not formally resolved to the liking of the AFL, heartened unions in other industries.

Another major battleground in the fight between organized labor and the War Department occurred in the railroad industry. In the summer of 1943, a series of meetings were held among railroad executives, the War Department, and the War Manpower Commission. In the meetings, discussions focused on whether POWs could be legally used in the railroad industry.[79] Union opposition to the use of prisoners on railroads was immediate and included a resolution of the Railway Labor Executives' Association of 16 July 1943. In the resolution, the RLEA, "representing substantially all the railway workers of our nation, declare their unqualified opposition to the use of prisoners of war as railroad track workers or in any other line of railroad employment."[80] In September, the WMC announced that prisoner labor would be used in track maintenance operations. Despite assurances from the WMC that prisoners would only be used when other labor was unavailable, and that wages, working conditions, and employment opportunities would remain unaffected, labor leaders were furious, and they argued that the nation's entire rail network would be opened to sabotage.[81] In mid-October, railway union locals across the nation adopted resolutions that threatened to shut down the American railways if prisoners were employed on the railroads in any capacity. That the nation was at war did not stop the unions from issuing this threat, despite a War Department assessment that fears of sabotage were without merit. Unions brought legal challenges against the use of prisoners, and union members refused to work in conjunction with prisoners. Again, the unions were successful in halting the use of prisoner labor in a vital industry. Despite massive manpower shortages in the railroad industry, the War Department and the WMC agreed that prisoners would not be used for railroads except in extreme emergencies.

The third sector in which prisoner labor provoked union unrest was the logging industry, specifically the production of pulpwood. In 1943, the pulp and paper industry was declared essential to the war effort. As such, its priority for manpower rose, and the question of using prisoner of war labor became pertinent. The pulpwood industry had been hit hard by manpower shortages, particularly in the South. Despite the pressing need for labor, the International Woodworkers of America protested the use of prisoners in forestry. The union attack on POW labor centered on the conditions of free labor in the industry. Prisoners, who had to be housed according to the provisions of the Geneva Convention, lived in a much more comfortable environment than free laborers performing the same work.[82] The IWA also argued that prisoners were being used to drive the wages of free labor down, despite the lower production of the average prisoner when compared with free laborers. However, in the pulpwood industry, unlike meatpacking or the railroads, the WMC and the War Department remained committed to the use of prisoners for labor. The government argued that previous efforts to recruit free labor had proven completely inadequate, and thus the production of pulpwood would be insufficient to meet the needs of the war effort without additional workers. Unlike in the meatpacking and railroad industries, the unions of the pulpwood industry were less unanimous in their condemnation of prisoner labor. In the South, some civilian employees welcomed prisoner labor as the only way to keep companies operating, and thus providing civilian jobs.[83] Despite the complaints of the IWA, which was affiliated with the Congress of Industrial Organizations (CIO), the national leadership of the CIO was more accepting of prisoner labor in the pulpwood industry than the AFL. The CIO, rather than directly opposing the use of prisoner labor in its entirety, sought to cooperate with the government on the issue and thus influence the ways and locations of prisoner use. However, the CIO still placed first priority on the improvement of free labor conditions within the industry in the hope that prisoner labor would not prove necessary.[84]

When they found the executive branch of the federal government unwilling to back down in the employment of prisoners, union leaders turned to legislators for assistance. On 1 June 1945, Senator Robert La Follette Jr. contacted Paul McNutt with the allegation that certain employers in Wisconsin had laid off all free labor in favor of German POWs.[85] McNutt promised that any such reports would be immediately investigated by the United States Employment Service (USES), and steps would be taken to prevent any repetitions in the future.[86] Such a preference for POW labor, though uncommon, was not an isolated incident. The USES investigation, launched immediately, showed that no free laborers had been laid off to date, but the prisoner allocation for the area should be reduced to prevent any future conflicts.[87] A more heated argument arose between Frank McNamee, acting chairman of the WMC in the summer of 1945, and Congressman Frank W. Boykin of Alabama. Boykin's assistance was enlisted by both organized labor and the employers of the pulpwood industry in Alabama. Labor unions complained that German and Italian POWs were being used in competition with free labor. Employers complained that they were being forced to pay artificially high wages to the War Department for POW labor. Despite the dual nature of Boykin's protests and his threat to launch a congressional investigation of the employment practices concerning prisoner labor, the WMC refused to alter its policies in the pulpwood industry. The pulpwood industry was the only major war industry in which the WMC successfully stood up to the efforts of organized labor to curtail the use of POW labor, and thus it was within the pulpwood industry that prisoners made the greatest nonagricultural effect on the American wartime economy.[88]

Some labor unions took the extreme step of condemning all prisoner labor within the United States. The Oklahoma City Building and Construction Trades Council called for all building trades councils to "join us in our fight to stir up this nation in stopping the use of war prisoners on any type of labor within the continental limits of the United States." The Council wished to compel the government to deport all POWs to Europe, before the surrender of Germany, through the use of an AFL-wide letter-writing campaign to senators and representatives.[89] After the German surrender, calls for the end of POW labor increased, despite assurances given by the WMC to employers that POW labor would not be withdrawn without advance notice.[90] The CIO Industrial Union Council of York, Pennsylvania, condemned the use of

"Nazi slave labor to the displacement of American labor" in August 1945.[91] In response to repeated calls for the end of the POW labor program, the War Department curtailed plans for the shipment of more prisoners to the United States as early as September 1944. Instead, prisoners captured in Europe were turned over to the governments of France, Belgium, and Holland for labor purposes behind the front lines.[92]

The prisoner experience in World War II once again demonstrated the improvisational nature of American POW policy and practice, as efforts to plan for the capture, maintenance, and utilization of enemy prisoners proved wholly inadequate. Although the United States managed to feed and shelter its prisoners, American commanders greatly underestimated the speed of captures in Europe and were completely unprepared to provide more than the most basic necessities for enemy prisoners. Millions of POWs remained in holding camps despite massive wartime labor shortages because no provisions had been made to transport them to the United States or house them on arrival, much less provide gainful employment. Even when the War Department transported enemy captives to the United States, their utilization was undermined by American labor groups, who perceived prisoner labor as a threat rather than an essential wartime measure. The labor program certainly benefited the United States, but it was much less successful than the potential represented by millions of enemy prisoners. Prisoners confined in the United States enjoyed a more comfortable existence than prisoners elsewhere in the world, but this was primarily the result of the high wartime standard of living in the United States. Quite simply, the United States had a higher capacity to treat its stateside captives well, and did so.[93]

THE POW LEGACY OF WORLD WAR II

In World War II, the United States did not base its treatment of enemy captives on reciprocity, as it had in earlier wars. Allegations and evidence of enemy mistreatment of American prisoners, including executions, torture, and orders for giving no quarter, did not prompt retaliation by the United States. Instead, American investigators gathered evidence from returning POWs regarding their treatment in German and Japanese prison camps, to be used at postwar trials of officers and government officials accused of violating the laws of war.[94] All civilians and prisoners of war repatriated from Japanese control filled out a war crimes questionnaire during their debriefing sessions. They reported that Japanese POW camp rules included a death penalty for any escaping prisoners, as well as any who assisted them or knew of the escape.[95] The final death rate of American prisoners in German and Italian camps was approximately 4 percent; in Japanese camps, the mortality rate was 27 percent.[96]

The use of prisoners for intelligence-gathering purposes proved much more successful than the interrogation efforts of World War I. For years after the end of the war, German prisoners remained of interest to American intelligence officers. In particular, any German prisoner released by the Soviet Union drew the attention of American commanders. Naval intelligence officers questioned hundreds of prisoners returned to the American zone of occupation in the postwar period. Most of the interrogations sought to ascertain the location and production capability of Soviet factories where POW labor had been utilized. As with the wartime interrogations, prisoners often provided maps of the area or detailed diagrams of equipment they had observed. These interrogations were conducted on a voluntary basis, but they demonstrated the continued usefulness of former prisoners to American intelligence efforts at the beginning of the cold war era.[97]

In the conflicts of the cold war era, the U.S. military again captured thousands of POWs, and again was accused by its own citizens of coddling enemy prisoners. The labor program utilized in World War II was the last American effort to obtain labor from enemy captives. In later conflicts, American commanders ignored the labor potential of captives and instead kept them idle in massive prison compounds. Prisoners during the cold war became tools of propaganda rather than labor. In the Korean War, fought just five years after World War II, American military planners ignored or forgot the lessons of World War II and developed an entirely new system of prisoner confinement, with disastrous results.

7

CONTAINING COMMUNISM

The Korean War

Stanley Weintraub volunteered for service in the U.S. Army in April 1951, accepting a commission in exchange for immediate active duty. Within a few months, he was sent to Pusan as the admissions officer for a POW hospital. He reported that American officers in the POW compound had no language familiarity with either Korean or Chinese, and thus had to rely on members of the prisoner population as translators. Unfortunately, most of the prisoners selected were specially trained political officers who had deliberately surrendered in order to enter the POW compounds and organize the prisoners for continued resistance behind the wire.[1]

In early 1952, the most hard-line communists of the prison compounds demanded that all prisoners of war be returned at the end of hostilities, as required by the Geneva Convention Relative to Prisoners of War of 1949. When it became clear that United Nations authorities would not compel the return of a prisoner against his or her will, the political organizers launched a massive uprising, seizing control of their compounds with stockpiles of improvised weapons, including spears and hand grenades. At Weintraub's hospital, POW amputees openly marched within the perimeter of the compound, brandishing their homemade weapons and denying access to prison authorities. In response, the hospital called for reinforcements, eventually receiving the assistance of an infantry regiment to help put down the resistance. In quashing the uprising, American troops resorted to the use of tear gas, concussion grenades, flamethrowers, and machine guns, all to suppress prisoners who had made no move to escape their confinement. In Weintraub's words, "eventually, the uprisings were put down, although in propaganda value they represented a great victory for the Communists."[2]

During the cold war, the nature of POW practices in the world changed radically, due in large part to the Geneva Convention Relative to Prisoners of War of 1949, a multilateral agreement designed to modify the 1929 Geneva

Convention. The United States presented a draft model for the convention that was adopted without substantial modifications, clarifying certain aspects of prisoner treatment that had proven troublesome during World War II. The new convention influenced American treatment of POWs in the Korean War, fought in Asia with the goal of containing the spread of communism. In the war, U.S. POW policy primarily consisted of holding enemy captives in overcrowded compounds while making almost no effort to utilize POW labor. Over the course of the Korean War, American political and military leaders gradually moved away from maintaining responsibility for POWs, shifting guard and supply responsibilities to allied nations whenever possible.

In Korea, the repatriation of prisoners became the primary disputed issue during armistice negotiations because the United States had adopted a new policy that no forced repatriation of prisoners to communist regimes would occur. Although the legality of this policy has been extensively debated, the practical result was that thousands of North Korean and Chinese prisoners did not return to their homes at the end of the conflict. American POWs repatriated after the armistice created a major controversy in the United States by reporting that many of their fellow captives actively assisted the enemy while prisoners through radio broadcasts and the creation of written propaganda.

During the Korean War, the North Korean and Chinese governments sought to use prisoners held by U.S. forces as propaganda tools by encouraging prisoners to provoke conflicts with American captors. These outbreaks of violence received extensive publicity as atrocities and provided leverage at diplomatic conferences. At the same time, American prisoners became helpless victims brutalized by their captors and coerced into serving a propaganda function for the enemy by signing forced confessions of war crimes or by actively denouncing the United States and its allies in a variety of formats.

MODIFYING INTERNATIONAL LAW

The U.S. State Department assumed the lead role in negotiating a new Geneva Convention in 1949. It began by polling diverse federal agencies for recommendations about what should be changed, added, or deleted from the 1929 convention. After drafting an initial proposal, American diplomats sought suggestions from foreign nations, relying primarily on France and Great Britain for international support. American officials feared that the Soviet Union might cause significant problems by insisting on major changes to the American draft, such as eliminating the International Committee of the Red Cross (ICRC) from participation at the conference, but the process ran smoothly at the international conference, and the new convention superseded the old in 1949.[3]

The Geneva Convention of 1949 sought to rectify the primary faults of the 1929 convention, exposed by the mistreatment of prisoners during World War II. Chief among the complaints was the use of nation-specific rather than absolute standards in regard to prisoner maintenance. The 1929 convention ensured that prisoners received rations equal in quantity to those given to garrison troops of the capturing nation. In 1949, the food provision was modified, and required that food rations be sufficient to maintain good health among prisoners, measured by the prevention of weight loss or nutritional deficiencies. Further, any prisoners required to labor for their captor were entitled to additional rations. To wealthy nations, this change presented the obvious solution to complaints that some native diets were insufficient to maintain the health of POWs from other global regions. In particular, the massive weight loss and high mortality rates of Allied prisoners held by Japan during World War II demonstrated that the equality standard of 1929 could not be universally applied.

The 1949 convention expanded the definition of prisoners of war to include individuals who accompanied armed forces without actually being members, such as the crews of merchant marine ships and civilian aircraft. Article 13 expanded the guarantee of "humane treatment" made in the 1929 convention by prohibiting "any unlawful act or omission by the Detaining Power causing death or seriously endangering the health of a prisoner of war in its custody." The use of prisoner labor, a pressing issue to any captor, presented a serious problem for the delegates—specifically, how to allow the use of prisoner labor without contributing to war efforts. Eventually, the solution adopted was to enumerate the classes of work on which prisoners might be compelled to labor. These classes included camp maintenance, agriculture, transportation of nonmilitary goods, arts and crafts, domestic service, and industries without a military character. No prisoners could be compelled to work at dangerous or unhealthy labor, but prisoners could volunteer for such work if they so desired.

The issue of repatriation, an extremely important matter in the armistice negotiations in Korea, remained somewhat ambiguous in the 1949 convention. Sick and wounded prisoners could be repatriated or interned in a neutral country before the end of hostilities. However, able-bodied prisoners were to be repatriated "without delay" at the end of hostilities. Ironically, at the time of the signing of the 1949 convention, some signatories still held German and Japanese prisoners of war four years after the close of World War II. The retention of prisoners for several years after the end of hostilities would clearly violate the 1949 convention.

Perhaps the greatest flaw of the 1929 convention was the lack of enforceability of its provisions. Only the threat of retaliation and the condemnation of world opinion served to enforce the convention, and neither had proven particularly coercive during World War II. In the 1949 convention, signatories agreed to supplement international law with the adoption of domestic legislation providing effective penal sanctions for persons committing or ordering grave breaches of the convention, specifically killing, torturing, or injuring prisoners, or depriving them of their rights under the convention.

THE KOREAN WAR

Unlike the world wars, in which combat occurred for years before American intervention, the Korean War surprised the United States and provoked a rapid American response. The United States did not have years to prepare for combat operations, but because the war began only five years after the conclusion of World War II, it is to be expected that American POW policy would remain consistent between the two wars. In fact, many of the lessons of World War II were ignored as U.S. forces scrambled to first save South Korea and next push back invading communist forces from North Korea and China. Because many of the individuals associated with POW operations in World War II had left military service by 1950, American POW commanders again resorted to improvising wartime practices.

Works discussing POW history in general have focused on two primary issues when discussing the Korean War: the issue of forced repatriation and the violent uprisings in camps. Prisoners during the Korean War have generated more discussion in general works about the conflict than was typical for earlier wars. This is undoubtedly partly the result of the central role of prisoners in armistice negotiations and the very public accusations of atrocities made by both sides. In 1987, Callum A. MacDonald argued that the primary victims of prolonged armistice negotiations were United Nations Command (UNC) POWs, who endured an extra year of captivity during the truce talks. He focused most of his discussion on communist confinement practices, but he noted that UNC POW facilities on Koje-do were overcrowded, often operating at double capacity, and understaffed, with only one American guard for every 180 prisoners. Stanley Sandler also saw a lack of guards as a contributing factor to unrest in U.N. camps, noting that "something approaching pandemonium prevailed in the UNC POW camps" and arguing that prisoners deliberately provoked guards to fire into POW compounds as a means of generating anti-American propaganda.[4] Lee Ballenger's *The Outpost War* made an interesting distinction of the capturing behavior of UNC forces, noting that most North Koreans and Chinese who were taken prisoner deliberately surrendered; they were not taken captive during firefights. He argued that U.N. troops viewed taking prisoners as problematic, and to avoid paperwork, they often turned prisoners over to South Korean troops, knowing the POWs might be mistreated or even executed. The UNC, coveting prisoners for their intelligence value, offered a one-week furlough to any troops making captures to counteract this behavior. Offering rewards to combat troops for captures resumed a practice initiated in the Pacific theater of World War II, when soldiers received furloughs and ice cream for taking prisoners.

Many works have discussed the plight of U.N. prisoners in North Korea, and special emphasis has remained on American soldiers.[5] The army's official army histories of the Korean War, with one exception, have largely ignored the issue of prisoners. Roy E. Appleman's *South to the Naktong, North to the Yalu* included a brief mention of enemy captures, noting that Eighth Army commanders discounted the intelligence provided by captured Chinese prisoners —and underestimated Chinese troop strength in Korea as a result—but he does not discuss the internment of prisoners. James F. Schnabel's *Policy and Direction* mentioned surrender demands and the number of enemy captures but did not discuss the fate of prisoners. Likewise, Billy C. Mossman's *Ebb and Flow* saw POWs largely in terms of intelligence value but provided no discussion of the disposition of captured enemies. Only Walter G. Hermes provided significant discussion of prisoners, and then only in terms of the repatriation issue. He argued that the major lesson of the war regarding prisoners was that they should not be under the control of the army commander, who should not be distracted from fighting by administrative matters.[6]

During the Korean War, the United States adopted the leadership of UNC military forces, and American policy decisions dominated the behavior of UNC forces toward POWs. Initially, American forces in Korea received little guidance regarding the capture and treatment of enemy prisoners. On 5 July 1950, General Douglas MacArthur ordered all U.S. military personnel to treat captured North Korean troops "in accordance with the humanitarian principles applied by and recognized by civilized nations involved in armed conflict."[7] Not until 16 August did MacArthur clarify that UNC forces would follow the provisions of the Geneva Convention of 1949, even though the agreement had not been ratified, and that summary executions were strictly forbidden, despite evidence that enemy forces had refused quarter to UNC personnel.[8]

THE UNC CAMP SYSTEM AND KOJE-DO

On 26 September 1950, the United States accepted responsibility for the maintenance of all prisoners taken by UNC forces.[9] UNC forces captured over 150,000 POWs during the war; of the total captured, 126,000 were taken in the last three months of 1950.[10] As had been the case in earlier conflicts, American commanders placed little emphasis on POW affairs and provided a limited number of trained custodial personnel for the guarding and maintenance of prisoners. They assumed that enemy captives would behave in a docile fashion, similar to the behavior of Japanese captives in World War II. By understaffing prison compounds, the U.S. leadership allowed the formation of massive underground prisoner organizations. Rather than meek, passive, or helpful behavior, the POWs held in UNC compounds acted as fanatical ideologues. Prisoner factions exerted ruthless control over the compounds, enforcing discipline and judicial punishments on any prisoners expressing political sentiments contrary to the leaders of the compound. Each compound soon had a distinct political ideology: some were hard-core communist, others strictly anticommunist. Interventions in the compounds by guard forces were rare and were almost always undertaken to stop violence rather than to prevent it. Camp commanders had virtually no control over camp behavior until the last year of the war.[11]

Enemy prisoners were initially unsegregated in the summer of 1950, first in temporary camps near Pusan and later in a massive prison complex on the island of Koje-do. No effort was made to separate communists from anticommunists, in the same manner that German Nazis and anti-Nazis had been separated in American camps during World War II. Despite ample evidence that thousands of South Koreans had been forced into North Korean service, U.N. forces made no attempt to free South Korean conscripts who had been captured. As Chinese forces entered the war, they were sent to a more distant prison locale, the island of Cheju-do, approximately 100 miles southwest of Koje-do. Here, too, the initial practice was to confine all prisoners together, regardless of political leanings.

South Korean prime minister John Myun Chang and president Syngman Rhee each requested in the spring of 1951 that South Korean POWs be segregated into separate camps, screened by the South Korean government, and released from custody. General Matthew B. Ridgway refused to release any POWs in UNC custody, regardless of nationality, but agreed to confine South Koreans in separate camps.[12] Provoked by Ridgway's refusal, Chang informed UNC that the South Korean government would no longer supply subsistence for the 150,000 POWs in South Korea, and full responsibility for feeding the prisoners immediately fell to the UNC.[13] On 16 October, Ridgway changed his position on South Korean prisoners, ordering them to be reclassified as civilian internees, eligible for release after screening by South Korean authorities. Although the Red Cross was notified of the status change, he allowed no publicity of the shift.[14]

The South Korean withdrawal of subsistence illustrated a larger problem within the U.N. war effort. The South Korean government often disagreed with U.N. POW policy during the war and refused to cooperate on a number of occasions. Rhee, in particular, proved difficult to accommodate. If the United States pursued a policy that contradicted Rhee's desires, it had to do so without the assistance of South Korea, even though the primary contingent of guard personnel at the prison compounds was supplied by the South Korean Army. This issue culminated in 1953, when Rhee forbade neutral observers from even entering South Korean territory and orchestrated the "escape" of thousands of prisoners under the guard of South Korean troops.

Agitation within the POW compounds at Koje-do occurred as a result of many factors, but a major contributor was simple overcrowding, often a problem in POW compounds in other wars. By June 1951, UNC POW Camp No. 1, at Koje-do, consisted of thirty-one compounds, some housing as many as 8,000 POWs. A total of approximately 150,000 POWs filled the compounds well beyond their designed capacity; they were guarded by only six military police companies.[15] The first major disturbance began on 19 June 1951, when officer POWs at Compound No. 72 refused to eat unless they were given complete control over the internal workings of all of the POW camps on the eastern end of the island. The UNC responded by deploying guards to withdraw the untouched morning meal. As the guards entered the compound, prisoners threw rocks and debris and rushed the gate. When warning shots did not deter the crowd, the threatened South Korean guards opened fire, killing three prisoners and wounding eight.[16] Prison riots became increasingly common in the summer of 1951 and spring of 1952. On 20 March

1952, the Koje-do commandant, Brigadier General Francis T. Dodd, noted that demonstrations by POWs were spreading through the compounds and requested permission to deny food to all POWs within compounds holding demonstrations. Dodd's superior, Brigadier General Paul F. Yount, approved the plan, but he thought that denial of food might convey propaganda advantages to the POWs more significant than any gained from demonstrations, which were already having an effect on armistice negotiations under way at Panmunjom.[17] In May, Dodd made the foolish decision to enter a POW compound without a military police escort and was taken hostage by the prisoners.

Dodd's capture by enemy POWs while inspecting the compound illustrated the complete lack of control by UNC forces. On 7 May 1952, Dodd approached Compound No. 76 at the behest of the camp's prisoner representative. As UNC guards watched, Dodd was seized by a rush of prisoners and quickly dragged into the compound, where he was held captive for three days. The prisoners announced that Dodd would be executed unless U.N. authorities agreed to publicly admit that prisoners had been killed in POW camps by guard personnel and to promise better treatment of prisoners in the future. The prisoners further demanded that the UNC agree to repatriate all prisoners at the end of the war, by force if necessary. They also desired visitations to the prison compounds by North Korean and Chinese representatives. Dodd admitted in a signed statement that some prisoners had been killed by guards during frequent prison riots, but he had no authority to agree to any other prisoner demands. Dodd's admission matched that of Brigadier General Charles F. Colson, assistant commandant at Koje-do, who assumed command and negotiated for Dodd's release. Dodd and Colson were both criticized for making any admissions worthy of communist propaganda, including that prisoners had been killed by prison guards and that tear gas had been used to quell disturbances. After three days of negotiations, the prisoners released Dodd without injury, and he and Colson were both demoted and returned to the United States.[18] Despite all of the riotous behavior, the UNC guard component at Koje-do was not increased until 2 January 1952, when Ridgway ordered an infantry battalion from the U.S. Eighth Army to provide additional security.[19]

General Mark Clark, who replaced Ridgway as the commander of U.N. forces in May 1952, ordered Brigadier General Haydon L. Boatner to reestablish control of the prison compounds at Koje-do by any means necessary, including the use of force. Boatner requested massive guard reinforcements and an engineering battalion. While the engineers built new prison compounds on Koje-do, Boatner led a series of raids on existing compounds to remove contraband, including communist propaganda, national flags, and portraits of Kim Il Sung, all of which had been smuggled in by prisoners surrendering with the purpose of organizing resistance in the prison camps. On 10 June, Boatner ordered guards to enter Compound No. 76 and forcibly remove the prisoners to a new, more secure compound. When the prisoners resisted, a melee ensued, resulting in the deaths of forty-three prisoners.[20] The remaining 6,500 prisoners were rounded up, divided into units of 500, and placed into the new facilities. Prisoners in other compounds, having witnessed the reduction of Compound No. 76, proved more tractable, and by the end of June, Boatner was in firm control of Koje-do.

After regaining control of all POW compounds and dispensing prisoners to smaller encampments on the island, Boatner issued a new standard operating procedure for POW enclosures on 15 August 1952. The new regulations forbade prisoners from singing outside the compound or at night. Physical exercise could not include any tactical military training. No prisoner could approach a fence line of any compound, and to keep a closer watch over prisoners, all tent flaps remained open except during inclement weather. The disciplinary measures available to enclosure commanders were curtailed in the regulations, dietary punishments were virtually eliminated, and the use of tear gas to quell disturbances was strongly discouraged, though not strictly banned. Boatner's insistence that all disobedient prisoners be immediately punished regained control of the intransigent prisoners and improved morale among guard personnel on Koje-do.[21]

On 31 March 1953, Boatner issued the final standard operating procedure for POWs at Koje-do. Almost three years had elapsed since the first capture of enemy prisoners, and the UNC finally issued comprehensive orders for the care and maintenance of enemy prisoners.[22] The orders modified the regulations used in German POW camps during World War II. For the first time, an effort to organize labor detachments occurred at Koje-do. The prisoners formed labor companies of twenty-five men, escorted by five guards. Work projects were determined entirely by enclosure commanders, as long as they conformed to the Geneva Convention of 1949. Boatner ordered all camp commanders to "aggressively implement" the work programs, "to insure the greatest possible efficiency in the utilization of prisoners of war."[23] In a letter written in 1959, Boatner declared the labor program to be an unmitigated failure, despite the fact that UNC studies in the spring of 1952 identified 10,000 skilled laborers among the POW population.[24] Boatner concluded the labor program failed because POWs remained too close to the combat zone and still considered themselves active in the fighting. As a result, he recommended that all prisoners be confined on Cheju-do if hostilities resumed in Korea, or even be shipped to Okinawa.[25]

Not all of the prisoners' misbehavior in UNC compounds was initiated by communist agitators.[26] By December 1951, anticommunists were in control of two-thirds of the compounds. These prisoners vowed to resist repatriation at all costs, suggesting that if the United Nations had adopted a policy of forced repatriation, even more violence in POW compounds would occur. Anticommunist POWs produced innumerable petitions, manifestoes, and testimonials attacking communism and the Chinese and North Korean governments. These statements were signed by thousands of prisoners, many including a drop of blood next to their name to indicate their commitment against communism. Many begged to join UNC and South Korean forces to resume fighting. For example, Kim Won Sang, a former teacher from Kaesong, begged for release from Compound No. 74 on Koje-do, stating, "I will sacrifice myself for the fatherland and fight against the Reds as long as my life shall last." Hundreds of Chinese officers claimed they had served in the Chinese Nationalist Army before the communist takeover of China and had been forced into service in Korea. Some of the prisoners requested release because they were Christians and feared communist oppression within the POW camps or after repatriation.[27] These petitions against forcible repatriation cannot be simply accepted at face value. Because anticommunist POWs controlled a majority of the camp compounds, they may not have been spontaneous declarations; rather, they may have represented a propaganda device encouraged by compound leaders or the South Korean government. Given the number of prisoners who refused repatriation from anticommunist compounds, however, the petitions also cannot be simply discarded as propaganda.

The motivation behind compound power struggles varied by location, but evidence shows that communist prisoners were motivated primarily by a desire for self-protection. Communist prisoners did not seek to ingratiate themselves with their captors or obtain special favors and privileges. Instead, they sought total control over compounds to be prepared for any action that might be required of them as events unfolded. They did not consider themselves removed from the fighting. Most believed the struggle continued in captivity. Even in communist-controlled compounds, most prisoners did not identify ideology as a major determinant of their behavior.[28] Many joined factions as a result of short-term issues and remained loyal to their faction because their personal safety came to depend on the success of their clique within the compound. There is no evidence to suggest that they intentionally planned mass escapes or even the systematic harassment of U.N. authorities. Rather, these became spontaneous group efforts.[29] The primary complaint of communist agitators within the compounds soon became the U.N. stance on repatriation. By the time the U.N. proposed free choice for prisoners regarding repatriation in January 1952, virtually every compound was firmly controlled by either communist or anticommunist factions. These factions submitted entire compounds to indoctrination regarding the repatriation issue, and the influence of the indoctrination can be seen in the proportion of prisoners who rejected repatriation from each compound.[30]

Certain complaints were common to all POW compounds under U.N. control, regardless of the political ideology or nationality of the inhabitants. Virtually every compound complained about the type, amount, and preparation of food provided, the regulations of each compound, and specific incidents of mistreatment by guard personnel. In addition, Korean POWs complained about clothing issues, especially when they were given red uniforms. The red clothing, associated in Korean culture with criminals, was considered dishonorable and infuriated North and South Koreans alike, who shredded their uniforms rather than wear them. Eventually, the camp commandants were informed of the significance of red clothing, and a new issue of POW uniforms rectified the error.[31]

THE ARMISTICE AND THE REPATRIATION QUESTION

The armistice convention to end the Korean War began on 10 July 1951 at Kaesong. The conference soon shifted to Panmunjom, where it lasted more than two years before delegates signed an armistice on 27 July 1953. The primary point of contention in the peace talks was the disposition of prisoners of war. POWs had never been such an important issue at an armistice negotiation. Typically, the return of prisoners after previous wars was included in armistices as an afterthought, and any serious discussion of POW repatriation revolved around the rate of return for prisoners or the payment of prisoner upkeep. In Korea, the primary issue was whether or not POWs would be forced to accept repatriation if they preferred not to return to their homeland.

The communist delegation at Panmunjom maintained that all prisoners must be repatriated, by force if necessary. They based their arguments on two key articles in the Geneva Convention of 1949, Articles 7 and 118. Article 7 prohibited any POW from renouncing any rights guaranteed by the convention. Article 118 ensured a rapid repatriation of all prisoners from all sides at the end of hostilities. Because all prisoners were guaranteed repatriation and could not renounce their rights, the communist position was for complete repatriation, regardless of the wishes of individual prisoners. The communist delegates insisted that the UNC agree to the release and exchange of all prisoners as a precondition to the exchange of any information on prisoners held.[32]

The UNC delegates argued that the Geneva Convention was created for the protection and benefit of individual prisoners, not for the benefit of the prisoners' original nations, and it would be wrong to force POWs to return to communist regimes, where previous postwar experiences suggested they would be mistreated by their own governments. Although no promises had been made to induce surrender in exchange for release in South Korea, psychological warfare officers suggested that any attempt to force repatriation would be met with violence, particularly from Chinese prisoners.[33] The UNC held nearly 150,000 prisoners, while the communists held barely 10,000. As such, a complete repatriation of all prisoners would provide a massive military advantage to the enemy, with no guarantee that all U.N. personnel would be returned. Rather, the UNC recommended a one-for-one exchange of prisoners, with the balance repatriated under parole not to participate for the duration of the Korean War.[34]

It is conceivable that the communist negotiators had no desire to consummate a peace agreement. By creating a thirty-day cease-fire, they halted U.N. advances and created a perfect propaganda outlet in the armistice negotiations.[35] Discussion of repatriating POWs began on 11 December 1951, when Rear Admiral Ruthven E. Libby recommended equal exchange of prisoners during the negotiations and requested visits to all POW camps by the Red Cross. Communist delegates immediately rejected both suggestions and substituted a recommendation to release all prisoners on both sides en masse.[36] Without a mass exchange agreement, North Korean and Chinese negotiators initially refused to exchange any data about U.N. prisoners in communist custody. When lists of prisoners were exchanged on 23 December 1951, the U.N. presented the names of 132,474 POWs, and received a list of 11,559. Earlier communist propaganda claimed 65,000 prisoners had been taken, but when asked to account for the discrepancy, the communist negotiators claimed that over 50,000 prisoners had been directly released at the front.[37] According to UNC figures, only 177 of those supposedly released at the front returned to UNC lines. While claiming to have released 50,000 prisoners, the communists accused the UNC of presenting a list missing 44,259 prisoners previously reported to the Red Cross. According to the UNC, 37,000 of the "missing" prisoners were civilian internees, not prisoners of war, who had been captured during the rapid U.N. advance in the autumn of 1950. They had initially been reported as POWs, but they were then reclassified by the South Korean government. The remainder were prisoners who had provided more than one name, who had escaped, or who had died in custody.

In April 1952, the UNC began screening POWs to determine how many would refuse repatriation. Prisoners were interviewed individually, using questions designed to encourage a maximum number of returnees. The first question was simply "Would you like to return to China/North Korea?" Prisoners who answered in the affirmative were designated for repatriation, and their interviews were immediately terminated. Prisoners who answered in the negative were then asked if they would forcibly resist repatriation, and if they were aware of the potential consequences of refusing repatriation. At no time did UNC interrogators promise to send nonreturnees to any specific location. The final question for any remaining POWs was the prisoners' specific intent if the UNC decided to forcibly repatriate him. If the prisoner did not mention an intent to resist, commit suicide, or perform a similar violent act, he was included on the repatriation list. After the completion of screenings, the UNC delegates presented the communists with a figure of 70,000 prisoners who would accept repatriation. Communist negotiators declared this figure completely unacceptable.[38]

As discussions at Panmunjom broke down, more riots erupted in compounds across Koje-do. American negotiators claimed the communist senior delegate, General Nam Il, orchestrated the riots to provide propaganda material and leverage for communist diplomats at the armistice negotiations. The riots cost hundreds of lives by provoking guards to fire on rioting POWs, allowing the communists to accuse the UNC of murdering POWs. Daily meetings did nothing to advance the peace talks, as neither side was willing to compromise on their fundamental position regarding repatriation. In June, the U.N. rescreened POWs, hoping to increase the number willing to accept repatriation. On 13 July, the UNC announced that rescreening brought the total number of potential repatriates up to 83,000, but the communist delegates continued to insist on full repatriation.[39] On 8 October 1952, the UNC delegates unilaterally recessed the armistice conference and refused to return until the communist delegates agreed to negotiate in good faith.[40] The conference remained in recess until 26 April 1953, although liaison and staff officers' meetings continued. On 22 February 1953, General Mark W. Clark requested an immediate exchange of all sick and wounded POWs in a letter to North Korean president Kim Il Sung and Chinese premier Peng Teh-huai. The communists agreed to Clark's request on 28 March, and from 20 April until 2 May, sick and wounded POWs were repatriated at Panmunjom. The repatriation, dubbed Operation Little Switch, included a swap of 6,670 communist POWs for 684 UNC personnel.[41]

The debate over the exchange of all remaining POWs continued until 8 June 1953, when delegates of each side signed the Terms of Reference for the Neutral Nations Repatriation Commission that were eventually annexed to the armistice agreement of 27 July 1953. Under these terms, each side agreed to turn over any POWs who refused repatriation to a Neutral Nations Repatriation Commission (NNRC), headed by delegates from India. This commission then took custody of nonrepatriate prisoners for ninety days. During that time, representatives of their home government met with each prisoner and explained the right of repatriation. If a POW decided to exercise his right of repatriation, his application was immediately processed. If a POW did not accept repatriation after ninety days, he was released from POW status as a civilian.

Rhee adamantly opposed the armistice agreement, and he refused permission for NNRC forces to enter South Korea. He viewed the entire armistice as a failure to unify the Korean peninsula, and he accused the UNC of appeasing the enemy rather than seeking a permanent peace. On 18 June, Rhee orchestrated the mass escape of 26,867 anticommunist North Korean POWs and encouraged the South Korean civilian population to shield the escapees from recapture by UNC forces.[42] On 20 June, the communist armistice delegates accused Clark and the UNC of negligence and demanded that steps be taken to recapture the escapees. Clark responded by blaming the South Korean government for the breakout and denied any UNC involvement in the escape. Although the communist negotiators continued to complain, Rhee's action presented a fait accompli, and virtually none of the escaped prisoners was recaptured.

On 27 July, the final version of the armistice was signed, and the NNRC began the process of screening the prisoners one final time to determine who would refuse repatriation. After ninety days of political harangues, threats, lectures, and appeals to patriotism by Chinese and North Korean political officers, 15,000 Chinese and 8,000 North Korean prisoners refused repatriation. A study by the U.S. Army revealed that POWs who refused repatriation were typically young and well educated, and had a brief period of service in the military before capture.[43]

The Chinese nonreturnees were transported to Taiwan to live under the

Nationalist government in exile, which had been driven from the mainland in 1949. The North Koreans who refused repatriation were allowed to settle in South Korea. In comparison, only twenty-two UNC soldiers refused repatriation and remained in North Korea. With nonreturnees finally identified, Operation Big Switch, the exchange of direct repatriates, began on 5 August and ended on 23 December 1953. The UNC returned 75,801 prisoners to communist control and received 12,773 in return.[44] Both sides accused the other of withholding prisoners from exchange and failing to account for missing personnel.[45]

As American personnel returned from captivity, a bleak picture of the communist POW camps and the behavior of American prisoners emerged. Although only 21 American prisoners refused repatriation, hundreds more actively collaborated with their captors as a means of gaining better treatment within the camps. An army investigation concluded that 425 returning prisoners could be tried for their acts of collaboration.[46] In response to the reports of collaboration, President Dwight D. Eisenhower issued Executive Order No. 10631 on 17 August 1955, prescribing a code of conduct for American service personnel. Under the code, members of the American military must never voluntarily surrender, must continue to resist the enemy while in captivity, must maintain discipline and faith in fellow prisoners, and must refuse to give information to enemy interrogators. The code became a fundamental aspect of American military training and is still issued to all American military forces.

As the repatriation of POWs commenced, the UNC POW command began a study of POW treatment with the idea of creating a guide for the future handling of Asian communist POWs. The study included a series of lessons learned in the Korean War. The most important lesson was that future camp commanders needed a greater understanding of communist POWs, including psychology, political organization, and responses to captivity. Also, POW planning must occur before the capture of thousands of prisoners, and thus camp locations should be carefully selected in advance, allowing prisoners to be segregated by ideology immediately after capture. Finally, camp commanders must retain firm control of the camp at all costs, punishing POW offenders and maintaining strict discipline, by force if necessary.[47] The result of the study was a new training course for all army personnel undertaking prisoner of war operations. More comprehensive than any previous course, it required 137 hours of instruction for all POW camp personnel.[48]

Because Korean and Chinese communist prisoners did not behave in the traditional or expected manner of POWs, by essentially waiting for exchange or the end of the war, the United States was forced to create new methods of holding captives. The experiences of the Korean War changed American POW policy by establishing a firm practice of refusing to forcibly repatriate prisoners. The United States had little effect on the treatment of American prisoners by the enemy because the enemy remained unconcerned by the fate of its own prisoners beyond their potential propaganda value, and thus any threat of retaliation remained empty.

8

THE DOMINOES BEGIN TO FALL

The Vietnam War

In April 1965, thirty-seven-year-old Nguyen Ngoc Vinh, a North Vietnamese soldier, volunteered to infiltrate South Vietnam and fight alongside the Vietcong. Two months later, he found himself in a battalion marching south, armed with a submachine gun and a hundred rounds. It took more than a month to reach the Laotian border and another two months to arrive at Binh Dinh province in South Vietnam. Conditions on the march proved excruciating, with poor food and no medical supplies. The volunteers received no pay during their first seven months. Eventually, they were given a few piasters per month. Vinh and his comrades feared their leaders, particularly the political commissars, who banned any outside contact, including listening to the radio.[1]

Vinh's first combat action was a disaster: the enemy had anticipated the attack and drove off the battalion with heavy losses, forcing the North Vietnamese volunteers to spend more than two months regrouping. On 28 January 1966, in only his third combat action, Vinh blundered into a squad of enemy troops; he was shot twice and captured. During five days of interrogation at Bong Son, Vinh received daily beatings from his captors, despite his willingness to answer all of the questions posed by the South Vietnamese intelligence specialists at the prison compound. He was moved to Qui Nhon jail for three weeks, then flown to Saigon for further interrogation and eventual confinement. At Saigon, he interacted with American interrogators for the first time, and once again proved willing to share his knowledge. Although American personnel did not engage in physical punishment, Vinh reported that South Vietnamese interrogators utilized beatings and electrodes to compel him to write propaganda letters for broadcast on Radio Saigon. Although he was willing to respond to interrogations, he showed no signs of defecting to the south, and he expressed his willingness to remain in captivity indefinitely rather than betray his cause and country.[2]

THE VIETNAM WAR

In Vietnam, American commanders abdicated responsibility for POW treatment by turning virtually all çaptives over to the care of the South Vietnamese government, which made little pretense of following the Geneva Convention. This decision was largely a matter of convenience; it freed American personnel for combat operations. As in Korea, American prisoners, though greatly outnumbered by enemy captives, shaped the American public's perception of the POW issue. Repatriated Americans reported extensive mistreatment by their captors, including the torture and execution of American prisoners.

In Vietnam, senior American personnel showed few signs of absorbing the lessons of the Korean War when dealing with communist prisoners, and instead, the United States essentially dodged the issue of prisoner maintenance in Vietnam by turning all captives over to South Vietnamese government control. In the Vietnam War, American involvement began in an advisory capacity and gradually evolved into full-scale combat operations. Although U.S. forces were responsible for the capture of thousands of prisoners, the United States did not retain custody of these prisoners. Instead, all POWs captured by American forces were turned over to the South Vietnamese government for internment by the Army of the Republic of Vietnam (ARVN). American personnel served as advisors for the ARVN prison compounds but had no authority to dictate policy to the South Vietnamese government. American advisors urged ARVN camp commanders to follow the provisions of the Geneva Convention of 1949, but compliance was spotty at best.

The transfer of prisoners from American to South Vietnamese control was allowed by the Geneva Convention of 1949, although the capturing power still maintained a legal responsibility to ensure the proper treatment of its former captives. In this regard, the United States Military Assistance Command, Vietnam (MACV), encountered great difficulty with the ARVN. Visits to ARVN prison camps by the International Committee of the Red Cross (ICRC) invariably resulted in complaints about camp conditions, and the complaints were rarely rectified in a timely manner. Particularly troubling were repeated allegations of torture, substantiated by ICRC investigators, that plagued the ARVN prison system.

The nature of the Vietnam War complicated the POW situation. Most of those captured were South Vietnamese rebels, members of the National Liberation Front, commonly referred to as the Vietcong. Although thousands of members of the North Vietnamese Army (NVA) also were captured, the Hanoi government maintained the fiction that no North Vietnamese troops were in South Vietnam, and it refused to discuss the exchange of prisoners or reciprocal actions regarding POW treatment.

In the Vietnam War, the practices of earlier American conflicts had little impact on the treatment of prisoners. The South Vietnamese government viewed enemy combatants as domestic insurgents subject to civil rather than military law. The North Vietnamese government unwittingly contributed to this approach when it insisted that no North Vietnamese troops were present in South Vietnam. This signaled that Hanoi would not protest any mistreatment of captured North Vietnamese Army troops. Throughout the war, the commanders of MACV attempted to mitigate the South Vietnamese approach to POW operations, but allegations of mistreatment, torture, and executions dogged the POW program for the duration of the war. At the same time, MACV commanders had no desire to assume responsibility for the maintenance of POWs, which would place tremendous strain on MACV logistics.

Most of the works devoted to POW history in general have focused on the conditions faced by American POWs captured by the Vietcong and the North Vietnamese. When authors address the camps for Vietcong or North Vietnamese prisoners, the general assumption is that the United States forced South Vietnam to strictly adhere to the provisions of the Geneva Convention.[3] Vernon E. Davis is the rare exception. In *The Long Road Home*, he argued that the South Vietnamese government hesitated to adhere to the Geneva Convention; they only agreed to do so after the promise of financial assistance from the United States.[4] He also believed that the South Vietnamese government greatly hampered American efforts to exchange prisoners by insisting that only "repentant" prisoners—those who renounced their allegiance to the Vietcong or North Vietnam—should be eligible for release before the end of the war.[5]

THE VIETNAM CAMP SYSTEM AND PHU QUOC

As in the Korean War, most enemy prisoners in Vietnam were held in large, overcrowded prison camps. Once again, a massive island prison complex was created for communist prisoners, this time on the island of Phu Quoc. Virtually no effort was made to utilize POW labor; prisoners were quickly interrogated and then dumped into wretched conditions. In the early years of major

American involvement, American advisors suggested that the government of South Vietnam should plan ahead for the capture of thousands of prisoners. Repeated American efforts to prompt the construction of POW camps failed. POWs were routinely held in civilian jails and prisons through 1967.[6]

Unfortunately, as the number of Vietcong captures rose, the ability of camp commanders to feed and maintain their prisoners, much less monitor their activities within each compound, declined rapidly. At the end of 1966, only 1,825 prisoners were in custody, 949 of whom were Vietcong; 711 were members of the North Vietnamese Army. By the end of 1967, the total number of prisoners had risen to 9,743, including 7,221 Vietcong prisoners. Over 10,000 prisoners were captured in 1968 and 1969, straining camp capacities to the breaking point. Construction of new camps proceeded slowly because the South Vietnamese government placed a low priority on prisoners of war.[7] American advisors stressed the need for expanded camp capacity or a form of POW release throughout 1969, with few results. Camp construction on Phu Quoc remained stagnant, primarily as a result of a lack of raw materials.[8] This situation illustrated the frustration MACV advisors faced: the inability to force action on South Vietnamese camp commanders.

Until 1966, South Vietnam refused to admit it had captured prisoners of war. Rather, the government referred to all POWs as Communist Rebel Prisoners (CRP), whom they defined as "all who carry or do not carry arms and belong to the following three categories: intruders from the North, returned from regroupment to the North, or joined the VC Armed Forces in the South." In short, any enemy combatant, regardless of origin or unit, was considered a CRP. Those not captured while fighting could be detained by the declarations of witnesses, because of their own statements, or simply for being in a region controlled by the Vietcong.[9] ARVN commanders made no mention of the provisions of the Geneva Convention, although ARVN camp personnel were prohibited from inhumane treatment or retaliation on enemy prisoners.[10] On 29 October 1966, in accordance with the Geneva Convention, MACV defined prisoners of war for American forces as those captured while engaging in combat or members of the North Vietnamese Armed Forces or the Vietcong. Despite fighting as allies, American and South Vietnamese units did not even have a consistent definition of prisoners of war, much less a coherent policy for their treatment.

On 19 October 1965, the South Vietnamese Joint General Staff (JGS), on the advice of MACV, issued JGS Memo No. 2537, which provided a standard operating procedure for the capture of communist insurgents. Captured Vietcong were briefly interrogated for tactical intelligence and soon evacuated to divisional collection points. At the division level, all captured Vietcong were given a lengthy interrogation, and their POW status was determined. Those in possession of valuable intelligence were sent to either the National Intelligence Center or the Combined Military Intelligence Center, depending on the nature of the intelligence. Vietcong with no intelligence value were shipped directly to a POW detention camp. Captured individuals deemed to be civilians by a military tribunal were returned to the place of capture and released.[11]

The JGS issued a new standard operating procedure for Vietcong prison camps on 25 May 1966, after consulting with American advisors and deciding that captured rebels should be held in camps separate from civil prison facilities. Vietcong POWs were defined as any rebels captured while openly bearing arms and resisting the ARVN. Any Vietcong who intentionally concealed his or her identity, as well as guerrillas operating outside the laws of war, were specifically exempted from POW status. The procedures required all Vietcong prisoners to be searched, interrogated, and fingerprinted on arrival at a prison camp. All Vietcong personnel were segregated by rank, sex, nationality, language, and political inclination.[12] Although the new procedures clearly defined who received POW status, they did not mention the disposition of captives exempted from POW status.

Each separate POW camp in South Vietnam received a MACV military police advisory team of one officer and four enlisted men to assist in supervising the confinement of up to 2,000 prisoners. The central POW camp at Phu Quoc, with a planned capacity of 20,000 POWs, received an advisory team of only seven officers and twenty-six enlisted men.[13] The standard guard force at each enclosure was a Quan Canh company of ARVN soldiers who received virtually no training in POW maintenance.

The POW advisors were coordinated at MACV headquarters, first by Colonel Richard O. Rowland and later by Colonel Charles D. Gooch. Rowland believed the Vietnamese government and ARVN earnestly wished to provide excellent POW care but were hampered by poor logistics. He appreciated the diplomatic aspect of POW care, noting "a signal failure in the PW program would create repercussions that could be disastrous." He especially feared that ARVN might insist on the United States assuming control of POWs if MACV advisors pushed too hard to improve POW conditions.[14] The American personnel were advisors only; they had no authority to order changes in the operation of ARVN POW camps, and they reported that camp commanders often ignored their suggestions, particularly in regard to the treatment of Vietcong prisoners.[15]

Once separated into camp compounds, enlisted Vietcong prisoners selected a prisoner representative for communications with camp officials and representatives of the ICRC. The election of representatives was done through secret ballots, but all Vietcong representatives required the approval of the camp commander. Officer camps automatically granted the position to the highest-ranking prisoner in the camp. The representative enjoyed wide latitude in the performance of official duties, but he maintained no disciplinary power over other POWs.[16]

Camp commanders were warned to prevent acts of opposition by Vietcong prisoners by maintaining an active guard presence in each camp. Any prisoner attempting to organize opposition to camp regulations, or any form of protest, whether active or passive, was immediately punished by camp authorities. Prisoners were prohibited from assembling in large groups, displaying propaganda, or chanting communist slogans within the camps. Fraternization between captives and guards or civilians was strictly forbidden. Camp commanders were authorized to use force to break up any demonstration of protest, to end POW refusals to work, or to prevent imminent riots.[17] American commanders expressed concern that Phu Quoc could become another Koje-do, with POWs virtually running their own compounds and guard personnel powerless to stop major incidents of violence.[18]

LABOR CONCERNS AND SPECIAL PRISONER CATEGORIES

Enlisted prisoners could be assigned labor duties, including camp maintenance, manual labor, transportation duties, and public benefit tasks of a nonmilitary nature within the provisions of the Geneva Convention of 1949. For the most part, South Vietnam exerted little effort to utilize prisoner labor, and virtually all labor details remained within the confines of POW camps.[19] Camps received insufficient guard personnel to maintain control over large working parties; thus, most prisoners had no opportunity to labor outside of the camps. Cao Van Vien observed in 1971 that at Phu Quoc, "the camp has only accomplished a vegetable planting project with a limited scope." He blamed a lack of funds, insufficient guard personnel, and a lack of U.S. military support for the failure to use prisoner labor.[20]

The only exceptions to the general nonuse of prisoner labor were two specialized vocational programs, the Chieu Hoi and Bien Hoa programs. Vietcong prisoners who were South Vietnamese citizens were eligible for a vocational training program that led to eventual release and resettlement on government-controlled territory. The Chieu Hoi (Open Arms) program sought to create productive, peaceful citizens out of former rebels through a program of political indoctrination, and it eased some camp overcrowding by allowing the release of thousands of Vietcong POWs.[21] Prisoners who had good conduct and who requested reclassification were screened by camp authorities. If camp commanders recommended a change in status, the returnees transferred to the control of the Ministry of Information for administration and release. By 1969, even a small number of North Vietnamese POWs entered the Chieu Hoi program.[22]

Adolescent prisoners presented a special problem for South Vietnamese and American captors. As of 7 March 1968, over 1,300 prisoners between the ages of eleven and eighteen were in custody, including eighty-eight women and forty-nine members of the NVA. The government transferred these young POWs to a special reeducation program, the Youth Rehabilitation Program at Bien Hoa, which contained a basic literacy program and a vocational training center, coupled with intense political indoctrination. Of the sixty-seven teachers at Bien Hoa, twenty-five specialized in political indoctrination, ten in literacy, and thirty-two in vocational training, including woodworking, tailoring, brickmaking, and gardening.[23]

Female POWs were sent to a single enclosure at Qui Nhon. Female prisoners had also been taken and segregated during the Korean War. However, in Vietnam, American medical officers reported that a high number of female POWs arrived at their compounds pregnant, presenting a new medical difficulty for guard personnel.[24] Discipline at Qui Nhon remained a problem throughout the war. Camp guards resorted to flogging female POWs for various offenses, a clear violation of the Geneva Convention.[25]

In 1968, the South Vietnamese government finally decided to completely segregate Vietcong prisoners from civil defendants and North Vietnamese POWs. To accomplish this task, a massive expansion of the prison facilities at Phu Quoc commenced. Further, South Vietnamese authorities removed the 5,000 prisoners deemed the most hard-core communists to the island prison at Con Son. This action followed the precedent created by the separation of fanatical Nazi prisoners during World War II and the segregation of ardent communists in the Korean War.[26] By creating a distinction between civil prisoners and POWs, South Vietnam submitted to an important legal issue pressed by MACV advisors, but this shift did not guarantee the Geneva Convention would be followed.

THE PROPAGANDA VALUE OF PRISONERS

The enemy sought to use POW mistreatment as a propaganda device in the Vietnam War in the same manner as that in the Korean War. However, in Vietnam, when prisoner riots did not provoke violent responses as they had on Koje-do, Vietcong rebels began attacking prison camps, killing their own prisoners with mortar shells and rocket fire, to demonstrate that the South Vietnamese government had not taken adequate measures to protect its captives. The island of Phu Quoc proved a poor choice for the prison compound: it was rife with Vietcong activity. In 1968 alone, the prison compounds were attacked or shelled thirty-four times. The prison was successfully breached only once, during the Tet offensive, when 2,665 POWs escaped after an assault on the fence line. Few escapees were recaptured; they successfully hid among the native population of the island.[27]

In late 1968, an inspection tour by members of the Office of the Provost Marshal revealed a number of glaring weaknesses in the Vietnamese POW program. No prisoner of war information center existed, despite the requirement for such a bureau by Article 122 of the Geneva Convention. Previous ICRC visits had little effect on camp conditions, regardless of American pressure to conform to ICRC requirements. The central camp at Phu Quoc remained overcrowded, and almost no effort to utilize POW labor existed. POW discipline remained lax, and guard personnel responded slowly to demonstrations by prisoners. In short, many problems remained in the POW system despite American efforts to assist the South Vietnamese government.[28] By October 1968, Phu Quoc operated with 40 percent more POWs than its normal capacity, and the rate of captures continued to climb. Even a simple list of POWs, as required by Article 122 of the Geneva Convention, remained incomplete at the end of 1969.[29]

A 1970 study conducted by the Army Concept Team in Vietnam concluded that American treatment of POWs from the period of capture to delivery to ARVN custody complied with the requirements of the Geneva Convention. American soldiers received reminder cards illustrating the major points of the Geneva Convention, and enemy prisoners were processed quickly but humanely into ARVN control.[30] Once POWs reached permanent enclosures, the situation changed. ICRC inspections of Phu Quoc in 1970 revealed inadequate food supplies, poor medical care, and physical beatings of prisoners. A separate MACV investigation corroborated the ICRC reports; it found that no corrective action occurred from February to October 1970. If anything, the situation of POWs worsened as camps became more crowded.

The MACV investigator concluded that the South Vietnamese government had neither the desire nor the ability to improve camp conditions; any improvements required direct U.S. assistance. He noted that the United States had an obligation under Article 12 of the Geneva Convention to ensure proper treatment of prisoners captured by U.S. forces but no facilities to assume direct control of the POWs.[31] The provost marshal ordered American advisors to notify ARVN camp commanders of any mistreatment of POWs and demand immediate corrective action, but the incidents continued unabated.[32]

On 11 August 1971, an American embassy investigator reported that beatings in the Phu Quoc compounds continued, and that anytime an American advisor became aware of a beating, the camp commanders merely transferred the victim to a different compound to hide the incident. Within ARVN, camp personnel were rated exclusively on the number of prisoner escapes. No attempt to discipline guards for mistreatment of prisoners occurred. Cao Van Vien, chief of the JGS, insisted that ICRC delegations falsely reported camp conditions, despite the concurrent findings of MACV and embassy investigators.[33]

Poor responses to ICRC camp visit complaints hurt the war effort and lowered world opinion of the South Vietnamese treatment of POWs. Few complaints received proper attention or follow-up, and changes in POW camp administration rarely occurred as the result of an ICRC visit. ICRC visits to Phu Quoc reported physical evidence of torture, including electrocution scars, food inadequacies, and nutritional deficiencies among the POW population.[34] Proposed ration scales for POWs published on 16 September 1968 suggested 2,024 calories per day for POWs in East and Southeast Asia, while recommending over 2,400 calories for prisoners from all other regions of the world. Corresponding lower standards for protein, fat, and vitamins also applied to the area, and rice comprised virtually the entire proposed ration for East Asian prisoners.[35] The ICRC visits, and subsequent complaints, demonstrated that American advice regarding the care of POWs remained unheeded by South Vietnamese camp commanders: ICRC visits to American-run camps during World War II and the Korean War typically resulted in no significant complaints about prisoner maintenance.

THE LEGACY OF THE VIETNAM WAR

American POW policy in Vietnam was largely driven by an overriding urge to free American POWs from enemy control. The MACV chief of POW operations, Colonel Henry Gibson, noted in 1968 that "the question of treatment of enemy prisoners of war is inexorably interwoven with the treatment of captured Americans by the enemy."[36] Because the Vietcong had no discernible central committee authorized to conduct exchange negotiations, and because the North Vietnamese government refused to regard captured American personnel as prisoners of war, arranging the liberation of American captives proved exceedingly difficult. The situation was further complicated by the South Vietnamese refusal to release any POWs who refused to swear fealty to the government and settle in a location under government control. In an attempt to free American personnel, U.S. commanders unilaterally released enemy prisoners on a number of occasions. They hoped that North Vietnam and the Vietcong would feel pressure to release an equivalent number of prisoners as a goodwill gesture. Although the "reciprocal releases" freed a few American prisoners, they did not lead to a regular exchange cartel or negotiations for repatriation. Neither the Vietcong nor the North Vietnamese government showed a particular interest in regaining POWs under South Vietnamese control.[37] Because the Vietcong and North Vietnamese expressed no concern for their prisoners in South Vietnam, any threat of retaliation for the mistreatment of American or South Vietnamese captives remained hollow. The United States made no such threats despite evidence that American prisoners received inadequate food and medical care while in captivity.

Maintaining the precedent established in Korea, the United States insisted that no enemy personnel, even if sick or wounded, would be repatriated by force. To avoid a drawn-out armistice negotiation, Ambassador Ellsworth Bunker recommended that any POW who did not desire repatriation should be reclassified before any negotiations, effectively preempting the question of voluntary repatriation. General Creighton Abrams rejected the suggestion, as it would violate the spirit of the Geneva Convention, if not its literal wording.[38] On 29 May 1971, the United States announced that 660 severely wounded and sick prisoners, eligible for immediate repatriation, would be screened by the ICRC, and those accepting repatriation sent to North Vietnam. Optimistic American planners believed that most American POWs held in North Vietnam were eligible for repatriation under the same provisions of the Geneva Convention, and that international public pressure could force the return of hundreds of American prisoners through the unilateral release of sick and wounded North Vietnamese prisoners. The ICRC finished its screening procedures in a single day and announced that only thirteen permanently disabled prisoners had elected to be repatriated. This outcome prompted North Vietnamese propaganda to announce that hundreds of prisoners had been offered repatriation by the United States, only to be held back, against their will, in an example of American cruelty.[39]

At the end of American involvement in the war, ARVN held 37,540 POWs, including 9,971 NVA and 26,927 Vietcong. The NVA prisoners were repatriated to Hanoi by air, but the Vietcong prisoners presented a greater problem. They were South Vietnamese citizens who represented a real threat to the government, and only 9,706 had agreed to join the Chieu Hoi program. The rest still opposed the Saigon government.[40] American diplomats expected North Vietnam to make POW exchange a difficult proposition, and they did not believe North Vietnam would release all of its prisoners within sixty days of the cease-fire.[41] In short, they believed North Vietnam would not bargain in good faith. Four key areas of contention existed. First, North Vietnam still claimed in 1972 that no NVA troops existed in South Vietnam; thus, it might refuse to accept the return of NVA POWs. Second, North Vietnam might insist that all 27,000 remaining Vietcong prisoners be freely released to settle anywhere in South Vietnam, including Vietcong-controlled areas in the countryside. Third, many NVA POWs might refuse repatriation and Vietcong prisoners might refuse to return to Vietcong-controlled areas, effectively refusing repatriation. Finally, members of the Chieu Hoi program would probably resist forcible return to Vietcong-controlled areas, and the North Vietnamese might argue they were held back against their will.[42]

In the end, the Paris peace accords called for an end to hostilities and an opportunity for the citizens of South Vietnam to self-determine their government. This allowed the United States to withdraw from Vietnam while declaring the successful preservation of the democratic South Vietnamese government. Such preservation proved illusory. Less than two years after the last American combat forces left the country, a massive North Vietnamese offensive overwhelmed ARVN defenses, captured Saigon, and established a unified Vietnamese government under a communist regime. This terminated any debate regarding the treatment of POWs by the United States, although it did not eliminate allegations that American prisoners had been held back from repatriation.

The Vietnam War represented a new approach by the United States in regard to the question of how to handle enemy prisoners. In this war, the American military essentially abdicated responsibility for prisoners by turning them over to the South Vietnamese government, even knowing that South Vietnam would not adhere to the requirements of the Geneva Convention. In every American war before Vietnam, guarding and maintaining enemy prisoners had been a thankless task given to poorly trained troops unsuited for combat. In Vietnam, this approach reached its apex. By giving custody of prisoners to the South Vietnamese, more American personnel remained available for combat duty. Any mistreatment of POWs could be blamed on the South Vietnamese because American camp personnel maintained only an advisory role and had no power to change the day-to-day operations of POW camps.

The advisory approach to POW operations in Vietnam certainly lightened the burden on American logistics, but it also ensured that the United States could not utilize POW labor, nor could it institute changes to POW policies without the acquiescence and active participation of South Vietnam's authorities. Most of the time, this did not represent a problem, but when American negotiators wished to exchange enemy prisoners for American captives, they required permission from the South Vietnamese government. American POW policy before Vietnam had been improvisational, but in Vietnam, any American improvisation was slowed by the need to convince South Vietnamese camp commanders to change their policies. This necessity resulted in a poorly functioning system strained to capacity from 1968 until 1973, continually beset by ICRC complaints and supply difficulties.

The American advisory approach to POW operations in coalition warfare continued; if anything, it increased after the end of the cold war. In the First Gulf War, which I discuss in the next chapter, American commanders planned for the construction of two massive POW compounds, where Iraqi prisoners could be rapidly interrogated and then transferred to Saudi Arabian custody, again freeing American personnel for combat operations.

The primary legacies of the cold war, from the standpoint of supervising POWs, are twofold. First, there was a sustained effort to transfer control and responsibility for enemy prisoners to less combat-effective allied troops, who often do not share American views on the efficacy of complying with the Geneva Convention. The practical result of massive, overcrowded compounds and little day-to-day control of prisoners became evident in Korea and Vietnam. Second, American commanders broadened the definition of POWs to include guerrillas and other combatants who do not necessarily represent a specific nation. Further, the previous assumption that only adult men served as combatants changed during the cold war. For the first time in American history, the captives held by the United States and its allies included many women and adolescents. Such nontraditional combatants have played an increasing role on the battlefields of the post–cold war era.

9

POW POLICY IN THE POST–COLD WAR ERA

By far the most famous prisoner of the global war on terror, Khalid Sheikh Mohammed, spent more than a decade planning, financing, and orchestrating terror attacks before his capture in Pakistan in 2003. He was uniquely suited to targeting American institutions: he possessed not only a technical understanding of target structures, but also a cultural understanding of the United States. Both educations were earned at North Carolina Agricultural and Technical State University, where Mohammed received a degree in mechanical engineering in 1986. He then moved to Afghanistan to join the mujahideen in their resistance against the Soviet military occupation. During this time, he met Osama bin Laden, the founder of Al Qaeda, and became interested in attacking Western civilization, which he considered to be a corrosive influence in the Muslim world.[1]

That Mohammed organized and led attacks, particularly against American targets, has never been in doubt. However, the question of whether he should be classified as a prisoner of war, an illegal enemy combatant, or simply a criminal illustrates the problem facing the United States and its allies in the global war on terror. International law is unfortunately muddled on the issue—Mohammed clearly engaged in acts of war by planning the 11 September 2001 attacks, given that some of the targets were military in nature. Likewise, he coordinated other, earlier attacks on military and government targets overseas, including a role in planning the 2000 attack on the USS *Cole*. On the other hand, Mohammed did not act in accordance with the international laws of war, including his decisions to target civilians in most of the attacks. As such, he cannot claim protection under the Geneva Convention Relative to Prisoners of War. Mohammed thus became a divisive subject—not for his participation in terror attacks, which he proudly admitted to during interrogations and military tribunal proceedings, but rather for the way he had been treated while in captivity, including allegations of torture during interrogations. His classification as a prisoner held by American military forces offers insight into the problems faced by American POW planners during the twenty-first century.

From 2003 until 2006, Mohammed was held in a variety of locations, including Jordan and Poland, before his transfer, along with thirteen other high-value suspects, to the detention facility at Guantánamo Bay, Cuba. During his captivity, Mohammed was interrogated almost constantly, including the use of the controversial waterboarding technique. According to Central Intelligence Agency officials, he was subjected to "harsh interrogation techniques" more than 100 times in the first year of his captivity.[2] Mohammed subsequently claimed that he admitted to various activities primarily to escape the interrogation methods. In his 2007 combatant status review tribunal, his prepared statement claimed responsibility for dozens of attacks and planned operations against American targets.[3] On 8 December 2008, Mohammed and four co-conspirators indicated that they would like to plead guilty to planning the 11 September attacks.[4] Such a plea would not necessarily indicate the defendants should not be considered prisoners of war, given that the Geneva Convention Relative to Prisoners of War allows criminal trials of prisoners for crimes committed before and during their captivity. However, the fact that Mohammed and his compatriots are facing criminal trials illustrates the broader point: that detainees from the global war on terror do not fit neatly into the category of POWs.

After the end of the Vietnam War, the United States next captured large numbers of military prisoners in 1990–1991 with the commencement of Operation Desert Shield. Once again, the United States faced an aggressor state, Iraq, in a distant and hostile terrain, as part of a coalition of military forces. As in Korea, the United States adopted a leadership role for the coalition forces to develop and implement a POW policy, particularly after the start of combat in Operation Desert Storm. Despite a four-month period of deployment and buildup, the United States entered combat unprepared for the capture of enemy forces, and it improvised ways to maintain Iraqi prisoners for what turned out to be the short period of combat after commencing land operations.

In 2001, after the 11 September terrorist attacks, the United States led a coalition to invade Afghanistan and Iraq as part of the war on terror. The Afghanistan invasion, begun with the intent of dismantling terrorist organizations, resulted in revised definitions for who received prisoner of war status. Interrogations of prisoners taken in Afghanistan led to reports of torture and violations of the Geneva Convention by U.S. interrogators. The Second

Gulf War further blurred the definition of POWs in the twenty-first century. Iraqi military and civilian captives were housed together in massive prison compounds and mistreated by poorly trained American guards. The resulting scandal provoked world outrage and fueled insurgents combatting the U.S. occupation of Iraq.

THE PERSIAN GULF WAR

Iraqi president Saddam Hussein launched an invasion of Kuwait on 2 August 1990, provoking immediate condemnation from other nations and a flurry of United Nations resolutions. Iraq's military occupied Kuwait and threatened the sovereignty of Saudi Arabia, destabilizing the region and disrupting the world's oil supply. Eventually, thirty-six nations deployed forces to participate in ousting Iraqi forces from Kuwait, including over 540,000 American troops. American planners anticipated the capture of thousands of Iraqi POWs, but they expected to hold them for a period of only one week before transferring them to Saudi Arabian control for detainment and eventual repatriation. To encourage surrenders, coalition planes dropped more than 32,000,000 surrender leaflets. Over 70 percent of prisoners cited the leaflets as a factor in the decision to surrender, and virtually all reported that they had seen the leaflets.[5] American forces captured over 60,000 Iraqi troops and accepted custody of 8,000 more captured by British and French forces, but they could not process them rapidly enough to transfer them to Saudi control for several weeks.[6] All told, coalition forces captured almost 87,000 Iraqi prisoners, most during the four days of ground combat.[7] Although American commanders dictated policies governing the treatment of Iraqi POWs, in practice, after capture, POWs remained an afterthought.

Construction of POW facilities in Saudi Arabia never matched demand. The first Iraqi prisoners captured during ground operations arrived at Camp Brooklyn within one hour of the completion of the first compound, and they were soon put to work building more facilities. As areas were completed, they were immediately occupied to capacity by prisoners. The U.S. Army had initially planned to construct four camps for POWs, each with a capacity to hold up to 24,000 prisoners, but captures greatly exceeded expectations. The Seventh Corps of the U.S. Army captured over 7,000 prisoners in the first two days of combat, and U.S. Marines reported 8,000 prisoners on the first day. The raw numbers overwhelmed transportation capacity to transfer prisoners to the enclosures in Saudi Arabia. Operational commanders feared that the rate of capture might hinder the ability of ground forces to rapidly advance into Iraq.[8] The lack of transportation became so extreme that disarmed prisoners routinely traveled to rear areas without a coalition escort.[9] Planners had selected sites in Saudi Arabia where prisoners could be processed, interrogated, and transferred to Saudi control. As prisoners flooded into the camps, they overwhelmed the identification and examination system. Each camp initially processed prisoners at a rate of fewer than 100 per day, although by the end of combat, the number rose to 1,500 per day through streamlined procedures.[10]

Despite the problems associated with the capture of 80,000 Iraqis by coalition forces in a ground war lasting only four days, Iraqi prisoners received exceptionally good treatment after capture. Most underwent a cursory interrogation and medical examination before transfer into a holding enclosure.[11] At the enclosures, the prisoners reported that they received better food, clothing, medical supplies, and shelter as prisoners of war than what they had been provided by their own army. Perhaps the most telling statistic is that only eight Iraqi prisoners died in U.S. custody, all from battle wounds or illnesses contracted before capture.[12] The International Committee of the Red Cross (ICRC) reported that the coalition forces adhered to international law and accepted practices, and pronounced, "The treatment of Iraqi prisoners of war by U.S. forces was the best compliance with the Geneva Convention by any nation in any conflict in history."[13]

American prisoners in Iraqi custody received far worse treatment during the conflict. Iraq captured only twenty-three American prisoners, mostly pilots, and twenty-four other coalition prisoners.[14] American repatriates reported physical abuse, malnourishment, insufficient protection from attacks, and poor medical care.[15] On a number of occasions, Iraqi interrogators forced coalition prisoners to appear before television cameras for propaganda purposes. These efforts backfired, provoking international condemnation without deterring coalition advances into Iraq.[16] Although coalition officials threatened to hold war crimes trials for the mistreatment of prisoners, they issued no threats of retaliation on Iraqi prisoners.[17]

The safe return of American prisoners remained a high priority for U.S. commanders, as had been the case in earlier conflicts. The first agenda item at the cease-fire negotiations was the immediate return of all coalition prisoners. Iraq repatriated all of its captives on 4 and 5 March 1991, the two days after the signing of the cease-fire agreement. The armistice made no mention of the disposition of Iraqi prisoners.[18] The insistence on returning coalition prisoners reflected a legacy of the Vietnam War and included the fear that some prisoners might be unaccounted for at the end of hostilities. One American aviator, Lieutenant Commander Michael Scott Speicher, was rumored to have been held back from exchange by Iraq. In January 2001, his status was officially changed from killed in action to missing in action. In 2009, Speicher's remains were discovered near the wreckage of his airplane.[19]

In keeping with established cold war policy, the United States vowed to refuse to use force to repatriate Iraqi prisoners. The coalition requested that the ICRC determine which prisoners wished to refuse repatriation; a total of over 13,000 elected to remain in Saudi Arabia. The repatriation of Iraqi POWs commenced on 6 March 1991, primarily relying on Saudi Arabian transportation. On 22 August, the last Iraqi POW left Saudi Arabian territory. The next day, all remaining prisoners legally became refugees and permanent residents of Saudi Arabia.[20]

The U.S. POW effort succeeded in the First Gulf War, despite inadequate planning, a shortage of trained personnel, and a lack of facilities, because it had ample assistance from the Saudi government in the form of supplies and transportation.[21] The relationship remained markedly different from the often adversarial relationships maintained with the South Korean and South Vietnamese governments of earlier wars. The short duration of the war contributed to the ease of prisoner maintenance; facilities designed to be temporary proved sufficient for the prisoners' needs. In the next American conflict in the Middle East, the treatment of military captives radically differed from the 1991 experience. Unlike Operation Desert Storm, which consisted of clear operational goals; a long period of preparation; and the careful incorporation of coalition forces, the war on terror, and the subsequent invasions of Afghanistan and Iraq, suffered from a lack of preparation and foresight regarding POW affairs.

THE GLOBAL WAR ON TERROR

On 11 September 2001, members of the Al Qaeda terrorist network hijacked four airplanes, eventually steering two into the World Trade Center in New York City and one into the Pentagon, and crashing one in rural Pennsylvania. On 21 September 2001, President George W. Bush presented an ultimatum to the Taliban, the radical Islamic government of Afghanistan. In it, he demanded the Taliban deliver Osama bin Laden and the leadership of Al Qaeda to American control, release all imprisoned foreign nationals, and close all terrorist training camps within the country. If the Taliban failed to comply, Bush vowed that it would "share their fate."[22] Such threats fell on deaf ears; the leadership of the Taliban refused to even respond to Bush's ultimatum. On 7 October 2001, American and British forces commenced an invasion of Afghanistan, aided by rebels of the Northern Alliance.

As in any conflict, American forces captured enemy combatants, provoking the first substantial POW question of the war on terror: Should members of Al Qaeda or other terrorist networks be considered prisoners of war? The Geneva Convention of 1949 is somewhat ambiguous on the subject, although a literal reading of the document suggests that members of terrorist organizations do not receive POW status on capture.[23] They typically do not wear identifiable uniforms, operate under the control of officers responsible for troop behavior, or adhere to the international laws of war. As such, for failing to meet the standards of POW status, captured members of Al Qaeda fell outside the legal definition of POWs and remained in captivity in Afghanistan. Those prisoners identified as having special intelligence value were transferred to Camp X-Ray, a prison established in January 2002 at Guantánamo Bay, Cuba. In the first three months of operation, American forces airlifted over 600 prisoners to Guantánamo for long-term interrogation.[24] The location was hardly an ideal one, but proposals for prison compounds in Eastern Europe, Germany, the Marshall Islands, Guam, Tinian, American Samoa, and Pakistan, or on board prison ships at sea, all met resistance within the military, the Department of Justice, or the State Department. The Bush administration did not wish to bring terror suspects to the United States, where constitutional protections might be applied to prevent successful interrogations. Likewise, Europe's court of human rights might intervene if prisoners were held in European nations. As such, Guantánamo became, in the words of Karen Greenberg, "the least worst place" to hold detainees.[25]

Had the Afghan conflict remained solely between the United States and Al Qaeda, it is unlikely any controversy would have emerged from Guantánamo. The invasion of Afghanistan provoked resistance from the military forces of the Taliban and necessitated a further definition of enemy captives. A White House legal counsel recommendation, endorsed by Bush, denied POW status to Taliban captives as well, on the grounds that the Taliban was a "failed state," despite the Taliban's de facto control of the nation for years before the conflict. Further, because Taliban units reportedly did not follow the Geneva Convention, they could not expect quarter from coalition forces. A clarification, issued 7 February 2002, announced that the United States would substantially adhere to the Geneva Convention regarding the maintenance of Taliban captives, but it would not accord them prisoner of war status.[26] Like captured Al Qaeda members, certain Taliban fighters faced prolonged captivity in Guantánamo for interrogation purposes, suggesting a blurring of the line between military units and terrorist groups.[27]

Interrogators at Guantánamo utilized Field Manual 34-52, which included a series of guidelines for the interrogation of enemy prisoners. Written in 1987 and modified in 1992, the guidelines contained a list of acceptable means of coercing responses from prisoners, including sleep and sensory deprivation. The guidelines expressly forbade physical beatings and certain threats or deceptions.[28] On 16 April 2003, Secretary of Defense Donald Rumsfeld broadened the acceptable interrogation methods to include forced nudity and the use of military dogs for intimidation purposes.[29] Physical means of intelligence extraction remained illegal, and the new means were intended solely for use at Guantánamo, not as a general shift in prisoner of war interrogation techniques used by American forces.

While coalition forces remained in Afghanistan seeking to destroy or negate Al Qaeda, the Bush administration turned its attention to Iraq. After making the case for military action at the United Nations, the invasion of Iraq commenced on 20 March 2003, ostensibly in a search for illegal weapons of mass destruction. The broad coalition support of 1991 had largely dissipated by 2003. Although thirty-nine nations officially supplied troops or matériel, the invasion remained overwhelmingly an American venture, with the largest foreign contribution of troops provided by Great Britain.[30] Noticeably absent were the regional neighbors of Iraq that had participated in the First Gulf War. American and coalition forces quickly invaded Iraq and captured the capital of Baghdad by 9 April, and in the process captured over 80,000 Iraqi troops.[31] Again, American planes rained millions of surrender leaflets on Iraqi forces, prompting many to surrender at the first sight of coalition troops.[32] Hussein fled before the advancing forces and directed an insurgent campaign to harass the occupying forces until his capture on 13 December.

As in Vietnam and the First Gulf War, the return of American POWs remained of paramount importance to American commanders. Although the Iraqi military captured few Americans, press reports on the fate of American POWs riveted the nation. In particular, the story of Private First Class Jessica Lynch, taken prisoner during an ambush of a supply convoy, became the symbol of American POWs during the war. Special operations forces raided the hospital where Lynch was held as a prisoner and successfully freed her from captivity. In the same operation, they discovered the bodies of seven American POWs who had died of wounds received in the ambush. Within hours of obtaining her freedom, Lynch's visage beamed from news broadcasts across the country.[33] Less than two weeks later, marines rescued seven U.S. prisoners held in Tikrit. The freed prisoners received a heroes' welcome on their release.[34]

If the status of terrorists and Taliban fighters confounded American legal analysts, no such controversy existed regarding Iraqi prisoners. Iraqi captives received POW status immediately, and no government or military official suggested that they did not deserve the protections guaranteed by the Geneva Convention. Living up to the requirements of the convention proved difficult because no location in Iraq remained secure from hostile action, and thus POWs could not be evacuated from the war zone without removing them from Iraq entirely. Because no other nation offered to house Iraqi prisoners as Saudi Arabia had done in 1991, they remained an American problem that continually confounded occupational authorities and tied down military forces.

Without a secure base of operations outside the combat zone, American commanders had no convenient area for the internment of captured Iraqi troops. The insurgency ensured that no location within Iraq remained safe from hostile operations. Pentagon expectations of a quick war followed by a brief occupation proved unfounded; the system of temporary facilities used in 1991 could not be applied. American commanders searched for a rapid solution to the problem of maintaining POWs and decided to use existing Iraqi prison facilities. The most ill-advised choice, Abu Ghraib, was a large prison compound outside of Baghdad. The use of Abu Ghraib indicated the improvised nature of POW operations in the Second Gulf War and a clear lack of understanding by American commanders regarding the nature of Abu Ghraib under Hussein's regime. The prison deserved its reputation as a hated symbol of the regime: it held thousands of political prisoners who were subjected to unspeakable tortures.[35]

The decision to place POWs in Abu Ghraib and other prison facilities in Iraq clearly violated the Geneva Convention. Article 22 states that prisoners may be placed in civil prison facilities only as a temporary expedient, but by October 2004, Abu Ghraib had been in operation as a POW compound for months, and the POW population exceeded 7,000. To maintain the prisoners, a military police (MP) force of only ninety-two reservists staffed the prison, resulting in a prisoner-to-guard ratio of 75:1.[36] The 800th MP Brigade, which provided the personnel for Abu Ghraib, had been converted from maintaining criminal prisoners to maintaining POWs, but brigade members received little practical instruction in the proper treatment of POWs. The unit also remained responsible for facility security and logistics, and they provided supply convoys for the prison. Insurgent forces shelled the prison repeatedly, but the guards' lack of heavy weapons and vehicles prevented a sufficient response to halt the attacks, further complicating the problem of protecting prisoners and sapping the morale of the guard personnel.

In the fall of 2003, Abu Ghraib's population reached 8,000 prisoners, many taken from their homes in the middle of the night, not captured on the battlefield. Journalist Mark Danner estimated that 70 to 90 percent of Abu Ghraib's prisoners had been arrested by mistake.[37] The line between prisoners of war and civilian detainees disappeared at Abu Ghraib because all remained confined together, and the entire prison population was vulnerable to abusive treatment. In February 2004, the ICRC released a report on the treatment of prisoners of war and other internees in Iraq. It concluded that brutality and mistreatment of prisoners constituted a widespread problem in Iraq at the hands of both coalition forces and Iraqi police. Interrogators used prohibited techniques to elicit information from prisoners, resulting in deaths and serious injuries to prisoners.[38] Most of these interrogators came from outside the 800th MP Brigade and neither reported to nor were held accountable by any member of the guard contingent. The ICRC report, though public, went largely unheeded by American reporters and citizens, but comparing the report with ICRC statements from 1991 indicates that American and coalition prisoner practices markedly declined in the Second Gulf War.

On 29 April 2004, the American public became aware of Abu Ghraib as a result of a CBS broadcast of a series of photographs showing American personnel abusing prisoners.[39] The pictures included naked prisoners chained together and forced to simulate homosexual acts, military dogs menacing terrified captives, and a hooded, shrouded figure connected to electrical leads, standing on a box with arms outstretched. The photographs, taken by American personnel participating in the abuse, became the icons of the Second Gulf War—images of guard personnel completely out of control. Bush and Rumsfeld had never authorized physical or sexual abuse in any capacity, yet both of these appeared at Abu Ghraib. Further, interrogation techniques reserved for Guantánamo detainees, such as the use of nudity and military dogs, had migrated to Iraq without official sanction.[40]

The abuse revelations from Abu Ghraib did not come as a surprise to the Pentagon or the White House. On 19 January 2004, Lieutenant General Ricardo Sanchez, commander of coalition forces in Iraq, had ordered an investigation into the treatment of detainees at Abu Ghraib. Investigators led by

Major General Antonio M. Taguba scrutinized the behavior of the 800th MP Brigade and found dozens of instances of abuse of prisoners by American personnel.[41] It also found members of the brigade—the same unit that oversaw POW operations in the First Gulf War—were inadequately trained for POW treatment. The brigade's commander, Brigadier General Janis Karpinski, did not provide sufficient oversight for prisoner affairs.[42] Taguba recommended that Karpinski and several subordinates be relieved of command.[43] Criminal investigations of enlisted personnel directly involved in the abuse followed the Taguba report.

After the public revelation of the abuses at Abu Ghraib, Sanchez ordered another investigation of the allegations. Lieutenant General Anthony Jones and Major General George R. Fay expanded the scope of the Taguba investigations by interviewing hundreds of detainees and coalition military personnel. Their report concluded that at the time of the abuse, only 600 of the Abu Ghraib inmates were prisoners of war; the remainder were civilian detainees who did not merit POW status.[44] Jones and Fay found that responsibility for the abuse rested with "a small group of morally corrupt soldiers and civilians." It was exacerbated by a failure of leadership and oversight at multiple levels of command, and it was encouraged by civilian and military intelligence agencies seeking to obtain actionable intelligence from the prisoners regarding the insurgency.[45] A classified portion of the report, leaked to the *New York Times*, indicated that Sanchez authorized the use of interrogation techniques at Abu Ghraib that had been specifically intended for Guantánamo.[46]

In the aftermath of the Abu Ghraib scandal, President Bush offered to demolish the prison, but the Iraqi interim government rebuffed the offer as a waste of resources. Insurgents remained in U.S. custody in Iraq in 2006, although the government has not released the number or location of detainees currently being held. Most were transferred from Abu Ghraib to Camp Bucca, a semipermanent detention facility on the outskirts of Umm Qasr that was originally constructed by British forces to serve as a temporary facility for captured Iraqi POWs. The U.S. Army accepted responsibility for the compound in April 2003; it replaced the temporary structures with cinder block barracks designed to hold thousands of prisoners on a long-term basis.

In 2004, the U.S. Supreme Court ordered that prisoners at Guantánamo were entitled to legally challenge their detention by the United States, in the case of *Rasul v. Bush.* Congress effectively overrode the Supreme Court decision by suspending the writ of habeas corpus for prisoners at Guantánamo with the passage of the Detainee Treatment Act on 31 December, 2005.[47] According to this act, the prisoners were not allowed to sue for their own release in U.S. courts, although existing lawsuits could go forward. The first such lawsuit, *Hamdan v. Rumsfeld*, reached the Supreme Court in the summer of 2006. The court ruled that the executive branch had no authority to create military tribunals to try captives in the war on terror. In essence, the U.S. military could not treat enemy captives as both prisoners of war and criminal defendants. In response, Congress passed the Military Commissions Act, essentially re-creating the military tribunals established by the Department of Defense. These military tribunals considered the status of some Taliban and Al Qaeda prisoners and ordered the release of some foreign nationals, but hundreds more awaited hearings or were ordered to remain in custody for further interrogation. Of the approximately 150 detainees released from custody before 2005, at least seven were recaptured or killed while fighting NATO forces in Afghanistan.[48]

On 12 June 2008, the Supreme Court ruled in *Boumediene v. Bush* that because the prisoners held at Guantánamo Bay had not been defined as prisoners of war, they should receive the legal protections of the U.S. Constitution, including the right to a speedy trial and the right to legal representation. Five months later, five detainees represented in the *Boumediene* case were ordered freed by a federal district court in Washington, D.C. This decision demonstrated that individual prisoners could now sue for release on a case-by-case basis.

In 2009, President Barack Obama announced that the United States would close the detention facility at Guantánamo Bay by the end of the calendar year. However, the announcement was not accompanied by a formal plan of where the prisoners would be sent, returning to the initial dilemma of 2001. In the first five months of the Obama administration, a number of detainees at Guantánamo were released from the facility, including the transfer of a few to captivity in allied nations. In June, Palau offered to accept custody of thirteen Chinese Uighur Muslims at Guantánamo, although the detainees in question balked at permanent residence in the Pacific island nation.[49] Likewise, Bermuda accepted four Uighur detainees in the same month, a move that triggered a vote of no confidence in the Bermudan prime minister and that angered British officials who had not been notified of the plan in advance.[50]

Because the Taliban no longer rules Afghanistan, repatriation to that nation presents both legal and ethical problems. The current government of Afghanistan will almost certainly punish former Taliban fighters, particularly those singled out for detention in Cuba. Members of Al Qaeda confined at Guantánamo cannot be expected to return to Afghanistan in the near future, and yet many have committed no overt act that could trigger a civil prosecution in an American court. They remain in legal limbo, awaiting a defined policy that could clarify their fate in the war on terror. Foreign nationals captured in Afghanistan might be repatriated to their home countries, but depending on their origin, they might face civil imprisonment, torture, or even execution for their activities. American citizens are certainly unwilling to accept the idea of transferring Guantánamo captives to the continental United States; even a proposal to place them in maximum-security prison facilities was met with strong opposition. Although President Obama vowed to close the detention facility, Congress voted against an appropriation to actually fund the closure, with leaders of both parties demanding a clear plan for the disposition of the prisoners before any action could be taken. The problems that Obama faces, although not of his making, demonstrate the fundamental difficulties that the United States faces in planning future POW operations. They also resonate in current operations in Afghanistan and Iraq, where American units continue to capture enemy combatants. Until the underlying issues are addressed, the problems are unlikely to disappear—and will in all likelihood increase if the conflict spreads to neighboring regions.

Conclusion

THE FUTURE OF AMERICAN POW POLICY

American POW policy and practice have always been improvisational. At no time in U.S. history has the nation entered a war fully prepared for the number of POWs captured in that war. This is unsurprising, given that the United States has rarely entered a war adequately prepared for initial combat, a much greater consideration. Circumstances have forced American commanders to create new POW systems to meet the needs of each conflict while engaged in combat operations. POWs have never been a major priority for the U.S. armed forces, and the officers given control of POWs have typically been unsuited for combat command as a result of age, inexperience, or disposition. The result has been an ongoing scramble to house and feed prisoners in every war, occasionally with disastrous results, as seen in Civil War camps, Koje-do, and Abu Ghraib. At the end of each conflict, prisoners have returned home, and little effort has been expended to assess POW operations, thus ensuring that the U.S. military remained unprepared for the next conflict. Improvisation does not make the United States unique; historically, POWs have remained a low priority for military forces worldwide. In most wars, the United States has maintained its captives in better fashion than its enemies and has had just cause to complain about the treatment of American prisoners. Nevertheless, the habit of American POW policy has been to pay lip service to high ideals of humane treatment, but not to allocate the resources necessary to guarantee such high standards.

The United States has maintained a keen interest in the treatment of captured Americans. This behavior has been present in every American war and has been of special note in conflicts after the Civil War, when U.S. forces have captured many more prisoners than the enemy in each conflict. The development of international law regarding prisoners has influenced American military practices and guaranteed that American decisions are not made in a vacuum, but it has also largely been driven by American diplomatic efforts and has created an international legal system that is unrealistic at best, and in many cases unworkable. For the most part, the War Department and the Department of Defense have explicitly followed the Hague and Geneva conventions (although some disagreements occurred regarding the proper interpretation of each document) and have expected similar compliance from enemies. When captors of U.S. prisoners openly mistreated POWs, the American response has consistently been the threat of retaliation or postwar trials.

The United States has never approached POW policy in the same way for two consecutive wars, and practice has maintained even less continuity between conflicts separated by decades or centuries. There is little evidence in the official records or the historiography of POW affairs to suggest that racism significantly affected POW policy, although it almost certainly influenced the decisions of some individuals involved in POW practice. Only during World War II did the United States capture significant numbers of prisoners of multiple ethnicities at the same time, and the treatment of German, Italian, and Japanese prisoners did not markedly differ. Racial comparisons between wars are difficult, if not impossible, because of the changes in American society and in the nature of warfare over time. One cannot compare the treatment of Iraqi POWs in 2003 with the treatment of British prisoners in 1813 and hope to make a convincing argument that racism is the overriding factor in the difference of treatment for each group.

As the United States grew in power and status, its ability to influence international law regarding prisoners grew as well. At the Hague conventions of 1899 and 1907, the United States participated as one among many nations. By 1929, the United States was one of the sponsoring powers of the Geneva Conference, pushing for an agreement to clarify the laws of prisoner care. At the 1949 Geneva Conference, the United States essentially proposed the new convention and gained ratification of the new treaty without substantial modifications. However, some have argued that in the period after 1949, the United States has set back POW affairs by not explicitly following the convention and by refusing to accede to the 1977 protocol establishing new standards for POW maintenance, including expanding the definition of POWs. The legal impact of the war on terror remains to be seen, but the abuse at Abu Ghraib and the allegations of mistreatment at Guantánamo have hurt American standing in the international community.

Despite improvisations, certain principles have guided American conduct toward military captives. At no time has the United States adopted collective punitive measures against all prisoners, nor has it ever been declared

U.S. policy or obvious practice to mistreat POWs. Even cases of deliberate abuse, such as the situation at Abu Ghraib, have been shown to be the actions of a few individuals, not the enforcement of a deliberate policy. If POWs held by the United States have had cause to complain about their treatment, it has been due to negligence, not a malign intent. At times, the principle of thrift has become too influential, resulting in overcrowded prison compounds and a driving desire by camp commanders to reduce the public burden represented by prisoners. One early example of economizing POW treatment came during the Revolutionary War, when states quartered British prisoners with citizens to save the cost of constructing POW encampments. Another occurred in the War of 1812, when marshals chose to lease prison ships rather than construct new facilities. In the Civil War, combinations of thrift and neglect led to the massively overcrowded prison pens at Andersonville, Elmira, and other locations, where prisoners received scant rations and little shelter.

Although the United States has often linked enemy POW treatment to the treatment of American prisoners and thus ceded the initiative regarding prisoners to the enemy, rarely has the United States carried out a policy of retaliation on enemy prisoners. Retaliatory acts occurred during the War of 1812 and the Civil War, but in later wars, the common U.S. practice consisted of warning the enemy of retaliation or possible war crimes trials for the mistreatment of American prisoners. Examples of retaliatory warnings occurred in the Philippine War and the Vietnam War. In both cases, commanders never ordered retaliatory measures. In the First Gulf War, President George H. W. Bush warned Iraq that it would be held accountable for the mistreatment of American prisoners, yet no war crimes trials occurred even after repatriated prisoners reported abuse while in captivity.

For those who seek policy implications, I draw the following conclusions from my analysis here. POW policies in the future must be clearly established before the capture of enemy troops, and facilities must be prepared well in advance of the arrival of prisoners. A standard operating procedure for the construction of camps, the interrogation of captives, and the standards for POW treatment are all vital to the future of POW operations. A clear definition of whom the United States regards as a prisoner of war, currently lacking, remains fundamentally important to the future of American POW policy. Waiting to determine a captive's status exacerbates any POW situation. Military units tasked with POW affairs require extensive training in both procedures and international law regarding prisoners. If these units are from the reserves or national guard, they must be specifically devoted to

POW operations. Attempts since 2003 to convert military police companies specializing in criminal affairs within the U.S. military and the detention of criminal prisoners have resulted in allegations of mistreatment such as those from Abu Ghraib and Guantánamo. Expecting the military to make POW affairs a top priority is unrealistic, but it is also foolish to assign insufficient personnel to oversee a large POW population in a hostile location. The scandals associated with prisoner abuse during the war on terror and the second invasion of Iraq must serve as a warning for the military leadership of the United States if it wishes to ensure the proper treatment of American prisoners in future conflicts. Continually entering wars unprepared for prisoners and improvising policies in the midst of combat can only result in future allegations of mistreatment of enemy prisoners and the prospect of international criticism for the United States. Although improvisation has been the standard behavior of U.S. POW policy, it cannot remain the standard in the American conflicts of the future if the United States hopes to maintain its role in international affairs as a leader in improving the humane treatment of war captives.

Internal improvements in the function of the American POW system are a vital, worthy goal, but a redefinition of international law is also in order. Although the United States has lost some credibility in the world as a result of the scandals associated with prisoners of the war on terror, it remains the sole superpower in the world, and the scandal has drawn attention to the need for, at minimum, a clarification of the laws of war regarding legal combatants. More likely, it will prove necessary to create an entirely new classification system, one that reflects the reality of modern warfare in an era of nonstate actors and multilateral belligerents. Such an agreement will have little force or legitimacy without the participation of the United States, which has shown little interest in diplomatic approaches to end the problem of terrorism in the world.

NOTES

INTRODUCTION: AMERICAN POW POLICY AND PRACTICE

1. One important exception arose in James Bacque, *Other Losses: The Shocking Truth behind the Mass Deaths of Disarmed German Soldiers and Civilians under General Eisenhower's Command* (New York: Prima, 1991), in which Bacque accused Dwight D. Eisenhower of deliberately mistreating German prisoners in 1945, leading to the deaths of hundreds of thousands of prisoners. This assertion was countered by Günter Bischof and Stephen E. Ambrose, eds., *Eisenhower and the German Prisoners of War* (Baton Rouge: Louisiana State University Press, 1992), and will be considered further in chap. 7.

2. J. Fitzgerald Lee, "Prisoners of War," *Army Quarterly* 3 (1921–1922): 348–356.

3. Herbert C. Fooks, *Prisoners of War* (Federalsburg, Md.: J. W. Stowell, 1924), 20–21.

4. William E. S. Flory, *Prisoners of War: A Study in the Development of International Law* (Washington, D.C.: American Council on Public Affairs, 1942).

5. George G. Lewis and John Mewha, *History of Prisoner of War Utilization by the United States Army, 1776–1945* (Washington, D.C.: Government Printing Office, 1955).

6. A. J. Barker, *Prisoners of War* (New York: Universe Books, 1974), 207.

7. Howard S. Levie, *Prisoners of War in International Armed Conflict*, Naval War College International Law Studies 59 (Newport, R.I.: Naval War College Press, 1977).

8. Richard Garrett, *POW* (London: David & Charles, 1981).

9. Lawrence H. Keeley, *War before Civilization* (New York: Oxford University Press, 1996), 83–88.

10. June Namias, *White Captives* (Chapel Hill: University of North Carolina Press, 1993), 3–5; J. Norman Heard, *White into Red* (Metuchen, N.J.: Scarecrow Press, 1973), 1–2; Kathryn Zabelle Derounian-Stodola and James Arthur Levernier, *The Indian Captivity Narrative, 1550–1900* (New York: Twayne Publishers, 1993), 2–8.

11. Hugo Grotius, *De Jure Belle ac Pacis*, trans. Francis W. Kelsey (1625; reprint,

1925), bk. 3, chap. 4, pt. 10–12, available at http://www.lonang.com/exlibris/grotius/.

12. Ibid., chap. 7, pt. 1, 2, 5, 9; chap. 14, pt. 3–5, 9; chap. 21, pt. 25.

13. Emmerich de Vattel, *The Law of Nations or the Principles of Natural Law* (1758), bk. 3, chap. 8, pt. 140–141, 149–154; chap. 18, pt. 287–294, available at http://www.lonang.com/exlibris/vattel/.

14. For a discussion of the colonial unwillingness to take prisoners and to kill noncombatants as well as enemy warriors, see John Grenier, *The First Way of War: American War Making on the Frontier, 1607–1814* (New York: Cambridge University Press, 2005), 29–52, 128–130; Douglas Edward Leach, *Flintlock and Tomahawk: New England in King Philip's War* (New York: Macmillan, 1958), 224–226; Robert Rogers, *Journals of Major Robert Rogers* (London: J. Millan, 1765), 40–46.

15. Richard Hutchinson, "The Warr in New-England Visibly Ended," in *Narratives of the Indian Wars*, ed. Charles H. Lincoln (New York: Charles Scribner's Sons, 1913), 103–106.

16. See Ian K. Steele, *Warpaths: Invasions of North America* New York: Oxford University Press, 1994), 131.

CHAPTER 1: STRUGGLING INTO EXISTENCE

1. Thomas Hughes, *A Journal by Thomas Hughes* (Cambridge: Cambridge University Press, 1947), 18–19 September 1777.

2. Ibid., 22 October 1777.

3. Ibid., 28 April 1778.

4. Ibid., 27 May–30 June 1778.

5. Ibid., 10 June 1781.

6. The first congressional mention of the importance of economy when caring for enemy prisoners came on 4 January 1776, in reference to prisoners held in Trenton, N.J. *Journals of the Continental Congress, 1774–1789*, ed. Worthington C. Ford et al. (Washington, D.C.: Government Printing Office, 1904–1937), 4:30–32. Hereafter cited as JCC.

7. For a discussion of colonial approaches to warfare with Native American populations, see John Grenier, *The First Way of War: American War Making on the Frontier, 1607–1814* (New York: Cambridge University Press, 2005), 1–52.

8. George Adams Boyd, *Elias Boudinot: Patriot and Statesman, 1740–1821* (Princeton, N.J.: Princeton University Press, 1952), 34, 45–46. If civilians and privateers are counted, the British held more captives than the Americans for almost the entire war. However, during the war, the term "prisoner of war" was understood to refer only to individuals captured while fighting with land forces. "Marine prisoners," as naval captures were called, were accorded an entirely different status by both the British and the Americans.

9. Among the works that summarize the POW situation are Carl Berger, *Broadsides and Bayonets: The Propaganda War of the American Revolution* (San Rafael,

Calif.: Presidio Press, 1976); John Tebbel, *Turning the World Upside Down: Inside the American Revolution* (New York: Orion Books, 1993); and Henry Steele Commager and Richard B. Morris, eds., *The Spirit of Seventy-Six: The Story of the Revolution as Told by Participants* (1958; reprint, New York: Da Capo Press, 1995).

10. Herbert Aptheker, *The American Revolution, 1763–1783* (New York: International Publishers, 1960), 115.

11. Some of the better-written narratives are Ethan Allen, *A Narrative of Colonel Ethan Allen's Captivity* (1779; reprint, Burlington, Vt.: H. Johnson, 1838); John Blatchford, *The Narrative of John Blatchford* (1865; reprint, New York: New York Times, 1971); Christopher Hawkins, *The Adventures of Christopher Hawkins* (1864; reprint, New York: New York Times, 1968); Charles Herbert, *A Relic of the Revolution* (1847; reprint, New York: New York Times, 1968); and Israel R. Potter, *The Life and Remarkable Adventures of Israel R. Potter* (1824; reprint, New York: Corinth Books, 1962). Works discussing the prison narratives of the revolution include Larry G. Bowman, *Captive Americans: Prisoners during the American Revolution* (Athens: Ohio University Press, 1976); Francis D. Cogliano, *American Maritime Prisoners in the Revolutionary War: The Captivity of William Russell* (Annapolis, Md.: Naval Institute Press, 2001); Sheldon S. Cohen, *Yankee Sailors in British Gaols: Prisoners of War at Forton and Mill, 1777–1783* (Newark: University of Delaware Press, 1995); and Robert John Dean, "Prison Narratives of the American Revolution" (Ph.D. diss., Michigan State University, 1980).

12. Boyd, *Elias Boudinot*, 33. Washington to Boudinot, 1 April 1777, *The Writings of George Washington from the Original Manuscript Sources, 1745–1799*, ed. John C. Fitzpatrick, 39 vols. (Washington, D.C.: Government Printing Office, 1931–1944), 7:343.

13. Gerald O. Haffner, "The Treatment of Prisoners of War by the Americans during the War of Independence" (Ph.D. diss., University of Indiana, 1952); Charles H. Metzger, *The Prisoner in the American Revolution* (Chicago: Loyola University Press, 1971).

14. Betsy Knight, "Prisoner Exchange and Parole in the American Revolution," *William and Mary Quarterly* 48 (April 1991): 201–222; Rembert Patrick, "British Prisoners of War in the American Revolution" (master's thesis, University of North Carolina, 1934).

15. Richard Sampson, *Escape in America: The British Convention Prisoners, 1777–1783* (Chippenham, U.K.: Picton Publishing, 1995); Harry M. Ward, *Between the Lines: Banditti of the American Revolution* (Westport, Conn.: Praeger, 2002); George W. Knepper, "The Convention Army, 1777–1783" (Ph.D. diss., University of Michigan, 1954); William M. Dabney, "After Saratoga: The Story of the Convention Army" (Ph.D. diss., University of New Mexico, 1954).

16. For a discussion of British recruitment practices during the war, see Edward E. Curtis, *The Organization of the British Army in the American Revolution* (1926; reprint, New York: AMS Press, 1969), 54–60. All recruits, voluntary or impressed, served for a period of three years or the duration of the war, at the discretion of the crown.

17. Washington still received dozens of such requests, but each was rejected out of fairness to all prisoners held by the enemy. For Washington's explanation, see Washington to Joseph Spencer, 2 September 1777, 9:161; Washington to John Beatty, 23 December 1779, 17:306–307, both in Washington, *Writings.*

18. Washington to Gage, 11 August 1775, Washington, *Writings,* 3:416–417.

19. Washington to the President of Congress, 17 November 1775, Washington, *Writings,* 4:73.

20. For a discussion of Boudinot's findings, consult David L. Sterling, "American Prisoners of War in New York: A Report by Elias Boudinot," *William and Mary Quarterly* 13 (July 1956): 376–393.

21. JCC 4 (1776), 264.

22. Washington to Nicholas Cooke, 3 March 1777, 6:242; Washington to Israel Putnam, 25 January 1778, 10:348–349; Washington to John Beatty, 29 December 1779, 17:306–307; Washington to Thomas Sim Lee, 4 May 1780, 18:328–329; all in Washington, *Writings.*

23. JCC 4 (1776), 370–373.

24. Washington to the President of Congress, 11 May 1776, 5:35; Washington to Boudinot, 1 April 1777, 7:343; both in Washington, *Writings.* JCC 7 (1777), 289; JCC 8 (1777), 491–492.

25. JCC 5 (1776), 452–458.

26. JCC 5 (1776), 630–632. Washington considered the possibility of enlisting enemy prisoners to be of dubious value, Washington to Pennsylvania Council of Safety, 12 January 1777, Washington, *Writings,* 6:504.

27. Washington to the President of Congress, 30 July 1776, 5:355; Washington to Abraham Skinner, 17 February 1781, 21:236–237; both in Washington, *Writings.* JCC 9 (1777), 776–777.

28. Paul Nelson puts the exact number at 5,791 prisoners, including 3,379 British and Canadian troops and 2,412 German troops. Paul David Nelson, *General Horatio Gates: A Biography* (Baton Rouge: Louisiana State University Press, 1976), 142. Ward claims the actual number of Germans was 2,492, for a total of 5,871 POWs; Harry M. Ward, *The American Revolution: Nationhood Achieved, 1763–1788* (New York: St. Martin's, 1995), 251. Sampson points out that four different returns exist for the British prisoners, with the numbers ranging from 2,923 to 3,198 soldiers, Sampson, *Escape in America,* 192. According to Washington, the total number of prisoners was 5,740; see Washington to Landon Carter, 27 October 1777, Washington, *Writings,* 9:451–455. Washington put the total losses caused the British by Burgoyne's campaign at 9,583 killed, captured, or deserted.

29. Samuel White Patterson, *Horatio Gates: Defender of American Liberties* (New York: Columbia University Press, 1941), 175–183; Nelson, *Horatio Gates,* 142–152.

30. JCC 9 (1777), 948–952, 1059–1064; JCC 10 (1778), 44–45, 48–53.

31. Sampson, *Escape in America,* 82–88. Sampson argues, "Congress had no sound or honest case for their action, and the 'stain' on their history remains" (86). For Washington's argument, see Washington to Horatio Gates, 14 November 1777, Washington, *Writings,* 10:61–63.

32. Washington to William Howe, 10 February 1778, Washington, *Writings,* 10:444–446. JCC 10 (1778), 197–198, 203, JCC 12 (1778), 1240; JCC 18 (1780), 1028–1031.

33. JCC 17 (1780), 753–754.

34. JCC 12 (1778), 1032–1033.

35. JCC 12 (1778), 1111–1112.

36. Washington to Heath, 29 April 1778, Washington, *Writings,* 11:320–322. Heath was the senior officer in Massachusetts, where the practice was especially prevalent. Washington also wrote to government officials in the state, attempting to end the practice. Washington to Jeremiah Powell, 2 May 1778, 11:424; Washington to Board of War, 19 September 1778, 12:470; both in Washington, *Writings.*

37. Washington to the President of Congress, 10 July 1780, 19:147–150; Washington to Skinner, 12 July 1780, 19:159–161; Washington to Skinner, 24 July 1780, 19:248–250; all in Washington, *Writings.* JCC 17 (1780), 704–706.

38. JCC 18 (1780), 1028–1031.

39. Washington to the President of Congress, 7 November 1780, 20:314–315; Washington to Board of War, 7 November 1780, 20:316; Washington to the President of Congress, 16 April 1781, 21:474–475; all in Washington, *Writings.*

40. JCC 19 (1781), 274, 299–302. Roger Kaplan has noted that the British practice of interrogating all prisoners who escaped American captivity and reached the British lines represented a major source of intelligence during the war. Roger Kaplan, "The Hidden War: British Intelligence Operations during the American Revolution," *William and Mary Quarterly* 47 (January 1990): 115–138.

41. JCC 15 (1779), 1288; Washington to John Beatty, 30 October 1779, 17:45–48; Washington to Francis Lewis, 19 February 1780, 18:26, both in Washington, *Writings.*

42. JCC 16 (1780), 47–52.

43. Michael C. Scoggins, *The Day It Rained Militia* (Charleston: The History Press, 2005), 112.

44. Washington to the Board of War, 7 November 1780, Washington, *Writings,* 20:316.

45. Henry Clinton, *The American Rebellion* (New Haven: Yale University Press, 1954), 166.

46. JCC 17 (1780), 753–754; David B. Mattern, *Benjamin Lincoln and the American Revolution* (Columbia: University of South Carolina Press, 1995), 107–110. Lincoln originally agreed to the surrender of only 1,500 Continentals and 500 militia, but Clinton's threat to search the city for arms caused the total number of surrenders to rise to over 5,000.

47. Bernard A. Uhlendorf, ed., *The Siege of Charleston* (New York: New York Times, 1938), 89–93, 281–289; Franklin B. Hough, *The Siege of Charleston* (Albany: J. Munsell, 1867), 78–80, 203–206.

48. Alice Noble Waring, *The Fighting Elder: Andrew Pickens* (Columbia: University of South Carolina Press, 1962), 41–43.

49. Dr. Robert Brownfield wrote a detailed account of the slaughter, contained in William Dobein James, *A Sketch of the Life of Brig. Gen. Francis Marion* (Charleston: Gould and Riley, 1821), appendix 1–7.

50. Franklin and Mary Wickwire, *Cornwallis: The American Adventure* (Boston: Houghton Mifflin, 1970), 182–184; Paul Hubert Smith, *Loyalists and Redcoats: A Study in British Revolutionary Policy* (Chapel Hill: University of North Carolina Press, 1964), 131.

51. Anne King Gregorie, *Thomas Sumter* (Columbia: R. L. Bryan, 1931), 94–95; Dan L. Morrill, *Southern Campaigns of the American Revolution* (Baltimore: Nautical & Aviation Publishing, 1993), 83.

52. W. Gilmore Simms, *The Life of Francis Marion* (New York: George F. Cooledge & Brother, 1846), 126; Robert D. Bass, *Swamp Fox: The Life and Campaigns of General Francis Marion* (New York: Henry Holt, 1959), 45. Simms put the number of Continentals who joined Marion at 3 of 150; Bass claims the number was actually 85.

53. Lyman C. Draper, *King's Mountain and Its Heroes* (Cincinnati: P. G. Thompson, 1881), 170–177; *State Records of North Carolina*, 26 vols. (Goldsboro, N.C.: Nash Brothers, 1886–1907), 15:105–106.

54. John S. Pancake, *This Destructive War: The British Campaign in the Carolinas, 1780–82* (Tuscaloosa: University of Alabama Press, 1985), 71. Pancake argues that most Americans fighting in South Carolina, regardless of allegiance, simply didn't understand the "so-called rules of war," including that a failure to accept an initial call to surrender might preclude any further offers of quarter. See also John C. Dann, ed., *The Revolution Remembered: Eyewitness Accounts of the American Revolution* (Chicago: University of Chicago Press, 1980), 189.

55. Henry Lee, *The American Revolution in the South*, ed. Robert E. Lee (New York: Arno Press, 1969), 449–462, 613–620.

56. Pancake, *This Destructive War*, 118–120; Isaac Shelby, "Battle of King's Mountain" (1823), 6, reprinted in Draper, *King's Mountain;* Morrill, *Southern Campaigns*, 101–113.

57. Robert D. Bass, *Gamecock: The Life and Campaigns of General Thomas Sumter* (New York: Holt, Rinehart, and Winston, 1961), 98–99.

58. Waring, *Fighting Elder*, 49–50.

59. Ibid., 111–119.

60. Theodore G. Thayer, *Nathanael Greene: Strategist of the American Revolution* (New York: Twayne, 1960), 329.

61. Pancake, *This Destructive War*, 217.

62. JCC 21 (1781), 829–831. For a discussion of British recruitment of American prisoners, see Philip Ranlet, "British Recruitment of Americans in New York during the American Revolution," *Military Affairs* 48 (January 1984): 26–28.

63. "General Orders," 4 October 1781, 23:171; "General Orders," 3 November 1781, 23:320–323; both in Washington, *Writings*. The second contains a summary of the courts-martial of American deserters captured during the surrender of Yorktown. Nine were hanged, fourteen were given 100 lashes, and three were granted POW status.

64. Washington to Nathanael Greene, 24 October 1781, 23:260–261; Washington to Greene, 31 October 1781, 23:311, both in Washington, *Writings*. Washington recommended that sailors captured by American privateers be exchanged for privateers held by the British.

65. Washington to the President of Congress, 18 February 1782, 24:4–6; Washington to the President of Congress, 20 February 1782, 24:9–12; "Instructions to Brigadier General Henry Knox and Gouverneur Morris," 11 March 1782, 24:55–59; all in Washington, *Writings.* Washington complained that privateers were releasing prisoners rather than delivering them to Continental control, and forbade Knox and Morris from agreeing to any exchange of British soldiers for American seamen.

66. Washington to Moses Rawlings, 12 December 1781, Washington, *Writings,* 23:383–384. For a comparison of the German and British prisoners in Pennsylvania and how they were perceived by the American inhabitants of the area, see Laura L. Becker, "Prisoners of War in the American Revolution: A Community Perspective," *Military Affairs* 46 (December 1982): 169–173.

67. JCC 21 (1781), 1150–1151; JCC 22 (1782), 76–77.

68. JCC 23 (1782), 463–464, 606–608, 852–853. Washington to Benjamin Lincoln, 18 August 1782, 25:35–37; Washington to the President of Congress, 28 August 1782, 25:72; both in Washington, *Writings.* While serving as a minister to France, Franklin took great interest in the situation of American prisoners, particularly those held in Britain. On his own initiative, he repeatedly attempted to negotiate exchange cartels, with no more success than Washington's representatives in America. For a complete description of Franklin's efforts, see Catherine M. Prelinger, "Benjamin Franklin and the American Prisoners of War in England during the American Revolution," *William and Mary Quarterly* 32 (April 1975): 261–294.

69. Washington to the President of Congress, 28 August 1782, Washington, *Writings,* 25:72; JCC 22 (1782), 76–77, 154–156.

70. JCC 22 (1782), 178, 372–373.

71. JCC 22 (1782), 274–276.

72. JCC 22 (1782), 321, 372–373.

73. JCC 22 (1782), 323–324, 335–336, 337.

74. JCC 22 (1782), 343–344.

75. JCC 23 (1782), 373–374, 785.

76. JCC 23 (1782), 555–559.

77. JCC 22 (1782), 421–422; JCC 23 (1782), 555–559.

78. JCC 23 (1782), 660–661.

79. JCC 23 (1782), 661.

80. JCC 23 (1782), 713.

81. JCC 23 (1782), 848.

82. JCC 24 (1783), 140.

83. JCC 24 (1783), 184.

84. JCC 24 (1783), 958, 959–960.

85. Washington to Gebhard, 1 July 1783, Washington, *Writings,* 27:41.

CHAPTER 2: THE FIRST DECLARED WAR

1. Department of the Treasury, "Copies of Marshals Accounts, Accounts of James Prince, Marshal for Prisoners, Massachusetts, 1812–1815," Entry 315, Record Group (RG) 217.

2. W. B. Irish to John Mason, 10 April 1814, no document number, Box 8, Entry 127, RG 94. Michael McClary to James Monroe, 15 October 1812, Document 42, and Michael McClary to James Monroe, 27 November 1812; both in Box 15, Entry 127, RG 94. McClary to Stephen Pleasonton, 17 November 1817, no document number, Box 15, Entry 127, RG 94.

3. For a thorough list of detention facilities, see Anthony Dietz, "The Prisoner of War in the United States during the War of 1812" (Ph.D. diss., American University, 1964), 145–149.

4. The only American diplomatic effort involving prisoners of war before 1812 was the Treaty of Amity and Commerce, signed by the United States and Prussia in 1785, which contained provisions regarding the treatment of prisoners in the event of a future conflict between the nations. The British often sought to apply precedents from the Napoleonic wars to the conflict with the United States but had only limited success.

5. Dietz, "Prisoner of War"; *U.S. Statutes at Large* 2 (1806): 359–371. Works discussing the War of 1812 have long considered the POW issue to be of minimal importance. The following works do not mention prisoners, even when discussing the Treaty of Ghent: Henry Adams, *The War of 1812* (New York: Charles Scribner's Sons, 1891); John R. Elting, *Amateurs, to Arms! A Military History of the War of 1812* (Chapel Hill, N.C.: Algonquin Books, 1991); J. C. A. Stagg, *Mr. Madison's War: Politics, Diplomacy, and Warfare in the Early American Republic, 1783–1830* (Princeton, N.J.: Princeton University Press, 1983); James Ripley Jacobs and Glenn Tucker, *The War of 1812: A Compact History* (New York: Hawthorn Books, 1969); Francis F. Beirne, *The War of 1812* (New York: E. P. Dutton, 1949); Reginald Horsman, *The War of 1812* (New York: Alfred A. Knopf, 1969); Alfred Thayer Mahan, *Sea Power in Its Relations to the War of 1812*, 2 vols. (Boston: Little, Brown, 1905); Harrison Bird, *War for the West, 1790–1813* (New York: Oxford University Press, 1971); and Robin Reilly, *The British at the Gates: The New Orleans Campaign in the War of 1812* (New York: G. P. Putnam's Sons, 1974). One rare exception is Donald R. Hickey, *The War of 1812: A Forgotten Conflict* (Urbana: University of Illinois Press, 1989), 175–180. Another monograph containing a detailed discussion of prisoner issues is Allan Everest's *The War of 1812 in the Champlain Valley*, but like Hickey, it focuses primarily on diplomatic activities concerned with the fate of a few prisoners of war, rather than the situation of all prisoners or American policy toward British prisoners in general. Allan S. Everest, *The War of 1812 in the Champlain Valley* (Syracuse, N.Y.: Syracuse University Press, 1981), 79–86.

6. Both unused and used forms of this type can be found in Box 18, Entry 127, RG 94. The forms were used with varying success by individual marshals, some of whom took no interest in the matter, while others kept meticulous records.

7. For a more thorough discussion of the British argument and the American legal response, see Ralph Robinson, "Retaliation for the Treatment of Prisoners in the War of 1812," *American Historical Review* 49 (October 1943): 65–70; Rising Lake Morrow, "The Early American Attitude toward Naturalized Americans Abroad," *American Journal of International Law* 30 (October 1936): 647–663. In a case study

of naval vessels at New York Station, Christopher McKee has found that more than half of the enlisted personnel in January 1808 were not born in the United States. Christopher McKee, "Foreign Seamen in the United States Navy: A Census of 1808," *William and Mary Quarterly* 42 (July 1985): 383–393.

8. Hickey, *War of 1812*, 11–16. For a discussion of the diplomatic importance of the affair, see Anthony Steel, "Impressment in the Monroe-Pinkney Negotiation, 1806–1807," *American Historical Review* 57 (January 1952): 352–369. See also Lawrence S. Kaplan, "Jefferson, the Napoleonic Wars, and the Balance of Power," *William and Mary Quarterly* 14 (April 1957): 196–217. For more detailed discussions of impressments and the *Chesapeake-Leopard* Affair, consult Daniel A. Frater, "Impressment in the 18th Century Anglo-American World" (master's thesis, Queens College, New York, 1995); Scott Thomas Jackson, "Impressment and Anglo-American Discord, 1787–1818" (Ph.D. diss., University of Michigan, 1976); David Scott Thompson, "'This Crying Enormity': Impressment as a Factor in Anglo-American Foreign Relations" (master's thesis, Portland State University, 1993); and James F. Zimmerman, *Impressment of American Seamen* (New York: Columbia University Press, 1966). Bradford Perkins has argued that the actual number of British sailors aboard the *Chesapeake* may have been as high as 150. Bradford Perkins, "George Canning, Great Britain, and the United States, 1807–1809," *American Historical Review* 63 (October 1957): 4; Anthony Steel, "Anthony Merry and the Anglo-American Dispute about Impressment, 1803–6," *Cambridge Historical Journal* 9, no. 3 (1949): 331–351.

9. Thomas Barclay to Stephen Decatur, 17 May 1813, and Decatur to Barclay, both in Document 4, Box 12, Entry 127, RG 94. Barclay complained that British prisoners served aboard several American ships, some of which were vessels of war.

10. Thomas Barclay to John Mason, 13 July 1813, Document 169, Box 6, Entry 127, RG 94.

11. Although all prisoners were delivered to the control of the War Department, specifically the Commissary General of Prisons and Prisoners, some of the most detailed records of British prisoners taken during the war can be found in records maintained by the Navy Department. Unlike the army, the navy preserved a complete list of all British POWs held in the United States, compiled in 1818 using the scattered records that existed at the time. A two-volume list of prisoners was created, organized by the first letter of the prisoner's last name. Each entry contained the prisoner's full name, when and where the prisoner was captured, where the prisoner was held, his rank and unit, the capturing unit, and the date and method of disposal. Navy Department, "Register of British POWs in the United States, July 1812–March 1815, v. 1," Entry 402, RG 45. See also Navy Department, "Military and Naval Prisoners Canadian Frontier," Document 300, Box 18, Entry 127, RG 94. This roster contains the name, rank, unit, capturing party, date of capture, custody location, and manner of disposal for each prisoner and is organized in a vaguely alphabetical fashion.

12. Winfield Scott to the Secretary of War, 30 January 1813, Document 10, Box 1, Entry 127A, RG 94; Henry Kelly to John Armstrong, 2 July 1813, Document 24, Box 1, Entry 127B, RG 94.

13. Navy Department, "List of 23 British Soldiers Held by the United States of

America, as Hostages for 23 American Soldiers Sent to England for Trial," n.d., Document 298, Box 18, Entry 127, RG 94. See also Navy Department, "List of 39 British officers, Prisoners of War," 28 February 1814, Document 299, Box 18, Entry 127, RG 94. By the time this list had been made, four officers had already escaped custody. Navy Department, "Descriptive List of Twenty Three Hostages, British Prisoners of War to the United States," 12 August 1814, no document number, Box 18, Entry 127, RG 94. This contains physical descriptions and biographical data for each hostage prisoner. One confinement order issued by the British is found in George Glasgow to Winchester, 29 October 1813, no document number, Box 19, Entry 127, RG 94. This particular order placed forty-six officers and NCOs in close confinement as hostages against the safety of twenty-three British soldiers in similar confinement. Not all of the hostages were forced to remain in close confinement. Officers of both sides were often allowed to give their parole in exchange for a certain degree of liberty, most commonly remaining under house arrest. "Sworn statement of Brigadier General William H. Winder to remain in a certain house and area of Beaufort," 17 December 1813, Document 295, Box 18, Entry 127, RG 94. Other such statements exist for officers of lower ranks at the same location; they were usually dependent on the attitude of the confining officer. Similar considerations were given to British officers held by American captors.

14. *American State Papers: Foreign Relations*, 3:726–730. Well after the conclusion of the war, the issue of the "Irish traitors" remained unsettled. In a brief letter to Winfield Scott, Stephen Pleasonton of the Treasury Department vowed that if the men taken for trial by Great Britain had not received the rations due to all prisoners by the Cartel of 12 May, the Treasury Department would seek redress for the prisoners in question from the government of Great Britain. General Scott was assured that the topic would be introduced at the upcoming conference to discuss the costs associated with prisoner upkeep on each side. Stephen Pleasonton to Winfield Scott, 11 July 1817, Document 185, Box 10, Entry 127, RG 94; Robinson, "Retaliation," 69–70.

15. Thomas Barclay to John Mason, 9 August 1814, Document 3, Box 12, Entry 127, RG 94.

16. John Mason to James Prince, 28 September 1814, Document 34, Box 19, Entry 127, RG 94.

17. James Prince to Caleb Strong, 4 February 1814, Document 33, Box 19, Entry 127, RG 94, and James Prince to John Mason, 4 February 1814, Document 32, Box 19, Entry 127, RG 94.

18. Anthony Walsh to Thomas Barclay, 12 April 1814, Document 26, Box 10, Entry 127, RG 94.

19. John Smith to John Mason, 29 April 1814, no document number, Box 16, Entry 127, RG 94.

20. "Cartel for the exchange of prisoners of war between Great Britain and the United States of America," 12 May 1813, Document 190, Box 10, Entry 127, RG 94. The rank equivalencies established by the cartel were as follows: commanding general, 60 enlisted men; major general, 40 men; brigadier general, 20 men; colonel, 15 men; lieutenant colonel, 10 men; major, 8 men; captain, 6 men; lieutenant, 4 men; NCOs,

2 men, and enlisted personnel on a man-for-man basis. See also "Equivalent rank according to the Cartel of the 12th of May," Document 43, Box 18, Entry 127, RG 94. This item, a small card, appears to have been a reference sheet for American officers who might be in a situation allowing an exchange.

21. Captures at sea, Detroit, and Queenston quickly gave the British a numerical advantage in prisoners held that was maintained throughout the war. *Annals of Congress,* 13th Cong., 1st sess., 1804–1807.

22. John Graham, "Account of the Exchange," 22 December 1812, Document 322, Box 19, Entry 127, RG 94. In the exchange, the Americans consisted of 1 brigadier general, 3 colonels, 4 lieutenant colonels, 1 major, 10 captains, 1 lieutenant, and 2 second lieutenants, for a total rank equivalency of 185 privates. The exchanged British consisted of 3 lieutenants, 9 sergeants, 6 corporals, 2 drummers, and 139 privates, for an equal exchange value. See also George Barton to John Mason, 10 December 1814, no document number, Box 2, Entry 127, RG 94. Barton, an appointed agent of the British government, requested that Mason loan his office the returns of all district marshals under Mason to create a master list of all prisoners taken throughout the war. Such a master list was not finished until 9 May 1818 and was completed under the direction of the Navy Department. For orders regarding the creation of the list, see T. T. Gantle, "Copy of Circular to the Marshals of the United States," 22 August 1815, Document 38, Box 1, Entry 127A, RG 94, and R. Rush, "Circular," 8 May 1817, Document 40, Box 1, Entry 127A, RG 94.

23. "Cartel for the exchange of prisoners," Articles 8–14, quotation from Article 14.

24. John Mason to Thomas Barclay, 10 November 1813, Document 88, Box 17, Entry 127, RG 94.

25. Thomas William Moore to John Graham, 17 February 1813, Document 77, Box 18, Entry 127, RG 94, has an example of such a request, in this case hoping that Lieutenant Heyman, confined in Petersburg, Va., could be sent to Bermuda via the cartel ship *Bostock*, recently arrived in New York with 400 American prisoners for exchange. Another example is found in Thomas Barclay to John Mason, 7 December 1813, Document 82, Box 6, Entry 127, RG 94. For a more uncommon example, see Joseph Bloomfield to Richard Bache, no document number, Box 5, Entry 127, RG 94, in which President Madison ordered the release of certain British officers to the nearest British outpost on Lake Champlain.

26. John Mason to Thomas Barclay, 22 December 1813, Document 93, Box 17, Entry 127, RG 94.

27. In one interesting case, James Monroe wrote to the marshal of Boston requesting the discharge of five Russian sailors, who were taken on board the British merchant vessel the *Mary* and held captive in Boston. Monroe ordered the marshal to deliver these unnamed sailors to the Russian consul in exchange for a declaration of Russian citizenship for the men, to avoid any unpleasant consequences from the Russian empire. James Monroe to the Marshal of the U.S., 17 September 1812, Document 4, Box 20, Entry 127, RG 94; "Cartel for the exchange of prisoners," Article 3.

28. "Cartel for the exchange of prisoners," Articles 5–7.

29. For an example of such an application, see Winslow Lewis to John Mason, 23 November 1814, no document number, Box 611, Entry 464A, RG 45. Lewis served in the capacity of "Agent for the private armed schooner David Porter," in this case demanding $200 for the delivery of two prisoners. See also J. Pleasonton to John Mason, 3 December 1814, no document number, Box 611, E 464A, RG 45, referring to receipts for nine prisoners delivered to different marshals, all captured by the privateer *Sabine.* See also John Mason to the Secretary of the Treasury, 17 December 1814, no document number, Box 611, Entry 464A, RG 45; John Mason to John Gooding, 6 December 1814, no document number, Box 611, Entry 464A, RG 45. Gooding, a lawyer, had requested Mason to release the brother of his client, David McCaughan, after having the vessel *Sabine* relinquish its claim to a bounty. Mason refused the request, on the grounds that to grant it would force an American citizen to remain in captivity who could be exchanged for the prisoner.

30. The allegations of mistreatment are found in Thomas Wake to William J. P. Nicholls, 19 October 1813, Document 311, Box 19, Entry 127, RG 94. The positive testimony is found in the testimonial of E. K. Lindo, Charleston, 27 October 1813, no document number, Box 19, Entry 127, RG 94.

31. Michael McClary to John Mason, 21 February 1814, Document 17, Box 15, Entry 127, RG 94.

32. Lawrence Williams to John Mason, 23 February 1814, Document 58, Box 12, Entry 127, RG 94. Williams, the Deputy Marshal of Ohio, had ordered the investigation one month earlier.

33. Navy Department, "Register of British POWs in the United States, July 1812–March 1815, v. 1," Entry 402, RG 45.

34. John Mason to Anthony St. John Baker, 18 July 1815, Document 212, Box 11A, Entry 127, RG 94. Mason claimed that the United States retained no "blacks or people of colour" captured during the war with the exception of former slaves, who were returned to captivity upon capture. See also John Mason to Secretary of the Treasury, 17 December 1814, no document number, Box 611, E 464A, RG 45.

35. Thomas Barclay to John Mason, 3 July 1813, no document number, Box 6, Entry 127, RG 94; Thomas Barclay to John Mason, 19 July 1813, no document number, Box 6, Entry 127, RG 94.

36. James Dick to Anthony Thomas Baker, 17 July 1815, Document 30, Box 8, Entry 127, RG 94, and Morton A. Waring to John Mason, 24 August 1815, which includes South Carolina District Court finding of John Drayton, 24 August 1815, Document 31, Box 8, Entry 127, RG 94.

37. Arnett G. Lindsay, "Diplomatic Relations between the United States and Great Britain Bearing on the Return of Negro Slaves, 1783–1828," *Journal of Negro History* 5 (October 1920): 391–419.

38. Joseph Bowen and eight other soldiers to Colonel Lewis, 28 March 1814, Document 3, Box 19, Entry 127, RG 94. For more information on the surrender of Fort Dearborn, see Milo M. Quaife, "The Fort Dearborn Massacre," *Missouri Valley Historical Review* 1 (March 1915): 561–573; Robert S. Quimby, *The U.S. Army in the War of 1812: An Operational and Command Study*, 2 vols. (East Lansing: Michigan

State University Press, 1997), 1:137–138; John K. Mahon, *The War of 1812* (Gainesville: University of Florida Press, 1972), 130–131. Roger Vose to John Mason, 15 February 1814; John Graham to John Mason, 10 November 1813; Lewis Cass to the Secretary of War, 21 October 1813; all found in Document 4, Box 1, Entry 127A, RG 94.

39. John R. Boyd to Francis Rottenburgh, 25 August 1813, no document number, Box 4, Entry 127, RG 94; John R. Boyd to Francis Rottenburgh, 13 August 1813, no document number, Box 4, Entry 127, RG 94; Rottenburgh, to John R. Boyd, 23 August 1813, no document number, Box 4, Entry 127, RG 94.

40. John R. Boyd to Francis Rottenburgh, 4 September 1813, no document number, Box 4, Entry 127, RG 94.

41. Thomas Barclay to John Mason, 1 February 1814, Document 69, Box 12, Entry 127, RG 94. For an examination of British exchange policies of the eighteenth century, see Olive Anderson, "The Establishment of British Supremacy at Sea and the Exchange of Naval Prisoners of War, 1689–1783," *English Historical Review* 75 (January 1960): 77–89. Anderson argues that British policy was to refuse mass exchanges unless the Royal Navy faced an extreme need for manpower, and to ignore agreements to exchange prisoners when it was to Britain's advantage to refuse exchanges. See also Thomas Barclay to John Mason, 13 July 1813, no document number, Box 6, Entry 127, RG 94.

42. George Barton to John Mason, 8 March 1815, no document number, Box 2, Entry 127, RG 94. See also George Barton to John Mason, 29 June 1815, no document number, Box 2, Entry 127, RG 94.

43. "Rules and Regulations," Frederick Town, Md., 14 September 1814, Document 4, Box 11A, Entry 127, RG 94.

44. Ibid.

45. Ibid.

46. In one interesting case, two hostage prisoners of war requested that "Major Melville [the American deputy marshal of Pittsfield, Mass.] will accept the tribute of their unfeigned acknowledgement for the very Gentlemanly & humane treatment which Major Melville has uniformly manifested towards them in the exercise of his official duties as Marshal and Agent of Prisoners of War." "Testimonial of Lt. Col. Grant and Major Powell (Hostage Prisoners of War)," 8 May 1814, no document number, Box 20, Entry 127, RG 94. Grant also wrote a personal letter to Major Melville attesting that Pittsfield prison was well kept, and requesting that Melville continue to act as the POW agent for British prisoners confined at the prison; C. W. Grant to Thomas Melville, 7 May 1814, Document 48, Box 20, Entry 127, RG 94. Another testimonial to Melville's conduct, written by six officers confined at Pittsfield, was sent to Thomas M. Moore, Agent for British Prisoners of War, 12 December 1813, no document number, Box 20, Entry 127, RG 94. See also Thomas Melville to George Prevost, 7 January 1815, Document 112, Box 20, Entry 127, RG 94, and Thomas Melville to George Prevost, 7 January 1815, Document 113, Box 20, Entry 127, RG 94.

47. Thomas Melville, "Abstract of Supplies made and to be made to British Prisoners of War," 27 November 1814, no document number, Box 20, Entry 127, RG 94. The total spent on "Supplies made" for rations was $14,655.75, and allotted for

"Supplies making by Approximations" for clothing was $19,827.30. One excellent example of these requests can be found in Thomas Melville to George Prevost, 24 November 1814, requesting the sum of $7,500 and reiterating a request for $16,000, placed in an earlier correspondence, no document number, Box 20, Entry 127, RG 94. Thomas Melville to Elisha Jenkins, 13 July 1813, Document 114, Entry 127, Box 4, RG 94.

48. Elisha Jenkins to John Armstrong, 13 July 1813, no document number, Box 4, Entry 127, RG 94.

49. John Mitchell to John Cochet, 15 September 1814; Mitchell to Cochet, 16 September 1814; Cochet to Mitchell, 17 September 1814, no document numbers, Box 7, Entry 127, RG 94; Hickey, *War of 1812*, 177.

50. "Copy of Sir George Prevost's proposition," 25 January 1814, no document number, Box 14, Entry 127, RG 94; Anderson, "Establishment of British Supremacy."

51. Jesse Williamson to Sutherland and Grant, 26 March 1815, Document 4, Box 13, Entry 127, RG 94. The document contains a bill for the cost of rations provided to American prisoners, with a daily tally of prisoners present and rations issued. The bill was to be paid by the United States to Williamson, the "United States Agent for the Exchange of American Prisoners of War."

52. "Convention between Brigadier General W. H. Winder and Colonel Edward Baynes on the part of Sir George Prevost," 15 April 1814, no document number, Box 10, Entry 127, RG 94; "Colonel Lear's Amendments to the foregoing made and confirmed July 16th, 1814," 16 July 1814, no document number, Box 10, Entry 127, RG 94; "Brigadier General W. H. Winder's Convention," 15 April 1814; "Colonel T. Lear's Amendments to Brigadier General W. H. Winder's Convention," 16 July 1814, Document 26, Box 1, Entry 127A, RG 94. See also Robinson, "Retaliation," 68–69. See Anderson, "Establishment of British Supremacy," for a discussion of the rarity of a complete exchange involving British forces.

53. Disslissis [spelling unclear] to John Mason, 24 March 1815, Document 41, Box 15, Entry 127, RG 94.

54. Robert Gardner, "Examination of British Deserters," 30 August 1814, no document number, Box 19, Entry 127, RG 94. The examination estimated that 6,000 British troops had attacked, including 4 regiments of infantry, 1,000 marines, 200 sailors, and a rocket company of 40 men, supported by only two or three small fieldpieces.

55. Ebenezer Learned, "Public Instrument of Protest," 9 June 1815, Documents 25–30, Box 5, Entry 127, RG 94.

56. For more on the Dartmoor prison riot, see Charles King to J. Q. Adams, 26 April 1815, Document 77, Box 9, Entry 127, RG 94, and Charles King and Francis Seymour Larpent, "Report on the Investigation at Dartmoor Prison," 26 April 1815, Document 18, Box 9, Entry 127, RG 94. See also Charles Andrews, *The Prisoners' Memoirs or Dartmoor Prison* (New York: Self-Published, 1815); *Horrid Massacre at Dartmoor Prison* (Boston: Nathaniel Conerly, 1815); Reginald Horsman, "The Paradox of Dartmoor Prison," *American Heritage* 26 (February 1975): 13–17; John Melish, *A Description of Dartmoor Prison, with an Account of the Massacre of the Prison* (Philadelphia: Self-Published, 1815).

57. Thomas Barclay to John Mason, 26 May 1814, no document number, Box 6, Entry 127, RG 94.

58. Treasury Department, "Statement of the appropriations for the safe keeping & accommodation etc. of prisoners of war," n.d., no document number, Box 18, Entry 127, RG 94. Beyond the initial appropriations, the statement contains the total bills presented by individual marshals, the cost of cartel ships, and the interest due on treasury notes used to finance the care of prisoners.

59. George Barton to John Mason, 27 February 1815, no document number, Box 7, Entry 127, RG 94.

CHAPTER 3: PRISONERS ON FOREIGN SOIL

1. Antonio Lopez de Santa Anna, *The Eagle: The Autobiography of Santa Anna*, ed. Ann Fears Crawford (Austin: Pemberton Press, 1967), 51–56.

2. Will Fowler, *Santa Anna of Mexico* (Lincoln: University of Nebraska Press, 2007), 167–168.

3. James L. Morrison Jr., *"The Best School in the World": West Point, the Pre–Civil War Years, 1833–1866* (Kent, Ohio: Kent State University Press, 1986), 91–93.

4. Quote is in Michael Howard, George J. Andreopoulos, and Mark R. Shulman, eds., *The Laws of War: Constraints on Warfare in the Western World* (New Haven, Conn.: Yale University Press, 1994), 88; see also Alfred Vagts, *A History of Militarism*, rev. ed. (New York: Meridian Books, 1959), 113–114; John A. Lynn, *The Bayonets of the Republic: Motivation and Tactics in the Army of Revolutionary France, 1791–94* (Urbana: University of Illinois Press, 1984), 97–118.

5. For a description of one of the worst continental prison compounds of the war, see Denis Smith, *The Prisoners of Cabrera: Napoleon's Forgotten Soldiers, 1809–1814* (New York: Four Walls Eight Windows, 2001). For French prisoners in Britain, see Gavin Daly, "Napoleon's Lost Legions: French Prisoners of War in Britain, 1803–1814," *History* 89 (July 2004): 361–380.

6. Joe Knetsch, *Florida's Seminole Wars, 1817–1858* (Charleston, S.C.: Arcadia Publishing, 2003), 40–41.

7. John Missall and Mary Lou Missall, *The Seminole Wars: America's Longest Conflict* (Gainesville: University Press of Florida, 2004), 137–141.

8. Kerry A. Trask, *Black Hawk: The Battle for the Heart of America* (New York: Henry Holt, 2006), 258; Joseph M. Street to Henry Atkinson, 31 July 1832, and Glendower M. Price to Gustavus Loomis, 6 August 1832, both in Ellen M. Whitney, ed., *The Black Hawk War, 1831–1832*, 3 vols. (Springfield: Illinois State Historical Library, 1975), 2:908–909, 2:947–948.

9. Trask, *Black Hawk*, 284–288.

10. Works that ignore or marginalize POWs during the Mexican war include Otis A. Singletary, *The Mexican War* (Chicago: University of Chicago Press, 1960); Horatio O. Ladd, *History of the War with Mexico* (New York: Dodd, Mead, 1882); John Edward Weems, *To Conquer a Peace: The War between the United States and Mexico*

(Garden City, N.Y.: Doubleday, 1974); Cadmus M. Wilcox, *History of the Mexican War* (Washington, D.C.: Church News Publishing, 1892); Philip Berry, *A Review of the Mexican War on Christian Principles* (New York: J. S. Ozer, 1849); John Porter Bloom, "With the American Army into Mexico, 1846–1848" (Ph.D. diss., Emory University, 1956); Robert S. Ripley, *The War with Mexico*, 2 vols. (New York: Harper and Brothers, 1849); and George G. Lewis and John Mewha, *History of Prisoner of War Utilization by the United States Army, 1776–1945* (Washington, D.C.: Government Printing Office, 1955), 25–26.

11. For examples, see Robert Ryal Miller, *The Mexican War Journal and Letters of Ralph W. Kirkham* (College Station: Texas A&M University Press, 1991); Frederick Zeh, *An Immigrant Soldier in the Mexican War*, ed. William J. Orr and Robert Ryal Miller (College Station: Texas A&M University Press, 1995); and Robert Ryal Miller, *Shamrock and Sword: The Saint Patrick's Battalion in the U.S.-Mexican War* (Norman: University of Oklahoma Press, 1989).

12. George Wilkins Kendall, *Dispatches from the Mexican War*, ed. Lawrence Delbert Cress (Norman: University of Oklahoma Press, 1999), 382–388.

13. One example of this relationship is contained in Randy W. Hackenburg, *Pennsylvania in the War with Mexico* (Shippensburg, Pa.: White Mane, 1992), 40, 54–55. The 2nd Pennsylvania Regiment was detailed to guard prisoners captured at Cerro Gordo and was not included in the Battle of Molino del Rey because of its guard duties. Contemporary accounts within the work suggest the soldiers of the guarding regiment were frustrated by not being allowed to join in the assault on the city and viewed guard duty as something of a punishment detail. In each case, the guard duty lasted a few days at most because prisoners at each location were paroled en masse.

14. Santa Anna maintained through his autobiography and other sources that he had not ordered the executions, which he regarded as Urrea's responsibility. See Santa Anna, *Eagle*, 51–52; Fowler, *Santa Anna*, 167–168.

15. Margaret Swett Henson, "Politics and the Treatment of the Mexican Prisoners after the Battle of San Jacinto," *Southwestern Historical Quarterly* 94 (October 1990): 193.

16. Ibid., 189–190. Santa Anna left in December 1836, when he was sent to Washington, D.C., to discuss the question of Texan independence with Andrew Jackson. See also Kenneth Rueben Durham Jr., *Santa Anna: Prisoner of War in Texas* (Paris, Tex.: Wright Press, 1986), 63–91.

17. William Preston Stapp, *The Prisoners of Perote*, ed. Joe B. Frantz (Austin: University of Texas Press, 1978), xviii. For two other works describing the Texan prisoners held at Perote, see Joseph D. McCutchan, *Mier Expedition Diary: A Texan Prisoner's Account*, ed. Joseph Milton Nance (Austin: University of Texas Press, 1978); and Samuel H. Walker, *Samuel H. Walker's Account of the Mier Expedition*, ed. Marilyn McAdams Sibley (Austin: Texas State Historical Association, 1978). For a discussion of the expeditions from the Mexican perspective, see M. A. Sanchez Lamego, *The Second Mexican-Texas War 1841–1843* (Hillsboro, Tex.: Texian Press, 1972).

18. Sam W. Haynes, *Soldiers of Misfortune: The Somervell and Mier Expeditions* (Austin: University of Texas Press, 1990), 123–127.

19. Stanley Siegel, *A Political History of the Texas Republic, 1836–1845* (Austin: University of Texas Press, 1956), 214, 217; Stapp, *Prisoners*, xix.

20. Stephen B. Oates, "Los Diablos Tejanos!," *American West* 2 (Summer 1945): 44–50; Walker, *Mier Expedition*, 10.

21. Taylor to the AG, 26 April 1846; Taylor to the AG, 3 May 1846; Thornton to W. W. S. Bliss, 27 April 1846; W. T. Hardee to Taylor, 26 April 1846; all found in *Messages of the President on the Subject of the Mexican* War, 30th Cong., 1st Sess., 1848, H. Exec. Doc. 60, Serial 520, 288–292. Hereafter cited as H. Doc. 60.

22. Taylor to the AG, 12 May 1846, H. Doc. 60, 297. The officers sent to New Orleans included General La Vega and a few members of his staff.

23. Marcy to Taylor, 9 July 1846, H. Doc. 60, 333.

24. Ibid.

25. Ibid., 334.

26. Ibid., 333.

27. Zachary Taylor to James K. Polk, 1 August 1846, H. Doc. 60, 336–338.

28. Mark E. Nackman, "The Making of the Texan Citizen Soldier, 1835–1860," *Southwestern Historical Quarterly* 78 (January 1975): 243.

29. Frank S. Edwards, *A Campaign in New Mexico with Colonel Doniphan* (Philadelphia: Carey and Hart, 1847), 155.

30. Zachary Taylor to the AG, 16 June 1847, H. Doc. 60, 1178.

31. Taylor to Ampudia, 24 September 1846, H. Doc. 60, 348–349.

32. Robert S. Ripley argues that the final terms of capitulation at Monterrey allowed the garrison to retire to the interior without giving paroles, and that they were not considered POWs. Ripley, *War with Mexico*, 1:237–246.

33. Taylor to Santa Anna, 5 November 1846, and Santa Anna to Taylor, 10 November 1846, H. Doc. 60, 437–438.

34. Ripley, *War with Mexico*, 1:379–380.

35. Hackenburg, *Pennsylvania in the War*, 40. Other estimates place the number captured at Cerro Gordo as high as 6,000 POWs; see J. Jacob Oswandel, *Notes of the Mexican War, 1846–47–48* (Philadelphia, 1885), 129; Miller, *Mexican War Journal*, 4; Kendall, *Dispatches*, 212. Cress notes that the official U.S. count was 199 officers and 2,837 enlisted men taken prisoner, and that another 1,000 POWs probably escaped U.S. custody before they could be processed.

36. Miller, *Shamrock*, 92. Miller's number of prisoners is supported by other sources, such as Kendall, *Dispatches*, 332, 343–344.

37. Miller, *Mexican War Journal*, 52.

38. W. L. Marcy to Winfield Scott, 21 April 1848, H. Doc. 60, 1233. Marcy cites a previous letter from himself to Scott, in which the president ordered Scott to end the parole of Mexican officers.

39. Ripley, *War with Mexico*, 2:160–161.

40. Hackenburg, *Pennsylvania in the War*, 54.

41. Miller, *Shamrock*, 114. Kendall puts the number captured at nearly 1,000 men, including 53 officers. See Kendall, *Dispatches*, 372–376.

42. Kendall lists the ranks and numbers of prisoners taken, including 5 generals,

3 colonels, and 100 lower-grade officers, with 800 enlisted personnel. Kendall, *Dispatches*, 387–388.

43. Arthur D. Howden Smith, *Old Fuss and Feathers: The Life and Exploits of Lt.-General Winfield Scott* (New York: Greystone Press, 1937), 271.

44. Henry W. Halleck, *International Law; or, Rules Regulating the Intercourse of States in Peace and War* (New York: D. Van Nostrand, 1861), 438–439.

45. Miller, *Shamrock*, 122.

46. Ibid.; Bauer, *The Mexican War*, 336–337.

47. Miller, *Shamrock*, 128.

48. Peter F. Stevens, *The Rogue's March: John Riley and the St. Patrick's Battalion* (Washington, D.C.: Brassey's, 1999), 2–3. In particular, the Irish were viewed as likely deserters. Approximately 20 percent of Irish soldiers deserted during the war.

49. General Orders No. 187, Puebla, 24 June 1847, found in Vol. 22, Entry 134, RG 94.

50. Werner H. Marti, *Messenger of Destiny: The California Adventures, 1846–1847 of Archibald H. Gillespie* (San Francisco: John Howell Books, 1960), 82–83.

51. James A. Crutchfield, *Tragedy at Taos: The Revolt of 1847* (Plano: Republic of Texas Press, 1995), 129–132, 135–147.

52. Philip Berry, *A Review of the Mexican War* (Columbia, S.C.: A. S. Johnston, 1849), 35.

53. Ripley, *War with Mexico*, 2:82.

54. Halleck, *International Law*, 438–439.

CHAPTER 4: BROTHER AGAINST BROTHER

1. William Hoffman to the Assistant Adjutant-General, 1 March 1861; General Orders No. 34, Department of the Gulf, 25 April 1863, both in U.S. War Department, *The War of the Rebellion: A Compilation of the Official Records of the Union and Confederate Armies*, 127 vols. (Washington, D.C.: Government Printing Office, 1880–1901), ser. 2, 1:10–12, 1:104. All references to this text will use the common designation OR, and all references are to series 2 unless otherwise noted. War Department (WD), General Orders No. 34, includes a summary of the surrender of all federal forces in Texas.

2. William Hoffman to the Adjutant-General, 14 November 1861, OR, 1:67.

3. Judah P. Benjamin to Benjamin Huger, 23 January 1862, OR, 1:98–99. See also John E. Wool to Benjamin Huger, 27 January 1862, OR, 1:78; William Hoffman to Edwin M. Stanton, 13 March 1862, OR, 1:81–82; Robert E. Lee to Benjamin Huger, 31 March 1862, OR, 1:102–103; John E. Wool to Benjamin Huger, 1 April 1862, OR, 1:86.

4. Montgomery C. Meigs to Simon Cameron, 3 October 1861, OR, 3:48; Special Orders No. 284, War Department, 23 October 1861, OR, 3:121.

5. Of the 674,000 prisoners taken, 462,634 were Confederates and 211,411 were federals. A total of 247,769 Confederates were paroled on the battlefield, as were 16,688 federals, leaving 214,865 Confederates and 194,743 federals held in captivity.

Lonnie R. Speer, *Portals to Hell: Military Prisons of the Civil War* (Mechanicsburg, Pa.: Stackpole Books, 1997), 341.

6. No discussion of Civil War POWs is complete without a thorough examination of the U.S. War Department's *The War of the Rebellion.* These volumes contain a record of letters, pronouncements, and orders organized chronologically and seek to draw together as much information about the war as was then possible. A full eight volumes, the entire second series of the set is devoted to prisoners of war.

7. Asa B. Isham, Henry M. Davidson, and Henry B. Furness, *Prisoners of War and Military Prisons* (Cincinnati: Lyman & Cushing, 1890), 475–476.

8. William Best Hesseltine, *Civil War Prisons: A Study in War Psychology* (Columbus: Ohio State University Press, 1930), ix.

9. Speer, *Portals,* xviii–xix.

10. Ibid., xix.

11. Charles W. Sanders Jr., *While in the Hands of the Enemy: Military Prisons of the Civil War* (Baton Rouge: Louisiana State University Press, 2005), 5.

12. A recent trend in Civil War POW historiography is the study of individual prisons. The Confederate prison at Andersonville has been the subject of dozens of works since the end of the war, most either vilifying the camp and its commanders as the worst example of POW mistreatment in the history of American warfare or attempting to defend the overseers of the prison as victims of circumstance who did the best they could with meager resources. For examples, see R. Randolph Stevenson, *The Southern Side; or, Andersonville Prison* (Baltimore: Turnbull Brothers, 1876); Ovid L. Futch, *History of Andersonville Prison* (Gainesville: University of Florida Press, 1968); Peggy Sheppard, *Andersonville, Georgia, USA* (Leslie, Ga.: Sheppard Publications, 1973); Joseph P. Cangemi and Casimir J. Kowalski, eds., *Andersonville Prison: Lessons in Organizational Failure* (Lanham, Md.: University Press of America, 1992); William Marvel, *Andersonville: The Last Depot* (Chapel Hill: University of North Carolina Press, 1994). Other prison camps, Union and Confederate, remained largely neglected until the 1980s and 1990s, when numerous histories of specific camps emerged. For examples, see Louis A. Brown, *The Salisbury Prison: A Case Study of Confederate Military Prisons, 1861–1865* (Baton Rouge: Louisiana State University Press, 1980); Willliam S. Peterson, "A History of Camp Butler, 1861–1866," *Illinois Historical Journal* 82 (Summer 1989): 74–92; Sandra V. Parker, *Richmond's Civil War Prisons* (Lynchburg, Va.: H. E. Howard, 1990); William O. Bryant, *Cahaba Prison and the Sultana Disaster* (Tuscaloosa: University of Alabama Press, 1990); George Levy, *To Die in Chicago: Confederate Prisoners at Camp Douglas, 1862–1865* (Evanston, Ill.: Evanston Publishing, 1994); Benjamin F. Booth, *Dark Days of the Rebellion,* ed. Steve Meyer (Garrison, Iowa: Meyer Publishing, 1995); Michael Horigan, *Elmira: Death Camp of the North* (Mechanicsburg, Pa.: Stackpole Books, 2002); Bryan Temple, *The Union Prison at Fort Delaware: A Perfect Hell on Earth* (Jefferson, N.C.: McFarland, 2003).

13. WD, Special Orders, No. 284, 23 October 1861, OR, 3:121.

14. Montgomery C. Meigs to William Hoffman, 26 October 1861, OR, 3:122–123.

15. WD, General Orders No. 67, 17 June 1862, OR, 4:30.

16. Arch Fredric Blakey, *General John H. Winder, CSA* (Gainesville: University of Florida Press, 1990), 47–48, 56, 196–197; E. J. Warner, *Generals in Gray: Lives of the Confederate Commanders* (Baton Rouge: Louisiana State University Press, 1959), 340–341.

17. Joseph P. Reavis to John Schofield, 30 August 1862, OR, 4:473.

18. J. M. Glover to John Schofield, 18 September 1862, OR, 4:532–539, contains the report of the investigators. No federal officer was punished for the incident.

19. William Hoffman to Peter Zinn, 4 December 1862, Vol. 2, Entry 167, RG 249. Zinn was the commandant of Camp Chase, Ohio.

20. Edwin M. Stanton to John E. Wool, 11 February 1862, OR, 3:254; John E. Wool to Benjamin C. Huger, 13 February 1862, OR, 3:259–260; Benjamin C. Huger to John E. Wool, 20 February 1862, OR, 3:289.

21. John A. Dix to Edwin M. Stanton, 23 July 1862, OR, 4:266–268. Dix's letter to Stanton contains a copy of the cartel.

22. Ibid., 267.

23. Jonathan H. Winder, "Prisoners of War," 16 July 1862, OR, 4:821, contains a tabulation of the number of Union prisoners held in Confederate prison camps in July 1862. "Abstract from monthly returns of the principal U.S. military prisons," OR, 8:987–1004, is a compilation of Union prisoner of war camp reports, providing a tally of the number of Confederate prisoners in the largest camps from July 1862 until November 1865.

24. "Proclamation of the President of the Confederate States," 23 December 1862, contained within WD, CSA, General Orders No. 111, 24 December 1862, OR, 5:905–908.

25. "Joint resolutions adopted by the Confederate Congress on the subject of retaliation April 30–May 1, 1863," OR, 5:940–941.

26. Edmund Kirby Smith to R. Taylor, 13 June 1863, Box 1, Entry 469, RG 109.

27. WD, General Orders No. 252, 31 July 1863, OR, 6:163.

28. Unsigned letter to E. A. Hitchcock, 25 September 1864, Box 2, Entry 149, RG 249.

29. O. O. Poppleton to Benjamin Butler, 5 January 1865, Box 2, Entry 149, RG 249; *Mobile Advertiser and Register*, 16 October 1864. See also *Richmond Examiner*, 11 October 1864, for a list of USCT prisoners to be reclaimed by former owners.

30. Benjamin Butler to Robert Ould, 12 October 1864; sworn testimony of Chapman Dinkins, 12 October 1864; sworn testimony of James F. McKnight, 12 October 1864; all found in Box 2, Entry 149, RG 249.

31. Robert E. Lee to Ulysses S. Grant, 19 October 1864; Ulysses S. Grant to Robert E. Lee, 20 October 1864; both found in Box 2, Entry 149, RG 249.

32. O. O. Poppleton to Benjamin Butler, 21 January 1865, Box 2, Entry 149, RG 249.

33. Henry W. Halleck to Robert E. Lee, 7 December 1863; Robert E. Lee to Henry W. Halleck, 12 December 1863; both in Box 3, Entry 149, RG 249.

34. Hesseltine, *Civil War Prisons*, 227–228.

35. John Ransom, *John Ransom's Andersonville Diary* (1881; reprint, New York:

Berkley Books, 1986), 40–41; John McElroy, *Andersonville: A Story of Rebel Military Prisons* (Toledo, Ohio: D. R. Locke, 1879), 192–195.

36. Entry 73, RG 249, is a list of all prisoners taken at Vicksburg. The surrender included 15 generals, 173 field-grade officers, 1,965 company officers, 3,992 noncommissioned officers, and 23,233 privates.

37. Robert Ould to S. A. Meredith, 20 October 1863; Robert Ould to S. A. Meredith, 27 October 1863; S. A. Meredith to E. A. Hitchcock, 29 October 1863; all in Box 2, Entry 149, RG 249.

38. E. A. Hitchcock to Edwin M. Stanton, 18 March 1864, Box 2, Entry 149, RG 249.

39. Benjamin Butler to Edwin M. Stanton, 3 May 1864, Box 2, Entry 149, RG 249.

40. Charles Alfred Humphreys, *Field, Camp, Hospital and Prison in the Civil War, 1864–1865* (Boston: George H. Ellis, 1918), 133.

41. William Hoffman to E. A. Hitchcock, 5 May 1864, Box 2, Entry 149, RG 249.

42. William Hoffman, "Statement of Federal and Rebel Prisoners of War," 16 April 1864, Box 2, Entry 149, RG 249.

43. Edwin M. Stanton to Robert Murray, 10 July 1862, OR, 4:162–163.

44. William Hoffman to Christian Thieleman, 25 February 1862, OR, 5:297.

45. William Hoffman to Ambrose Burnside, 20 June 1863, OR, 6:31.

46. William Hoffman to H. M. Lazille, 2 August 1863, Entry 16, RG 249.

47. William Hoffman to William S. Rosencrans, 26 August 1863, OR, ser. 3, 3:722; William Hoffman to Rosencrans, 29 August 1863, OR, ser. 3, 3:737–738.

48. W. R. Holloway to Edwin M. Stanton, 3 September 1863, OR, ser. 3, 3:766; Edwin M. Stanton to Oliver P. Morton, 19 September 1863, OR, ser. 3, 3:824.

49. Benton McAdams, *Rebels at Rock Island: The Story of a Civil War Prison* (DeKalb: Northern Illinois University Press, 2000), 137.

50. Abraham Lincoln to Ulysses S. Grant, 22 September 1864, OR, ser. 3, 4:740; Ulysses S. Grant to Edwin M. Stanton, 25 September 1864, OR, ser. 3, 4:744.

51. Dee Alexander Brown, *The Galvanized Yankees* (Urbana: University of Illinois Press, 1963), 1–2. Brown's work provides a complete description of the recruitment, service, and campaigns of the six regiments formed from Confederate prisoners.

52. Samuel Jones to Braxton Bragg, 13 September 1864, OR, 7:821–822.

53. D. W. Vowles to Commanding Officer, CSA Military Prison, Camp Lawton, 8 November 1864, OR, 7:1113–1114.

54. WD, CSA, Special Orders, No. 8, 16 January 1865, Vol. 19, Entry 106, RG 249.

55. Isham et al., *Prisoners of War*, 365–366.

56. It is impossible to provide an accurate number of Union POWs who joined Confederate ranks, but the number is certainly in the thousands. Dee Brown estimated that between 1,500 and 2,000 federal POWs enlisted into Confederate ranks, but found that most surrendered to Union troops as quickly as possible, and they did not represent a significant source of manpower to the Confederacy; see Brown, *Galvanized Yankees*, 211–217. Brown's estimate is too low, given that 2,169 POWs joined from a single prison. See "Register of Federal POWs who enlisted in CSA, Salisbury, NC," Vol. 1, Entry 136, RG 249. The inside cover notes that recruiting was done by "Irish Catholic of Yorke's Louisiana Brig."

57. WD, General Orders No. 100, 24 April 1863, OR, 5:671–682; Leon Friedman, ed., *The Law of War: A Documentary History*, 2 vols. (New York: Random House, 1972), 1:158–186.

58. Frank B. Freidel, *Francis Lieber, Nineteenth Century Liberal* (Baton Rouge: Louisiana State University Press, 1947), 329.

59. WD, Special Orders No. 399, 17 December 1862, OR, ser. 3, 2:951.

60. General Orders No. 100, Article 49; Friedman, *Law of War*, 1:168.

61. General Orders No. 100, Articles 49–51, 81–82; Friedman, *Law of War*, 1:168, 1:173.

62. General Orders No. 100, Articles 60–66; Friedman, *Law of War*, 1:170.

63. General Orders No. 100, Article 48; Friedman, *Law of War*, 1:167.

64. Henry W. Halleck to E. A. Hitchcock, 12 August 1863, Box 2, Entry 149, RG 249.

65. Ibid; S. A. Meredith to Robert Ould, 24 August 1863, Box 2, Entry 149, RG 249.

66. Robert Ould to S. A. Meredith, 24 August 1863, Box 2, Entry 149, RG 249. Article 131 provided that any paroled officer whose government disapproved of his parole must return to captivity. Thus illegal paroles did not nullify a prisoner's capture, and if one side released all parolees, the other side was justified in doing so as well.

67. Richard Shelly Hartigan, *Lieber's Code and the Law of War* (Chicago: Precedent, 1983), 2.

68. Ibid., 22; Freidel, *Lieber*, 340–342.

69. Hartigan, *Lieber's Code*, 23.

70. Homer B. Sprague, *Lights and Shadows in Confederate Prisons: A Personal Experience, 1864–5* (New York: G. P. Putnam's Sons, 1915), 43.

71. Alonzo Cooper, *In and Out of Rebel Prisons* (Oswego, N.Y.: R. J. Oliphant, 1888), v.

72. Junius Henri Browne, *Four Years in Secessia* (New York: Arno, 1970), 276; William C. Harris, *Prison-Life in the Tobacco Warehouse at Richmond* (Philadelphia: G. W. Childs, 1862), 120; William Hartley Jeffrey, *Richmond Prisons, 1861–1862* (St. Johnsbury, Vt.: Republican Press, 1893), 115.

73. Cangemi and Kowalski, *Andersonville Prison*, 17–18.

74. Ibid., 18; McElroy, *Andersonville*, 118–125; Ransom, *Andersonville Diary*, 112–122.

75. Cangemi and Kowalski, *Andersonville Prison*, 11.

76. Ibid.

77. Stevenson, *Southern Side*, 404. Stevenson served as the chief surgeon of the Andersonville hospital and was tasked with recording the cause of death for every prisoner.

78. Ibid.

79. Speer, *Portals*, 332; Cangemi and Kowalski, *Andersonville Prison*, 14; Record and Pension Office, "Andersonville Georgia Confederate Military Prison," 15 January 1900, Box 1, Entry 105, RG 249. This record places the total number of prisoners received at Andersonville at 44,928.

80. "Minutes of meeting of sergeants commanding detachments at Andersonville," undated; undated petition, Citizens of Pittsburg to Abraham Lincoln; both in Box 4, Entry 149, RG 249.

81. Thomas R. Cord to Colonel Sherman, 9 September 1864, Box 2, Entry 149, RG 249, contains a thorough description of the conditions at Andersonville, sent to the commander of the 19th U.S. Infantry Regiment.

82. WD, CSA, Orders No. 13, 27 July 1864, OR, 7:588; John Worrell Northrop, *Chronicles from the Diary of a War Prisoner in Andersonville* (Wichita, Kans.: John Northrop, 1904), 104.

83. H. A. M. Henderson to J. D. Imboden, 23 January 1865; WD, CSA, General Orders No. 2, 15 February 1865; both found in Box 7, Entry 107, RG 249.

84. William Hoffman, "Regulations for POW Compounds," Circular, 7 July 1862, Box 1, Entry 105, RG 249.

85. Speer, *Portals*, 323–340.

86. General Orders No. 190, 3 May 1864, Box 1, Entry 105, RG 249.

87. McAdams, *Rebels at Rock Island*, 214–215.

88. William Hoffman, "Circular No. 4," 10 August 1864, Box 1, Entry 105, RG 249.

89. John Henry King, *Three Hundred Days in a Yankee Prison* (Kennesaw, Ga.: Continental Book Co., 1959), 78.

90. William W. Ward, *"For the sake of my country": The Diary of Colonel W. W. Ward*, ed. R. B. Rosenburg (Murfreesboro, Tenn.: Southern Heritage Press, 1992), 16.

91. In particular, Ward, *"For the sake of my country,"* and William Hyslop Sumner Burgwyn, *A Captain's War: The Letters and Diaries of William H. S. Burgwyn, 1861–1865*, ed. Herbert M. Schiller (Shippensburg, Pa.: White Mane, 1994), stress monetary matters.

92. A. Schoepf to Edwin M. Stanton, 19 August 1863, Box 4, Entry 149, RG 249.

93. Montrose A. Pallen to Edwin M. Stanton, 19 December 1863; William Pierson to William Hoffman, 25 December 1863; both in Box 4, Entry 149, RG 249.

94. James I. Robertson Jr., "The Scourge of Elmira," in *Civil War Prisons*, ed. William B. Hesseltine (Kent, Ohio: Kent State University Press, 1972), 80–81.

95. Berry Benson, *Berry Benson's Civil War Book: Memoirs of a Confederate Scout and Sharpshooter*, ed. Susan Williams Benson (Athens: University of Georgia Press, 1962), 132.

96. "Consolidated Returns for Elmira, NY," Box 16, Entry 208, RG 109.

97. F. Lee Lawrence and Robert W. Glover, *Camp Ford CSA: The Story of Union Prisoners in Texas* (Austin: Texas Civil War Centennial Advisory Committee, 1964), 75–76.

98. Gene Eric Salecker, *Disaster on the Mississippi: The Sultana Explosion, April 27, 1865* (Annapolis, Md.: Naval Institute Press, 1996), xi.

99. William Hoffman to Brigadier General Schoepf; William Hoffman to L. H. Lee; William Hoffman to H. A. Allen; William Hoffman to T. Ingraham; William Hoffman to Charles B. Pratt; all dated 21 July 1865, Vol. 3, Entry 25, RG 249.

100. William Hoffman to J. C. McKee, 3 August 1865, Vol. 3, Entry 25, RG 249.

101. "Roll of Prisoners in Confinement," 20 October 1863, Entry 16, RG 249.

102. Marvel, *Andersonville*, 244; *New York Daily Tribune*, 28 November 1865.

103. Speer, *Portals*, 291–292.

104. Cangemi and Kowalski, *Andersonville Prison*, 29–33.

CHAPTER 5: AMERICA BECOMES A WORLD POWER, 1865–1919

1. Geronimo, *Geronimo's Story of His Life*, ed. S. M. Barnett (1906, reprint; Alexander, NC: Alexander Books, 1999), 127–129; Alexander B. Adams, *Geronimo: A Biography* (New York: G. P. Putnam's Sons, 1971), 312–315.

2. Jason Betzinez, *I Fought with Geronimo* (New York: Bonanza Books, 1959), 198–199.

3. Edwin Wildman, *Aguinaldo: A Narrative of Filipino Ambitions* (Boston: Lothrop Publishing, 1901), 363–367; Brian M. Linn, *The Philippine War, 1899–1902* (Lawrence: University Press of Kansas, 2000), 274–276, 296.

4. John F. Hutchinson, *Champions of Charity: War and the Rise of the Red Cross* (Boulder, Colo.: Westview Press, 1996), 123–126.

5. During the Spanish-American War, Red Cross societies provided nurses and supplies for American training camps, but they did not assist in the maintenance of Spanish prisoners; Hutchinson, *Champions of Charity*, 223, 229; Caroline Moorehead, *Dunant's Dream: War, Switzerland and the History of the Red Cross* (New York: Carroll & Graf, 1998), 103–105.

6. Howard S. Levie, ed., *Documents on Prisoners of War*, Naval War College International Law Studies 60 (Newport, R.I.: Naval War College Press, 1979), 58.

7. Ibid., 59; Leon Friedman, ed., *The Law of War: A Documentary History*, 2 vols. (New York: Random House, 1972), 1:198–199.

8. "Laws and Customs of War on Land, 1907," *United States Statutes at Large*, 36:2277, Treaty Ser., No. 539, Article 2.

9. According to the 1899 convention, prisoner labor "shall have nothing to do with the military operations." In the 1907 convention, the wording was changed to "shall have no connection with the operations of the war." "Laws and Customs of War on Land, 1899," *United States Statutes at Large*, 32:1803, Treaty Ser., No. 403, Article 6; "Laws and Customs, 1907," Article 6.

10. George G. Lewis and John Mewha, *History of Prisoner of War Utilization by the United States Army, 1776–1945* (Washington, D.C.: Government Printing Office, 1955), 48.

11. Ibid., 49; J. Fred Rippy, *The United States and Mexico* (New York: Alfred A. Knopf, 1931), 349–358.

12. James L. Haley, *The Buffalo War: The History of the Red River Indian Uprising of 1874* (Austin: State House Press, 1998), 211–212.

13. George W. Baird, "The Capture of Chief Joseph and the Nez Perces," *International Review* 7 (August 1879): 214.

14. U.S. Congress, House, "Report of the Secretary of War, Miscellaneous Reports," *Annual Reports of the War Department, 1898*, 55th Cong., 3rd sess., 1898, H. Doc. 2, serial 3744, 25–26.

15. Ivan Musicant, *Empire by Default: The Spanish-American War and the Dawn of the American Century* (New York: Henry Holt, 1998), 474–475, 480–481, 507; Graham A. Cosmas, *An Army for Empire: The United States Army in the Spanish-*

American War (Columbia: University of Missouri Press, 1971), 232; Frank B. Freidel, *The Splendid Little War* (Boston: Little, Brown, 1958), 252–254; David F. Trask, *The War with Spain in 1898* (New York: Macmillan, 1981), 315–318.

16. Leon Wolff, *Little Brown Brother* (1960; reprint, New York: Oxford University Press, 1991), 233–234, 252–254, 305–307; William Thaddeus Sexton, *Soldiers in the Sun: An Adventure in Imperialism* (Harrisburg, Pa.: Military Service Publishing, 1939), 240–241; Russell Roth, *Muddy Glory: America's "Indian Wars" in the Philippines, 1899–1935* (West Hanover, Conn.: Christopher Publishing House, 1981), 86–87.

17. Stuart Creighton Miller, *"Benevolent Assimilation": The American Conquest of the Philippines, 1899–1903* (New Haven, Conn.: Yale University Press, 1982), 88–90, 187–188.

18. David Howard Bain, *Sitting in Darkness: Americans in the Philippines* (Boston: Houghton Mifflin, 1984), 84–87, at 85.

19. Andrew J. Birtle, *U.S. Army Counterinsurgency and Contingency Operations and Doctrine, 1860–1941* (Washington, D.C.: Center of Military History, 1998), 129–132.

20. Brian M. Linn, *The U.S. Army and Counterinsurgency in the Philippine War, 1899–1902* (Chapel Hill: University of North Carolina Press, 1989), xi–xii; Linn, *Philippine War*, ix–x.

21. Ibid., 221–224.

22. The Teller Amendment attached to the declaration of war guaranteed that the United States would not attempt to annex Cuba as a result of the war; Musicant, *Empire by Default*, 186–187; Elbert J. Benton, *International Law and Diplomacy of the Spanish-American War* (Baltimore: Johns Hopkins Press, 1908), 97–98.

23. Fred J. Buenzle, "The Collier *Merrimac*," *United States Naval Institute Proceedings* 66 (October 1940): 1447–1453.

24. "Report of Major-General Shafter, Commanding the Troops in Cuba," *Annual Reports, 1898*, 66; Freidel, *Splendid Little War*, 138.

25. Ibid., 240–242.

26. Ibid., 66.

27. For a description of the conditions at Annapolis and Portsmouth, see Charles J. Dutton, "American Prison Camp," *Commonweal* 33 (3 January 1940): 270–272. Thirty-one prisoners died at Portsmouth; their remains were exhumed and repatriated in 1916. C. S. Kempff to Chief of the Bureau of Navigation, 13 March 1934, Box 585, Entry 464A, RG 45.

28. "U.S. Navy Academy," 21 July 1898, Box 594, Entry 464A, RG 45, contains a list of all Spanish naval prisoners held at the Naval Academy.

29. "Report of the Quartermaster's Department," *Annual Reports, 1898*, 163–164, 393–394.

30. Pedro Lopez de Castillo to the Soldiers of the American Army, 21 August 1898, Center of Military History, *Correspondence Relating to the War With Spain*, 2 vols. (1902, reprint; Washington, DC: Government Printing Office, 1993), 1:249–250.

31. William R. Day to John D. Long, 8 August 1898, Box 594, Entry 464A, RG 45.

32. F. V. McNair to Pascual Cervera, 31 August 1898; Pascual Cervera to F. V. McNair, 1 September 1898, both in Box 594, Entry 464A, RG 45.

33. Pedro Ramil, Luis Fabra, Aquilino Amigo, and Miguel Olivares to John D. Long, 16 August 1898, Box 594, Entry 464A, RG 45.

34. U.S. Congress, Senate, "Statement of Brigadier General Robert P. Hughes," *Affairs in the Philippine Islands*, 57th Cong., 1st sess., 1902, 3 vols., serial 4242–4244, 1:515 (hereafter cited as *Affairs*); "Statement of General Elwell S. Otis," *Affairs*, 1:793–794.

35. "Statement of Robert P. Hughes," *Affairs*, 1:505, 515–516.

36. Linn, *Philippine War*, 211–212.

37. U.S. Congress, House, "Report of Major-General E. S. Otis," *Annual Reports of the Secretary of War, 1900*, 56th Cong., 2nd sess., 1900, serial 4073, 182.

38. Antonio Luna, "To the Field Officers of the Territorial Militia," 7 February 1899, *Affairs*, 2:1214–1216; Linn, *Philippine War*, 59, 136–137.

39. Arthur MacArthur to Theodore Schwan, 13 November 1899, *Annual Reports, 1900*, 250–251.

40. Ibid., 200.

41. Lewis and Mewha, *Prisoner of War Utilization*, 46.

42. U.S. Congress, House, "Report of the Lieutenant General Commanding the Army," *Annual Reports of the Secretary of War, 1901*, 57th Cong., 1st sess., 1901, serial 4272, 94–95, 227; "Statement of Governor William H. Taft," *Affairs*, 309–310.

43. "Report of the Lieutenant General," 95; "Statement of Governor William H. Taft," 68.

44. The records of trials conducted by the American provost courts in the Philippines are maintained in the National Archives. For examples, see Boxes 1–3, Entry 2398; Box 1, Entry 2381; Box 1, Entry 2394; all found in RG 395.

45. "Report of the Lieutenant General," 98–99; Wildman, *Aguinaldo*, 362–363. Wildman put the total captures at 21,415 insurgents, 11,346 rifles, 80 fieldpieces, 3,000 shells, 700,000 rounds of ammunition, 20 tons of gunpowder, and 408 bolos in the same time period.

46. "Report of the Lieutenant General," 102.

47. "Report of Brigadier General George W. Davis, USA, provost-marshal-general, on military affairs," *Annual Reports, 1901*, 227.

48. "Report of the Lieutenant General," 100–101.

49. "Report of Brigadier General George W. Davis," 228.

50. Linn, *Philippine War*, 304, 321.

51. Lewis and Mewha, *Prisoner of War Utilization*, 46.

52. "Testimony of William Lewis Smith," *Affairs*, 3:1538–1540; "Testimony of Grover Flint," *Affairs*, 3:1767–1768; "Testimony of D. J. Evans," *Affairs*, 3:2061–2062; "Testimony of Isadore H. Dube," *Affairs*, 3:2249–2250; "Testimony of Januarius Manning," *Affairs*, 3:2252–2253; "Testimony of William J. Gibbs," *Affairs*, 3:2305.

53. "Testimony of Leroy E. Halleck," *Affairs*, 3:1969–1970; "Testimony of Richard V. Hughes," *Affairs*, 3:2236–2237; "Testimony of Isadore H. Dube," *Affairs*,

3:2243; Frederick Funston to Henry Cabot Lodge, 2 May 1902, *Affairs*, 3:2259–2260; R. P. Hughes to H. C. Corbin, 8 May 1902, *Affairs*, 3:2441.

54. Examples include "Testimony of Leroy E. Halleck," *Affairs*, 3:1972–1973, 1985; "Testimony of Januarius Manning," *Affairs*, 3:2254.

55. "Testimony of Robert P. Hughes," *Affairs*, 1:660; "Testimony of Leroy E. Halleck," *Affairs*, 3:1983–1984; "Testimony of D. J. Evans," *Affairs*, 3:2063; "Testimony of William J. Gibbs," *Affairs*, 3:2306–2307; "Testimony of Fred McDonald," *Affairs*, 3:2775–2776.

56. Elihu Root to Henry Cabot Lodge, 17 February 1902, *Affairs*, 2:949–951.

57. Cornelius Gardener to William H. Taft, 16 December 1901, *Affairs*, 2:884.

58. "Statement of David P. Barrows," *Affairs*, 1:723; "Statement of Maj. Gen. E. S. Otis, USA," *Affairs*, 1:731.

59. J. M. Spaight, *War Rights on Land* (London: Macmillan, 1911), 265.

60. "Prisoners of War in Germany and the other Central States," Box 378, Entry 464B, RG 45.

61. Carl P. Dennett, *Prisoners of the Great War* (Boston: Houghton Mifflin, 1919), 13, 228–229.

62. Richard B. Speed III, *Prisoners, Diplomats, and the Great War: A Study in the Diplomacy of Captivity* (New York: Greenwood Press, 1990), 76, 82, 101, 138, 209.

63. Ibid., 16, 194–195.

64. Ibid., 107–122.

65. Ibid., 26.

66. Jacob B. Lishchiner, "Origin of the Military Police: Provost Marshal General's Department, AEF, World War I," *Military Affairs* 11 (Summer 1947): 69–70.

67. Ibid., 69.

68. U.S. Army, *United States Army in the World War, 1917–1919*, vol. 15, *Reports of the Commander-in-Chief, Staff Sections and Services* (Washington, D.C.: Center of Military History, 1991), 329; "Prisoner of War Companies, Orders and Instructions," 19 January 1918, Box 444, Entry 472, RG 120; these instructions were simplified and distributed as "Prisoners of War Regulations and Instructions, 1918," 1 July 1918, Box 282, Entry 66, RG 120, and "Manual for Prisoners of War," 1 July 1918, Box 444, Entry 72, RG 120.

69. U.S. Army, *Army in the World War*, 15:329–330.

70. Ibid., 15:330. No captured German troops were shipped from Europe to the United States; only the crews of German warships in American ports at the outbreak of war were interned in the continental United States. These 1,356 naval officers and men were joined by 2,300 merchant sailors and 2,300 alien enemies in four internment camps. None provided a significant source of labor for the government. William B. Glidden, "Internment Camps in America, 1917–1920," *Military Affairs* 37 (December 1973): 137–141.

71. "Prisoners of War Regulations," 2.

72. Ibid., 4.

73. "Prisoner of War Companies," 1; "Prisoners of War Regulations," 6.

74. "Prisoner of War Companies," 6; "Prisoners of War Regulations," 11.

75. "Manual for Prisoners," 1.

76. U.S. Congress, House, "Final Report of General John J. Pershing," *Annual Reports of the War Department, 1919*, 66th Cong., 2nd sess., 1919, serial 7682, 631.

77. "Lists of German Prisoners of War Assigned to Prisoner of War Company Commanders," Box 445, Entry 65, RG 120, contains the muster roll for each labor company; "Prisoner of War Labor Companies," 8 March 1919, Box 444, Entry 72, RG 120 lists each company and commanding officer.

78. "Method of Handling Prisoners of War by the Provost Marshal General, AEF," no date, Box 282, Entry 66, RG 120.

79. U.S. Army, *Army in the World War*, 15:332.

80. William S. Sims to Josephus Daniels, 30 March 1918; "Disposal of Prisoners of War Captured by the United States Naval Forces in European Waters," 5 April 1918; and Josephus Daniels, "Instructions Concerning the Disposition of Prisoners of War Captured by U.S. Naval Forces in European or Other Waters," 9 May 1918; all in Box 378, Entry 464B, RG 45; Glidden, "Internment Camps," 140.

81. U.S. Army, *Army in the World War*, 15:330.

82. Ibid., 331.

83. "History of Central Prisoner of War Enclosure No. 1," 2, Box 290, Entry 68, RG 120.

84. Ibid., 3.

85. "Prisoner of War Labor Company No. 6 Menu for Week from March 9–15, 1919," "PWL Co. No. 5 Menus from March 31st, 1919 to April 6th, 1919," "Menu for week of March 16, 1919, PWL Co. #27," "Menu of the week March 16th to 22nd 1919, PWL Co. 26," "PWL Co. #8, Bill of Fare," all in Box 444, Entry 72, RG 120.

86. "History of Central Prisoner of War Enclosure No. 1," 4–5.

87. Office of the Provost Marshal General, "History of Officer Prisoners of War Enclosure," 10, Box 290, Entry 68, RG 120.

88. Ibid., 1, 19–25, quotation at 1. The prison at Richelieu contained an all-time high of 880 officer prisoners on 5 March 1919, attended by 44 noncommissioned officers and 453 privates; "Officers POW Enclosure (Richelieu)," Box 285, Entry 66, RG 120.

89. Basil D. Spalding, "Prison Order No. 1," 24 December 1918; Basil D. Spalding, "Prison Order No. 1," 6 January 1919; Basil D. Spalding, "Prison Order No. 5," 2 February 1919; all in Box 282, Entry 66, RG 120.

90. "Prisoner of War Regulations," 16.

91. Basil D. Spalding, "Prison Order No. 7," 15 February 1919; Basil D. Spalding, "Prison Order No. 8," 26 February 1919; both in Box 282, Entry 66, RG 120.

92. Basil D. Spalding, "Prison Order No. 4," 17 January 1919; Basil D. Spalding, "Prison Order No. 21," 19 July 1919; both in Box 282, Entry 66, RG 120.

93. "Report of CPWE 1," 18 July 1918; "Report of CPWE 1," 3 October 1918; "Field Reports of Prisoners Captured by Different Organizations"; all in Box 434, Entry 64, RG 120.

94. Lewis and Mewha, *Prisoner of War Utilization*, 64.

95. H. H. Tebbetts to Commanding General, Services of Supply, 24 August 1919; Order No. 17, PWE Co. #223, 16 September 1919; both in Box 235, Entry 68, RG 120.

96. "Manual for Prisoners," 22.

97. "Questions Asked German Prisoners," Box 433, Entry 64, RG 120, contains a list of standard interrogation questions used by the Second Division. Box 432, Entry 64, RG 120, contains hundreds of interrogation reports from various divisions in the First Army.

98. C. A. Willoughby, "Identification of German Prisoners of War," *Infantry Journal* 15 (September 1918): 181–184. Willoughby included pictures of German insignia, descriptions of regional dialects, and lists of uniform types to aid interrogators in the identification of enemy units.

99. Speed, *Prisoners*, 179.

100. Ibid., 179.

101. H. H. Tebbetts, "Repatriation of Prisoners of War," 7 September 1919; John J. Pershing to Commanding Officer, Intermediate Section, 9 and 10 September 1919; all in Box 235, Entry 68, RG 120.

102. "History of Central Prisoner of War Enclosure No. 1," "Prisoner of War Enclosure, Number 5," and "History of Prisoner of War Enclosure #3," all in Box 235, Entry 68, RG 120.

CHAPTER 6: AMERICA BECOMES A SUPERPOWER

1. Georg Gaertner and Arnold Krammer, *Hitler's Last Soldier in America* (New York: Stein & Day, 1985), 15–16, 29–35, 59–60.

2. Ibid., 20–28, 57–59.

3. HQ EUCOM to the Provost Marshal General Department, 18 March 1949, Box 88, Entry 452, RG 389, presents the total number of prisoners handled by U.S. forces as 7,200,000.

4. George G. Lewis and John Mewha, *Prisoner of War Utilization by the United States Army, 1776–1945* (Washington, D.C.: Government Printing Office, 1955), 126–127, 146–147.

5. Judith M. Gansberg, *Stalag USA: The Remarkable Story of German POWs in America* (New York: Thomas Y. Crowell, 1977); Ron Robin, *The Barbed-Wire College: Reeducating German POWs in the United States during World War II* (Princeton, N.J.: Princeton University Press, 1995).

6. Arthur L. Smith Jr., *The War for the German Mind: Re-educating Hitler's Soldiers* (Providence, R.I.: Berghahn Books, 1996), viii.

7. Arnold P. Krammer, *Nazi Prisoners of War in America* (New York: Stein & Day, 1979).

8. James Bacque, *Other Losses: The Shocking Truth behind the Mass Deaths of Disarmed German Soldiers and Civilians under General Eisenhower's Command* (New York: Prima, 1991), 2; Albert E. Cowdrey, "A Question of Numbers,"

in *Eisenhower and the German POWs,* ed. Gunter Bischof and Stephen E. Ambrose (Baton Rouge: Louisiana State University Press, 1992), 84.

9. Enemy Prisoner of War Information Bureau, "Prisoner of War Records," 21 September 1948, Box 1, Entry 467E, RG 389, shows that over 600,000 German prisoners were transferred to European nations. Of the 749,785 prisoners held in Europe at the end of the war, 141,939 died in American custody, but this figure includes only 5,266 who died of causes other than battlefield wounds. See also HQ EUCOM to the Provost Marshal General Department, 18 March 1949, Box 88, Entry 452, RG 389, which lists transfers of over 2,000,000 POWs to British, Russian, and French control, as well as the discharge of 1,721,367 prisoners without documentation from the Volkssturm, civilian, and deserter categories.

10. John Hammond Moore, *The Faustball Tunnel* (New York: Random House, 1978); Reinhold Pabel, *Enemies Are Human* (Philadelphia: John C. Winston, 1955).

11. Allan Kent Powell, *Splinters of a Nation: German Prisoners of War in Utah* (Salt Lake City: University of Utah Press, 1989); David Fiedler, *The Enemy among Us: POWs in Missouri during World War II* (St. Louis: Missouri Historical Society Press, 2003); Richard E. Holl, "Swastikas in the Bluegrass State: Axis Prisoners of War in Kentucky, 1942–46," *Register of the Kentucky Historical Society* 100 (Spring 2002): 139–165; Merrill R. Pritchett and William L. Shea, "The Afrika Korps in Arkansas, 1943–1946," *Arkansas Historical Quarterly* 37 (Spring 1978): 3–22; Richard Paul Walker, "Prisoners of War in Texas during World War II" (Ph.D. diss., North Texas State University, 1980).

12. Lewis H. Carlson, *We Were Each Other's Prisoners: An Oral History of World War II American and German Prisoners of War* (New York: HarperCollins, 1997); see also Frederick Joseph Doyle, "German Prisoners of War in the Southwest United States during World War II: An Oral History" (Ph.D. diss., University of Denver, 1978); and Claire Swedberg, *In Enemy Hands: Personal Accounts of Those Taken Prisoner in World War II* (Mechanicsburg, Pa.: Stackpole Books, 1997).

13. Prominent examples include Jeffrey E. Gerger, *German Prisoners of War at Camp Cooke, California: Personal Accounts, 1944–1946* (Jefferson, N.C.: McFarland, 1996); Allen V. Koop, *Stark Decency: German Prisoners of War in a New England Village* (Hanover, N.H.: University Press of New England, 1988); Michael R. Waters, *Lone Star Stalag: German Prisoners of War at Camp Hearne* (College Station: Texas A&M University Press, 2004); and Donald Mace Williams, *Italian POWs and a Texas Church: The Murals of St. Mary's* (Lubbock: Texas Tech University Press, 1992).

14. Geneva Convention Relative to the Treatment of Prisoners of War, 1929, Articles 29–31. *Treaty Series,* No. 846, signed at Geneva, 27 July 1929 (Washington, D.C.: Government Printing Office, 1932).

15. The United States investigated British practice before entering the war; see "Interview by Colonel William Cattron Rigby, FAGD, U.S. Army, with Lieutenant J. Turner, Adjutant, Featherstone Park, Haltwhistle (Invasion Camp)," 7 November 1941, Box 1435, Entry 457, RG 389.

16. Lewis and Mewha, *Prisoner of War Utilization,* 83. In December, the United States held 1,881 enemy prisoners.

17. William F. Ross and Charles Romanus, *The Quartermaster Corps: Operations in the War against Germany*, The United States Army in World War II (Washington, D.C.: Center of Military History, 2004), 531–532, 631–632.

18. A report of the provost marshal general's office estimated in October 1943 that the United States could house 383,000 prisoners by 1 July 1944; "Maintenance, Transhipment, and Disposal of Prisoners of War," undated, Box 1442, Entry 458, RG 389.

19. Joseph Bykofsky and Harold Larson, *The Transportation Corps: Operations Overseas*, The United States Army in World War II (Washington, D.C.: Center of Military History, 2003), 361–362.

20. Earl F. Ziemke, *The U.S. Army in the Occupation of Germany, 1944–1946* (Washington, D.C.: Center of Military History, 1975), 291; Bischof and Ambrose, *Eisenhower and the German POWs*, 5.

21. Office of the Provost Marshal, "Summary of PW Activities," 1 May 1947, Box 87, Entry 452, RG 389; Ross and Romanus, *Quartermaster Corps*, 532, puts the number of German POWs in American hands on 20 May 1945 at 2,884,762.

22. "Total Number of German, Italian, and Japanese Prisoners of War and Protected Personnel Received in Continental United States from November 1942 through May 1945," Box 1442, Entry 458, RG 389. On 1 June 1945, 374,480 German prisoners, 50,582 Italian prisoners, and 4,337 Japanese prisoners had been sent to the United States. According to data reported in 1950, the peak number of enemy POWs in the United States was 378,898 Germans, 51,156 Italians, and 5,413 Japanese, Enemy Prisoner of War Information Bureau, "Prisoner of War Records," 1 January 1950, Box 1, Entry 467E, RG 389.

23. James Richard Keen, "The Captive Enemy? Italian Prisoners of War in Texas during World War II" (master's thesis, University of Texas of the Permian Basin, 1988), 15–17.

24. Louis E. Keefer, *Italian Prisoners of War in America, 1942–1946: Captives or Allies?* (New York: Praeger, 1992), 74–75.

25. Lewis and Mewha, *Prisoner of War Utilization*, 96, Keefer, *Italian Prisoners*, 75–76.

26. Lewis and Mewha, *Prisoner of War Utilization*, 99–100.

27. Keefer, *Italian Prisoners*, 104.

28. Ibid., 127, 168; John M. Eager to Vito Marcantonio, 29 June 1945, Box 1467, Entry 458, RG 389.

29. Matthias Reiss, "Bronzed Bodies behind Barbed Wire: Masculinity and the Treatment of German Prisoners of War in the United States during World War II," *Journal of Military History* 69 (April 2005): 498–499; Bill Cunningham, "Blizzard Nets One Bad Story," *Boston Herald*, 12 February 1945; John Hammond Moore, "Italian POWs in America: War Is Not Always Hell," *Prologue* (Fall 1976): 151; "What Did Army Expect When It Let Them Go to Dances? Ask Parted Wives of POWs," *Washington Daily News*, 11 July 1945, 26; Z. C. Steakley to C. H. Smith, 4 May 1945, Box 3, Entry 268, RG 38; "Speech to be given by Lt. Comdr. C. H. Smith, III," 3, Box 4, Entry 268, RG 38.

30. Keefer, *Italian Prisoners*, 161.

31. Arnold P. Krammer, "Japanese Prisoners of War in America," *Pacific Historical Review* 52 (February 1983): 70.

32. "Total number of Japanese P.W. enlisted men in prisoner of war camps," 16 July 1945, Box 2, Entry 1004, RG 389.

33. John W. Dower, *War without Mercy: Race and Power in the Pacific War* (New York: Pantheon Books, 1986), 35.

34. For examples, see E. B. Sledge, *With the Old Breed at Peleliu and Okinawa* (New York: Presidio Press, 1981), 33–34; Henry Berry, *Semper Fi, Mac: Living Memories of the U.S. Marines in World War Two* (New York: Arbor House, 1982), 74–75; William F. Halsey and Joseph Bryan III, *Admiral Halsey's Story* (New York: McGraw-Hill, 1947), 123; William Manchester, *Goodbye, Darkness: A Memoir of the Pacific War* (Boston: Little, Brown, 1980), 439; Martin Caidin, *The Ragged, Rugged Warriors* (New York: Dutton, 1966), 36–37.

35. Simon P. MacKenzie, "The Treatment of Prisoners of War in World War II," *Journal of Modern History* 66 (September 1994): 488.

36. Ulrich Strauss, *The Anguish of Surrender: Japanese POWs of World War II* (Seattle: University of Washington Press, 2003), 6.

37. William J. Donovan to Allen W. Gullion, 3 July 1944; Arthur L. Lerch to William J. Donovan, 17 July 1944; Arthur L. Lerch to William J. Donovan, 11 August 1944; all in Box 1435, Entry 457, RG 389.

38. Allison Gilmore, *You Can't Fight Tanks with Bayonets: Psychological Warfare against the Japanese Army in the Southeast Pacific* (Lincoln: University of Nebraska Press, 1998), 150–156; "Check-List for Use in Interrogations on Morale," no date, Box 908, Entry 177, RG 165.

39. Ibid., 49.

40. Ibid., 55; Krammer, "Japanese Prisoners," 80.

41. Lewis and Mewha, *Prisoner of War Utilization*, 258, Krammer, "Japanese Prisoners," 89; "Tabulation of POWs Processed in the Philippines and Okinawa by Month of Capture," 15 January 1946, Box 7, Entry 1004, RG 389; Walter P. McMinn to O. J. Magee, 24 March 1948, Box 88, Entry 452, RG 389.

42. AG to all Interrogators, memorandum, 18 December 1943, Box 908, Entry 177, RG 165; see also "IV Army Corps School for Interrogation of P.W.—German," 1 July 1941, Box 923, Entry 177, RG 165; "Notes on Interrogating Technique," 27 March 1942, Box 924, Entry 177, RG 165; "Interrogation in the Field," no date, Box 924, Entry 177, RG 165.

43. Gansberg, *Stalag USA*, 15; "Japanese Officer Prisoners of War," no date, Box 2, Entry 1004, RG 389; Ikuhiko Hata, "From Consideration to Contempt: The Changing Nature of Japanese Military and Popular Perceptions of Prisoners of War through the Ages," in *Prisoners of War and Their Captors in World War II*, ed. Bob Moore and Kent Fedorowich (Washington, D.C.: Berg, 1996), 272–273.

44. "Miscellaneous Questions of Current Importance," 1 September 1944, Box 908, Entry 177, RG 165.

45. Examples of technological interrogations include "Peenemuende Experimental

Center," 14 December 1944, which included detailed information on jet engines, V-1 and V-2 missiles, and helicopters, as well as a map of the experimental facility at Peenemuende; "Static Flamethrowers," 20 November 1944; and "Information on German Tanks," 29 December 1944; all found in Box 647, Entry 177, RG 165; "Final Session of the Research Group Training School," 22 August 1945, Box 909, Entry 177, RG 165. Luis de Florez to the Secretary of the Navy, 19 June 1945, and H. G. Bowen to the Provost Marshal General, 3 October 1945, both in Box 109, RG 298.

46. "Japanese Biological Warfare," 12 April 1945; "Bacteriological Warfare," no date; both in Box 908, Entry 177, RG 165.

47. "Psychological Study of an S.S. Deserter," 30 May 1944, Box 660, Entry 179, RG 165.

48. "Extract from Report on Opinions of 1700 German Ps/W on Politics, Postwar Division and Occupation of Germany," 8 March 1945; "Suggestions for Classification of Prisoners of War," 18 April 1945; both in Box 924, Entry 177, RG 165.

49. Box 658, Entry 179, RG 165, contains dozens of individual interrogation reports of anti-Nazi prisoners who volunteered information to assist in the destruction of Nazi Germany; see also "Extract from Report on Opinions of 1700 German Ps/W," 8 March 1945, Box 924, Entry 177, RG 165.

50. U.S. War Department, *Enemy Prisoners of War*, 5 October 1944, Technical Manual 19-500, 1.1.

51. Ibid., 2.2.

52. Arthur L. Lerch to Colonel Gerhardt, 5 September 1944, Box 1439, Entry 457, RG 389.

53. U.S. War Department, *Enemy Prisoners*, 2.12.

54. Sidney Shalett, "Prisoner Coddling Is Denied by Army," *New York Times*, 7 May 1944, 14; "Deny 'Coddling' of War Prisoners," *New York Times*, 8 October 1944, 14; "Coddling of War Prisoners Is Denied by Gen. Lerch at a Legion Meeting Here," *New York Times*, 17 April 1945, 30; Frederick C. Othman, "Nazis Smell Pretty and General's Glad," *Washington Daily News*, 1 May 1945; "Defend Treatment of War Prisoners," *New York Times*, 1 May 1945, 9.

55. Krammer, *Nazi Prisoners*, 62; "The YMCA War Prisoners' Aid Offers Educational Assistance," *School and Society* 59 (6 May 1944): 325; U.S. War Department, *Enemy Prisoners*, 2.31–32.

56. U.S. War Department, *Enemy Prisoners*, 2.49–53.

57. Edward Shils and Morris Janowitz, "Cohesion and Disintegration in the Wehrmacht in World War II," *Public Opinion Quarterly* 12 (1948): 280–315; Richard Holmes, *Acts of War: The Behavior of Men in Battle* (New York: Free Press, 1985); William C. Bradbury, Samuel M. Meyers, and Albert D. Biderman, *Mass Behavior in Battle and Captivity: The Communist Soldier in the Korean War* (Chicago: University of Chicago Press, 1968); and Omar Bartov, *Hitler's Army: Soldiers, Nazis, and War in the Third Reich* (New York: Oxford University Press, 1991).

58. "Death and Treason," *Newsweek*, 5 February 1945, 47; "Seven by the Rope," *Newsweek*, 23 July 1945, 27; "War Prisoners: How Should They Be Treated?" *Senior Scholastic*, 12 February 1945, 3.

59. "Screening of cooperative prisoners of war," 12 December 1945; "Special Regulations for the Special Project Center, Fort Eustis, Virginia," 10 January 1946; both in Box 1, Entry 467D, RG 389; "Memorandum on the Use of Civilian Personnel in German POW Camps," no date, Box 672, Entry 437, RG 389; Robert P. Patterson to the Secretary of State, 15 April 1945, Box 673, Entry 437, RG 389; Dean Acheson to Henry L. Stimson, 4 April 1945, Box 673, Entry 437, RG 389.

60. Carlson, *We Were Each Other's Prisoners,* 114; Howard M. Jones to B. F. Bryan Jr., 23 May 1945, Box 673, Entry 437, RG 389.

61. Office of War Information and the War Manpower Commission, "Information Plan," no date, 5–6, Box 19, Entry 23, RG 211.

62. The War Manpower Commission never considered POWs to be more important than many other sources of emergency labor. For examples of other contemplated sources, see U.S. Employment Service, *A Short History of the War Manpower Commission,* preliminary draft (Washington, D.C.: U.S. Department of Labor, 1948), 88–91.

63. Minutes of the Commandant's Conference, 8 December 1944, Box 1, Entry 268, RG 38; "A Few Interesting Facts about POW's," *Base Maintenance Notes* (January 1945): 9, Box 5, Entry 268, RG 38; "General Training Program for Prisoner of War Work Supervisors," no date, 4, Box 2, Entry 268, RG 38.

64. "Prisoner of War Labor Program," undated, Box 9, Entry 11, RG 211.

65. A. M. Ross to William Haber, 16 August 1943, Box 44, Entry 115, RG 211.

66. Minutes of the Labor-Management Committee, 27 July 1943, Box 44, Entry 115, RG 211; see also Frank P. Fenton to Marjorie G. Russell, 13 August 1943, Box 3, Entry 11, RG 211.

67. Lawrence Appley to All Regional Directors, 21 June 1943, Box 21, Entry 126, RG 211. Appley's orders specifically forbade the use of prisoner labor in jobs made vacant by labor disputes, regardless of the causes or particulars of the dispute.

68. Byron Fairchild and Jonathan Grossman, *The Army and Industrial Manpower,* The United States Army in World War II (Washington, D.C.: Office of the Chief of Military History, 1959), 189–196.

69. Although all POWs were guarded by the army, thousands worked and lived on naval installations. Minutes of Conference Re: Use of German Prisoners of War, no date; E. C. Peterson to the Assistant Secretary of the Navy, 5 March 1945; both in Box 1, Entry 268, RG 38.

70. U.S. War Department, *Enemy Prisoners,* 5.1–4.

71. John E. O'Gara to Brigadier General Pearson, 10 March 1943; Blackshear M. Bryan, "Labor of Prisoners of War," 2 April 1943; Paul B. Clemens, "Employment of Prisoners of War in Agriculture," 24 September 1943; all in Box 1435, Entry 457, RG 389.

72. For examples, see Selma Rice to Edward D. Hollander, 20 July 1943; Selma Rice to Fay W. Hunter, 26 July 1943; both in Box 19, Entry 89, RG 211.

73. "War Prisoner Labor Fought," *New York Times,* 16 November 1944, 8.

74. "War Prisoner Pay Is Held Inviolate," *New York Times,* 12 February 1944, 15.

75. W. Parkinson to Jerpe Commission Company, 29 March 1944; J. J. Guenther to Frank M. Rarig, 8 April 1944; both in Box 9, Entry 11, RG 211.

76. U.S. War Department, *Enemy Prisoners,* 5.6–7.

77. Frank Rarig to John J. Guenther, 12 April 1944, Box 9, Entry 11, RG 211.

78. Ibid.

79. War Department policy allowed POWs to work in the railroad industry in a maintenance capacity only; U.S. War Department, *Enemy Prisoners*, 5.7.

80. J. G. Luhrsen to Nelson H. Cruikshank, 24 July 1943; "Resolution Adopted by the Railway Labor Executives' Association," 16 July 1943; both in Box 19, Entry 23, RG 211.

81. "Draft of Proposed Letter to Officials of Railway Labor Organizations Concerning Prisoners of War," 7 September 1943, Box 19, Entry 23, RG 211.

82. Contractors using POW labor were also required to supply supervisors, trainers, and tools for the prisoners, and could not use POWs for high climbing, swamp logging, top felling, slash burning, or the operation of power machines; U.S. War Department, *Enemy Prisoners*, 5.6.

83. Fairchild and Grossman, *Army and Industrial Manpower*, 191–193; James E. Fickle and Donald W. Ellis, "POWs in the Piney Woods: German Prisoners of War in the Southern Lumber Industry, 1943–1945," *Journal of Southern History* 56 (November 1990): 696.

84. "CIO Victory Production Committee Report on Employment of War Prisoners," undated, Box 13, Entry 11, RG 211.

85. Robert M. La Follette Jr. to Paul V. McNutt, 1 June 1945, Box 1, Entry 175, RG 211; similar allegations had already occurred, including Ben H. Kinch to Franklin D. Roosevelt, 13 November 1943, Box 3, Entry 11, RG 211.

86. McNutt to Paul C. Kirk, 13 June 1945, Box 1, Entry 175, RG 211. Kirk, the president of the Federation of Labor of Sturgeon Bay, Wisc., had originally contacted La Follette with his complaints.

87. W. H. Spencer to Executive Director, War Manpower Commission, 20 June 1945, Box 1, Entry 175, RG 211.

88. Boykin to McNutt, 13 July 1945; McNamee to Boykin, 19 July 1945; McNamee to Boykin, 23 July 1945; Boykin to McNamee, 27 July 1945; McNamee to Boykin, 10 August 1945; all found in Box 38, Entry 155, RG 211.

89. W. A. Meyer to all Building Trades Councils, 29 March 1945, Box 163, Entry 171, RG 211.

90. McNutt to Henry L. Stimson, 19 May 1945, Box 163, Entry 171, RG 211.

91. CIO Industrial Union Council of York County to Paul McNutt, 7 August 1945, Box 163, Entry 171, RG 211.

92. Memorandum, Robert P. Patterson to Henry Stimson, 26 September 1944, in Box 1438, Entry 457, Record Group 389.

93. MacKenzie, "Treatment of Prisoners," 490.

94. Dwight D. Eisenhower to George C. Marshall, 13 January 1945, Box 1437, Entry 457, RG 389, contains a list of atrocities by German commanders, including no-quarter orders and prisoner executions; see also "Anger at Nazi Atrocities Is Rising but U.S. Treats Prisoners Fairly," *Newsweek*, 7 May 1945, 58.

95. H. G. Teel, "Rules for POWs in Japanese Camps," no date; "War Crimes Office," no date; both in Box 1447, Entry 458, RG 389.

96. Hata, "From Consideration to Contempt," 266.

97. Boxes 49–52, Entry "Prisoner of War Interrogation Records," RG 38, contains hundreds of interrogation reports of German prisoners released by the Soviet Union and returned to the U.S. occupation zone.

CHAPTER 7: CONTAINING COMMUNISM

1. Stanley Weintraub, "Behind the Wire," in *No Bugles, No Drums: An Oral History of the Korean War*, ed. Rudy Tomedi (New York: John Wiley, 1993), 191–193.

2. Ibid., 194–195.

3. "Geneva Convention Files"; Embassy of France to the Department of State, 19 January 1949; both in Box 124, Entry 472, RG 353; Interdepartmental Committee on Prisoners of War, "United States Draft for the Revision of the Geneva Convention Relative to the Treatment of Prisoners of War," 4 March 1949, Box 673, Entry 437, RG 389.

4. Stanley Sandler, *The Korean War: No Victors, No Vanquished* (Lexington: University Press of Kentucky, 1999), 212–215.

5. Lee Ballenger, *The Outpost War* (Washington, D.C.: Brassey's, 2000), 103–105. Many works have discussed the plight of U.N. prisoners in North Korea, with special emphasis on the captivity experiences of American soldiers. For examples, see Eugene Kinkead, *In Every War but One* (New York: Norton, 1959), 170–186, which concluded that American service personnel suffered in communist-run camps as a result of a pronounced lack of discipline and training in the army. He claimed that one-third of all American POWs collaborated with the enemy, and more than 13 percent were guilty of "serious collaboration." See also Albert Biderman, *March to Calumny: The Story of American POWs in Korea* (New York: Arno Press, 1979), 36–37, 42–43, which systematically countered Kinkead's thesis and observed that the military convicted only ten American repatriates for collaboration, and argued that most American POWs neither collaborated with nor actively resisted the enemy. Raymond B. Lech's *Broken Soldiers* (Urbana: University of Illinois Press, 2000) relied on transcripts of army interrogations and debriefings of returning American POWs to examine their mistreatment in communist camps. He considered the period of captivity as a "methodical and calculated program of torture," an attempt to destroy individuality and retrain the prisoners as "proper thinkers" (4). Lewis H. Carlson used oral interviews with surviving American POWs to document the situation in North Korean and Chinese camps. He accused the communist captors of deliberately mistreating American prisoners, with the result that 40 percent died while in captivity. See Lewis H. Carlson, *Remembered Prisoners of a Forgotten War: An Oral History of Korean War POWs* (New York: St. Martin's Press, 2002), xiii.

6. Roy E. Appleman, *South to the Naktong, North to the Yalu (June–November 1950)*, U.S. Army in the Korean War (Washington, D.C.: Office of the Chief of Military History, 1961), 751–756; James F. Schnabel, *Policy and Direction: The First Year*, U.S. Army in the Korean War (Washington, D.C.: Office of the Chief of Military History, 1972); Billy C. Mossman, *Ebb and Flow: November 1950–July 1951* (Washington, D.C.: Center of Military History, 1990), 440–445, 479–480; Walter G. Hermes, *Truce*

Tent and Fighting Front, U.S. Army in the Korean War (Washington, D.C.: Office of the Chief of Military History, 1966), 233–237, 260–261.

7. Douglas MacArthur to all American forces in Korea, 5 July 1950, Box 477, Entry EUSAK, RG 338.

8. Douglas MacArthur, "Circular Number 19," 16 August 1950, Box 477, Entry EUSAK, RG 338.

9. Callum A. MacDonald, *Korea: The War before Vietnam* (New York: Free Press, 1986), 134.

10. R. C. Partridge to Charles J. Kersten, 23 September 1953; Office of the Provost Marshal General, "Tabulation of the Number of Korean and Chinese Communist Prisoners of War," 28 July 1953; both in Box 92, Entry 452, RG 389; Office of the Provost Marshal General, "Recapitulation of Prisoner of War Strength," 24 September 1953, Box 89, Entry 452, RG 389.

11. Samuel M. Meyers and William C. Bradbury, "The Political Behavior of Korean and Chinese Prisoners of War in the Korean Conflict: A Historical Analysis," in *Mass Behavior in Battle and Captivity: The Communist Soldier in the Korean War*, ed. William C. Bradbury, Samuel C. Meyers, and Albert D. Biderman (Chicago: University of Chicago Press, 1968), 209–211.

12. Syngman Rhee to John B. Coulter, 3 May 1951; John Myun Chang to John B. Coulter, 7 May 1951; both in Box 801, Entry EUSAK, RG 338; James A. Van Fleet to Matthew B. Ridgway, 20 April 1951; John Myun Chang to John B. Coulter, 24 May 1951; James A. Van Fleet to Paul F. Yount, 21 May 1951; all in Box 800, Entry EUSAK, RG 338.

13. John Myun Chang to John B. Coulter, 24 May 1951; James A. Van Fleet to Matthew B. Ridgway, 1 June 1951; James A. Van Fleet to Paul F. Yount, 4 July 1951; all in Box 800, Entry EUSAK, RG 338.

14. Matthew B. Ridgway to James A. Van Fleet, 16 October 1951; James A. Van Fleet to Paul F. Yount, 25 October 1951; H. I. Hodes to John J. Muccio, 25 October 1951; all in Box 800, Entry EUSAK, RG 338.

15. "A Study of the Administration and Security of the Oriental Communist Prisoner of War during the Conflict in Korea," 13–14, 25 September 1953, Box 14, Entry PMG POWD, RG 472.

16. Ibid., 18–19.

17. Francis T. Dodd to Paul F. Yount, 20 March 1952; Paul F. Yount to Matthew B. Ridgway, 22 March 1952; both in Box 837, Entry EUSAK, RG 338; Mark Clark to James A. Van Fleet, 29 January 1952, Box 836, Entry EUSAK, RG 338.

18. "Statement of Brigadier General Charles F. Colson Regarding the Negotiations Conducted with the P.W. Leaders in Compound 76," 20 February 1953, Box 837, Entry EUSAK, RG 338.

19. "Eighth Army Regiment in P.W. Command," 19 February 1953, Box 862, Entry EUSAK, RG 338.

20. "Study of the Oriental Communist Prisoner," 40.

21. "Standard Operating Procedures for POW Enclosures," 2–3, 15 August 1952, Box 838, Entry EUSAK, RG 338.

22. Memorandum No. 13, 31 March 1953, Box 14, Entry PMG POWD, RG 472.

23. Ibid., 39.1.

24. Matthew B. Ridgway to James A. Van Fleet, 24 February 1952, Box 837, Entry EUSAK, RG 338.

25. David P. Schorr Jr. to Haydon L. Boatner, 16 July 1959; Haydon L. Boatner to David P. Schorr Jr., 31 July 1959; David P. Schorr Jr. to Haydon L. Boatner, 30 September 1959; Haydon L. Boatner to David P. Schorr Jr., 20 October 1959; all in Box 87, Entry 452, RG 389.

26. Meyers and Bradbury, "Political Behavior," 267–271.

27. "Petition of Kim Won Song," 25 July 1951, Box 838, Entry EUSAK, RG 338; "Petition," 18 July 1951; "Petition," 5 August 1951; "The Petition," 22 August 1951; "The Supplication," no date; "No. 77 Brigade Church Christian Petition," 15 July 1951; all found in Box 502, Entry EUSAK, RG 338.

28. Meyers and Bradbury, "Political Behavior," 280; "Demographic Study of Korean and Chinese P.W.s," no date, Box 87, Entry 452, RG 389.

29. "Draft Technical Report," 13 June 1956, Box 87, Entry 452, RG 389.

30. Ibid., 14.

31. Examples of the clothing complaints are contained in Lee Hak-Kyoo to Francis T. Dodd, 26 July 1951; Lee Hak-Kyoo to James A. Van Fleet, 26 July 1951; Paul F. Yount to James A. Van Fleet, 30 July 1951; all in Box 477, Entry EUSAK, RG 338. Colonel Lee served as the prisoner representative for North Korean officer POWs on Koje-do. The impact of the clothing issue is detailed in Meyers and Bradbury, "Political Behavior," 265, 269–270.

32. "Chronology of Principal Events in Korean Armistice Negotiations," 20, Box 1, Entry 61, RG 333.

33. R. C. Dalquist to Robert A. Gelwick, 23 October 1951, Box 1, Entry 61, RG 333.

34. Ibid., 23. See also "UNC Proposal on Agenda Item 4 Presented to the Communists," 2 January 1952; "UNC Proposal on Agenda Item 4 Presented to the Communists," 8 January 1952; "UNC Proposal on Agenda Item 4 Presented to the Communists," 28 January 1952; all in Box 1, Entry 61, RG 333; Matthew B. Ridgway to James A. Van Fleet, 30 July 1951, Box 800, Entry EUSAK, RG 338.

35. William H. Vatcher Jr., *Panmunjom: The Story of the Korean Military Armistice Negotiations* (New York: Praeger, 1958), 118–119.

36. Libby's request was followed by a request from Ridgway, also rejected as unnecessary by the communist leadership. Matthew B. Ridgway to Kim Il Sung and Peng Teh-huai, 21 December 1951; Kim Il Sung and Peng Teh-huai to Matthew B. Ridgway, 24 December 1951; both in Box 1, Entry 61, RG 333.

37. Vatcher, *Panmunjom*, 129; "Chronology of Armistice Negotiations," 25.

38. "Chronology of Armistice Negotiations," 35; "Description of the Process of Screening Communist Prisoners of War by the UNC," 28 May 1952, Box 1, Entry 61, RG 333.

39. On 31 March 1953, UNC guards at Koje-do received orders to segregate any prisoners who claimed to be anticommunists and who intended to resist repatriation. Memorandum No. 13, 45.

40. Mark Clark to Kim Il Sung and Peng Teh-haui, 19 October 1952, Box 1, Entry 61, RG 333.

41. A copy of Clark's proposal is included in Mark Clark to the AG, 8 April 1953, Box 862, Entry EUSAK, RG 338.

42. Mark Clark to JCS, 22 April 1954, Box 92, Entry 452, RG 389.

43. "Demographic Study."

44. "History of MAC Prisoner of War Activities," 1, Box 5, Entry 61, RG 333.

45. Ibid., 4; "UNCMAC Estimate of the Situation," 2, 9 April 1957, Box 5, Entry 61, RG 333; J. A. Rell, "Illegal Detention of Prisoners of War," 1–2, 17 April 1954, Box 3, Entry 61, RG 333.

46. Julius Segal, "Factors Related to the Collaboration and Resistance Behavior of U.S. Army P.W.'s in Korea," Army Technical Report 33, December 1956, Box 87, Entry 452, RG 389.

47. "Standard Operating Procedure for the Operation of United Nations Prisoner of War Camps," 25 September 1953, 2–5, Box 14, Entry PMG POWD, RG 472; Pitman B. Potter, "Repatriation of Korean Prisoners of War," *American Journal of International Law* 47 (October 1952): 661–662; Office of the Provost Marshal General, "Repatriation of Prisoners of War," Box 92, Entry 452, RG 389.

48. Department of the Army, "Prisoner of War Operations," 26 June 1956, Box 90, Entry 452, RG 389.

CHAPTER 8: THE DOMINOES BEGIN TO FALL

1. Susan Sheehan, *Ten Vietnamese* (New York: Alfred A. Knopf, 1968), 190–195.

2. Ibid., 196–203.

3. Stuart I. Rochester and Frederick Kiley, *Honor Bound: American Prisoners of War in Southeast Asia, 1961–1973* (Annapolis, Md.: Naval Institute Press, 1999), 203; Tom Philpott, *Glory Denied: The Saga of Jim Thompson, America's Longest-Held Prisoner of War* (New York: Norton, 2001), 77.

4. Vernon E. Davis, *The Long Road Home: U.S. Prisoner of War Policy and Planning in Southeast Asia* (Washington, D.C.: Office of the Secretary of Defense, Historical Office, 2000), 63–64.

5. Ibid., 90–94.

6. U. Alexis Johnson to Ngueyn Cao Ky, 9 August 1965; "Year-End Wrap-up 1967," no date; "A Plan for the Development of Procedures and Facilities for Handling Combat Captives in SVN," no date; all in Box 2, Entry PMG POWD, RG 472.

7. Box 2, Entry PMG POWD, RG 472, contains monthly returns of prison compounds from 1965 until 1972.

8. Richard O. Rowland to Charles D. Gooch, 25 July 1969; Charles D. Gooch, "RVN Prisoner of War Camp Status," 28 September 1969; both in Box 4, Entry PMG POWD, RG 472.

9. Cao Van Vien, "Control, Follow-up, and Report of the CRP's (Communist Rebel Prisoner) Status," 30 June 1966, Box 1, Entry PMG POWD, RG 472.

10. Nguyen Huu Co, "Instruction on Prescription of the Policies Concerning the Treatment of Rebel Communist Prisoners," 16 December 1965, Box 1, Entry PMG POWD, RG 472.

11. JGS Memorandum 2537, 19 October 1965, Box 1, Entry PMG POWD, RG 472.

12. JGS Memorandum 333, 9–10, 25 May 1966, Box 1, Entry PMG POWD, RG 472.

13. MACJ Supplemental Data Sheet, no date, Box 1, Entry PMG POWD, RG 472; Franklin M. Davis Jr., "Plan for a Model Prisoner of War System," no date, Box 2, Entry PMG POWD, RG 472.

14. Richard O. Rowland to Charles D. Gooch, 9 June 1969, Box 4, Entry PMG POWD, RG 472.

15. Richard E. Abercrombie, "End of Tour Report," 30 May 1969, Box 4, Entry PMG POWD, RG 472.

16. JGS Memorandum 333, 11.

17. "Use of Force for P.W. Riot Control," 7 May 1968, Box 2, Entry PMG POWD, RG 472.

18. Carl C. Turner to Henry W. Gibson, 22 April 1968; Carl C. Turner to William Brandenburg, 8 July 1968, both in Box 2, Entry PMG POWD, RG 472.

19. William H. Brandenburg to Carl C. Turner, 26 July 1968, Box 2, Entry PMG POWD, RG 472.

20. Cao Van Vien to Creighton W. Abrams, no date, Box 15, Entry PMG POWD, RG 472.

21. Richard O. Rowland to Charles D. Gooch, 25 July 1969, Box 4, Entry PMG POWD, RG 472; Nguyen Hieu Trung, "Change from P.W. Status to Returnee Status, 7 April 1969, Box 6, Entry PMG POWD, RG 472.

22. Cao Van Vien, "Change to Returnee Status," 17 July 1967; "P.W.'s in the Chieu Hoi Program," no date; W. E. Colby, "P.W.'s in Chieu Hoi Program," 17 May 1969; Robert H. Ivey, "North Vietnam P.W.s and Chieu Hoi Program," 25 February 1969; all in Box 6, Entry PMG POWD, RG 472.

23. "POW Status Report," 1 April 1969, Box 3, Entry PMG POWD, RG 472.

24. Nguyen Trong Mae to Nguyen Van Cau, 1 December 1967, Box 2, Entry PMG POWD, RG 472; Nguyen Ca, "Detention of Female P.W.s Who Have Babies at the P.W. Camps," 30 August 1967, Box 7, Entry PMG POWD, RG 472.

25. Memorandum of Conversation, Christian Hauser, George H. Aldritch, Robert I. Starr, 15 May 1969, Box 7, Entry PMG POWD, RG 472.

26. "Civilian Detention Activities in 1968," 30 January 1969, Box 8, Entry PMG POWD, RG 472.

27. Milton K. Campbell, "Phu Quoc P.W. Camp and V.C. Activity on Phu Quoc," no date, Box 4, Entry PMG POWD, RG 472; Sam A. Roberts to Major General Davidson, 5 February 1969, Box 4, Entry PMG POWD, RG 472; "Civilian Detention Activities in 1968," 30 January 1969, Box 8, Entry PMG POWD, RG 472; CORDS-R Berkeley to State Department, 29 January 1969, Box 5, Entry PMG POWD, RG 472.

28. Richard Rowland, "Trip Report on Visit to Vietnam," 16 October 1968, Box 2, Entry PMG POWD, RG 472.

29. Frank B. Clay to Creighton W. Abrams, 14 October 1968, Box 3, Entry PMG POWD, RG 472. G. Warren Nutter to John Thorton and Richard O. Rowland, 5 November 1969; Frank A. Sieverts to Ellsworth Bunker, 6 October 1969; both in Box 4, Entry PMG POWD, RG 472.

30. Army Concept Team in Vietnam, "Accountability, Classification, and Record/Reporting System for Captured Enemy Personnel," June 1970, Box 9, Entry PMG POWD, RG 472.

31. Thorton E. Ireland, "ICRC Inspection of Central Prisoner of War Camp," 12 October 1970; Ellsworth Bunker to the Secretary of State, 14 October 1970; J. P. Dunbar to Thornton E. Ireland, 30 October 1970; "Conditions at Phu Quoc P.W. Camp," 28 September 1970; all in Box 10, Entry PMG POWD, RG 472.

32. Warren H. Metzner to Alan D. Holland, 20 March 1970, Box 12, Entry PMG POWD, RG 472; Charles D. Gooch to Warren H. Metzner, 25 February 1970, Box 13, Entry PMG POWD, RG 472.

33. Stephen Winship, "Observations on Visit to Phu Quoc P.W. Camp, July 29–30, 1971," 11 August 1971; Cao Van Vien to Creighton W. Abrams, 29 July 1971; both in Box 14, Entry PMG POWD, RG 472.

34. Kenneth G. Wickham to Creighton W. Abrams, 25 November 1968, Box 3, Entry PMG POWD, RG 472; Frank A. Sieverts to Ellsworth Bunker, 6 October 1969, Box 4, Entry PMG POWD, RG 472. ICRC, "Report on Visit made to Phu Quoc P.W. Camp," 8 March 1968; ICRC, "Annex to Report on Visit to Phu Quoc P.W. Camp," 18 March 1968; both in Box 1, Entry PMG POWD, RG 472.

35. "Proposed Ration Scales," 16 September 1968, Box 15, Entry PMG POWD, RG 472.

36. Henry Gibson to the provost marshal, 19 March 1968, Box 3, Entry PMG POWD, RG 472.

37. "Proposed Planning Guidance for CINCUSARPAC, CINCPAC, and COMUSMACV on Enemy P.W. Repatriation Planning," no date, Box 2, Entry PMG POWD, RG 472; "Reciprocal Repatriation of NVN Naval Personnel," 5 March 1968, Box 3, Entry PMG POWD, RG 472.

38. Creighton W. Abrams to Ellsworth Bunker, 29 November 1968, Box 3, Entry PMG POWD, RG 472.

39. Davis, *Long Road Home*, 280–282.

40. "Repatriation of Enemy Prisoners of War," 15 January 1973, Box 18, Entry PMG POWD, RG 472.

41. Allegations that North Vietnam retained American POWs after the war have abounded for three decades, despite numerous government investigations that have discovered no evidence of such prisoners. For a thorough discussion of the POW-MIA debate, see H. Bruce Franklin, "The POW/MIA Myth," in *The Lessons and Legacies of the Vietnam War*, ed. Walter L. Hixson (New York: Garland, 2000), 189–210.

42. Josiah W. Bennett to Charles S. Whitehouse, 11 November 1972, Box 18, Entry PMG POWD, RG 472.

CHAPTER 9: POW POLICY IN THE POST–COLD WAR ERA

1. "Profile: Al Qaeda 'Kingpin,'" 21 January 2009, BBC News, available at http://news.bbc.co.uk/2/hi/south_asia/2811855.stm; Office of the Director of

National Intelligence, "Biographies of Detainees," available at http://www.odni.gov/announcements/content/DetaineeBiographies.pdf, 13.

2. Scott Shane, "Waterboarding Used 266 Times on Two Subjects," *New York Times,* 19 April 2009.

3. "Verbatim Transcript of Combatant Status Review Tribunal Hearing for ISN 10024," 10 May 2007, available at http://www.aclu.org/pdfs/safefree/csrt_ksm.pdf.

4. "Sept. 11 Defendants Ask to Plead Guilty," *New York Times,* 8 December 2008.

5. Tom Clancy and Chuck Horner, *Every Man a Tiger* (New York: G. P. Putnam's Sons, 1999), 477; Rick Atkinson, *Crusade: The Untold Story of the Persian Gulf War* (Boston: Houghton Mifflin, 1993), 377.

6. M. S. White, ed., *Gulf Logistics: Blackadder's War* (London: Brassey's, 1995), 217, 234.

7. U.S. Department of Defense, *Final Report to Congress on the Conduct of the Persian Gulf War* (Washington, D.C.: Government Printing Office, 1992), 86, 473, 577; Atkinson, *Crusade,* 481; Dominic J. Caraccilo, *The Ready Brigade of the 82nd Airborne in Desert Storm* (Jefferson, N.C.: McFarland, 1993), 164; Clancy and Horner, *Every Man,* 477; Stephen A. Bourque, *Jayhawk! The VII Corps in the Persian Gulf War* (Washington, D.C.: Department of the Army, 2002), 455; Peter Rowe, ed., *The Gulf War 1990–91 in International and English Law* (London: Routledge, 1993), 202.

8. James F. Dunnigan and Austin Bay, *From Shield to Storm: High-Tech Weapons, Military Strategy, and Coalition Warfare in the Persian Gulf* (New York: William Morrow, 1992), 273; Caraccilo, *Ready Brigade,* 117; Bourque, *Jayhawk!,* 237.

9. Michael R. Gordon and Bernard Trainor, *The Generals' War: The Inside Story of the Conflict in the Gulf* (Boston: Little, Brown, 1995), 363, 368; Bourque, *Jayhawk!,* 319; Caraccilo, *Ready Brigade,* 150–155.

10. U.S. Department of Defense, *Final Report,* 585.

11. Norman Friedman, *Desert Victory: The War for Kuwait* (Annapolis, Md.: Naval Institute Press, 1991), 198.

12. U.S. Department of Defense, *Final Report,* 578.

13. Ibid., 577.

14. Andrew Leyden, *Gulf War Debriefing Book: An After-Action Report,* ed. Camille Akin (Grants Pass, Ore.: Hellgate Press, 1997), 291–292.

15. John Norton Moore, *Crisis in the Gulf: Enforcing the Rule of Law* (New York: Oceana, 1992), 70. One American POW, Major Rhonda Cornum, reported an attempted sexual assault in her autobiography: Rhonda Cornum, *She Went to War: The Rhonda Cornum Story,* ed. Peter Copeland (Novato, Calif.: Presidio Press, 1992), 49–50.

16. John Mueller, *Policy and Opinion in the Gulf War* (Chicago: University of Chicago Press, 1994), 343–344.

17. Ken Matthews, *The Gulf Conflict and International Relations* (London: Routledge, 1993), 152–155; Lawrence Freedman, "The Theory of Limited War," in *International Perspectives on the Gulf Conflict, 1990–91,* ed. Alex Danchev and Dan Keohane (New York: St. Martin's Press, 1994), 214.

18. See also Dennis Menos, *Arms over Diplomacy: Reflections on the Persian Gulf War* (Westport, Conn.: Praeger, 1992), 93; Moore, *Crisis in the Gulf*, 255; Robert H. Scales, *Certain Victory: The U.S. Army in the Gulf War* (Washington, D.C.: Office of the Chief of Staff of the Army, 1993), 323; Gordon and Trainor, *Generals' War*, 444.

19. Amy Waters Yarsinske, *No One Left Behind: The Lieutenant Commander Michael Scott Speicher Story* (New York: Dutton, 2002), 241; Lon Wagner and Amy Waters Yarsinske, "Dead or Alive?" *Virginian-Pilot*, 4 January 2002; Sara A. Carter, "Speicher Remains Found in Iraq, Identified," *Washington Times*, 3 August 2009.

20. A total of 13,227 enlisted and 191 officer POWs refused repatriation. U.S. Department of Defense, *Final Report*, 587; Adam Roberts, "The Laws of War," in Danchev and Keohane, *International Perspectives*, 276; Gordon and Trainor, *Generals' War*, 413–414.

21. Scales, *Certain Victory*, 65.

22. President George W. Bush, "Transcript of President Bush's Address," CNN.com/U.S., 21 September 2001, available at http://archives.cnn.com/2001/US/09/20/gen.bush.transcript.

23. Adam Roberts and Richard Guelff, eds., *Documents on the Laws of War*, 2nd ed. (Oxford: Oxford University Press, 1989), 411–414.

24. Rosemary Foot, *Human Rights and Counter-terrorism in America's Asian Policy*, Adelphi Paper 363 (New York: Oxford University Press, 2004), 13–14.

25. Karen Greenberg, *The Least Worst Place: Guantánamo's First 100 Days* (New York: Oxford University Press, 2009), 4–5.

26. Steven Strasser, ed., *The Abu Ghraib Investigations: The Official Reports of the Independent Panel and the Pentagon on the Shocking Prisoner Abuse in Iraq* (New York: Public Affairs, 2004), 4–5; George Bush, "Humane Treatment of al Qaeda and Taliban Detainees," 7 February 2002, in *Torture and Truth: America, Abu Ghraib, and the War on Terror*, ed. Mark Danner (New York: New York Review of Books, 2004), 105–106.

27. Paul Rogers, *A War on Terror: Afghanistan and After* (London: Pluto Press, 2004), 165–166.

28. Department of the Army, "Intelligence Interrogation," 8 May 1987, Field Manual 34-52, chap. 1, available at http://www.globalsecurity.org/intell/library/policy/army/fm/fm34-52/toc.htm.

29. Strasser, *Abu Ghraib Investigations*, xvi–xvii, 32–33; Donald Rumsfeld to James T. Hill, 16 April 2003, in Danner, *Torture and Truth*, 199–204; Karen J. Greenberg and Joshua L. Dratel, eds., *The Torture Papers: The Road to Abu Ghraib* (New York: Cambridge University Press, 2005), 1239.

30. Iraq Coalition Troops, http://www.globalsecurity.org/military/ops/iraq_orbat_coalition.htm#.

31. John Keegan, *The Iraq War* (New York: Alfred A. Knopf, 2004), 81; Sara Beck and Malcolm Downing, eds., *The Battle for Iraq: BBC News Correspondents on the War against Saddam* (Baltimore: Johns Hopkins University Press, 2003), 22; Anthony H. Cordesman, *The Iraq War: Strategy, Tactics, and Military Lessons* (Washington, D.C.: Center for Strategic and International Studies, 2003), 247.

32. Cordesman, *Iraq War*, 512; Nicholas E. Reynolds, *Basrah, Baghdad, and*

Beyond: The U.S. Marine Corps in the Second Iraq War (Annapolis, Md.: Naval Institute Press, 2005), 43.

33. Rick Bragg, *I Am a Soldier, Too: The Jessica Lynch Story* (New York: Alfred A. Knopf, 2003), 129–132; Peter Baker, "Iraqi Man Risked All to Help Free American Soldier," *Washington Post*, 4 April 2003.

34. Dexter Filkins, "7 U.S. POWs Are Found Alive by Marines," *International Herald Tribune*, 14 April 2003.

35. Beck and Downing, *Battle for Iraq*, 156–157; John Lee Anderson, *The Fall of Baghdad* (New York: Penguin Press, 2004), 109, 364, 370–371.

36. Strasser, *Abu Ghraib Investigations*, xiv.

37. Danner, *Torture and Truth*, 3.

38. "Report of the International Committee of the Red Cross on the Treatment by the Coalition Forces of Prisoners of War and Other Protected Persons by the Geneva Conventions in Iraq during Arrest, Internment, and Interrogation," February 2004, in Danner, *Torture and Truth*, 252.

39. Bing West, *No True Glory: A Frontline Account of the Battle for Fallujah* (New York: Bantam Books, 2005), 213.

40. Strasser, *Abu Ghraib Investigations*, xvi–xviii.

41. "Article 15-6 Investigation of the 800th Military Police Brigade (The Taguba Report)," in Danner, *Torture and Truth*, 289–290.

42. Ibid., 312–313.

43. Ibid., 319–324.

44. "Investigation of Intelligence Activities at Abu Ghraib," in Danner, *Torture and Truth*, 404–405.

45. Ibid., 405.

46. Douglas Jehl and Eric Schmitt, "Army Report: Gen. Sanchez Approved Torture at Abu Ghraib," *New York Times*, 27 August 2004, A1.

47. *Rasul et al. v. Bush, President of the United States, et al.*, October term, 2003, available at http://www.cdi.org/news/law/rasul-decision.pdf; Tom Curry, "Senate Wrests Detainee Issue from Courts," 14 November 2005, MSNBC.com, http://www.msnbc.msn.com/id/10039267/from/RL.2; Eric Schmitt, "Senate Approves Limiting Rights of U.S. Detainees," *New York Times*, 11 November 2005, A1; Mark Sappenfield, "Senate Affirms Path of Antiterror Tribunals," *Christian Science Monitor*, 18 November 2005.

48. John J. Lumpkin, "7 Ex-Detainees Return to Fighting," *Boston Globe*, 18 October 2004.

49. Tomoko Hosaka, "Uighurs Trigger Public Backlash in Palau," *Miami Herald*, 12 June 2009.

50. Carol Rosenberg, "Surprise: Four Chinese Detainees Sent from Guantánamo to Bermuda," *Miami Herald*, 11 June 2009.

BIBLIOGRAPHY

U.S. GOVERNMENT RECORD GROUPS, NATIONAL ARCHIVES, WASHINGTON, D.C.

RG 38. Records of the Office of the Chief of Naval Operations.
RG 40. General Records of the Department of Commerce.
RG 45. Naval Records Collection of the Office of Naval Records and Library.
RG 94. Records of the Adjutant General's Office, 1780s–1917.
RG 111. Records of the Office of the Chief Signal Officer, 1860–1962.
RG 120. Records of the American Expeditionary Forces (World War I).
RG 165. Records of the War Department General and Special Staffs.
RG 208. Records of the Office of War Information.
RG 211. Records of the War Manpower Commission.
RG 217. Records of the Accounting Officers of the Department of the Treasury.
RG 249. Records of the Commissary General of Prisoners.
RG 333. Records of International Military Agencies.
RG 389. Records of the Office of the Provost Marshal General, 1941–.
RG 395. Records of the U.S. Army Overseas Operations and Commands, 1898–1942.
RG 407. Records of the Adjutant General's Office, 1917–.
RG 472. Records of the United States Forces in Southeast Asia, 1950–1975.

GOVERNMENT PUBLICATIONS AND DOCUMENTS

American State Papers: Foreign Affairs. 6 vols. 1789–1828.
American State Papers: Military Affairs. 7 vols. 1789–1838.
Annals of Congress.
Continental Congress. *Journals of the Continental Congress, 1774–1789.* Edited by Worthington C. Ford et al. 34 vols. Washington, D.C.: Government Printing Office, 1904–1937.
State Records of North Carolina. 26 vols. Goldsboro, N.C.: Nash Brothers, 1886–1907.

U.S. Army. *United States Army in the World War, 1917–1919.* 17 vols. Washington, D.C.: Center of Military History, 1988–1991.

U.S. Congress. House. *Messages of the President on the Subject of the Mexican War.* 30th Cong., 1st sess., 1848. H. Doc. 60, Serial 520.

U.S. Congress. House. *Annual Reports of the War Department, 1898.* 55th Cong., 3rd sess., 1898. H. Doc. 2, Serial 3744.

U.S. Congress. House. *Annual Reports of the Secretary of War, 1900.* 56th Cong., 1st sess., 1900. Serial 4073.

U.S. Congress. House. *Annual Reports of the Secretary of War, 1901.* 57th Cong., 1st sess., 1901. Serial 4272.

U.S. Congress. House. *Annual Reports of the War Department, 1919.* 66th Cong., 2nd sess., 1919. Serial 7682.

U.S. Congress. Senate. *Affairs in the Philippine Islands.* 57th Cong., 1st sess., 1902. Serial 4242–4244.

U.S. Department of Defense. *Final Report to Congress on the Conduct of the Persian Gulf War.* Washington, D.C.: Government Printing Office, 1992.

U.S. Employment Service. *A Short History of the War Manpower Commission.* Preliminary Draft. Washington, D.C.: U.S. Department of Labor, 1948.

U.S. War Department. *Enemy Prisoners of War.* 5 October 1944. Technical Manual 19-500.

U.S. War Department. *The War of the Rebellion: A Compilation of the Official Records of the Union and Confederate Armies.* 127 vols. Washington, D.C.: Government Printing Office, 1880–1901.

NEWSPAPERS AND MAGAZINES

Army and Navy Journal
BBC News Online
Boston Herald
Commonweal
Cosmopolitan
Miami Herald
Mobile Advertiser and Register
New York Daily Tribune
New York Times
Newsweek
Richmond Examiner
School and Society
Senior Scholastic
The Times (London)
Time
Washington Daily News
Washington Post

Washington Times
The World Today

PRINTED SOURCES

Adams, Alexander B. *Geronimo: A Biography*. New York: G. P. Putnam's Sons, 1971.

Adams, Henry. *The War of 1812*. New York: Charles Scribner's Sons, 1891.

Addington, Larry H. *The Patterns of War since the Eighteenth Century*. 2nd ed. Bloomington: Indiana University Press, 1994.

Allen, Ethan. *A Narrative of Colonel Ethan Allen's Captivity*. 1779. Reprint, Burlington, Vt.: H. Johnson, 1838.

Anderson, Chandler. "Agreement between the United States and Germany Concerning Prisoners of War." *American Journal of International Law* 13 (January 1919): 97–101.

Anderson, John Lee. *The Fall of Baghdad*. New York: Penguin Press, 2004.

Anderson, Olive. "The Establishment of British Supremacy at Sea and the Exchange of Naval Prisoners of War, 1689–1783." *English Historical Review* 75 (January 1960): 77–89.

Andrews, Charles. *The Prisoners' Memoirs or Dartmoor Prison*. New York: Self-Published, 1815.

Appleman, Roy. *South to the Naktong, North to the Yalu (June–November 1950)*. U.S. Army in the Korean War. Washington, D.C.: Office of the Chief of Military History, 1961.

Aptheker, Herbert. *The American Revolution, 1763–1783*. New York: International Publishers, 1960.

Atkinson, Rick. *Crusade: The Untold Story of the Persian Gulf War*. Boston: Houghton Mifflin, 1993.

Bacque, James. *Other Losses: The Shocking Truth behind the Mass Deaths of Disarmed German Soldiers and Civilians under General Eisenhower's Command*. New York: Prima, 1991.

Bain, David Howard. *Sitting in Darkness: Americans in the Philippines*. Boston: Houghton Mifflin, 1984.

Baird, George W. "The Capture of Chief Joseph and the Nez Perces." *International Review* 7 (August 1879): 209–215.

Ballenger, Lee. *The Outpost War*. Washington, D.C.: Brassey's, 2000.

Barker, A. J. *Prisoners of War*. New York: Universe Books, 1974.

Bartov, Omar. *Hitler's Army: Soldiers, Nazis, and War in the Third Reich*. New York: Oxford University Press, 1991.

Bass, Robert D. *Gamecock: The Life and Campaigns of General Thomas Sumter*. New York: Holt, Rinehart, and Winston, 1961.

———. *Swamp Fox: The Life and Campaigns of General Francis Marion*. New York: Henry Holt, 1959.

Bauer, K. Jack. *The Mexican War, 1846–1848*. New York: Macmillan, 1974.

Beck, Sara, and Malcolm Downing, eds. *The Battle for Iraq: BBC News Correspondents on the War against Saddam.* Baltimore: Johns Hopkins University Press, 2003.

Becker, Laura L. "Prisoners of War in the American Revolution: A Community Perspective." *Military Affairs* 46 (December 1982): 169–173.

Beirne, Francis F. *The War of 1812.* New York: E. P. Dutton, 1949.

Benson, Berry. *Berry Benson's Civil War Book: Memoirs of a Confederate Scout and Sharpshooter.* Edited by Susan Williams Benson. Athens: University of Georgia Press, 1962.

Benton, Elbert J. *International Law and Diplomacy of the Spanish-American War.* Baltimore: Johns Hopkins Press, 1908.

Berger, Carl. *Broadsides and Bayonets: The Propaganda War of the American Revolution.* San Rafael, Calif.: Presidio Press, 1976.

Berry, Henry. *Semper Fi, Mac: Living Memories of the U.S. Marines in World War Two.* New York: Arbor House, 1982.

Berry, Philip. *A Review of the Mexican War.* Columbia, S.C.: A. S. Johnston, 1849.

———. *A Review of the Mexican War on Christian Principles.* New York: J. S. Ozer, 1849.

Betzinez, Jason. *I Fought with Geronimo.* New York: Bonanza Books, 1959.

Biderman, Albert. *March to Calumny: The Story of American POWs in Korea.* New York: Arno Press, 1979.

Bird, Harrison. *War for the West, 1790–1813.* New York: Oxford University Press, 1971.

Birtle, Andrew J. *U.S. Army Counterinsurgency and Contingency Operations Doctrine, 1860–1941.* Washington, D.C.: Center of Military History, 1998.

Bischof, Gunter, and Stephen E. Ambrose, eds. *Eisenhower and the German Prisoners of War.* Baton Rouge: Louisiana State University Press, 1992.

Blakey, Arch Fredric. *General John H. Winder, CSA.* Gainesville: University of Florida Press, 1990.

Blatchford, John. *The Narrative of John Blatchford.* 1865. Reprint, New York: New York Times, 1971.

Bloom, John Porter. "With the American Army into Mexico, 1846–1848." Ph.D. diss., Emory University, 1956.

Booth, Benjamin F. *Dark Days of the Rebellion.* Edited by Steve Meyer. Garrison, Iowa: Meyer Publishing, 1995.

Bourque, Stephen A. *Jayhawk! The VII Corps in the Gulf War.* Washington, D.C.: Office of the Chief of Staff of the Army, 1993.

Bowman, Larry G. *Captive Americans: Prisoners during the American Revolution.* Athens: Ohio University Press, 1976.

Boyd, George Adams. *Elias Boudinot: Patriot and Statesman, 1740–1821.* Princeton, N.J.: Princeton University Press, 1952.

Bradbury, William C., Samuel M. Meyers, and Albert D. Biderman, eds. *Mass Behavior in Battle and Captivity: The Communist Soldier in the Korean War.* Chicago: University of Chicago Press, 1968.

Bragg, Rick. *I Am a Soldier, Too: The Jessica Lynch Story.* New York: Alfred A. Knopf, 2003.

Brown, Dee Alexander. *The Galvanized Yankees.* Urbana: University of Illinois Press, 1963.

Brown, Louis A. *The Salisbury Prison: A Case Study of Confederate Military Prisons, 1861–1865.* Baton Rouge: Louisiana State University Press, 1980.

Browne, Junius Henri. *Four Years in Secessia.* New York: Arno, 1970.

Bryant, William O. *Cahaba Prison and the Sultana Disaster.* Tuscaloosa: University of Alabama Press, 1990.

Buenzle, Fred J. "The Collier *Merrimac.*" *United States Naval Institute Proceedings* 66 (October 1940): 1447–1453.

Burgwyn, Wiliam Hyslop Sumner. *A Captain's War: The Letters and Diaries of William H. S. Burgwyn, 1861–1865.* Edited by Herbert M. Schiller. Shippensburg, Pa.: White Mane, 1994.

Bykofsky, Joseph, and Harld Larson. *The Transportation Corps: Operations Overseas.* The United States Army in World War II. Washington, D.C.: Center of Military History, 2003.

Caidin, Martin. *The Ragged, Rugged Warriors.* New York: Dutton, 1966.

Cangemi, Joseph P., and Casimir J. Kowalski, eds. *Andersonville Prison: Lessons in Organizational Failure.* Lanham, Md.: University Press of America, 1992.

Caraccilo, Dominic J. *The Ready Brigade of the 82nd Airborne in Desert Storm.* Jefferson, N.C.: McFarland, 1993.

Carlson, Lewis H. *Remembered Prisoners of a Forgotten War: An Oral History of Korean War POWs.* New York: St. Martin's Press, 2002.

———. *We Were Each Other's Prisoners: An Oral History of World War II American and German Prisoners of War.* New York: HarperCollins, 1997.

Carnahan, Burrus M. "Lincoln, Lieber and the Laws of War: The Origins and Limits of the Principle of Military Necessity." *American Journal of International Law* 92 (April 1998): 213–231.

Cavadaa, Frederic F. *Libby Life.* Philadelphia: King & Baird, 1864

Center of Military History. *Correspondence Relating to the War with Spain.* 2 vols. 1902. Reprint, Washington, D.C.: Government Printing Office, 1993.

Clancy, Tom, and Chuck Horner. *Every Man a Tiger.* New York: G. P. Putnam's Sons, 1999.

Clinton, Henry. *The American Rebellion.* New Haven: Yale University Press, 1954.

Cogliano, Francis D. *American Maritime Prisoners in the Revolutionary War: The Captivity of William Russell.* Annapolis, Md.: Naval Institute Press, 2001.

Cohen, Sheldon S. *Yankee Sailors in British Gaols: Prisoners of War at Forton and Mill, 1777–1783.* Newark: University of Delaware Press, 1995.

Commager, Henry Steele, and Richard B. Morris, eds. *The Spirit of Seventy-Six: The Story of the Revolution as Told by Participants.* 1958. Reprint, New York: Da Capo Press, 1995.

Cook, Ruth Beaumont. *Guests behind the Barbed Wire: German POWs in America—A True Story of Hope and Friendship.* Birmingham, Ala.: Crane Hill, 2006.

Cooper, Alonzo. *In and Out of Rebel Prisons.* Oswego, N.Y.: R. J. Oliphant, 1888.

Cordesman, Anthony H. *The Iraq Wars: Strategy, Tactics, and Military Lessons.* Washington, D.C.: Center for Strategic and International Studies, 2003.

Cornum, Rhonda. *She Went to War: The Rhonda Cornum Story.* Edited by Peter Copeland. Novato, Calif.: Presidio Press, 1992.

Cosmas, Graham A. *An Army for Empire: The United States Army in the Spanish-American War.* Columbia: University of Missouri Press, 1971.

Cowdrey, Albert E. "A Question of Numbers." In *Eisenhower and the German POWs.* Edited by Gunter Bischof and Stephen E. Ambrose, 78–92. Baton Rouge: Louisiana State University Press, 1992.

Cozzens, Peter, ed. *Eyewitnesses to the Indian Wars, 1865–1890.* 5 vols. Mechanicsburg, Pa.: Stackpole Books, 2001–2005.

Crutchfield, James A. *Tragedy at Taos: The Revolt of 1847.* Plano: Republic of Texas Press, 1995.

Curtis, Edward E. *The Organization of the British Army in the American Revolution.* 1926. Reprint, New York: AMS Press, 1969.

Dabney, William M. "After Saratoga: The Story of the Convention Army." Ph.D. diss., University of New Mexico, 1954.

Daly, Gavin. "Napoleon's Lost Legions: French Prisoners of War in Britain, 1803–1814." *History* 89 (July 2004): 361–380.

Danchev, Alex, and Dan Keohane, eds. *International Perspectives on the Gulf Conflict, 1990–91.* New York: St. Martin's Press, 1994.

Dandridge, Danske. *American Prisoners of the Revolution.* Charlottesville, Va.: Michie, 1911.

Dann, John C., ed. *The Revolution Remembered: Eyewitness Accounts of the American Revolution.* Chicago: University of Chicago Press, 1980.

Danver, Mark, ed. *Torture and Truth: America, Abu Ghraib, and the War on Terror.* New York: New York Review of Books, 2004.

Davis, Gerald H. "Prisoners of War in Twentieth-Century War Economies." *Journal of Contemporary History* 12 (October 1977): 623–634.

Davis, Vernon. *The Long Road Home: U.S. Prisoner of War Policy and Planning in Southeast Asia.* Washington, D.C.: Office of the Secretary of Defense, Historical Office, 2000.

Dean, Robert John. "Prison Narratives of the American Revolution." Ph.D. diss., Michigan State University, 1980.

Dennett, Carl P. *Prisoners of the Great War.* Boston: Houghton Mifflin, 1919.

Derounian-Stodola, Kathryn Zabelle, and James Arthur Levernier. *The Indian Captivity Narrative, 1550–1900.* New York: Twayne Publishers, 1993.

Dietz, Anthony. "The Prisoner of War in the United States during the War of 1812." Ph.D. diss., American University, 1964.

Döhla, Johann Conrad. *A Hessian Diary of the American Revolution.* Translated by Bruce E. Burgoyne. Norman: University of Oklahoma Press, 1990.

Dower, John W. *War without Mercy: Race and Power in the Pacific War.* New York: Pantheon Books, 1986.

Dowling, Morgan E. *Southern Prisons.* Detroit: Graham, 1870.

Doyle, Frederick Joseph. "German Prisoners of War in the Southwest United States during World War II: An Oral History." Ph.D. diss., University of Denver, 1978.

Draper, Lyman C. *King's Mountain and Its Heroes.* Cincinnati: P. G. Thompson, 1881.

Dunnigan, James F., and Austin Bay. *From Shield to Storm: High-Tech Weapons, Military Strategy, and Coalition Warfare in the Persian Gulf.* New York: William Morrow, 1992.

Durham, Kenneth Rueben, Jr. *Santa Anna: Prisoner of War in Texas.* Paris, Tex.: Wright Press, 1986.

Dutton, Charles J. "American Prison Camp." *Commonweal* 33 (3 January 1940): 270–272.

Dyer, Brainerd. "The Treatment of Colored Union Troops by the Confederates, 1861–1865." *Journal of Negro History* 20 (July 1935): 273–286.

Edwards, Frank S. *A Campaign in New Mexico with Colonel Doniphan.* Philadelphia: Carey and Hart, 1847.

Elting, John R. *Amateurs, to Arms! A Military History of the War of 1812.* Chapel Hill, N.C.: Algonquin Books, 1991.

Everest, Allan S. *The War of 1812 in the Champlain Valley.* Syracuse, N.Y.: Syracuse University Press, 1981.

Fairchild, Byron, and Jonathan Grossman. *The Army and Industrial Manpower.* The United States Army in World War II. Washington, D.C.: Office of the Chief of Military History, 1959.

Falk, Richard A. "International Law Aspects of Repatriation of Prisoners of War during Hostilities." *American Journal of International Law* 67 (July 1973): 465–478.

Fickle, James E., and Donald W. Ellis. "POWs in the Piney Woods: German Prisoners of War in the Southern Lumber Industry, 1943–1945." *Journal of Southern History* 56 (November 1990): 695–720.

Fiedler, David. *The Enemy among Us: POWs in Missouri during World War II.* St. Louis: Missouri Historical Society Press, 2003.

Flory, William E. S. *Prisoners of War: A Study in the Development of International Law.* Washington, D.C.: American Council on Public Affairs, 1942.

Fooks, Herbert C. *Prisoners of War.* Federalsburg, Md.: J. W. Stowell, 1924.

Foot, Rosemary. *Human Rights and Counter-Terrorism in America's Asian Policy.* Adelphi Paper 363. New York: Oxford University Press, 2004.

Fowler, Will. *Santa Anna of Mexico.* Lincoln: University of Nebraska Press, 2007.

Franklin, H. Bruce. "The POW/MIA Myth." In *The Lessons and Legacies of the Vietnam War.* Edited by Walter L. Hixson, 189–210. New York: Garland, 2000.

Frater, Daniel A. "Impressment in the 18th Century Anglo-American World." Master's thesis, Queens College, New York, 1995.

Freedman, Lawrence. "The Theory of Limited War." In *International Perspectives on the Gulf Conflict, 1990–91.* Edited by Alex Danchev and Dan Keohane, 201–223. New York: St. Martin's Press, 1994.

Freidel, Frank B. *Francis Lieber, Nineteenth Century Liberal.* Baton Rouge: Louisiana State University Press, 1947.

———. "General Orders 100 and Military Government." *Mississippi Valley Historical Review* 32 (March 1946): 541–556.

———. *The Splendid Little War.* Boston: Little, Brown, 1958.

Friedman, Leon, ed. *The Law of War: A Documentary History.* 2 vols. New York: Random House, 1972.

Friedman, Norman. *Desert Victory: The War for Kuwait.* Annapolis, Md.: Naval Institute Press, 1991.

Futch, Ovid L. *History of Andersonville Prison.* Gainesville: University of Florida Press, 1968.

Gaertner, Georg, and Arnold Krammer. *Hitler's Last Soldier in America.* New York: Stein & Day, 1985.

Gansberg, Judith M. *Stalag USA: The Remarkable Story of German POWs in America.* New York: Thomas Y. Crowell, 1977.

Garrett, Richard. *POW.* London: David & Charles, 1981.

Gerger, Jeffrey E. *German Prisoners of War at Camp Cooke, California: Personal Accounts, 1944–1946.* Jefferson, N.C.: McFarland, 1996.

Geronimo. *Geronimo's Story of His Life.* Edited by S. M. Barnett. 1906. Reprint, Alexander, N.C.: Alexander Books, 1999.

Gilmore, Allison. *You Can't Fight Tanks with Bayonets: Psychological Warfare against the Japanese Army in the Southeast Pacific.* Lincoln: University of Nebraska Press, 1998.

Glazier, Willard. *The Capture, the Prison Pen, and the Escape.* Hartford: H. E. Goodwin, 1867.

Glidden, William B. "Internment Camps in America, 1917–1920." *Military Affairs* 37 (December 1973): 137–141.

Gordon, Michael R., and Bernard E. Trainor. *The Generals' War: The Inside Story of the Conflict in the Gulf.* Boston: Little, Brown, 1995.

Goss, Warren L. *The Soldier's Story of His Captivity at Andersonville.* Boston: Lee and Shepard, 1866.

Gray, Michael P. *The Business of Captivity: Elmira and Its Civil War Prison.* Kent, Ohio: Kent State University Press, 2001.

Greenberg, Karen. *The Least Worst Place: Guantánamo's First 100 Days.* New York: Oxford University Press, 2009.

Greenberg, Karen J., and Joshua L. Dratel, eds. *The Torture Papers: The Road to Abu Ghraib.* New York: Cambridge University Press, 2005.

Gregorie, Anne King. *Thomas Sumter.* Columbia: R. L. Bryan, 1931.

Grenier, John. *The First Way of War: American War Making on the Frontier, 1607–1814.* New York: Cambridge University Press, 2005.

Grotius, Hugo. *De Jure Belle ac Pacis.* Translated by Francis W. Kelsey. 1625. Reprint, 1925. Available at http://www.lonang.com/exlibris/grotius/.

Hackenburg, Randy W. *Pennsylvania in the War with Mexico.* Shippensburg, Pa.: White Mane, 1992.

Haffner, Gerald O. "The Treatment of Prisoners of War by the Americans during the War of Independence." Ph.D. diss., University of Indiana, 1952.

Haley, James L. *The Buffalo War: The History of the Red River Indian Uprising of 1874*. Austin: State House Press, 1998.

Halleck, Henry W. *International Law; or, Rules Regulating the Intercourse of States in Peace and War.* New York: D. Van Nostrand, 1861.

Halsey, William F., and Joseph Bryan III. *Admiral Halsey's Story.* New York: McGraw-Hill, 1947.

Harris, William C. *Prison-Life in the Tobacco Warehouse at Richmond.* Philadelphia: G. W. Childs, 1862.

Hartigan, Richard Shelly. *Lieber's Code and the Law of War.* Chicago: Precedent, 1983.

Hata, Ikuhiko. "From Consideration to Contempt: The Changing Nature of Japanese Military and Popular Perceptions of Prisoners of War through the Ages." In *Prisoners of War and Their Captors in World War II.* Edited by Bob Moore and Kent Fedorowich, 253–276. Washington, D.C.: Berg, 1996.

Hawkins, Christopher. *The Adventures of Christopher Hawkins.* 1864. Reprint, New York: New York Times, 1968.

Haynes, Sam W. *Soldiers of Misfortune: The Somervell and Mier Expeditions.* Austin: University of Texas Press, 1990.

Heard, J. Norman. *White into Red.* Metuchen, N.J.: Scarecrow Press, 1973.

Henson, Margaret Swett. "Politics and the Treatment of the Mexican Prisoners after the Battle of San Jacinto." *Southwestern Historical Quarterly* 94 (October 1990): 189–230.

Herbert, Charles. *A Relic of the Revolution.* 1847. Reprint, New York: New York Times, 1968.

Hermes, Walter G. *Truce Tent and Fighting Front.* U.S. Army in the Korean War. Washington, D.C.: Center of Military History, 1966.

Hersh, Seymour M. *Chain of Command: The Road from 9/11 to Abu Ghraib.* New York: HarperCollins, 2004.

Hesseltine, William Best. *Civil War Prisons: A Study in War Psychology.* Columbus: Ohio State University Press, 1930.

———, ed. *Civil War Prisons.* Kent, Ohio: Kent State University Press, 1972.

Hickey, Donald. *The War of 1812: A Forgotten Conflict.* Urbana: University of Illinois Press, 1989.

Hixson, Walter L., ed. *The Lessons and Legacies of the Vietnam War.* New York: Garland, 2000.

Holl, Richard E. "Swastikas in the Bluegrass State: Axis Prisoners of War in Kentucky, 1942–46." *Register of the Kentucky Historical Society* 100 (Spring 2002): 139–165.

Holmes, Richard. *Acts of War: The Behavior of Men in Battle.* New York: Free Press, 1985.

Horigan, Michael. *Elmira: Death Camp of the North.* Mechanicsburg, Pa.: Stackpole Books, 2002.

Horrid Massacre at Dartmoor Prison. Boston: Nathaniel Conerly, 1815.
Horsman, Reginald. "The Paradox of Dartmoor Prison." *American Heritage* 26 (February 1975): 13–17.
———. *The War of 1812.* New York: Alfred A. Knopf, 1969.
Hough, Franklin B. *The Siege of Charleston.* Albany: J. Munsell, 1867.
Howard, Michael, ed. *Restraints on War: Studies in the Limitation of Armed Conflict.* Oxford: Oxford University Press, 1979.
Howard, Michael, George J. Andreopoulos, and Mark R. Shulman, eds. *The Laws of War: Constraints on Warfare in the Western World.* New Haven, Conn.: Yale University Press, 1994.
Hughes, Thomas. *A Journal by Thomas Hughes.* Cambridge: Cambridge University Press, 1947.
Humphreys, Charles Alfred. *Field, Camp, Hospital and Prison in the Civil War, 1864–1865.* Boston: George H. Ellis, 1918.
Hutchinson, John F. *Champions of Charity: War and the Rise of the Red Cross.* Boulder, Colo.: Westview Press, 1996.
Hutchinson, Richard. "The Warr in New-England Visibly Ended." In *Narratives of the Indian Wars.* Edited by Charles H. Lincoln. New York: Charles Scribner's Sons, 1913.
Isham, Asa B., Henry M. Davidson, and Henry B. Furness. *Prisoners of War and Military Prisons.* Cincinnati: Lyman & Cushing, 1890.
Jackson, Scott Thomas. "Impressment and Anglo-American Discord, 1787–1818." Ph.D. diss., University of Michigan, 1976.
Jacobs, James Ripley, and Glenn Tucker. *The War of 1812: A Compact History.* New York: Hawthorn Books, 1969.
James, William Dobein. *A Sketch of the Life of Brig. Gen. Francis Marion.* Charleston: Gould and Riley, 1821.
Jeffrey, William Hartley. *Richmond Prisons, 1861–1862.* St. Johnsbury, Vt.: Republican Press, 1893.
Johnson, Hannibal A. *The Sword of Honor: From Captivity to Freedom.* Providence, R.I.: The Society, 1903.
Joslyn, Mauriel. *Immortal Captives: The Story of 600 Confederate Captives and the United States Prisoner of War Policy.* Shippensburg, Pa.: White Mane, 1996.
Kaplan, Lawrence S. "Jefferson, the Napoleonic Wars, and the Balance of Power." *William and Mary Quarterly* 14 (April 1957): 196–217.
Kaplan, Roger. "The Hidden War: British Intelligence Operations during the American Revolution." *William and Mary Quarterly* 47 (January 1990): 115–138.
Keefer, Louis E. *Italian Prisoners of War in America, 1942–1946: Captives or Allies?* New York: Praeger, 1992.
Keegan, John. *The Iraq War.* New York: Alfred A. Knopf, 2004.
Keeley, Lawrence H. *War before Civilization.* New York: Oxford University Press, 1996.
Keen, James Richard. "The Captive Enemy? Italian Prisoners of War in Texas during World War II." Master's thesis, University of Texas in the Permian Basin, 1988.

Kendall, George Wilkins. *Dispatches from the Mexican War.* Edited by Lawrence Delbert Cress. Norman: University of Oklahoma Press, 1999.

Kent, James. *Commentaries on American Law.* 4th ed. 4 vols. New York: E. B. Clayton, 1840.

King, John Henry. *Three Hundred Days in a Yankee Prison.* Kennesaw, Ga.: Continental Book Co., 1959.

Kinkead, Eugene. *In Every War but One.* New York: Norton, 1959.

Knauss, William H. *The Story of Camp Chase.* Nashville: Smith & Lamar, 1906.

Knepper, George W. "The Convention Army, 1777–1783." Ph.D. diss., University of Michigan, 1954.

Knetsch, Joe. *Florida's Seminole Wars, 1817–1858.* Charleston, S.C.: Arcadia Publishing, 2003.

Knight, Betsy. "Prisoner Exchange and Parole in the American Revolution." *William and Mary Quarterly* 48 (April 1991): 201–222.

Koop, Allen V. *Stark Decency: German Prisoners of War in a New England Village.* Lebanon, N.H.: University Press of New England, 1988.

Krammer, Arnold P. "Japanese Prisoners of War in America." *Pacific Historical Review* 52 (February 1983): 67–91.

———. *Nazi Prisoners of War in America.* New York: Stein & Day, 1979.

Ladd, Horatio O. *History of the War with Mexico.* New York: Dodd, Mead, 1882.

Lawrence, F. Lee, and Robert W. Glover. *Camp Ford, CSA: The Story of Union Prisoners in Texas.* Austin: Texas Civil War Centennial Advisory Committee, 1964.

Leach, Douglas Edward. *Flintlock and Tomahawk: New England in King Philip's War.* New York: Macmillan, 1958.

Lech, Raymond B. *Broken Soldiers.* Urbana: University of Illinois Press, 2000.

Lee, Henry. *The American Revolution in the South.* Edited by Robert E. Lee. New York: Arno Press, 1969.

Lee, J. Fitzgerald. "Prisoners of War." *Army Quarterly* 3 (1921–1922): 348–356.

Levie, Howard S. *Prisoners of War in International Armed Conflict.* Naval War College International Law Studies 59. Newport, R.I.: Naval War College Press, 1977.

———, ed. *Documents on Prisoners of War.* Naval War College International Law Studies 60. Newport, R.I.: Naval War College Press, 1979.

Levy, George. *To Die in Chicago: Confederate Prisoners at Camp Douglas, 1862–1865.* Evanston, Ill.: Evanston Publishing, 1994.

Lewis, George G., and John Mewha. *History of Prisoner of War Utilization by the United States Army, 1776–1945.* Washington, D.C.: Government Printing Office, 1955.

Leyden, Andrew. *Gulf War Debriefing Book: An After Action Report.* Edited by Camille Akin. Grants Pass, Ore.: Hellgate Press, 1997.

Lindsay, Arnett G. "Diplomatic Relations between the United States and Great Britain Bearing on the Return of Negro Slaves, 1783–1828." *Journal of Negro History* 5 (October 1920): 391–419.

Linn, Brian M. *The Philippine War, 1899–1902.* Lawrence: University Press of Kansas, 2000.

———. *The U.S. Army and Counterinsurgency in the Philippine War, 1899–1902.* Chapel Hill: University of North Carolina Press, 1989.

Lishchiner, Jacob B. "Origin of the Military Police: Provost Marshal General's Department, AEF, World War I." *Military Affairs* 11 (Summer 1947): 66–79.

Lynn, John A. *The Bayonets of the Republic: Motivation and Tactics in the Army of Revolutionary France, 1791–94.* Urbana: University of Illinois Press, 1984.

MacDonald, Callum A. *Korea: The War before Vietnam.* New York: Free Press, 1986.

MacKenzie, Simon P. "The Treatment of Prisoners in World War II." *Journal of Modern History* 66 (September 1994): 487–520.

Mahan, Alfred Thayer. *Sea Power in Its Relations to the War of 1812.* 2 vols. Boston: Little, Brown, 1905.

Mahon, John K. *The War of 1812.* Gainesville: University of Florida Press, 1972.

Manchester, William. *Goodbye, Darkness: A Memoir of the Pacific War.* Boston: Little, Brown, 1980.

Marti, Werner H. *Messenger of Destiny: The California Adventures, 1846–1847, of Archibald H. Gillespie.* San Francisco: John Howell Books, 1960.

Marvel, William. *Andersonville: The Last Depot.* Chapel Hill: University of North Carolina Press, 1994.

Mason, John Brown. "German Prisoners of War in the United States." *American Journal of International Law* 39 (April 1945): 198–215.

Mattern, David B. *Benjamin Lincoln and the American Revolution.* Columbia: University of South Carolina Press, 1995.

Matthews, Ken. *The Gulf Conflict and International Relations.* London: Routledge, 1993.

McAdams, Benton. *Rebels at Rock Island: The Story of a Civil War Prison.* DeKalb: Northern Illinois University Press, 2000.

McCarthy, Daniel. *The Prisoner of War in Germany.* New York: Moffat, Yard, 1917.

McCutchan, Joseph D. *Mier Expedition Diary: A Texan Prisoner's Account.* Edited by Joseph Milton Nance. Austin: University of Texas Press, 1978.

McElroy, John. *Andersonville: A Story of Rebel Military Prisons.* Toledo, Ohio: D. R. Locke, 1879.

McKee, Christopher. "Foreign Seamen in the United States Navy: A Census of 1808." *William and Mary Quarterly* 42 (July 1985): 383–393.

Melish, John. *A Description of Dartmoor Prison, with an Account of the Massacre of the Prison.* Philadelphia: Self-Published, 1815.

Menos, Dennis. *Arms over Diplomacy: Reflections on the Persian Gulf War.* Westport, Conn.: Praeger, 1992.

Meron, Theodor. "Prisoners of War, Civilians and Diplomats in the Gulf Crisis." *American Journal of International Law* 85 (January 1991): 104–109.

Metzger, Charles H. *The Prisoner in the American Revolution.* Chicago: Loyola University Press, 1971.

Meyers, Samuel M., and William C. Bradbury. "The Political Behavior of Korean and Chinese Prisoners of War in the Korean Conflict: A Historical Analysis." In *Mass Behavior in Battle and Captivity: The Communist Soldier in the Korean War.*

Edited by William C. Bradbury, Samuel C. Meyers, and Albert D. Biderman, 209–338. Chicago: University of Chicago Press, 1968.

Miller, Robert Ryal. *Shamrock and Sword: The Saint Patrick's Battalion in the U.S.-Mexican War.* Norman: University of Oklahoma Press, 1989.

———, ed. *The Mexican War Journal and Letters of Ralph W. Kirkham.* College Station: Texas A&M University Press, 1991.

Miller, Stuart Creighton. *"Benevolent Assimilation": The American Conquest of the Philippines, 1899–1903.* New Haven, Conn.: Yale University Press, 1982.

Millett, Allan R., and Peter Maslowski. *For the Common Defense: A Military History of the United States of America.* Rev. ed. New York: Free Press, 1994.

Millis, Walter. *Arms and Men: A Study in American Military History.* New Brunswick, N.J.: Rutgers University Press, 1981.

Missall, John, and Mary Lou Missall. *The Seminole Wars: America's Longest Conflict.* Gainesville: University Press of Florida, 2004.

Moore, Bob, and Kent Fedorowich, eds. *Prisoners of War and Their Captors in World War II.* Washington, D.C.: Berg, 1996.

Moore, John Hammond. *The Faustball Tunnel.* New York: Random House, 1978.

———. "Italian POWs in America: War Is Not Always Hell." *Prologue* 8 (Fall 1976): 141–151.

Moore, John Norton. *Crisis in the Gulf: Enforcing the Rule of Law.* New York: Oceana, 1992.

Moorehead, Caroline. *Dunant's Dream: War, Switzerland and the History of the Red Cross.* New York, Carroll & Graf, 1998.

Morrill, Dan L. *Southern Campaigns of the American Revolution.* Baltimore: Nautical & Aviation Publishing, 1993.

Morrison, James L. *"The Best School in the World": West Point, the Pre–Civil War Years, 1833–1866.* Kent, Ohio: Kent State University Press, 1986.

Morrow, Rising Lake. "The Early American Attitude toward Naturalized Americans Abroad." *American Journal of International Law* 30 (October 1936): 647–663.

Mossman, Billy. *Ebb and Flow: November 1950–July 1951.* U.S. Army in the Korean War. Washington, D.C.: Center of Military History, 1990.

Mueller, John. *Policy and Opinion in the Gulf War.* Chicago: University of Chicago Press, 1994.

Musicant, Ivan. *Empire by Default: The Spanish-American War and the Dawn of the American Century.* New York: Henry Holt, 1998.

Nackman, Mark E. "The Making of the Texan Citizen Soldier, 1835–1860." *Southwestern Historical Quarterly* 78 (January 1975): 231–253.

Namias, June. *White Captives.* Chapel Hill: University of North Carolina Press, 1993.

Nash, Gary B. *Red, White and Black: The Peoples of Early North America.* 4th ed. Upper Saddle River, N.J.: Prentice Hall, 2000.

Nelson, Paul David. *General Horatio Gates: A Biography.* Baton Rouge: Louisiana State University Press, 1976.

Northrop, John Worrell. *Chronicles from the Diary of a War Prisoner in Andersonville.* Wichita, Kans.: John Northrop, 1904.

Oates, Stephen B. "Los Diablos Tejanos!" *American West* 2 (Summer 1945): 44–50.
Oswandel, J. Jacob. *Notes on the Mexican War, 1846–47–48.* Philadelphia, 1885.
Pabel, Reinhold. *Enemies Are Human.* Philadelphia: John C. Winston, 1955.
Pancake, John S. *This Destructive War: The British Campaign in the Carolinas, 1780–82.* Tuscaloosa: University of Alabama Press, 1985.
Parker, Sandra V. *Richmond's Civil War Prisons.* Lynchburg, Va.: H. E. Howard, 1990.
Patrick, Rembert. "British Prisoners of War in the American Revolution." Master's thesis, University of North Carolina, 1934.
Patterson, Samuel White. *Horatio Gates: Defender of American Liberties.* New York: Columbia University Press, 1941.
Perkins, Bradford. "George Canning, Great Britain, and the United States, 1807–1809." *American Historical Review* 63 (October 1957): 1–22.
Peterson, William S. "A History of Camp Butler, 1861–1866." *Illinois Historical Journal* 82 (Summer 1989): 74–92.
Philpott, Tom. *Glory Denied: The Saga of Jim Thompson, America's Longest-Held Prisoner of War.* New York: Norton, 2001.
Potter, Israel R. *The Life and Remarkable Adventures of Israel R. Potter.* 1824. Reprint, New York: Corinth Books, 1962.
Potter, Pittman B. "Repatriation of Korean Prisoners of War." *American Journal of International Law* 47 (October 1953): 661–662.
Powell, Allan Kent. *Splinters of a Nation: German Prisoners of War in Utah.* Salt Lake City: University of Utah Press, 1989.
Prelinger, Catherine M. "Benjamin Franklin and the American Prisoners of War in England during the American Revolution." *William and Mary Quarterly* 32 (April 1975): 261–294.
Pritchett, Merrill R., and William L. Shea. "The Afrika Korps in Arkansas, 1943–1946." *Arkansas Historical Quarterly* 37 (Spring 1978): 3–22.
Quaife, Milo M. "The Fort Dearborn Massacre." *Missouri Valley Historical Review* 1 (March 1915): 561–573.
Quimby, Robert S. *The U.S. Army in the War of 1812: An Operational and Command Study.* 2 vols. East Lansing: Michigan State University Press, 1997.
Radley, Kenneth. *Rebel Watchdog: The Confederate States Army Provost Guard.* Baton Rouge: Louisiana State University Press, 1989.
Ranlet, Philip. "British Recruitment of Americans in New York during the American Revolution." *Military Affairs* 48 (January 1984): 26–28.
Ransom, John. *John Ransom's Andersonville Diary.* 1881. Reprint, New York: Berkley Books, 1986.
Reilly, Robin. *The British at the Gates: The New Orleans Campaign in the War of 1812.* New York: G. P. Putnam's Sons, 1974.
Reiss, Matthias. "Bronzed Bodies behind Barbed Wire: Masculinity and the Treatment of German Prisoners of War in the United States during World War II." *Journal of Military History* 69 (April 2005): 475–504.
Reynolds, Nicholas E. *Basrah, Baghdad, and Beyond: The U.S. Marine Corps in the Second Iraq War.* Annapolis, Md.: Naval Institute Press, 2005.

Riconda, Harry P. *Prisoners of War in American Conflicts.* Lanham, Md.: Scarecrow Press, 2003.

Ripley, Robert S. *The War with Mexico.* 2 vols. New York: Harper and Brothers, 1849.

Rippy, J. Fred. *The United States and Mexico.* New York: Alfred A. Knopf, 1931.

Roberts, Adam. "The Laws of War." In *International Perspectives on the Gulf Conflict, 1990–91.* Edited by Alex Danchev and Dan Keohane, 259–294. New York: St. Martin's Press, 1994.

Roberts, Adam, and Richard Guelff, eds. *Documents on the Laws of War.* 2nd ed. Oxford: Oxford University Press, 1989.

Robin, Ron. *The Barbed-Wire College: Reeducating German POWs in the United States during World War II.* Princeton, N.J.: Princeton University Press, 1995.

Robinson, Ralph. "Retaliation for the Treatment of Prisoners in the War of 1812." *American Historical Review* 49 (October 1943): 65–70.

Rochester, Stuart I., and Frederick Kiley. *Honor Bound: American Prisoners of War in Southeast Asia, 1961–1973.* Annapolis, Md.: Naval Institute Press, 1999.

Rogers, Paul. *A War on Terror: Afghanistan and After.* London: Pluto Press, 2004.

Rogers, Robert. *Journals of Major Robert Rogers.* London: J. Millan, 1765.

Rose, David. *Guantánamo: America's War on Human Rights.* London: Faber and Faber, 2004.

Ross, William F., and Charles Romanus. *The Quartermaster Corps: Operations in the War against Germany.* The United States Army in World War II. Washington, D.C.: Center of Military History, 2004.

Roth, Russell. *Muddy Glory: America's "Indian Wars" in the Philippines, 1899–1935.* West Hanover, Conn.: Christopher Publishing House, 1981.

Rowe, Peter, ed. *The Gulf War 1990–91 in International and English Law.* London: Routledge, 1993.

Salecker, Gene Eric. *Disaster on the Mississippi: The Sultana Explosion, April 27, 1865.* Annapolis, Md.: Naval Institute Press, 1996.

Sampson, Richard. *Escape in America: The British Convention Prisoners, 1777–1783.* Chippenham, U.K.: Picton Publishing, 1995.

Sanchez Lamego, Miguel A. *The Second Mexican-Texas War, 1841–1843.* Hillsboro, Tex.: Texian Press, 1972.

Sanders, Charles W., Jr. *While in the Hands of the Enemy: Military Prisons of the Civil War.* Baton Rouge: Louisiana State University Press, 2005.

Sandler, Stanley. *The Korean War: No Victors, No Vanquished.* Lexington: University Press of Kentucky, 1999.

Santa Anna, Antonio Lopez de. *The Eagle: The Autobiography of Santa Anna.* Edited by Ann Fears Crawford. Austin: Pemberton Press, 1967.

Scales, Robert H. *Certain Victory: The U.S. Army in the Gulf War.* Washington, D.C.: Office of the Chief of Staff of the Army, 1993.

Schnabel, James F. *Policy and Direction: The First Year.* U.S. Army in the Korean War. Washington, D.C.: Office of the Chief of Military History, 1972.

Scoggins, Michael C. *The Day It Rained Militia.* Charleston: The History Press, 2005.

Sexton, William Thaddeus. *Soldiers in the Sun: An Adventure in Imperialism.* Harrisburg, Pa.: Military Service Publishing, 1939.

Sheehan, Susan. *Ten Vietnamese.* New York: Alfred A. Knopf, 1968.

Sheppard, Peggy. *Andersonville, Georgia, USA.* Leslie, Ga.: Sheppard Publications, 1973.

Shils, Edward, and Morris Janowitz. "Cohesion and Disintegration in the Wehrmacht in World War II." *Public Opinion Quarterly* 12 (1948): 280–315.

Siegel, Stanley. *A Political History of the Texas Republic, 1836–1845.* Austin: University of Texas Press, 1956.

Simms, W. Gilmore. *The Life of Francis Marion.* New York: George F. Cooledge & Brother, 1846.

Singletary, Otis A. *The Mexican War.* Chicago: University of Chicago Press, 1960.

Sledge, Eugene B. *With the Old Breed at Peleliu and Okinawa.* New York: Presidio Press, 1981.

Smith, Arthur D. Howden. *Old Fuss and Feathers: The Life and Exploits of Lt.-General Winfield Scott.* New York: Greystone Press, 1937.

Smith, Arthur L. *The War for the German Mind: Re-educating Hitler's Soldiers.* Providence, R.I.: Berghahn Books, 1996.

Smith, Denis. *The Prisoners of Cabrera: Napoleon's Forgotten Soldiers, 1809–1814.* New York: Four Walls Eight Windows, 2001.

Smith, Paul Hubert. *Loyalists and Redcoats: A Study in British Revolutionary Policy.* Chapel Hill: University of North Carolina Press, 1964.

Spaight, J. M. *War Rights on Land.* London: Macmillan, 1911.

Speed, Richard B., III. *Prisoners, Diplomats, and the Great War: A Study in the Diplomacy of Captivity.* New York: Greenwood Press, 1990.

Speer, Lonnie R. *Portals to Hell: Military Prisons of the Civil War.* Mechanicsburg, Pa.: Stackpole Books, 1997.

Sprague, Homer B. *Lights and Shadows in Confederate Prisons: A Personal Experience, 1864–5.* New York: G. P. Putnam's Sons, 1915.

Stagg, J. C. A. *Mr. Madison's War: Politics, Diplomacy, and Warfare in the Early American Republic, 1783–1830.* Princeton, N.J.: Princeton University Press, 1983.

Stapp, William Preston. *The Prisoners of Perote.* Edited by Joe B. Frantz. Austin: University of Texas Press, 1978.

Starkey, Armstrong. *European and Native American Warfare, 1675–1815.* Norman: University of Oklahoma Press, 1998.

Steel, Anthony. "Anthony Merry and the Anglo-American Dispute about Impressment, 1803–6." *Cambridge Historical Journal* 9, no. 3 (1949): 331–351.

———. "Impressment in the Monroe-Pinkney Negotiation, 1806–1807." *American Historical Review* 57 (January 1952): 352–369.

Steele, Ian K. *Warpaths: Invasions of North America.* New York: Oxford University Press, 1994.

Sterling, David L. "American Prisoners of War in New York: A Report by Elias Boudinot." *William and Mary Quarterly* 13 (July 1956): 376–393.

Stevens, Peter F. *The Rogue's March: John Riley and the St. Patrick's Battalion.* Washington, D.C.: Brassey's, 1999.

Stevenson, R. Randolph. *The Southern Side; or, Andersonville Prison.* Baltimore: Turnbull Brothers, 1876.

Strasser, Steven, ed. *The Abu Ghraib Investigations: The Official Reports of the Independent Panel and the Pentagon on the Shocking Prisoner Abuse in Iraq.* New York: Public Affairs, 2004.

Strauss, Ulrich. *The Anguish of Surrender: Japanese POWs of World War II.* Seattle: University of Washington Press, 2003.

Swedberg, Claire. *In Enemy Hands: Personal Accounts of Those Taken Prisoner in World War II.* Mechanicsburg, Pa.: Stackpole Books, 1997.

Tebbel, John. *Turning the World Upside Down: Inside the American Revolution.* New York: Orion Books, 1993.

Temple, Bryan. *The Union Prison at Fort Delaware: A Perfect Hell on Earth.* Jefferson, N.C.: McFarland, 2003.

Thayer, Theodore G. *Nathanael Greene: Strategist of the American Revolution.* New York: Twayne, 1960.

Thompson, David Scott. "'This Crying Enormity': Impressment as a Factor in Anglo-American Foreign Relations." Master's thesis, Portland State University, 1993.

Tomedi, Rudy, ed. *No Bugles, No Drums: An Oral History of the Korean War.* New York: John Wiley, 1993.

Trask, David F. *The War with Spain in 1898.* New York: Macmillan, 1981.

Trask, Kerry A. *Black Hawk: The Battle for the Heart of America.* New York: Henry Holt, 2006.

Uhlendorf, Bernard A., ed. *The Siege of Charleston.* New York: New York Times, 1938.

Vagts, Alfred. *A History of Militarism.* Rev. ed. New York: Meridian Books, 1959.

Vatcher, William H., Jr. *Panmunjom: The Story of the Korean Military Armistice Negotiations.* New York: Praeger, 1958.

Vattel, Emmerich de. *The Law of Nations or the Principles of Natural Law.* 1758. Available at http://www.lonang.com/exlibris/vattel/.

Walker, Richard Paul. "Prisoners of War in Texas during World War II." Ph.D. diss., North Texas State University, 1980.

Walker, Samuel H. *Samuel H. Walker's Account of the Mier Expedition.* Edited by Marilyn McAdams Sibley. Austin: Texas State Historical Association, 1978.

Ward, Harry M. *The American Revolution: Nationhood Achieved, 1763–1788.* New York: St. Martin's Press, 1995.

———. *Between the Lines: Banditti of the American Revolution.* Westport, Conn.: Praeger, 2002.

Ward, William W. *"For the sake of my country": The Diary of Colonel W. W. Ward.* Edited by R. B. Rosenburg. Murfreesboro, Tenn.: Southern Heritage Press, 1992.

Waring, Alice Noble. *The Fighting Elder: Andrew Pickens.* Columbia: University of South Carolina Press, 1962.

Warner, E. J. *Generals in Gray: Lives of the Confederate Commanders.* Baton Rouge: Louisiana State University Press, 1959.

Washington, George. *The Writings of George Washington from the Original Manuscript Sources, 1745–1799.* 39 vols. Edited by John C. Fitzpatrick. Washington, D.C.: Government Printing Office, 1931–1944.

Waters, Michael R. *Lone Star Stalag: German Prisoners of War at Camp Hearne.* College Station: Texas A&M University Press, 2004.

Webb, Henry J. "Prisoners of War in the Middle Ages." *Military Affairs* 12 (Spring 1948): 46–49.

Weems, John Edward. *To Conquer a Peace: The War between the United States and Mexico.* Garden City, N.Y.: Doubleday, 1974.

Weigley, Russell F. *The American Way of War: A History of United States Military Strategy and Policy.* New York: Macmillan, 1973.

———. *History of the United States Army.* New York: Macmillan, 1962.

Weintraub, Stanley. "Behind the Wire." In *No Bugles, No Drums: An Oral History of the Korean War.* Edited by Rudy Tomedi, 189–195. New York: John Wiley, 1993.

West, Bing. *No True Glory: A Frontline Account of the Battle for Fallujah.* New York: Bantam Books, 2005.

White, M. S., ed. *Gulf Logistics: Blackadder's War.* London: Brassey's, 1995.

Whitney, Ellen M., ed. *The Black Hawk War, 1831–1832.* 3 vols. Springfield: Illinois State Historical Library, 1975.

Wickwire, Franklin and Mary. *Cornwallis: The American Adventure.* Boston: Houghton Mifflin, 1970.

Wilcox, Cadmus M. *History of the Mexican War.* Washington, D.C.: Chuch News Publishing, 1892.

Wildman, Edwin. *Aguinaldo: A Narrative of Filipino Ambitions.* Boston: Lothrop Publishing, 1901.

Williams, Donald Mace. *Italian Prisoners of War and a Texas Church: The Murals of St. Mary's.* Lubbock: Texas Tech University Press, 1992.

Willoughby, C. A. "Identification of German Prisoners of War." *Infantry Journal* 15 (September 1918): 181–202.

Wolff, Leon. *Little Brown Brother.* 1960. Reprint, New York: Oxford University Press, 1991.

Yarsinske, Amy Waters. *No One Left Behind: The Lieutenant Commander Michael Scott Speicher Story.* New York: Dutton, 2002.

"The YMCA War Prisoners' Aid Offers Educational Assistance." *School and Society* 59 (6 May 1944): 325.

Zeh, Frederick. *An Immigrant Soldier in the Mexican War.* Edited by William J. Orr and Robert Ryal Miller. College Station: Texas A&M University Press, 1995.

Ziemke, Earl F. *The U.S. Army in the Occupation of Germany, 1944–1946.* Washington, D.C.: Center of Military History, 1975.

INDEX

8/14 (3) 4/12
12/17 (4) 10/17